The Life of
ALEKSANDR BLOK

———

VOLUME II
The Release of Harmony
1908–1921

ИЗДАТЕЛЬСТВО „АЛКОНОСТЪ"

The Life of
ALEKSANDR BLOK

VOLUME II
The Release of Harmony
1908–1921

AVRIL PYMAN

OXFORD   LONDON   NEW YORK
OXFORD UNIVERSITY PRESS
1980

Oxford University Press, Walton Street, Oxford OX2 6DP

OXFORD LONDON GLASGOW
NEW YORK TORONTO MELBOURNE WELLINGTON
IBADAN NAIROBI DAR ES SALAAM CAPE TOWN
KUALA LUMPUR SINGAPORE JAKARTA HONG KONG TOKYO
DELHI BOMBAY CALCUTTA MADRAS KARACHI

British Library Cataloguing in Publication Data

Pyman, Avril
  Aleksandr Blok.
  Vol. 2: The release of harmony, 1908–1921
  1. Blok, Aleksandr Aleksandrovich – Biography
  2. Poets, Russian – 20th century – Biography
  I. Title
891.7'1'3 PG3453.B6Z/ 79-40501

ISBN 0-19-211763-7

A list of errata in volume I
will be found at p. 423

Printed in Great Britain by
Butler and Tanner Ltd, Frome and London

CONTENTS

LIST OF ILLUSTRATIONS

Plates

Illustrations in the text

The design reproduced on the first half-title is the colophon of
Alkonost, drawn by Annenkov

CHAPTER I

The Theme of Russia

(Spring 1908 – Spring 1909)

... My theme, and I know that now for certain, without any doubts whatsoever, is a living, real theme, it is not only *bigger than me*, it is bigger than all of us put together; and it is a theme common to us all. All of us who are *alive* come to it one way or another. If we do not come to it, it will come to us, *it is already advancing....*

That is how my theme stands before me, *the theme of Russia* (and in particular, the question of the intelligentsia and the people). To this theme I deliberately and irrevocably *dedicate my life.*

(Letter to Stanislavsky of 9 December 1908; VIII. 265)

1

Blok had been right, after all, when he wrote to Meyerhold in the autumn of 1906 that it would be through the theatre that he would effect the breakout from self-contained lyricism; that in his association with the live stage there was 'a kind of catharsis' (VIII. 169–72). Not only the staging of his own *Puppet Booth,*[a] but the whole two years of close involvement with the modern theatre had, by bringing him face to face with the problem of communication and the relationship between the artist and his public, given him the impetus '... to break the window and, thrusting out head and shoulders, to see that life was simple (joyful, difficult, complicated) ...' (*Z.K.*75).

It was through the theatre that Blok came to his theme of the schism between the intelligentsia and the people, a theme which he sought to express in the spring of 1908 not only in his writing for the theatre (the play *The Song of Fate*), but in a lecture about the theatre (v. 241–76) which marked an entirely new departure in his public life. For it was in the spring of 1908, when educated Russia,

[a] See vol. I, chapter x.

discouraged by oppression from above and indifference from below, was fast losing all hope of the society of which it formed a part, that Aleksandr Blok first emerged as a serious civic thinker and public speaker.

The main contention of his paper, read to the Theatre Club in April 1908 and based on his experience of the past few years, was that drama had ceased to be a popular art. The very prominence given to the producer—as though an intermediary was now essential between author and actor, between play and public—was a sign that those who wrote for the stage were ignorant not only of the mechanics of spectacle but of the requirements of their public. It was essential that modern drama should learn to cater for a more democratic audience. 'If not today, then tomorrow,' Blok concluded, 'we shall have knocking at the doors of our theatres not this blasé audience composed of the contemporary intelligentsia but a new audience: alive, demanding, and bold. Let us be ready to meet this *youth*. It will solve our complications, it will raise the burden from weary shoulders, it will give us wings, or destroy' (v. 276).

It was this nostalgia for a wider, simpler audience that caused Blok—in spite of the fact that his own drama was the *ne plus ultra* of lyrical obscurity—to turn away from Meyerhold (although, as he had heard through his wife, the young director was ardently in sympathy with the views expressed in his paper), to the better established and more businesslike Stanislavsky, founder-director of the Moscow Art Theatre, whose famous production of Chekhov's *The Seagull* he and Lyuba had seen during their visit to Moscow in 1904.[b]

In 1908 Meyerhold and Stanislavsky still had much in common. Both insisted on the importance of the producer. Both had declared war on the star system and sought to combine intelligent acting with carefully calculated group effects and ensembles. Both were seeking to express the dreamy, immaterial atmosphere of modernist drama. Meyerhold, however, was the more inventive and the bolder. He was also more of an adventurer, more abstract, more intellectual. His every production was a gamble, treading the knife-edge between success and failure. Stanislavsky was a practical man. His first love and care was not the idea of the theatre in its purest form but the actual theatre he had succeeded in building up and was running as a paying concern, a troupe of actors incomparably more distinguished than any Meyerhold had up to that time been able to scrape

[b] It was from this production, which made theatrical history, that the Moscow Art Theatre derived its emblem of a stylized seagull in flight.

together; a troupe that needed to have full confidence in the financial viability of their theatre. Stanislavsky, in fact, walked a different knife-edge: that between the fear of stagnation and the fear of a box-office flop. In a sense, this appealed to Blok as the more popular, more realistic approach. He considered that Meyerhold's constant experimenting, particularly his 'modernism in doubtful taste', ought to be confined to the studio.[c]

In May 1908, the Moscow Art Theatre visited Petersburg, and Blok arranged to read his *Song of Fate* to Stanislavsky and some of his colleagues. In the poet's reading, the play gripped the Muscovite visitors, especially the urban scenes where the demonic heroine, Faina, dominates a vast and vulgar Vanity Fair, a World Exhibition of Technical Progress and the Wonders of Science. Nemirovich-Danchenko kept exclaiming: 'What talent! What a talented boy!' and Stanislavsky took the text of the play back to Moscow with a half-promise to stage it that autumn.

The play had an importance for Blok which far exceeded its objective merits. As Stanislavsky was to discover when he reread it without the author, the characters were allegorical and almost totally lacking in psychology, but for the poet himself *The Song of Fate* marked the discovery of 'the theme of Russia': of her peculiar history and present position and of the doom inherent in the cultural dichotomy between the peasantry and the educated classes—or, as he was to put it that autumn, between 'the people' and 'the intelligentsia', between 'the element' (*stikhiya*) and 'culture'.

Before reading his play to Stanislavsky, Blok had written to his mother: 'It is the first of my works in which I began to feel the ground beneath my feet—not shifting and not only lyrical. That is how I define the importance of *The Song of Fate* for myself and that is why I love it more than anything else I have written ...' (VIII. 240).

That spring, as if to celebrate this winning out on to firmer ground, Blok wrote a series of masterly lyrics anathematizing his recent enthralment to romantic passion.[d] Their burthen is that passion cloys and that, however delightful the pleasures of love, 'it is more worthy to walk behind the heavy plough through the fresh dews of early morning' (III. 161). In these poems, Blok sometimes echoes the

[c] In fact, Meyerhold had already tried this, with Stanislavsky's backing, but the experiment had failed, both for financial reasons and because the two creative personalities were too different and too powerful to get along together even in such a loose affiliation as the Moscow Art Theatre and its pre-1905 Studio.

[d] See vol. I, chapters X and XI, for Blok's infatuation for the actress Natal'ya Nikolayevna Volokhova.

hedonistic 'anthological verses' of Pushkin and Batyushkov. Yet
here, as ever, the 'sunshine of Hellas' eluded him. In classical poetry
it is sober considerations of mortality and the passing of time which
lead to a certain scepticism with regard to physical delights. The
canker at the root of Blok's pleasures is not the simple knowledge
that all things change and pass. His beauties have mad eyes and the
roses at their breast are 'eternally crushed'. He and his fellow poets,
though they drink wine and weave wreaths of flowers in the best
Anacreontic tradition, present their flowers to the mistresses of other
men (III. 161). Passion itself is seen as a cruel and repetitive rite to which
celebrant and victim are alike foredoomed:

> The same soft words, the same caresses,
> The trembling lips so often seen ...
> A glimpse of shoulder—No! The Earth is
> Empty, and passionless, and clean!
>
> And, filling all my lungs with laughter,
> From topmost snowy heights above,
> I send down roaring avalanches
> To those ravines where I made love.
>
> (III. 160)

Together with his obsession with romantic passion, Blok shook
off that concern for the subtleties of friendship and devious literary
alliances and schisms which even the previous autumn had seemed
so important. In the course of this lonely spring, he became a man
obsessed by one thought, long foreseen but only now, at last, clearly
understood: he became a man with a message.

When the second Duma had been dissolved the previous year, its
appeal for widespread civic action had fallen on deaf ears. Political
action was left to divided parties and individuals and, over the year
1908, a record 782 political prisoners were tried by court martial and
executed by hanging. The Tsar's new Prime Minister, Stolypin, in
contrast to the majority of liberals and revolutionaries, had a realistic
programme of reform based on his own bureaucratic administrative
experience and moderate enough to be implemented without being
stalled by the court and the great land-owners (as Count Witte's radical proposals for land reform had been in 1906). Stolypin succeeded
in splitting the opposition and, in the general hush imposed by the
disciplinary clamp-down, it became only too evident that neither
the parliament nor the revolutionary parties had really enjoyed the
support of the electorate. Only very briefly, in 1905, had the whole
country been united in opposition to the absolute and inefficient

regime which had led it to defeat at the hands of Japan. Now, the people were apathetic; the Duma had been tamed by an anticonstitutional revision of the franchise which brought about the return of a very moderate assembly which, in any event, held little power; the hard-core opposition were in exile, or prison; the moderate liberals and professional classes seemed anxious only to forget their disappointments and to seek distraction and excitement elsewhere— even in that refined 'decadent' art, with its overtones of eroticism and mysticism, which only a few years before they had condemned as shocking.

For Blok, awareness of these developments had coincided with the discovery that the theatre and, indeed, the other arts were becoming increasingly élitist, trivial, and moribund. What had been genuine intuitive foreboding had degenerated into flabby pessimism or mystical mumbo-jumbo. The split between the people and the intelligentsia, he now felt more consciously than he had even in 1905, went deeper than politics. It was fundamental—and the next revolution would be social, not merely political, and would sweep away not only the evils of the old regime, but its most precious values and achievements. To prepare to meet this calamity, to welcome it in the name of youth and renewal and to rise above all personal sense of loss, was the duty of the individual to society; to give warning of its approach was the task Blok tried to take upon himself.

2

It is one thing to know what should be done, and quite another to do it. Humanly, Blok yearned for his wife, still on tour with Meyerhold and his company in the provinces. He never grew accustomed to being homeless and without Lyuba there could be no home. Her brief visit during Passion Week had decided 'absolutely nothing',[1] but they had both been in good form and she had promised to come back again either on St. Thomas's Sunday or, at latest, sometime in May.

The day of Doubting Thomas, however, came and went. Blok, who had kept quite sober for almost a month after Lyuba's departure in February, began to drink more often and more heavily, and confessed to his mother that he was 'getting sick of living alone' (VIII. 239). He was worried. Lyuba's letters had a forced gaiety. He felt a slackening-off of her attention, her spiritual presence which, at the same time the year before, when he had stayed on alone in Petersburg and she had been living at Shakhmatovo, had still sustained and enveloped him.

Now that she was gone he thought of her constantly. When, on 1 May, he had read *The Song of Fate* to his friends he had been surprised that no one commented on the figure of the wife, Elena, and noted in his diary: 'So be it: my darling will remain hidden from human eyes' (*Z.K.* 106). Later in May he thought of a new ending to *The Song of Fate*:

Weary Elena enters the log cabin where sits a neglected, discouraged Germann (a filthy life). She rushes to him. Germann puts her sternly aside, repeating *these* words. She remains by him, bearing in mind the words of the monk: 'And, at the end of the road—the soul of Germann.' (*Z.K.* 107)

'*These* words' were a scrap of verse also written in May and entitled 'In the Spirit of Orthodoxy':

> Unrecompensed and unrequited,
> No answer will you get of me.
> But you your solemn word have plighted
> The mistress of my house to be.   (II. 339)

The Song of Fate is the most directly autobiographical of Blok's works and Elena is undoubtedly modelled on Lyubov'. Nevertheless, it would be wrong to say that this autocratic quatrain expressed Blok's actual 'demands' on his wife; he was too conscious of his own guilt towards her, too sophisticated and ironical to make demands. On the contrary, he always emphasized that she must consider herself completely free. Yet, in spite of everything, the verse did express what he saw to be her supreme 'duty'.

Just now, however, Lyubov's abundant vitality and natural high spirits had broken bounds. She was only twenty-seven and had borne for five difficult years the heavy burden of the poet's complex love, his neurasthenia, infidelity, occasional cold cruelty, constant concern and tenderness. On her own, Lyubov' was filled with euphoria. The fact that, for the first time in her grown-up life, no one was requiring her to live up to some impossible ideal and that she was at liberty to indulge in self-discovery; the sheer sense of well-being she felt strolling alone through anonymous provincial towns in the spring, with their lilac, dusty streets, and the warm sun of the South; the undemanding cameraderie of her fellow actors; the restfulness of being a junior member of an organized group with no decisions to make, no one else's burdens to bear: she loved it all—not as a great actress loves her vocation but as a wild bird long captive glories in flight and woodland noises.

Blok disapproved of all this, metaphysically and ethically. One did not take holidays from a vocation—whether it was poetry or marriage. He disapproved not so much of his wife's half-rakish, half-immature experiments in passion^e as of her happiness, her repose, her forgetfulness of that high platonic anamnesis over which his own soul stood guard, 'a sentry unrelieved'. 'Do not forget duty,' he wrote to her. 'It is the only music' (VIII. 233).

For the moment, however, not unlike a great healthy dog that has every intention of returning to its master in its own good time but finds it convenient to pretend not to hear his call, Lyubov' shut her ears to the music of duty. She was sorry for Sasha and she did come back to see him for a further ten days in the middle of May. This time, however, they found no peace in one another's company; on the last day of her visit he wrote:

I go to bed only every other night and am wasting much energy on wine, boating on the sea, wandering about fields and forests, women. It's very hot. For all these reasons I'm tired. I am just going to see Lyuba off at the station, so that means that as from tomorrow I shall be alone again.[3]

On 4 June he left to join his mother at Shakhmatovo. But here, too, there was no rest without Lyuba. Now it was he who gave her news of their garden: 'there will be a great flowering of jasmine, irises, and lilies. Only the roses were damaged by frost. But they are recovering' (VIII. 242). By the middle of June, she filled all his thoughts:

... I think about you every day, I miss you every day and all my life just now is waiting for you. I still cannot decide whether I ought to live alone; I am very conscious of this lonely life now and I know that it is very fine but barren—there is no other word for it. Possibly we need to be together sometimes. Now it often seems to me that we might be together all the time, but—I don't know. It is very quiet here—hot, damp, and proliferous. Our garden is growing. I am often alone. I am reworking *The Song of Fate*. Perhaps I will even have finished it by the time I get back to Petersburg. The city draws me. It is hard for me to live here without you.... Will there ever come a time when we shall not be parted any more?

(VIII. 243–4)

---

^e For those who are interested, Lyubov' Dmitriyevna makes the most of these in her account of this theatrical season in her memoirs, published in 1977 by I. Paul'mann and L. S. Fleyshman.[2] The text of this edition corresponds more or less to the copy of the memoirs in my possession (frequently cited in vol. I), though the order of the fragments is somewhat different and, on occasion, the exact wording. Until the original manuscript is published, there are no differences sufficient to warrant a textual comparison with this modest and conscientious publication.

He had definitely broken with Volokhova and told Lyuba so in this letter, but the news left her indifferent.

As the spring passed into summer his impatience mounted:

... Time creeps by without you, dull, somehow, and barren. The rain hardly ever stops here—grey, autumnal. I am beginning to feel thoroughly depressed. I am worried about you. I think about you constantly.... Why do you write that you have prepared torments for yourself? I am very worried about that; and don't like you saying that you are not sure what sort of a welcome I shall give you.... There are so many things in which I need your help. It is a long time since the poetry in my exercise-books was written out in your hand. It is ages since I read you anything aloud. For a long time now there have been strangers in our flat. The *lampadki* don't get lit. It all seems so cold somehow.... I so need, so very much need to be with you, but you—do you want to be with me? Much of all this I don't say to anyone, not even to Mama. And if you don't understand, then let it be—I'll go on as I am.

(VIII. 244–5)

3

That month at Shakhmatovo, whatever Blok might say about the aridity of life alone, was far from barren. It was here that the poet's foreboding of the coming clash between the people and the intelligentsia first found sustained poetic expression in the cycle *On the Field of Kulikovo*. The central symbol had come to him while writing *The Song of Fate* and, a true symbol rather than a felicitous comparison, had sunk into the depths of his mind to come bubbling up again and again, in articles, in poetry, in letters and conversations.[4]

The battle of Kulikovo Field was fought in 1380 between the forces of the Muscovite Prince Dmitriy and the Tartar Khan Mamay. Dmitriy, with the blessing of St. Sergius of Radonezh and two stalwart soldier-monks to help him, led his Christian host against the Golden Horde, the Tartars who had occupied all the grassy steppe-lands of south and middle Russia and had, for two centuries, been exacting tribute from the thickly forested regions to the north and west of Vladimir-Suzdal, amongst the most bitterly disputed outposts of Eastern Christendom. The battle proved a decisive victory for the Russians and marked the beginning of the end of their long submission to an alien power.

This battle, wrote Blok, was 'one of the symbolic events of Russian history. Such events are fated to come again. What they stand for, only the future will reveal.'[5] There is a contemporary account of the battle, the *Zadonshchina*, images from which haunted Blok's memory, and he wove them into all his writing on the subject, even as the fourteenth-century author had introduced echoes from older oral sources. And so, in *The Song of Fate*, in Germann's vision of the battle, behind the very personal sense of foreboding, there is a long perspective of years:

... as though these days I were living the life of all times, living the torment of my native country. I remember the dreadful day of the battle of Kulikovo ... the wind drove away the mist and an autumn morning came, a morning like this one, and I remember there was a smell of burning. And the gleaming banner of the Prince moved forward from the hilltop. And when the first warriors fell, the monk and the Tartar, the hosts closed with one another and fought the whole day long, fighting with their swords, tearing one another to pieces like dogs ... and the fresh troops had to sit in ambush all through the day, permitted only to watch and to weep, impatient for battle ... and the leader repeated, warning us: it is too soon, our time has not yet come.... I don't know what to do, action is against my duty, my time has not yet come!—That is why I don't sleep at night. My whole being is always waiting for someone who will come and say: 'Your hour has come! It is time!'

(IV. 148–9)

And now your hour has come—To prayer!

(III. 253)

is the last line of the cycle *On the Field of Kulikovo*, which Blok wrote between 7 June and 23 December 1908.

It is at once the steppes of southern Russia that he evokes in this poem and the gentler countryside about Shakhmatovo. Blok's river Nepryadva, meandering between underwashed banks of yellow clay, is more like his native Lutosni than a river of the South. The image of the galloping mare comes not from the ancient chronicles but from a recurrent nightmare of his mother's, of being borne on and on beyond the edge of exhaustion by a runaway horse. The vision described in the central poem, the third of the cycle, a poem Blok copied out and sent to Lyubov' from Shakhmatovo, is not a vision of the Mother of God, such as a devout soldier in the Russian army of that time might have had, but of the Most Beautiful Lady. Yet it is told in terms taken from the ancient texts. In the fourth poem the lyrical persona is again lost and waiting, like 'the soldier of the reserve' in *The Song of Fate*—or perhaps no longer a warrior at all but just the familiar lyrical hero of all Blok's early poetry, running lonely on his white horse like a wolf beneath a waning moon, separated from the main battle, blinded by the 'dark fire' of his own

and his country's passions.*f* In the last poem, the only one not
written at Shakhmatovo, there is night, darkness, and certainty:

> And now your hour has come—To prayer!

Shakhmatovo had become a prism through which Blok saw the
whole of Russia, glimpses of past and future and all the vast lands
stretching south to the Black Sea and east to the foot of the Urals—
and beyond. It is something like the little land-bound lake near the
village of Sergiyevo which, according to one of the local peasants,
had no bottom: 'Sometimes boards with foreign inscriptions rise to
the surface—flotsam from broken ships. It is an overflow from the
ocean' (*Z.K.* 108).

4

At the beginning of July, Blok returned to Petersburg. Having heard
no more from the Moscow Art Theatre, he sought other opinions
on *The Song of Fate*. Zhenya Ivanov, who had disliked the work from
the beginning, continued to say so in no uncertain terms. Meyerhold,
now back in Petersburg, came out with more constructive criticism.
Blok decided to let the play lie fallow for a while before sending
Stanislavsky a finally reworked version.

Meanwhile, the theatre continued to claim much of his time. With
Aleksandr Benois, who was doing the décor for *Die Ahnfrau*,*g* he
went to measure up the stage and Benois, most scholarly of artists,
made several suggestions to bring his translation more into line with
the original German. He also saw a good deal of Chulkov, and of
Pyast and Gorodetsky, both recently married. The Merezhkovskys
were back from Paris, but Blok avoided them. Chulkov, having run
into Filosofov at one of their publishers', had treated Blok to a lively
account of the 'rustling whirl of rumours' about all their private lives
which the Merezhkovskys had brought back with them from Paris,
rumours which made Blok write cattily to his mother: 'It's quite understandable: they have no lives of their own, so they feed on fantastic
stories about the way other people live.'*6*

Still Lyuba did not come. As if to invoke her return, he set about
putting their flat in order, knocking two small rooms into one and

f Indeed, it was in the middle of his work on *On the Field of Kulikovo* that Blok came
out with the mischievous suggestion: 'I might try publishing my "personal songs", and
my "objective songs". I'd like to see anybody divide the one from the other, though—
the devil himself might break his leg at it!' (*Z.K.* 109).

g Grillparzer's play, which Blok had translated for Kommissarzhevskaya's theatre the
year before; see vol. I, chapter XI.

re-papering after the temporary tenants. This done, he returned to his aimless, insomniac existence, wandering about the outskirts of Petersburg.

18 July

I am sitting drinking in Ozerki. Today I wrote Lyuba a letter. The day was miserable and hot—I'm getting drunk: 'Mistress of my house'. And the house is all made new again. The horror of last winter has been exorcised. I don't know, I don't know ... A quiet day ...

(Z.K. 110)

The letter he wrote that day was near-desperate:

The way I am living now is useless, cold, and empty. Surely you have not become like me? You write 'the wave of my madness' as if it were a matter of course.... Do you know what I want to say to you? If I am to go on living as I am now, without anything much happening, getting drunk every now and again, trusting only one person in depth—Evgeniy Ivanov, not having one living soul by me, I shan't last long, the soul grows old and grey.... For one whole day I rode across the shining fields between Shakhmatovo, Rogachevo, and Boblovo. Not long ago. In the forest between Pokrovskoye and Ivlevo there were just the same slender shoots of bracken, the standing water shone, the meadows were all in flower. And the infinite distance, and the high road, and all those tantalizing, heart-rending twists and turns on the road where I was always *alone* and at one with something Great, before you knew me, and when you came to know me and now, again, when you are forgetting me. Yet all is as it was, and I still bear in myself that same profound secret known *to me* alone, and I bear it *alone*. Nobody in the whole world knows about it. And you don't want to know. But without you I would never have discovered that secret. So it was to you I applied the words: 'For all things, all, to thee my thanks I render....'[h] Indeed, everything I have written, perhaps, everything I have thought, lived by, everything which has made my soul so weary—applies to you.

Try to understand with what feeling I send you this letter. I have not altogether unlearnt how to feel.

(VIII. 346–7)

As he wrote here to Lyuba, the only person with whom Blok felt really at peace was Zhenya Ivanov. He spent long hours with him learning to ride a bicycle in Tsarskoye Selo, the beautiful Petersburg Versailles, where Zhenya was now living. The opulent eighteenth-century royal palace, the Lycée where Pushkin had studied and

---

[h] The epigraph to 'Invocation by Fire and Darkness', from M. Yu. Lermontov. No doubt Blok was sincere in this back-dating of the epigraph to his wife, but the original poem was undoubtedly inspired by Volokhova. The words which follow, however, go far towards explaining the anomaly.

written his first poetry, the swans on the lake, the park with its Grecian statues gleaming amongst transparent northern foliage, were all evocative of the carefree youth of Russian literature. 'It smells of Pushkin,' Blok thought with profound satisfaction, wobbling determinedly after the enthusiastic Zhenya between gardens of flowering limes and rambling roses.

Indeed, that summer Blok's growing awareness of historical continuity made him peculiarly receptive to the lucid influences of the Russian classics. His verses began to recall Pushkin: Pushkin Byronic, in the romantic 'Mary' cycle (III. 165–6), and Pushkin classic, in the strict simplicity of the poem to his absent wife begun on 1 August and completed at the end of the year: 'Of virtue and of valiant deeds and glory ...' (III. 64–5).

The aristocratic, sauntering life of the past two summers led him also to the themes of friendship and poetry, and of friendship between poets, so beloved by Batyushkov, Zhukovsky, and the Pushkin Pleiade. But he filled them with a pungent satirical content peculiar to his own generation and to the year 1908. In the poem 'To my Friends' (III. 125–6) Blok gave free rein to his feelings of guilt and self-disgust, seeming to see the prime function of his generation as that of a caustic to burn out the rot of society, yet at the same time afflicted by the awful fear that they and their verses might be nothing but emanations from the general putrefaction. On the same day, he wrote a second poem, 'The Poets' (III. 127–8), in which, after sketching in an even more devastating picture of the cynical debauchery of the artist's life, he proceeded in no uncertain terms to condemn the vanity of philistine preoccupations and to reaffirm the integrity of his strange vocation:

> So you'll be content with yourself and your wife
> And your dock-tailed, lop-eared constitution,
> But the poet, at one with the world and with life,
> Asks more than a mere constitution.

> And though I may die in the ditch like a dog,
> Though life may erase and efface me,
> I believe: I was shrouded in snow by my God
> And the blizzard blown round to embrace me.

(III. 127–8)

He and his friends, he had claimed in the first poem, were losing their wits from laughter. Death, betrayal, adultery: there was a funny side to them all and they only had to catch one another's eyes to see it. On 22 July, sitting alone in the heat of the summer, drinking, hating himself, missing Lyuba, he read Heine and copied out some words from the *Journey through the Harz Mountains* which he later quoted in an article on 'Irony'. 'All of us, poets of our time', he wrote,

are carriers of a terrible epidemic. We are all infected by Heine's provocative irony. . . . Who else knows that condition of which Heine in his solitude once spoke: *'I cannot make out where irony ends and heaven begins!'* Don't you see?—that is a cry for help.

People like to laugh with those who suffer from irony. But they don't believe them or they are already ceasing to believe them. A man says he is dying and no one believes him. And so the man who laughs dies alone. Well, perhaps that's as it should be? 'For a dog—a dog's death.'[i]

(v. 348–9)

In the midst of this 'welter of wine and passions' (III. 64), this lonely dog's life, it was good to be reminded that some people, at least, had retained a monolithic, if quixotic, sense of human dignity. On 2 June 1908, many Russian newspapers, risking fines and confiscation, had defied the censor to publish Lev Tolstoy's 'I Cannot Keep Silent', a denunciation of the revival of the death penalty and the official counter-terror that was being implemented throughout the country.

'It is impossible to go on living like this', the old man had written. 'At least, I can't live like this. I can't and I won't.' Simply and sanely, basing his arguments, even as Blok's grandfather would have done, on the inherent goodness of mankind, Tolstoy had spoken out so benevolently and so reasonably on the counter-productive unreasonableness of organized cruelty and the joy of purposeful self-sacrifice, that Blok felt as though a sudden ray from the fast-sinking sun of nineteenth-century humanism had shone out to illumine his own times. 'The Sun over Russia' was the title he gave to an article he wrote that August to mark the occasion of Tolstoy's eightieth birthday, an event which, he considered, had been insufficiently celebrated by the nation at large.[7]

The poet had begun to feel the world in which he was living as a vampire world[j] in which an 'undead' bureaucracy subsisted on the living blood of the people. The thought of Tolstoy, actually daring the authorities to put him in prison 'where', as he had written, 'I

---

[i] Words written by Nicholas I on the report of Lermontov's death in a duel.

[j] Blok found the 'vampire' formula later that summer when, on the recommendation of Zhenya Ivanov, he gave himself the chilly pleasure of reading the story of Count Dracula ('I read it two nights running and was terribly frightened', VIII. 251), but his fear and disgust at the way things were going in Russia after the revolution had been steadily building up since the previous autumn; the vampire legend simply offered a convincing symbol at the precise psychological moment.

would know clearly that it is not for *my* sake these horrors are being perpetrated', actually offering his 'scraggy old neck' for the noose, came to Blok as a justification of the old culture and a profound personal reassurance.

It often occurs to me: it's all right, everything is simple and comparatively unfrightening so long as Lev Tolstoy is alive.... For as long as Tolstoy lives and treads the furrow, following the plough behind his little white horse, the morning is still fresh and dewy, not frightening, the vampires are asleep and—glory be to God. Tolstoy is out and about—the sun is out and about—that's what it means when you come to think about it. But if the sun sets, Tolstoy dies, the *last genius departs*—what will happen then?

(v. 302–3)

The frail and distant presence of this last believer in the social efficacy of individual morality, however, was not enough. Blok's faith in himself, in the ability to be a man and to cope with life on his own of which he had written to Bely only the year before,[k] appeared as yet to be ill-founded. On 23 July he wrote again to Lyuba:

I am writing to you absolutely ill and exhausted by drunkenness. All this time I am being eaten up by some inner sickness of the soul, and I can see no reason whatsoever for going on living as everybody else does as though they could count on a long life. There is quite definitely nothing to catch hold of; the only thing that I imagine might prove salutary is your presence, but even that only under conditions that are scarcely possible now: I need to have you by my side, but not indifferent, I need you to take some part in my life and even in my work; to find some means to heal me of this hopeless depression which is my permanent state just now.... Understand that, except for you, there is no one I can look to for support, because Mama's love for me is full of anxiety, and I can't subsist on mother-love alone, anyway. I need to have by me a live, young human being, a woman who loves me actively; if that is not to be, then there is nothing before me but empty, yawning darkness....

I doubt that there has ever been a worse time in Russia than this. I am tired of ineffective curses. I need a human being to breathe *life* into me, not just words and praise and insults and treachery, which is what I see going on around me all the time. Perhaps I am like that, too; all the more as in my heart I hate all my own circle; it is they, after all, who so assiduously cultivated those evil seeds which might not have sprung up so luxuriously in my soul. From irony, lyricism, fantasy, false hopes and promises it is not so very far to madness.—But surely you have not become like this too? ... It always seemed to me that you were a high-souled woman incapable of descending to the depths to which I have fallen....

[k] See vol. I, chapter X, p. 294.

I wrote in an acute fit of despair then lay down to rest. Now I have a temperature, I think—caught a chill, probably. I have no serious feelings. God knows why I am sending you this letter. You won't get it in less than a week, anyway. I'll send you money as soon as all that filthy literary and theatrical crowd stop letting me down, but just now I haven't a copeck to call my own. If you have decided not to throw me over altogether, come as soon as you possibly can. Never in my life have I experienced *such* feelings of loneliness, of being abandoned. Probably my suppositions are correct, you no longer remember me.

I reread this letter, and still I am going to post it. Send me a telegram when you get it. I am completely exhausted. If only I could talk to you as soon as possible, but what then—I don't know. I'm prepared to talk about the stage, too.

(VIII. 248–9)

Blok's indisposition, which was not entirely imagined, proved salutary. It forced him to rest and after a few days at home he felt calmer. Also, his financial situation improved. He had indeed been writing round for honorariums owed to him from various sources, and earlier that summer had been reduced to borrowing money from his father—always a distasteful expedient—to buy his ticket to Shakhmatovo. Now Kommissarzhevskaya at last sent the 200 roubles due to him for the Grillparzer translation and he was able to dispatch the promised help to Lyuba. More important, he received a letter from her, promising to return in the middle of August, at the end of the season. 'You will tell me everything about yourself and the theatre,' he wrote eagerly:

It is essential for us to be together and to talk about so many things, to help one another. No one but you will help me, either in life or in art.... Write what day you are coming. I had hoped that we might spend August at Shakhmatovo.... Still, we'll spend September there at least, perhaps, and we'll dig the earth. The earth explains a lot of things....

(VIII. 250–1)

Two days later, on 4 August, came a telegram from Lyuba announcing that she was already on her way home and would be in Petersburg on 9 August. This was followed by daily telegrams from various stations all the way from the Caucasus.

'Mama,' Blok wrote the afternoon he received the first of these, 'I've just got your letter and a wire from Lyuba. She is coming, most probably, on the NINTH, has already left and is glad to be on her way. Now—*basta!* I am no longer the drunken ruffian I was yesterday and the day before!'[8]

He did not stop drinking altogether, but his depression vanished.

Zhenya came for the night and took him back to Tsarskoye Selo where they went for a 25-verst bicycle ride: even the weather seemed fresh and bracing. *The Song of Fate*, revised and typed, was sent off to Stanislavsky. On the very day of Lyuba's arrival, Blok was to read a lecture about *Die Ahnfrau* to Kommissarzhevskaya's troupe. The editor of *Zolotoye Runo*, Ryabushinsky, had shown his appreciation of the poet's contributions by sending 200 roubles (more than was due to him) in response to his threat to leave the journal if they did not stop 'ruining his summer' by withholding his pay. The newspapers *Slovo* and *Rech'* were ready to take any work he could give them and two new periodicals, *Satirikon* and *Obrazovaniye*, were providing outlets for his verse and critical prose. Suddenly, all these trivia seemed interesting again.

Then Lyuba came. It was as though he had known it all along. She was four months pregnant.

5

Lyubov' Dmitriyevna had experienced a grand passion for a young actor to whom she refers in her memoirs as 'Page Dagobert'—a torrid affair, patently conditioned by the new theatrical and literary cult of the 'pure' and 'beautiful' human body and rather touchingly reminiscent of Elinor Glyn. 'Page Dagobert' himself is a shadowy figure who never enters the story of Lyubov's life with Blok except as a kind of anonymous catalyst and as a contributor to the idea rather than the character of the page in the play *The Rose and the Cross*. When Lyubov' returned she was all alone, unrepentant but rather frightened, expecting a child she did not want and half intended to abort.

Once again, Blok had nothing to offer but 'theory'. The upsurge of feeling he had experienced for her while she was away had been platonic in the strictest sense of the word. Now he was all gentleness, all kindness. Lyuba was only pretending to be an experienced woman of the world. The family doctor told her she had left things too late for an abortion; Blok said it would be wrong. She was to have her baby and he would acknowledge it and they would bring it up together.

Lyuba was touched, awed, grateful. The unhappy woman in her might well have preferred reproaches and a rough reassertion of marital rights, but it was her lot to live in the light of Blok's chivalry, and she gathered her battered dignity and responded as best she could. Besides, she loved him.

The part she now had to play was not an easy one. She hated the physical process of pregnancy, and felt no desire for the child. Blok's mother and Aunt Maria had to be told, as by now they knew only too well the unlikelihood of Blok himself being the father. Aleksandra Andreyevna, for all her love for her son, was quite capable of observing him dispassionately and put the blame for what had happened fairly and squarely on 'Sasha's lack of family feeling, over a whole period of his life'.[9] Zhenya Ivanov, who enjoyed the absolute confidence of both Aleksandra Andreyevna and Lyuba, was privy to this secret as to so many others.

On the whole, however, it was extraordinarily well kept. For once, tongues in Petersburg did not wag; the Beketov ladies were discreet; Lyuba, as always, was silent; and who could suspect the true state of affairs when Blok was patently looking forward to becoming a father? As Zinaida Hippius wrote of him later:

... There was a time when I remember a simple, human Blok whose face was lit from within as never before. In general, I don't remember his smile; it just flickered across his face unremarked. But at that time it is precisely the smile that I do remember, concerned and tender. And the voice was different, warmer.

That was when he was waiting for his child and most of all during the first few days after it was born.[10]

This expectant hope half touched, half exasperated Lyubov'. A very articulate expression of her feelings is contained in a letter written on 12 November to Blok's mother:

I want to write about myself; I know what you want to know, although you do not ask. I have got used to the thought of my child; I feel he is *mine* and *nobody* else's, and Sasha accepts him; well then, he will be ours. Sasha still wishes that I should not tell even Mama of all the bitterness connected with him. It was one of the most difficult questions for me—to find the truth, to find a way to act with real simplicity, integrity, without defiance or anything forced. I think Sasha is right. Why should others know about something that anyway they will never understand, and to humiliate and punish myself would be at least half a form of defiance and unnaturalness. I want everything to be as Sasha decides. Let those who know about my misfortune in connection with the child know, and as for the others— he will simply be *ours*. I beg of you, if you can without loss of your own integrity, speak of it as we do.... There is no point, now that he is to be ours, in trying to keep quiet about the nearness of the birth of the child, and for that matter no one who saw me could help noticing, but to let all the relations know—why should we? It is still painful to me to talk about it all, and if outsiders begin to speak of it, oh Lord! The more chance I am given to get used to it, the better and more simply shall I be able to cope, and you and Auntie do want to help me, don't you? I shan't be able to talk to Sasha's aunt, so please will you write?[11]

At the same time, it must have been burdensome to be the focus of so much Beketov good will. It was as though, somewhere deep down, the family were still hoping for an heir; but how could she provide them with an heir all on her own, she who had never been given the chance to bear a child of their blood? There is anger against her husband, as well as gratitude and respect, in her recollections of this period.

At Shakhmatovo, however, there were compensations. She and Blok did, as he had dreamt they would, spend the Golden Autumn together there,[1] and he did 'dig the earth'. At the same time, he turned the soil of his cultural heritage, rereading Turgenev and Tolstoy, chewing over 'that tasty cud of the intelligentsia—[Saltykov-] Shchedrin, Belinsky, Dobrolyubov'. On rereading Tolstoy's novel *Resurrection*, Blok noted Nekhludov's acknowledgement of the Russian peasantry as the *'vrai grand monde'*. In Turgenev's *A Nest of Gentlefolk*, it was the theme of the 'repentant nobleman', the languid Westernism and mildly self-indulgent sentiments of the hero on his return from abroad to his native estates, that fired his imagination (*Z.K.* 114).

He also became interested in the ideas of Lyuba's father, Dmitriy Mendeleyev, who had been a firm believer in the immense potential of the Russian land (animal and vegetable but above all mineral and chemical), and of the Russian people.[m] It must have been as balm to Lyuba, who prided herself on her own optimism and 'abundant mental health', to see her husband fastening eagerly on to these very qualities in her father's popular treatises.[12]

---

[1] '...I have a very firm hope that we might be able to spend the Golden Autumn together here', Blok had written Lyuba on 14 June. The extremes of the Russian climate make for a concentrated period (usually in the first fortnight of October or, by the old calendar, from mid-September) when the leaves turn all together before they are carried off by the first really hard frosts. This is called the 'golden autumn' and has intense brevity-value.

[m] The works that particularly interested Blok were *K poznaniyu Rossii: Zavetnye Mysli*, and *Materialy dlya suzhdeniya o spiritizme*. Mendeleyev maintained that Russian culture should be neither Slavophile nor Westernizing, but should rather develop step by step to keep pace with economic and technical development. The potential wealth of the Russian Empire was, he was certain, more than equal to that of the United States. Given wise politicians, whose task he saw as the reconciliation of apparently hostile interests and the cultivation of a sense of responsible citizenship, Russia would soon be a leading economic and cultural power.

This September, Blok dreamt 'of founding a periodical in the civic tradition of Dobrolyubov's *Sovremennik* [The Contemporary]' (*Z.K.* 113) which would take a completely different line from the decadent press. It would boycott contemporary European art and exclude the erotic near-pornography which was becoming so fashionable in his own circle. He would enlist non-aligned writers such as Leonid Andreyev, and would himself contribute an article on re-establishing contact with the 'soul of the people' as the only possible escape from impotent isolation.

Of more value, perhaps, to his poetry was the mere fact of living in the country again with Lyuba. Not for a long time had he felt Shakhmatovo so acutely. Things seen were stored away in his memory and notebooks to re-emerge in prose and verse as lasting images. In early October he noted: 'Seen: threshing floor with tumble-down barn. A little old man skirts a boggy patch. Light rain. *Siverko.*" Suddenly all the golden leaves come rustling down from a young lime tree growing in the bog ... and you want to cry ...' (*Z.K.* 115).

This image crops up in an article written later that autumn and the whole of these heartbreaking, sober weeks of looking back and turning over things long known yielded Blok's second great love poem to his country: not 'Rus'' this time, but 'Rossíya':

> Again, as in those years of wonder,
> Three work-worn traces shake and strain,
> The painted wheel-spokes sink and founder
> In churned and puddled ruts again ...
>
> Rossíya, beggarly Rossíya,
> Your wind-borne songs are to my ears
> As to my eyes your weathered *izbas*°
> Still sacrosanct as love's first tears!
>
> I know not how to cherish, spare you,
> I simply bear my cross with care ...
> Let any sorcerer you fancy
> Your outlaw loveliness ensnare!
>
> Though he mislead you and deceive you,
> You shall not perish, shall not fail ...
> But rather, over your fair features,
> Sorrow may draw a passing veil ...

" A cold autumn wind. There is a picture with this title by the *Mir Iskusstva* artist Polenov.
° Log houses.

But what of that? One sorrow more,
The river swelled by one more tear ...
Still—field and forest, patterned brow-band
Above the eyes—you're as you were ...

And easy runs the long, long roadway,
And the impossible's at hand
When, for one moment, from the roadside,
The eyes flash from beneath the band,
When, with the convicts' longing loaded,
The coachman's song swells through the land.

(III. 254–5)

The optimism which shines through this near-lament like a bright, pale sun through ragged clouds stems from Mendeleyev and his perfectly practical material hopes for the future of Russia, from Tolstoy's passionate reverence for the Russian peasant, and from the thought of the child who was growing in secret and would soon awake: the child of Russia herself, in whom she had 'invested all her freedom'.[p]

6

It was the tragic theme of the intelligentsia and the people, however, that continued to dominate Blok's thoughts, and he naturally became increasingly sensitive to any outward stimuli which bore upon this preoccupation. Since the previous autumn, he had been receiving letters from a peasant poet, Nikolay Kluyev, who had originally addressed him with a request for help in publishing his poetry. Kluyev had thought to address himself to Blok because, he said, 'a comrade who was in "Piter"[q] on business concerned with timber' had brought him back one of Blok's books. This book, Kluyev wrote, seemed to tell of a time when there should 'be no more Death on the earth, nor Want knocking at the door, nor Doubts at the mind', granting a glimpse of 'a New Life ... like the ocean, like waves, like stars, like the foaming wake of winged ships!'[13]

---

[p] All these themes, excluded from the finished poem, are present, explicitly or implicitly, in the variants. The legendary Siegfried motif of 'the son' growing up in obscurity, which seems first to have come to Blok with Lyuba's pregnancy, was to go on seeking but never obtaining expression in his poetry for the rest of his life.

[q] Workman's slang for Petersburg.

Blok, moved by this unexpected tribute from the depths of pro-vincial Olonetsk, had replied' asking Kluyev to write more about himself and the peasants, for, aware of the difficulty of communica-tion, he hoped to have found an interpreter in this raw army recruit who wrote of things like timber and hay-making yet had responded so lyrically to his own poems. The peasant poet, however, was offended by his Petersburg colleague's obvious feeling of unbridge-able apartheid—and hastened to assure him that this was not caused by peasant timidity:

The likes of us are not in the least shy of 'you', but simply envy you and hate you, and if we put up with your presence amongst us it is only for so long as we see some 'profit' to be had of you. Oh, how fierce is the pain of your presence, what an infinite-accursed sorrow it is to know that there is still no doing without 'you'. This knowledge is what is at the root of the sorrow, the yearning, the angry brooding that gnaws away at us. . . . The awareness that we cannot do without 'you' is the only reason for our failure to communicate with you, and rarely, rarely do you see cases of slavish devotion on the part of nannies and batmen, spoilt by waiting in the halls of the gentry. . . . The awareness that 'you' are everywhere, that 'you' can whereas we 'must', that is the insurmountable barrier that prevents us from entering into communication with you. But what reasons are there on your side? None—except for profound contempt and purely physical revulsion.'⁴

Blok, deeply struck by this letter, had quoted from it in print, and in May 1908 Kluyev, who was by no means so obscure or so naïve as his letters would seem to indicate, and who patently feared the authorities might blacklist him for expressing anti-establishment sentiments, objected sharply. In June 1908 Blok had written him a long letter about the 'soul of the people' which he had read, he said, 'with embarrassment'. Castigating the poet's already exacerbated class-consciousness, Kluyev described *Free Thoughts*, in one of the three books Blok had sent him, as the thoughts of a gentleman holidaymaker 'taking his ease in the bosom of Nature'. The village girls, he said brutally, laughed at Blok's Russian dances (*plyaski*) as though a young lady from the town with curls and lorgnette had suddenly come to join their country revels. His letter ended, how-ever, on a very different note:

I believe that spring will come, that the soul will find the light of the sun of truth, will make its own the great 'reality', and in the meantime let the cracked bell ring and sing, its sound will carry with the snowstorm by forest

' Unfortunately, Blok's letters to Kluyev have not been preserved.

paths and ravines to the lights of native villages and it will flare up like
a St. John's candle[5] in the twilight of men's souls.... Forgive me if I have
said anything wrong. I am so sorry to take leave of you.

Peace be with you.

N. KLUYEV[15]

Blok, guiltily aware of his own attachment to the subtleties and
comforts of education and privilege, was deeply impressed by
Kluyev's criticisms, which he received after he and Lyubov' returned
to Petersburg in the autumn of 1908. In the midst of a veritable whirlwind of new impressions and commitments, including writing two
newspaper articles and a lecture as well as talking over with Leonid
Andreyev the possibility of the new journal of which he had dreamt
at Shakhmatovo, Blok wrote to his mother in Revel on 2 November
that, though all the week had been very busy,

... The most important thing FOR ME was that Kluyev wrote me a long
letter about *The Earth in Snow*, in which he accuses me of intelligentsia-
type pornography (not throughout the book, of course, but in *Free
Thoughts*, for instance). And I believed him that even I, much as I detest
pornography, have indeed come under its influence in so far as I am an
intelligent. Perhaps this is even a good thing, but what is still better is that
it is Kluyev and no one else who has told me so. I would not have believed
anyone else as I believe him.

(VIII. 257–8)

Blok's family thought that he paid too much attention to this self-
confident village poet who, it seemed to them, was indeed out to
obtain 'some "profit"' from the impression he had produced on so
well-established and romantic a figure as Aleksandr Blok, whose
photograph was now on sale on postcards in Petersburg, for all the
world like a popular matinée idol.

Blok himself did not exclude such a possibility, but his mind was
subtle and cold and he had a water-diviner's response to hidden
truths. The truth he found in his relationship with Kluyev, behind
the strong mutual attraction and the almost equally strong antagon-
ism, was that they had startlingly little in common. His world was
not Kluyev's world, nor could the peasant poet enter into it, for it
was the product not only of a lifetime of leisured reading and study,
but of heredity, upbringing, and environment. Kluyev's world, on
the other hand, had plenty of room for Blok: the people; the tilling
of the earth and the gathering of crops, the prayerful Christian life

---

[5] According to Russian legend, on Midsummer Eve the sites of buried treasure are
marked by ghostly lights called St. John's candles.

and the eschatological vision; grinding poverty; huge forests; snow-covered plains; long, dusty roads.

To this world Kluyev called Blok with words rough and warm as the sun on the bark of old pines:

... If I wrote you that I shall go on pilgrimage' that does not mean that I am seeking to escape life, we go from monastery to monastery because they are the most convenient places: people 'from many provinces' live on holiday together for a few days, time enough to read *The Word of God to the People* for instance and one or two other 'needful' things. And so I too have a desire to go and would refuse none and it's worth going, because it is convenient and strong and unwithstandably holy. It is something no one can do without.[16]

Blok was too much of an individualist and too sure of the end for which he had come into the world—not as the son of priest or peasant but as one of the last scions of Russian aristocratic liberalism—to embark upon the kind of pilgrimage to which Kluyev was calling him. Nevertheless, to Russian ears the call was a very ancient and infinitely seductive one." He explained to his mother what was so important to him in Kluyev's letter:

... It is not just about 'pornography', but about something more complex which, in the last analysis, I love in myself. It is not even that I consider it valuable, it is just a part of me myself. I trust him, and at the same time I trust myself as well. It follows ...: *between the 'intelligentsia' and 'the people' there is an 'infrangible barrier'. It is probable that we feel that which is of most value in them as hostile to ourselves, and they feel the same way about us.*"

(VIII. 258–9)

The following day, he added a postscript: 'This is roughly the theme of a lecture I am writing for the Religious-Philosophical Society for next Tuesday, 11 November.' Blok's renewed interest in the Religious-Philosophical Society was the direct result of the

---

' *Po monastyryam*, lit. 'from monastery to monastery'.

" The poets Dobrolyubov and Semyёnov entered this vast 'holy' peasant world, only to melt into it, disappearing almost without trace, remembered for the fact that they had once belonged to the Petersburg avant-garde and written refined and subtle verse (see vol. I, pp. 185, 305). Even the normally cynical Bryusov had been impressed by Dobrolyubov's sustained renunciation. Kuzmin had spent many months in an enclosed Old Believer monastic community. The artist Kupreyanov, whom Blok did not meet until 1915 but who was another typical child of his class and time, spent a whole summer on such a 'pilgrimage', sketching the monasteries. And Lidia Dmitriyevna Zinov'eva-Annibal, in this same autumn of 1908, the last of her life, was seized with an intense longing to follow the pilgrims who came to beg at her dacha 'to the furthest hermitage, and from there on and on...'.[17]

" Italics mine. A. P.

return of the Merezhkovskys. They met and talked frankly about their differences and the mutual suspicions and misunderstanding which had grown up between them during the past two years, and this talk paved the way to a whole-hearted reconciliation. The Merezhkovskys, fresh from Paris, felt most forcibly the contrast between the revolutionary excitement of 1905 and the apathy of 1908, and Blok warmed to their genuine concern for what was going on in the country.

During their absence, however, the Merezkhovskys' place at the centre of the capital's aesthetic life had been taken by a new genera-tion, content and even eager to keep art and literature separate from sociology and religion. Blok attended an evening devoted to plan-ning a new journal, to be called *Apollon*, at the home of Sergey Makovsky, a young aesthete with the appearance of an immensely tall microcephalous cherub. In no way did the future journal look like corresponding to Blok's dream of a revival of the traditions of the Sixties. The choice of Apollo rather than Dionysus as the patron of the project was indicative rather of a growing Parnassian nostalgia for measure and harmony. Blok, feeling strongly that the time was not ripe for harmony, felt drawn to his older friends and mentors who, together with the serious, sociologically-minded Filosofov, were directing their energies towards regalvanizing the Religious-Philosophical Society.

Although, this autumn, Blok felt that he 'had definitely nothing to ask of the Church', he appreciated the Merezkhovskys' urgent sense of contemporaneity and both he and Lyuba became quite deeply involved in their projects. He needed, moreover,

... to come into contact with a wider audience, to try by any and every means to find out what they are thinking. Even by reading a paper myself and hearing out the criticism. . . . It must be understood that everything is extraordinarily, terrifyingly unsettled. And the most important thing I want to say is that we, the intelligentsia, must hurry, because it may be that the time is already past for questions of *theory*, that they are already an impossibility, because *deeds* have already, and awesomely, overtaken us.

(*Z.K.* 118–19)

Yet, even as he contemplated it, this self-imposed task of waking up a society whose only desire was to be lulled to sleep after con-vulsive and fruitless exertions seemed altogether beyond his strength: 'I must admit the thought of suicide can be soothing—the most vivid thought of all. Quiet! To disappear, to lose yourself, "having done all you could"' (*Z.K.* 118).

Blok's lecture[w] was read at an open session of the Religious-Philosophical Society on 13 November 1908. It took the form of a reply
to the opening lecture of the season on the theme of 'demotheism'
(the divinization of the people) by Germann Baronov. Baronov's
thesis was that, in the confusion of thought and values after the 1905
revolution, thinkers of Social Democratic inclination (notably
Gorky and Lunacharsky) had tended to confound the 'religious process' with the 'economic process', to perceive the historic laws of
cause and effect in the light of a vague teleological mystique, and
to substitute the idea of the 'people' for the idea of God.

Blok in his reply did not seek to dispute the wrong-headedness
of 'deifying' the people. 'We are not barbarians', he said disdainfully,
'to make a god out of the unknown and frightening.' Lunacharsky,
whose passion for 'pretentious slogans' was typical of the contemporary intelligentsia as a whole, might have influenced Gorky's
thinking, but the great writer's heart, like Gogol's, was 'full of
anxiety and love, the people's kind of love, the kind of love it is
possible to feel for a mother, a sister or a wife in one person, in Russia'
(v. 321). Gorky, like every true artist, was of the people; more than
this, every true scientist, whose business was the study of the elements, the earth and the sky, was of the people.

The intelligentsia, on the other hand, Blok saw and depicted in
his speech as a kind of old-boy network[x] of 'people of culture', people
given to hurried, contradictory and abstract theories. Yet Blok himself, throughout this winter, persistently and firmly identified with
the intelligentsia, calling himself an 'intelligent by blood' (almost a
contradiction in terms), and maintaining steadfastly that the intelligentsia had its own truth, its own duty and insights, unattainable
to the people and threatened by them.

In Blok's thought, there were always two truths: the sober concern
for the good of the country as a whole which was the truth of the
people, and the subtle, individual, freedom-loving truth which was
the truth of the intelligentsia. Tragedy lay in the fact that ideal truth
was somewhere between the two on the arc of the swinging pendulum, and that to grasp it firmly and to perpetuate it in any other
form than that of tension, anxiety, and concern, would be to halt
time, and with it the historical process.

If the 'people' have one consistent characteristic in Blok's thought
it is their *youth*. The intelligentsia, he felt, had had two centuries

[w] Originally entitled 'Russia and the Intelligentsia' but printed as 'The People and the
Intelligentsia'.
[x] In Russian, *krugovaya poruka*.

to do what it could for Russia. Now it was being overtaken by youth (again: the people), and Ibsen, on whom he had lectured twice that same autumn, had said: 'Youth is retribution'. From the depths of his own self-knowledge and of his knowledge of his friends' lives, Blok spoke of the intelligentsia's 'will to die'.[y]

> In the people there is nothing remotely like this.... If the intelligentsia is becoming more and more imbued with 'the will to die', then the people have always been bearers of 'the will to live'. This being so, it is easy to understand why the unbeliever turns for help to the people, seeking the strength to go on living: simply by the instinct of self-preservation; he turns to them in all urgency, only to come up against sarcasm and silence, against contempt and condescending pity, against the 'infrangible barrier'; and perhaps against something more terrible and unexpected still.
>
> It pleased Gogol and many Russian writers to picture Russia as the very embodiment of quiet and sleep; but this sleep is ending; the quiet is being replaced by a distant and growing roar quite unlike the cacophonous roar of the town.
>
> The same Gogol also pictured Russia as a flying troika.... Even as we cast ourselves at the feet of the people, we are casting ourselves straight under the hooves of the furious troika, to certain death.... The world around us is already dark. It is already possible to imagine that, just as it happens in bad dreams and nightmares, this darkness has overshadowed us because we are already directly beneath the shaggy chest of the centre horse and the heavy hooves are ready to come crashing down....
>
> (v. 327–8)

On this note of doom, Blok concluded his speech to the Religious-Philosophical Society. The long-term reception was mixed: the immediate result sensational. As a group of Sectarians, the most democratic and dissident section of the audience, surged forward to ply the speaker with questions and to invite him to talk further at their own homes,[z] the police, always represented at public discussions at

[y] Vladimir Pyast, in his memoir of Blok, gives his account of this tendency in Blok's own character:

> ... We happened to be eating oysters. I told him how much I liked them. Blok too, but at the same time he said 'Do you know? Oysters are actually *good* for you. There's iron in them and things like that. That is their tragedy.'
>
> Not so much a tragedy for the oysters, of course, as for those who enjoyed eating them. And this was very typical of him and of the demon of perversity in him....
>
> And one more thing. Blok once told me, that the doctor had said to him: 'Your organism is exceptionally strong, but you have done everything in your power to undermine it.' Blok liked tea as black as coffee; wine, sleepless nights, everything sharp and spicy, for the simple reason that such things were harmful.[18]

[z] On 29 November, Blok took up this invitation, spending 'several hours' with the Sec-

this time and empowered to close down the proceedings whenever they judged fit, intervened and forbade further polemics.

Blok went home to take tea with Zhenya Ivanov. As they settled down to discuss the excitements of the evening the doorbell rang. It was an eighteen-year-old girl, the daughter of a priest, so impressed by the poet's tragic existential sincerity that, like Liza Pilenko the previous winter, she had followed him home, 'to ask (not directly but indirectly, not so much of me as of the "power" that she perceived in me) whether or not she should shoot herself. I think she left us a little more serene than she came' (VIII. 261).

Many people, however, were indignant at what they had understood as a speech *against* the intelligentsia. Pyëtr Struve, the editor of *Russkaya Mysl'*, in which Blok's paper was originally to have been published, flatly refused to compromise the rational, progressive reputation of his journal by printing the 'naïve' forebodings of a decadent poet who, he said scathingly, 'had only just woken up' (III. 261). Unexpectedly, this produced a very real consolidation of Blok's newly mended friendship with Merezhkovsky. The older man, although he took the opposite view from Blok—considering that the people and the intelligentsia would inevitably discover more and more common ground as Enlightenment returned full circle, bringing its own insights to the basic religious truths which the peasantry had never abandoned—was nevertheless so incensed at Struve's refusal to publish that he, and of course Zinaida Hippius as well, withdrew their co-operation from his journal. Blok, Merezhkovsky felt, had something of the utmost importance to say, although he 'had not had sufficient voice' to put it across.[20]

With their usual tenacity, the Merezhkovskys insisted on a discussion of the paper, albeit at a 'closed' session of the Religious-Philosophical Society (Blok could not even obtain admittance for Aunt Maria, who was not a member), on 25 November. At this session, Chulkov took it upon himself to defend the intelligentsia,[21] and Vyacheslav Ivanov, and others with him, maintained that the very concept of class was outdated, that there were now only more or less enlightened individuals.[22] Thus, paradoxically, Blok's warning passed over the heads of those to whom it was addressed, the liberal intelligentsia and his own fellow decadents, but was perfectly understood by the more extreme representatives of the 'two opposing

tarians in the company of Aleksey Remizov. He was extremely interested but unfortunately recorded nothing of what they talked about.[19] That the connection was maintained seems likely from the poet's subsequent references to illegal Sectarian pamphlets.

camps': the watchdogs of law and order who had closed down the original meeting and the disaffected, plebeian Sectarians.

Thanks to the excellent advertisement of police intervention, Blok was invited by S. A. Vengerov, a scholarly publisher for whom he had previously undertaken various academic commissions,[aa] to read his paper again, before a much wider audience, at the Literary Society. In spite of the poet's doubts as to the suitability of his theme ('It goes too far beyond the bounds of literature,' he warned Vengerov on 4 December), the second reading did take place on 12 December, under a new title suggested by the organizer: 'The Divinization of the People in Literature'.

Lyubov' was present and, obviously relieved to escape the subject of baby clothes and her own painful situation, sent a vivid account of the evening to her mother-in-law:

It's a long time since there has been anything so fine and interesting as last Friday at the Literary Society when Sasha read his paper, after which everybody talked until two in the morning. Only you would never have stayed until the good part, I'm certain, because even I wanted to get up and leave at the beginning of the discussion. Cheap tub-thumpers from the S. D. [Social Democrat] lot were treating not only the paper but Sasha himself with such outrageous, brazen impertinence. Non-scientific, vague, childish, naïve, 'Where were you when the social movement was going on?' 'You would have seen the intelligentsia dying shoulder to shoulder with the people', and all this with gestures and interrupted by bursts of applause. The audience consisted entirely of people outside our circle,[bb] from the *Russkoye Bogatstvo* and the *Mir Bozhiy*[cc] groups, with perhaps ten supporters, no more. Chulkov only added to the horror.... He said that Blok should speak only for lyric poets like himself, cut off from the national element, and not about the intelligentsia, but that it was a welcome sign that a lyric poet had addressed himself to society. I was quite disgusted, Z. Hippius too, though admittedly that does not prove anything. The audience clapped. Then there were some more noisy orators and then Merezhkovsky got up to speak. Very warmly, simply, from the depths, the essence of what he said is conveyed quite well in *Slovo*, he got tremendous applause. Then the more serious orators got going and things became really interesting. He [Blok] was much attacked and it was very hurtful and

[aa] See vol. I, p 277n. Vengerov, editor of the Biblioteka Velikikh Pisateley (Library of Great Writers) and literary editor of the Brokgauz-Efron Encyclopedia, was a friend of Blok's grandfather and had first met the poet in October 1905. Blok more than once had occasion to enlist the older man's help for political exiles and petitions for clemency on behalf of persons condemned to death for political offences.[23]

[bb] In Russian, '*Vsya ne svoya*'.

[cc] Two 'thick journals' of Populist and Marxist sympathies (for Blok's first encounter with *Mir Bozhiv*, misleadingly described as liberal, see vol. I, p. 74).

wounding that there was a great deal of truth in what they said—that was about his present transition from one set of opinions to another, from the Tsar to the revolution, and: 'Where are your deeds?' Whereas the unbelieving[dd] intelligentsia that you are pillorying has already made a revolution, shed blood. . . . I meant to write about each one in detail, but I see that I don't remember everything . . . but what I am really leading up to is Korolenko and the other old men, Annensky, Gradovsky, Vengerov, and their attitude. Korolenko[ee] was in the chair and he gave the concluding speech, oh, so well. With such purity, 'holding high the standard', for instance, he just cannot pronounce the words 'the way' without adding 'ahead', and always with emotion and reverence! And then he quoted Heine, applied to Sasha and to his paper, on the significance of lyric poetry and poets—'If there is a crack in the heart of the poet it is because the world is split.' And at the end he thanked him for putting his theme so vividly. . . . And when we went into the next room after the end of the meeting I saw how all these old men were treating Sasha with tender affection like grandfathers, just as though they had recognized in him something of the very best in themselves. And when we went out on the street the snow was still falling heavily, it had been going on all day and all our window is blocked with snow. . . . It was such a good, wide-awake feeling, as though even if it was still only words at least they had touched on life, gone straight to the heart of things. . . .[24]

Blok, also writing to his mother, added his own evaluation of some of the speakers:

What I valued most was: Korolenko's speech, the fiery tirade of Stolpner,[ff] Merezhkovsky's defence, and the charming way the old men from *Russkoye Bogatstvo* treated me. . . . They fed me with sweets, clapped and generally treated me like a favourite grandson, with such transparent disinterestedness, trust and courtesy. The room was full. Vengerov says that there has never been such a tense atmosphere at any meeting of the Literary Society. I was terribly excited with a good, inner excitement relating to the theme rather than to the audience. I have finally become accustomed to an audience.

(VIII. 269; letter of 14 December 1908)

[dd] Although Blok later made it clear in print that he did not consider himself 'a representative of the new religious consciousness' (v. 331), he was appearing that evening in an alien, agnostic milieu as a representative of the Religious-Philosophical Society and so naturally came in for a lot of brickbats aimed rather at Merezhkovsky's 'new Christianity' than at himself.

[ee] Vl. G. Korolenko (1852–1921), a revered Populist writer and militant humanitarian journalist who had suffered arrest and exile in the 1870s and 1880s.

[ff] B. G. Stolpner was a Marxist philosopher who, according to Lyuba, had 'almost understood what Sasha is trying to say' and, had he done so, would have 'defended him as hotly as he attacked him'.

On 30 December Blok again read a paper at the Religious-Philosophical Society, this time entitled 'The Element and Culture'. A
series of earthquakes in Italy which had killed thousands of people
and destroyed the town of Messina gave him the image for which
he had been groping, at the same time confirming his premonition
of the sudden and dreadful reversals of fate which awaited the twentieth-century world.[gg] The image of the volcano, more pertinent and
less allegorical than Gogol's troika image, suggested the idea of
Russia as a shifting, molten mass contained beneath a thin crust of
culture, or 'civilization', as Blok later came to call it, using the word
in a derogatory sense as of something materialistic and ossified. In
the hearts of people of sensibility, as on the seismograph before an
earthquake, the needle was recording tremors that promised untold
destruction and catastrophic change. Answering the critics of his first
paper, Blok replied soberly: 'My questions are not put by me—they
are put by the history of Russia' (v. 350).

7

Throughout the winter, in articles, speeches and five- or six-hour-
long conversations, Blok continued to put 'Questions, Questions,
Questions'.[hh] Symbolism, as he saw it, no longer existed. There were
individual writers who occasionally produced works of value; those
who had once been Symbolists had, perhaps, something sacred, fragile, and profoundly personal to remember *for themselves*, but for
their readers this subjective experience was neither instructive nor
interesting—if only because it was essentially incommunicable.

In every article he returned to the leitmotiv of the intelligentsia's
unfitness for life: this is the basic theme of 'Irony' (v. 345–9), where
he defines the root cause of his own and his colleagues' attitudes as
the depersonalization and mechanization of life which had been
going on throughout the nineteenth century. 'Do not listen to our
laughter,' he begged. 'Listen to the pain behind it' (v. 349). Yet
through all this foreboding, he preserved a vision of an ideal Russia,
a Russia reborn 'in the spirit of music'.[ii]

[gg] The lecture was first published in full in the almanac *Italy* (Petersburg, 1909), a literary
collection in aid of victims of the earthquake at Messina.

[hh] The title of Blok's usual survey for *Zolotoye Runo*, no. 11–12, for the end of the year
1908 (v. 329–45), in which he wrote of the new spirit informing the Religious-Philosophical Society, of the problem of words and deeds, and these same 'high-minded six-hour-
long conversations'.

[ii] Cf. the brief article 'The Child of Gogol' (v. 376–9), written in March 1908.

Chukovsky recalled how, at that time,

... he was literally possessed by this thought of the catastrophe that over-shadowed us and, whatever the subject of conversation, would return to it again and again. Once—it was at the Anichkovs' in their pretentious and heterogeneous literary salon—it was already dawn when many of the guests took their leave and five or six of us were left, half-asleep in our chairs, somnolent from the dullness of fruitless, all-night discussions, when Blok, who had said nothing all night—in large gatherings he usually was silent—unexpectedly spoke up in a wide-awake, early-morning voice, not address-ing anybody in particular, almost as if to himself, saying that, if not today then tomorrow, the vengeance of the people would come upon us, ven-geance for our apathy and our falsity, 'for this evening we have just spent, just now' and 'for our verses . . . for mine and yours . . . the better, the worse . . .'

He spoke at length and, as always, on one note, with an immobile and apparently dispassionate face, occasionally accompanying his gloomy speech with a scarcely perceptible, strangely amused little laugh. The words were frightening, but he was listened to with indifference, even, it seemed with boredom. . . . When we took leave of her, our hostess[ii] murmured in the hall as if apologizing for Blok's tactlessness: 'Aleksandr Aleksandrovich . . . off again.' The guests shrugged sympathetically.[25]

Blok, overcome with the urgency of his theme, had not given himself time to find the essential form to express his ideas. His muse, used to total freedom, would not run smoothly in a prophet's har-ness, and he who only last winter had appeared to everybody as the epitome of the romantic poet, elusive and courteous, with an air that impressed men and women, Russians and foreigners, had very nearly become a bore.

8

Superficially, Blok was now behaving in an altogether more respect-able and responsible fashion. His craze for the theatre was over. The fashion for play-acting, however, had now spread throughout the modernist world, and he was beset by invitations: to listen to Remi-zov reading a new play; to take part in amateur theatricals at Solo-gub's; to stage The Song of Fate with Meyerhold, now rather uneasily attached to the Aleksandrinsky Theatre, or with Leonid Andreyev. He refused them all, and those contacts with the theatre that he could not avoid filled him with spleen and boredom.

[ii] Anichkov's wife was better known under her literary pseudonym as the Populist writer Ivan Strannik.

He found relaxation in the cinema ('the best substitute for the lately deceased theatre', VIII. 256) and enjoyed visiting it in comfortable anonymity with Lyuba. He saw a great deal of the Merezhkovskys, of Zhenya Ivanov, and of other serious people who were not directly concerned with art and literature. The element of *commedia dell'arte* was gone from his life. Instead, the picture conjured up by his letters and diaries of the last months of 1908 is that of a hard-working young man making a serious effort to straighten out his thoughts and his finances—and watching himself do so with a certain wry humour.

On his birthday, he wrote to his mother:

I am sitting here savouring the fact that I am now 28 years old. From Lyuba I received a present of a purse but there is nothing to put in it, Auntie promised in advance to give me Turgenev, contriving to forget that she had already done so on 30 August[kk] and from my dear Mama, there is not so much as a birthday card.

(VIII. 261)

However, when conscience-stricken Mama responded with a gift of 25 roubles he protested that it was 'too much', that they had plenty for everyday needs and therefore he would spend it on something pleasant rather than useful. He then proceeded to render a meticulous account of the judiciously spent windfall: a year's subscription to Benois's antiquarian magazine, *Starye Gody*; the *Collected Works* of Goethe and of a Russian author, Reshetnikov; large envelopes for keeping manuscripts.

Nevertheless, Blok's accounts for the rest of the month do show the degree to which he was dependent on the treadmill of articles, reviews, and lectures:

1 November	Rech' (Vyach. Ivanov)	31r. 39k
2 November	Ibsen (Kommissarzhevskaya's theatre)	30r.
15 November	Zolotoye Runo	83r. 5k
21 November	Ibsen (theatre)	30r.
22 November	Rech' (Ahnfrau)	49r. 32k
24 November	from Mama	25r.

There had to be a reverse side to his unnatural preoccupation with civic themes and family economics:

The hand of the clock creeps nearer and nearer to midnight
The candles have surged up in a wave of light
My thoughts have surged up in a wave of darkness
Happy New Year, my heart! I love you in secret,

[kk] Blok's name day.

Evenings without resonance, dumb back-alleys.
I love you in secret, my dark mistress,
My vicious youth, and all this burnt-out life of mine.

(III. 170)

Lurching, drunken rhythms inform his poetry:

Ya p'yán—davnó
Mne vsÿë—ravnó

(III. 168)

and Gogol's mysterious troika appears to the drunken man not only
in the visionary light of doom but in a fearful silver stardust com-
pounded of snow and wine and the sparks of iron-shod hooves on
Petersburg cobbles.

The notebooks themselves contain the occasional give-away: for
instance, a drawing of a crenellated wall above which is written the
one word NEURASTHENIA, signed *Aleksandr Blok, 4 November, SPb*.
Even suicide, the great *summus passus* of the autumn of 1902, no
longer seemed really worth it.

And, for the umpteenth time, we go on living
And laugh and cry.
The day's like any day; the problem's settled:
All men die.

(III. 68)

Later that November, he began work on the draft of another autobiographical play, never continued:

Act One

A writer. Study with heavy curtains at the windows. Books. Flowers.
Scent. A woman. He understands everything. She lives an intense intellectual life. Half-shut eyes, the teeth gleam through half-open lips. He puts
out the light, opens the curtains. An alien street, on alien life. Subtle
thoughts.

Visitors.

He is expecting his wife who wrote amusing letters and then stopped.

Return of wife. A child. He understands. She weeps. He has understood
and forgiven everything in advance. That is what she is crying about. She
reverences him, considering him the best of men and the cleverest.

But he has been seen not only at (literary) evenings, in his study amongst
piles of books, proud and authoritative. Not only riding by with that other
woman. His reputation is not confined to the mysterious aura of women's
love.

He has been seen at night—on the wet snow—helplessly staggering along
under the moon, shelterless, bent, weary, despairing of everything. He himself

knows the sickness of depression that is eating him away and secretly he loves it and is tormented by it. Sometimes he thinks of suicide. Some people he listens to and some he trusts—for most of his life he knows nothing. He only hopes in some kind of Russia, in some kind of universal rhythms of passion, yet he himself every single day betrays both Russia and passion. And he does *not understand* the formula of Ibsen and Gogol[ll] which torments and persecutes him. Or better, understanding it (as everybody else does), he fails to apply it. He is spoilt (an *intelligent*).

YET THE CHILD GROWS.

(*Z.K.* 120–1)

'Yet the child grows.' To this hope he clung, but dully. Throughout December, Blok seems to have been haunted, sleeping and waking, by the fear of syphilis. This was a recurrent terror, but now he feared it for Lyubov', for the child. Yet he did little to help Lyuba live through the lonely winter of waiting: he was always writing, reading, or out; sometimes drunk; often out until the small hours of the morning. The talk in their home was all of abstract subjects. There were moments when his wife was frightened, utterly lonely.

The public readings, moreover, were beginning to exhaust Blok. He had deliberately sought outside criticism of his ideas in the readings of 'The People and the Intelligentsia' and found it stimulating. The criticism of 'The Element and Culture' had, on the contrary, made him feel acutely isolated, almost physically sick. Yet he was now in the grip of his own commitments and continued to spend much time giving and attending talks.

In December, he finally heard from Stanislavsky, in a long, carefully worded personal letter, that the Moscow Art Theatre had decided against staging *The Song of Fate*. It began to look as though his success of the last two years had been a mere flash in the pan; as though his great theme were going to prove beyond his strength.

Christmas, however, was peaceful. He and Lyuba had a big Christmas tree that smelt of the forest and there was at least an illusion of cosiness. 'We met the New Year together, quietly, serenely and sadly' (*Z.K.* 128).

Yet as the winter deepened, he was yielding more and more often to the dull sensuality which served as a kind of thudding accompaniment to weariness and depression.

25 January. 3 a.m. The second time.

She is called Marta. She has two fat chestnut plaits, greenish-black eyes, a pock-marked face, all the rest is hideous except for the divine, passionate

[ll] This is the same formula of which Blok wrote in the article 'Irony': the artist's obligation to 'renounce himself'.

body. She is a stupid German girl. Laughs and speaks stupidly. But when
I speak of Goethe and Faust she begins to think and to fall in love. 'Even
if you were a crook, even if they arrested you, I would look for you everywhere.' I talk to her jokingly, in German, intrigue her. Who I am she has
no idea. When I spoke to her of passion and death she began by roaring
with laughter, and then fell deep into thought. With her woman's mind
and feeling she had essentially already come to believe it all and she would
believe all the rest if I wished. My system—of transforming shallow pro-
fessionals into passionate and tender women in three hours—has scored
another triumph.

All this is so mysterious. Her absolutely simple, rough soul becomes a
harp from which one can draw any note. Today she became so tender that
she struck several really deep notes on the old broken grand piano in her
room.... The only thing is that, alas, I am the second one she has actually
fallen in love with.

With curious detachment, he adds:

Perhaps I am already falling headlong into degradation. My wife does not
always have the strength and the will-power to pull me up or to be angry
with me (it is a fearful thing to put this in writing). Or is it because the
Child will soon come and she has withdrawn into thoughts of Him?
I don't know.

(Z.K. 129)

Blok, while he undoubtedly felt the whole sordid business of
prostitution as 'degrading', did not look upon the idea of passion
as necessarily sinful and had, indeed, taught Lyubov' his own attitudes. In this, they were very much children of their generation, only
perhaps unusually unsparing of themselves,[mm] making fewer allowances for themselves and for one another than many a modern couple
would do. On the other hand, they did think a good deal about
physical passion and, immediately after making the entry about his
wife's failure to restrain him, Blok was musing on about physical
love with no particular feeling of guilt—though, as always, he dif-
ferentiated between sensuality and true passion:

How seldom we achieve a great passion. When it does come it leaves nothing behind it but an all-embracing song. Legs, and arms and every member
sing and sing one single song of praise.

When there is no passion for a long time (for months), its place is taken
by accursed sensuality, heavy thought; then unease a whole night long
comes as an omen of its approach. And quite suddenly the wind of passion

[mm] The Freudian conception of sexuality and the unconscious were, however, a *terra in-
cognita* for them. It was not till after Blok's death that Lyubov' began to think in terms
of Freudian analysis.

is upon one. 'The Tempest'. There is nothing else—you are all passion, and 'she' is all passion. Still more rare is the passion that sets you free, a jubilation of the body. There is a passion that is a storm, too, but in a kind of closed circle of misery. But there is a passion that is a liberating storm, when you see the whole world from a high mountain. And at that moment the world is mine. It is a joy to feel a sense of possession in passion—an innocent joy.

(Z.K. 130)

There is no such jubilation—whether of the flesh or of the spirit— in the poetry of this winter. Quiet songs of despair and forgetfulness, flying snow, light as thistledown, dancing to rhythms as exquisite and delicate as Shelley's songs; night and death and—again—the dancing lightness of despair; then the stumbling, lurching tread of a man who knows nothing any more—neither why he came into the world nor whither he is going:

> Where yesterday went I've forgotten today,
> By morning my evenings are fled far away,
> And the lamps I forget in the light,
> And the days I forget at night.

(III. 69)

Two things he clung to still: Lyubov' and Russia.

> What if, yet spellbound, I should stumble
> Over the broken thread of life
> And come back home, contrite and humbled—
> Would you be able to forgive?
>
> You, who know well to what far beacon
> I set my course so long ago,
> Will you forgive my raving fevers,
> My darkness, poetry, storms of snow?
>
> Or can you, better, unforgiving,
> Set bells aclamour, that I might
> Not drift too far out from my homeland
> In this uncharted, pathless night?

(III. 9)

On 27 January Blok was drunk; 'I hope', he wrote that day, 'for the last time'. But, on the next: 'Ah, no!' (Z.K. 130)

The 29th of January was the première of Die Ahnfrau. On his return from Kommissarzhevskaya's theatre, Blok found Lyuba in labour. Dazedly, he recalls taking her to the nursing home:

The quiet waiting-room of the nursing home. Three o'clock at night, the all-pervading smell. Somewhere close by they are talking quietly to Lyuba, preparing a bath. The midwife is talking to the doctor over the phone. And far away, upstairs beyond the quiet and the half-darkness (the desperate distant cry of a woman in childbirth).*" Or is it a baby crying? Then it became just a sound in my own ears. Tiled vaults, cleanliness. The smell has got into my fur collar.

(Z.K. 130)

On 2 February, after a long, difficult, and painful labour, the baby was born: 'the image of his father', Lyubov' later recorded in her memoirs with a certain bleak satisfaction. Blok, however, thoroughly shaken and humbled, sought comfort in the reassuring grandfather-figure of Lev Tolstoy and copied out the words of Levin in *Anna Karenina*: 'But now everything will go differently. It is nonsense that life will not allow it to. It is necessary to make the effort to live better, much better' (Z.K. 131).

Above this entry is a record of Lyubov's temperature that tells a grim tale:

morning—39.4
at 3 p.m.—39.6
6 p.m.—39.3
9 p.m.—39.2

There was little he could do while the doctors struggled to save Lyuba and the child. He spent much time with the Merezhkovskys, whose abstract interests were probably restful and who were, in spite of Hippius's predilection for gossip, extremely kind. Hippius recalled these days:

Blok sat in our flat with the quietly radiant face I have already described. The child was weak, toxic, but Blok did not believe it would die: 'He's so big.' He had chosen him a name, Dmitriy, in honour of Mendeleyev.*⁰

In our dining room, over tea, Blok sat silently, looking unusually happy and absent-minded.

'What are you thinking about?'

'Well, you see ... about ... how to ... how ... well, how to bring him up ... Mitya ...'

That unfortunate little Mitya died on the tenth day.

Blok explained conscientiously, in detail, why he could not live, had been bound to die. He told it all very simply, but his face looked lost, unbelieving, suddenly grown dark, scared and astonished.

He came to see us once or twice again after that, then disappeared.[26]

---

*" This last entry evidently describes a product of Blok's fevered imagination, as he later crossed it out, writing firmly: 'Nonsense!'

*⁰ Dmitriy was also the other name Blok's mother had considered for him and the name is bound up with the dream that this child should grow up as the self he had failed to become.

Blok's mother, who had come from Revel, originally to attend the première of *Die Ahnfrau*, left again on 16 February. She was ill herself and could be of little help either to her son or his wife. On the occasion of Mitya's burial, Blok wrote a poem which echoes the words of the Orthodox funeral service for infants who, blessed in that they have committed no sin, are promised sure salvation with the souls of the saints. Laying claim to this salvation for the child, almost as though holding God to a gentleman's agreement, Blok continues to assert his own independence: he will not bend the knee, and he will mourn the 'blessed' infant without seeking comfort of their Maker.

Throughout February and March, he continued to write tragic, stunned poetry, the gist of which is that everything is over, that life is slowly running down and will soon grind to a halt. The only hope is in the slow growth of 'the people', coming into ear like corn in the field. Though the present is hungry and dark, 'the year of the Lord will surely come' which, the poet affirms, falling into the dignified idiom of the liturgy, 'is acceptable to us also' (III. 88).

The liturgical language, however, implied no reconciliation with official religion. Blok visited his mother at Easter and the annual surge of joy in the Resurrection affected him more negatively than ever. He positively choked on it 'like the devil on incense', spitting out a diatribe of indignation against the easy appeasement of his fellow citizens:

> They neither sleep, trade, nor remember.
> Above the black town, like a groan,
> Rings out to rend the midnight stillness
> The solemn Paschal carillon.
>
> Over the works of men that others
> Have trodden back into the earth,
> Over the pain, the death, the squalor,
> They ring and ring for all they're worth . . .
>
> Over the whole world's silly shambles,
> Over all things they can't put right . . .
> They ring, too, over the fur mantle
> That you were wearing on that night. . . .

(III. 89)

Lyuba, one painful gynaecological operation behind her and a second to follow later that year, had returned home on 26 February. Blok's first impulse after Mitya's death had been to go away somewhere: to Kluyev in the Olonetsk district; to wander about the fields and forests with the nature writer, Prishvin; to join the Sectarians, somewhere in the depths of Russia. But for this, too, it was too late. He could not now leave Lyuba. Instead, they decided to sell a couple of Mendeleyev pictures and go abroad together: to Italy, as Lyuba had wished to do two years earlier.

Until they left, Blok continued a desultory pursuit of the interests of that winter but, partly as a reaction against the prolonged effort to express his thoughts about Russia in coherent prose and partly at Lyuba's instigation, he began to think seriously of cutting down on articles and lectures and 'returning to art' (VIII. 278). The only obstacle to this was money. Poetry alone would not provide the two of them with a living.

Meanwhile, they were too drained and exhausted even to find comfort in one another's company. Lyuba kept to her own rooms, bored, singing to herself 'like a captive bird' (III. 74). Blok continued to drink alone, though 'moderately' and 'boringly' (VIII. 282), and to wander about the town by night. One wonders whether Chukovsky really had met him at such times, '... in some mouldering back street, along which he was making his way home with unsteady steps, stony-faced and staring-eyed',[27] or whether the image is in fact a persona, the 'homeless wanderer' who at that time figured as the singer of his songs.

When their maid Dunya left, the Bloks' home life threatened to crumble altogether. They were reduced to eating out like students, and as often as not went to different places, Lyuba, for some reason, favouring a vegetarian restaurant. The flat grew dingy, there was no one to clean the windows.

They left in some disarray. Blok's bicycle, affectionately known as Vas'ka, was safely bestowed in Tsarskoye Selo with Zhenya Ivanov. No one offered to rent the flat, but their one idea was now to get away: from everyone and everything. Blok even shrunk from the thought of returning to Shakhmatovo. 'I can't imagine it and don't love it ...' he wrote to Aleksandra Andreyevna before leaving.[28]

The last impressions of the season were of a farewell visit to the Merezhkovskys, of whom Blok noted: 'I love them in spite of everything—all three; they have taste, anger and will-power' (VIII. 281), and of the Moscow Art Theatre's remarkable performance of Chekhov's *Three Sisters*:

It is a corner of the great art of Russia—fortuitously preserved by some happy chance amongst all the befouled corners of my resentful, filthy, dull

and bloody country which tomorrow, praise be to God, I intend to leave.
... I shall make every conceivable effort to forget all about Russian
'politics', all Russian lack of ability, the whole back-water, in order to
become a man and not just a machine for the manufacture of spleen and
hatred. ... I feel I have the right to wash my hands [of it all] and to devote
myself to art. Let them get on with their hangings, the swine, let them
lie down and die in their own filth.

(VIII. 281–2)

CHAPTER II

Italy — Nauheim — Russia

(Spring 1909 – December 1909)

To the West I owe the fact that the spirit of enquiry has
awoken in me, and the spirit of modesty....
(*Z.K.* 153, entry for 12 July 1909, Tarakanovo)

1

After the long train journey through Russia and the Balkans, Blok's
arrival in Venice was at once a holiday and a homecoming. It was
supremely relaxing to know nobody and to have nothing to do. At
the same time, the town reminded him of Petersburg: a maritime
city, not quite a part of Italy, even as Petersburg was not quite a
part of Russia. It was easy to acquire the geography of the place,
there was a measured rhythm about the life of its citizens which
soothed and suited him:

Our rooms look out on to the sea, which we see through the flowers in
the window-boxes. If you look from the Lido, all the north is edged with
huge snowy mountains, some of which we came through on our way here.
The water is all green. One knows all this from books, yet it is quite new,
only not with any startling novelty, but rather soothing and refreshing....

Every Russian artist has the right if only for a few years to stop his ears
against everything Russian and to see his other motherland—Europe, and
Italy in particular....

(VIII. 283–4)

So Blok wrote happily to his mother on 7 May, a week after their
arrival. Lyuba's presence cushioned him against loneliness. At the
same time, they were sufficiently independent to wander off by
themselves if they wished, and Blok moved in a dream of historic
'memories', lazily letting time slip through his fingers like a child
playing in the dry sand. He was happy to abandon himself to the

fascination of the city and of its pictures: 'You want to be an artist here rather than a writer,' he wrote in the same letter to his mother. Days spent in museums and galleries, interspersed with restful interludes on the seashore or wandering about the town, confirmed the Russian poet in opinions cultivated through years of close communication with Olga Solov'eva,[a] the *Mir Iskusstva* group, and the Merezhkovskys. He rejected Titian, Tintoretto, and Veronese but gratefully took to his heart Bellini and Carpaccio. In these he found a tremulous youth and sense of promise which he associated with the best contemporary art in his own country (the Moscow Art's production of *Three Sisters*, for instance), and this filled him with hope that the sources of art were not running dry as he had feared, but that 'everything was still to be done' (VIII. 383).

In a brilliant, complex poem of 9 May he sang of Venice, his 'latest Adriatic love' with whom he 'had sailed far out to sea', till shore and loved ones were lost to view and totally forgotten. Closely interwoven by rhyme and rhythm are the motifs of the red sail on the green sea and the black steering-wheel worked into the lacy Venetian shawl—the sacred shawl, as he was to call it more than once in other contexts. There is a Christ in this poem, weary of carrying His cross, Who seems to beg association with the poet-Christ 'carefully' bearing His cross in the other love poem of the previous autumn: 'Rossíya'. Ages past and to come must have thronged Blok very closely in Venice, for he pictures his own spirit as outside time yet within the city. In 'Venice 2', the poet—'sick and young'—sees Salome slinking along a moonlight arcade on St. Mark's Square, and the head she bears upon a charger is his own;[b] in 'Venice 3', he is carried out on the tide into a velvety black limbo from which the spirit contemplates reincarnation in the past (or future?) of this enchanting city which, for a brief while, had even made him forget the sorrows of his own land.

This intensely personal, mystical reaction to Venice was undoubtedly conditioned by a kind of ultra-refinement of nervous exhaustion. All too soon, the circular-tour ticket bought in Russia bore Blok and Lyuba on upon their carefully budgeted journey; the

[a] An ardent propagandist for the English Pre-Raphaelites, and translator of Ruskin.

[b] A significant commentary on this image is supplied from Blok's prose by Dr. Lucy Vogel in her full-length study of *The Journey to Italy*[1]: 'Only the work that amounts to a confession, only a creative work in which the writer has *burnt himself to ashes*—whether to be reborn in order to create new things or to die—only that kind of work can be truly great. If this charred soul, presented on a platter as a beautiful work of art to the surfeited and disdainful crowd—to Herodias—is a mighty one, it will stir more than one generation, one nation or one century' (v. 278).

moment of enchantment fell back in time, whole and exquisite and unspoilt by use.

The effect of the change of scene was wholly salutary. Both he and she had quickly begun to recover from their appalling winter. By the time they reached their next stop, Ravenna, Blok, sunburnt, in his immaculate white suit and panama hat, had begun to look appreciatively at the supple carriage, soft baby curls, and dark, inviting eyes of the Italian girls. Lyuba, too, smart in her best Parisian suit, had shaken off the aftermath of pain and loss and begun to enjoy herself. Her statuesque beauty and brilliant colouring brought murmurs of 'Che bella' and Blok noted that wherever she went the Italians addressed her as 'Signorina' rather than 'Signora': 'baryshnya', he translated to himself with evident satisfaction. At meals they talked in low voices like a honeymoon couple—'perhaps from old habit...' (Z.K. 134). But they kept separate rooms.

Ravenna had been the happy suggestion of Valeriy Bryusov. It touched off other chords in Blok's memory: not personal and mystical as in Venice, but historical. The graves of Theodoric and of Galla Placidia reminded him of the solemn fall of Rome. The sleepy provincial town became a prism through which he found himself looking into the depths of the past, perceiving moments of doom and change and the men and women, now sleeping like the city itself 'in the arms of Eternity', who had been fated to act out these moments on the stage of history. The classical poem describing their burial places is hushed with an unspoken, apocalyptic foreboding. Keeping his own voice low so as not to wake the sleepers before their time, the poet catches an echo of their tragedies and passions in the Latin lettering, singing 'like a trumpet from the stone' of their silent tombs.'

Ravenna's association with Dante—first poet of the Eternal Feminine—pleased Blok. So did the provincial stillness, the untroubled antiquity of the place. 'It is easy to understand why Dante found

---

' There are three excellent translations of this poem, 'Ravenna', by Oliver Elton, Jon Stallworthy, and Robin Kemball.[2] On his return to Russia, Blok wrote of it to Bryusov:

...I feel that the poem I am sending you is inspired not only by Ravenna, but by your poetry....I like it, even though I believe the sea ebbed away from Classe before Theodoric's time and Galla and Plakida are one and the same person; but I could not devote less than two lines to the Empress who until this day exercises invisible dominion over Ravenna. I think that she looked like that Egyptian girl whose image has been preserved on wood in the Alexandrian room of the Florentine archaeological museum. There is, by the way, a picture by Carlo Dolci in the Uffizi: Placidia with a cross. But here she is more of a Roman, whereas I think she was a Greek type with Byzantine brows, arched, like that Egyptian's. And she was quite definitely Plakida and not Placidia.

(VIII. 294)

refuge in Ravenna. It is a town of rest and quiet death' (VIII. 294). The two days he spent there remained a well of inspiration, cool and tranquil through parched years of fire and destruction.

The little town is fast asleep, and everywhere there are churches and religious paintings from the first centuries of Christianity. Ravenna has preserved better than any other town this early art of the transition from Rome to Byzantium. And I am very glad that Bryusov sent us here; we have seen the grave of Dante, old sarcophagi, astonishing mosaics, the palace of Theodoric. In a field outside Ravenna—buried in roses and wistaria— is the tomb of Theodoric. On the other side of the town, a very ancient church, where they were actually in the process of uncovering from under the earth a mosaic floor of the 4th–6th centuries. It is damp, the smell is like the smell in a railway tunnel, and everywhere there are tombs. One I found under the altar in a dark stone crypt where there is standing water on the floor. Light fell on it from a little window; the stone slabs are a soft lilac covered by a soft green mould. And there is an awesome silence all round. Amazing Latin inscriptions.

(VIII. 284)

Florence was totally different. There they stayed for almost a fortnight, and the experience was not one of relaxation, but of mounting tension.

On arrival, Blok's first impression was of the size and busyness of the town: cracking whips, clattering trams, crowds of chattering people. Immediately he felt that neither he nor Lyuba was as fully recovered as they had thought. He found it took some time to learn his way about, and memories of the winter spent here in his childhood left him with only the faintest sense of general directions and a feeling of recognition on his first sight of the Arno. A few days spent in a good hotel gave them the opportunity to take baths— a luxury not always available in the more modest *pensioni* and guest-houses—but the hotel was too noisy for Blok and, oddly, it offended his latent puritanism.

There was much to enchant him: above all the picture galleries, the art of Fra Angelico, Botticelli, Bellini ... looking at pictures absorbed him. He looked 'actively', seeking his own themes, his own faces, or, on occasion, some pleasant contrast such as the black-headed, plump Madonna by Sustermans with her curly-headed, black-eyed infant. Raphael inspired him with reverent boredom; Leonardo fascinated him, originally because of a shared discovery about the air of Florence being 'black'; of Michelangelo he liked only 'some drawings'. Occasionally, an artist would be ungenerously rejected: 'Fat, red Rubens', vile G. de la Tour', or remembered for some chance detail. Always, however, he returned to Fra Angelico: the bitter almonds in *The Kiss of Judas*; the angel unfolding glimpses of paradise to unworthy sinners; and, in *The Naming of St. John the Baptist*, the dark passageway in the background with a glimpse of sunlit green beyond. Here, Blok felt, the painter had anticipated something he was constantly struggling to suggest in his own art (*Z.K.* 137–8). The 'youth' and freshness of the Quattrocento colours were a source of pure joy; the high Renaissance he admired, but did not feel at home in; the seventeenth century, almost everywhere, struck him as decline and degradation.

It was here in Florence that the twentieth century, happily eluded, almost forgotten in Venice and Ravenna, came welling back in a swirl of débris, machine oil, and putrefaction, and before he knew it depression again had him by the throat. The key episode was, as usual, a perfectly real happening:

(15 May Florence)

I step out of the café into a great hooting of motor horns. A hand cart. People pulling along a dead body on springs. A man with a torch walks before them. They bore it across the Cathedral square and shut the gates. Now they will have pulled it off, the dead legs hang down, they undress it.

That is what Florence is like from the other side. None of those who pass by *after* this know that behind those gates there is a naked corpse. The street lamps flicker.

(*Z.K.* 135)

This grim glimpse of the Venerable Company of the Misericordia going about their charitable business of giving Christian burial to the destitute gave form to the growing conviction that Florence, the birthplace of humanism, the cradle of modern European culture, was secretly dead: not gracefully and naturally dead like Ravenna, but still ghoulishly, lustfully animated. The men with the dead body were masked:

...Everything is masks, and the masks all hide something of another nature. And the pale blue irises in the Cascine—whose masks are they? When a chance breath of wind blows up in the stillness of a heat wave they all bend one way like blue flames, as though they wanted to fly away....

(v. 389–90)

In Florence, Blok began to drink again:

16 May

Sunday morning, the day after. Again the devil caught me and tortured me this night. I am sitting in an armchair—oh, if only one could always sleep. I see the tiled roofs of Florence and the sky. There they are—the black spots. I'm still not quite sober and that is why the truth about the black air leaps to the eye. There's no hiding it.

(Z.K. 136)

So, almost from the first day, Blok was filled with a dual love and hatred for Florence. The delicate pale blue irises in the Cascine park still held some recollection of the youth of the world, 'the blue dream of Fra Beato', but at the same time, the smart hotels, honking motor cars and proliferation of guides and tourists seemed designed to emphasize the inglorious mercantile pettiness of the present. These contradictory impressions lend bitter zest to the fine kaleidoscopic cycle of verses which Blok devoted to the city.

The first poem of the cycle is a denunciation worthy of Savonarola, and indeed the burning of the 'holy monk' is one of the things with which the poet reproaches the city. Florence was a Judas from the beginning. She exiled Dante, and now she has delivered herself up to the 'yellow dust' of modern Europe, trading the memory of her beauty like an ancient whore, building her brothels—the hotels—in the very shadow of the Cathedral.[d] He consigned the city to anathema, bidding her die and dissolve into the limbo of time, and declaring irrevocably:

> In the hour of love I shall forget you,
> In the hour of death it is not you I shall be with!

(III. 106)

This anathema, however, was pronounced with genuine anguish. 'It is a suffered experience' (VIII. 295), Blok was to write to Sergey Makovsky, the ultra-European editor of *Apollon* who—he rightly foresaw—would object to so 'blasphemous' a dismissal of a city which had always been particularly dear to the Russian Enlightenment.[3] Indeed, the poet does not sit in judgement on Florence. Almost, he identifies with it:

> How sweet to live and dream with you apart;
> To let your age-old heat waves, lazy, tender,
> Absorb and steal away my ageing heart ...

> But we must part, for so our paths are fated,
> And I shall dream of you, and it will seem
> From far away as though youth, new-created,
> Bloomed with your smoky iris in my dream. . . .

---

[d] The last insult Blok later took back, himself deleting these 'thoroughly ill-tempered lines' (VIII. 295). For these and other rejected variants see III. 532–3.

It is with a sense of loss, and in a clash of wild music echoing the very words and rhythms of a serenade he had heard sung in the Piazza della Signoria that, in the last poem, a furious gipsy dance, Blok breaks with Florence. Almost, it is a symbolic repetition of *The Snow Mask* and his break with his own youth, a miniature tarantella to drown out the pain of parting, a rite he was destined to perform again and yet again. Art (in the sixth poem) offers an ark in which to escape the boredom of the world but, as always, Blok rejected all arks. Better to weep in some deserted back street with the sorrowful soul of the real city (III. 106–9).

Not all the Italian poems were written at the time. Some—the first 'Florence', for instance, the anathema, and the sixth about the saving ark of art—demanded to be written at once. Others came more slowly, weeks or even months after the event. All, however, were written in the summer of 1909, between 9 May ('Venice I') and August, with the single exception of Blok's translation of the epitaph of Fra Filippo Lippi, made 17 March 1914, with which he finally chose to conclude the cycle.

The journey to Italy was thus a time of intensely creative concentration, and it was not only the heat and the mosquitoes—of which he complained bitterly towards the end of their fortnight in Florence that made Blok feel increasingly weary. It was, however, the heat which made him and Lyuba decide not to press on to Rome. Instead, they went on brief expeditions to places round about Florence: Settignano (the setting of a most perfect piece of free verse, III. 110) and Fiesole, the birthplace of Guido di Pietro, Blok's beloved Fra Angelico; and then to Perugia, Foligno, Assisi, Spoleto, and Siena.

After Perugia, Blok, carried away by the whirling red garments, bold, dark face and 'audacious' lily of the angel in Manni's fresco of *The Annunciation*, wrote two mischievous and passionate poems—the second entitled 'The Annunciation'—which testify vividly to the pitfalls of blasphemy which await the careless devotee of the cult of the Eternal Feminine (III. 116–19). In Siena, too, the long, half-closed eyes of the Madonnas teased his imagination. Indeed the whole impact of Catholic Mariolatry as bodied forth in the essentially humanist, half-pagan art of the Renaissance seems to have stirred a demonic sexuality of which he had previously been only half aware, removing the last barriers and preparing the way for the almost systematic, orgiastic debauch of the next few years. Yet the poems themselves are graceful pieces, suggesting the foolish frolics of some fundamentally innocent troubadour rather than the truly demonic

poetry of the ensuing years. Nevertheless, Blok was aware of trans-
gression. It was difficult not to be, with an ecclesiastical censorship
with which he had had constant trouble since his first publication
from the *Verses about the Most Beautiful Lady* in *Novyy Put'*, though
possibly the very existence of such a body gave blasphemy something of the dash and attraction of political free-thinking.

There was, however, to be one more moment of beatitude on this
Italian journey—for which Blok had to thank not art, but nature.
He later retold it in his own words. On their arrival in Spoleto,
oppressed by thunder, jaded from the journey, he and Lyuba had
been shown the remains of an underground Roman bridge, an experience which had awed, yet somehow refreshed their imagina-
tions. . . .

Immediately, as so often after a shock, all our tiredness vanished and, eager
to see something new and different, we climbed up through the town and
went out the other side, where rises the round, steep hill of Monteluco,
all covered in low, curly trees; for a long time it has been compared to
a head by Michelangelo.

Approaching the hill with the intention of climbing it we stopped by
an ancient aqueduct, conducted along a bridge over a grassy hollow. It was
a place completely sheltered from every breath of wind but, at the same
time, not dried up by the sun thanks to the mountain shadows, springs
and bushes; it was a happy corner of the earth, a blessed land: the kind
of paradise and peace which you come across here at home in the central
part of Russia in forest clearings, where the stumps have been overgrown
by young seedlings, high clumps of rose-bay willow herb, the white and
lilac caps of the silver-berries, and, nearer to the edge of the old forest, carpets of corn-wheat and frankincense. The wanderer in this land becomes
clear of soul and light of body and to him comes flying the great, rare,
bright butterfly with scalloped wings: the swallow-tail.

And so, by the old aqueduct, before climbing the mountain, we became
clear of soul and light of body. . . .

(v. 399–400)

He and Lyuba, who in this account appears almost symbolically
as 'my companion', [c] set off straight up a steep, grassy slope through
a tangle of curly alders, literally pulling themselves from trunk to
trunk. Struggling up the pathless mountainside for over an hour,
they reached a considerable height; the grass grew shorter and
tougher, the trees and bushes more gnarled, and they began to come
across great outcrops of rock.

[c] *Sputnitsa.*

... A bit further on and before me rose a wall of rock of more than my own height. My companion was walking away out to my left and I set off to the right, looking for a break in the rock wall.

Suddenly I found myself at the top of a completely sheer fall of rock. There were no trees, I looked round me, my heart sank and I myself almost went hurtling down.

Before me I had caught a glimpse of an unexpectedly immense view; the little town of Spoleto lay quite tiny at my feet, the church standing out in the fields about two versts from the town was precisely in position, like on a map.

I seized hold of a root growing out from the rock and then realized that above me, on a stony ledge, my companion was already standing and reaching down her hand to me. The fascination of the drop was so powerful that it required a real effort not only of the arms but of the will to clamber up by roots and juts of rocks to grasp the saving hand....

(v. 401)

When they reached the mountain meadow at the very summit of Monteluco,

... Everything around was new, and we were too. At the edge of the deep blue sky, where, as far as I can recall, not a trace of the thunderstorm remained, a snow-white tower of cloud had formed. Almost on a level with us shone the snowy summits of the Apennines. Never have I breathed such fresh, exhilarating air in such brilliant sunshine. We drank our fill and washed at an ice-cold spring. It was already late afternoon.

(v. 402)

They came down the mountain by a proper path, re-entering the town in a twilight made darker by the returning thunder, the first heavy drops of the storm just catching them as they ran for shelter to their hotel....

2

It was in Siena that Blok first faced up to the idea of going home. On 7 June (European style) he wrote to Zhenya Ivanov:

... We are in Siena, which is already our *eleventh* town. The imagination grows weary. My mood is still rather turgid. Tomorrow we go on to the sea, perhaps to get some bathing. In the Italian papers I read nothing but the most depressing news about Russia. How to return is beyond my comprehension but it is still further beyond my comprehension how to remain here. There is no earth here, only the sky, art, mountains and vineyards. There are no people. But how to go on living in Russia I don't really know

either. The most terrifying and regal town in the world is still, as far as
I can see, Petersburg. We will go up the Rhine when our money runs out,
and that will be quite soon. Well, good-bye, give both our loves to your
family.

Is the bicycle standing you in good stead?

(VIII. 287–8)

Marina di Pisa proved an unmitigated bore. Having dutifully sur-
veyed the leaning tower and whatever other objects of interest Pisa
itself had to offer, Blok shut himself up in his hotel room and settled
down to read *War and Peace* and to take stock of his life so far. The
experience was unpleasant.

Waking up at midnight to the sound of wind and sea, under the influence
of the reawakened memory of Mitya's death, of Tolstoy and of a certain
quiet that has come back to me from some time long ago, I think about
how for the last three or four years I have been drawn, without really noticing it myself, into an atmosphere of people who are altogether alien to
me, of political intrigue, boastfulness, haste, busyness. The cause of all this
is the Russian revolution, the results may be and indeed are already
threatening to become terrible.

(Z.K. 145)

To free himself from all the 'haste' and 'busyness' of the last few
years, however, he would have to find some non-literary source of
income, some way of keeping 'money' and 'weary, hard-pressed art'
in separate compartments. 'How Lyuba could help me in this,' he
noted wistfully (*Z.K.* 146). At the same time, the thought of taking
on a regular job not connected with writing had become utterly
daunting. In 'this alien, ailing Italy and particularly in this dull, im-
personal Marina di Pisa', where for some reason they did not get
any bathing and, to make matters worse, disliked their landlady, he
became more nervy, tired, and ill-tempered from day to day, and
at night woke up to worry about his own future and his work, about
his mother and Shakhmatovo—before he left there had again been
talk of selling it—and about everything else that was going on in
Russia. For the first time he began to long for news from home.

The Bloks arrived in Milan on 16 June, tired and almost incapable
of doing further battle with the omnipresent English for a sight of
Da Vinci's *Last Supper*. On the 19th, Blok wrote to his mother:

... I must admit that this journey has not been in the least relaxing. On
the contrary, we are both terribly tired and on edge to the last degree. Milan
is our thirteenth town and everywhere we have been we have looked at
almost everything. It is true that now I can absorb no more except art,

the sky and sometimes the sea. People are repulsive to me and all life—terrible. European life is just as revolting as Russian and, in general, all human life throughout the world seems to me nothing but a monstrous, dirty puddle....

The only place where I can live, after all, is Russia, yet a worse state of things than there, to judge from the newspapers and my own recollections, is not, I think, to be met with anywhere. It is of some slight consolation to me (and Lyuba) that everyone (whom we respect) feels equally bad—increasingly so.

I often feel a dreadful apathy. It is hard to return, and sometimes it seems that there is *nowhere to return to*: at the customs they'll rob you, in the midst of Russia they'll hang you or put you in prison, insult you, the censor won't pass what I've written....

More than ever I see that never until death will I accept anything of modern life and never will I submit to anything. Towards the whole shameful edifice I feel nothing but repulsion. It is too late to change anything—no revolution will change it. *All* people will *rot*, *one or two* human beings will remain. I love only art, children and death. Russia for me is still the same lyrical immensity. But in reality she is not, never has been or will be.

For a long time now I have been reading *War and Peace* and have reread almost all Pushkin's prose. That exists.

(VIII. 288–9)

Blok's last impressions of Milan were of children and art:

> 20 June before nightfall
> Milano
>
> Tomorrow morning we leave Italy. Thank God! The last, *beautiful* impression today: Ambrosiana[f] and the children up to mischief in the garden.
> To the future.

(Z.K. 148)

From Milan the Bloks went on to spend a quiet week at Bad Nauheim. By this time, Blok was pretty well acquainted with his own peculiar poetic temperament. In Marina di Pisa, at his most irritable and exhausted, he had written: '... all this may betoken either the approach of new misfortunes, events, losses, humiliations, or a passing crisis, the beginning of something new again (?), a renewal of life, the return of inspiration' (Z.K. 147).

Now, in the cool and quiet of the dull little German resort, the inspiration came. It came from the past in the form of a new cycle of lyrics, 'Twelve Years Later', dedicated to 'K. M. S.'.[g] The first

---

[f] i.e., Leonardo da Vinci.

[g] Kseniya Mikhailovna Sadovskaya (see vol. I, chapter III), who had long since ceased to keep up with her schoolboy lover, did not realize until she was on her deathbed that

five were written there and then in Bad Nauheim, the last three the following March in St. Petersburg—again touched off by the memory of a rendezvous, this time on Elagin Island (III. 182–6). These poems have the charm of period pieces, of unashamed romantic sentiment more characteristic of the nineteenth than of the twentieth century. Blok was a spontaneous poet and the theme of Sadovskaya obviously 'sung itself' in the cadences of those nineteenth-century romances which she herself sang so well; yet he was not entirely self-indulgent and did remove some of the more obviously 'dated' words:

(25 June)
Bad Nauheim

With all that are bound up words like 'enchanting' and 'divine', all those which it is improper for a Russian gentleman to allow to cross his lips, but which it is pleasant to remember in solitude and sometimes to use in verse—in secret.

(Z.K. 149)

Blok was very much a Northerner and one part German, reared on German literature. After the heat and dust of Italy, Germany struck him as exquisitely clean and well ordered, and he poured out these first impressions to Aleksandra Andreyevna:

... I was amazed by the beauty of Germany and by my feeling of kinship for it, a way of life I understand and the lofty lyricism that permeates everything. Now it is quite clear to me that half my weariness and apathy came from the fact that it is impossible to live in Italy. It is the most unlyrical country—there is no life, only art and the ancient world. And therefore, as you emerge from a church or museum, you feel yourself plunged into a kind of incongruous barbarity. Italians are not people at all, but noisy, grubby little animals. A typical Italian has the senseless, good-natured face of a monkey, shrilly whistling lips, hands thrust into the pockets of his invariably unbuttoned trousers. An Italian city is almost always an uncared-for water-closet, in Italian: *latrina*, as the notices inform you in strident letters wherever you go. There is no open country, so the only escape from the *latrinas* is along a dusty road bordered by hideous vines. There are few

---

he had not only remembered her in the prime of his life in poetry but had given the memory lasting form in this very personal cycle of verses. After her husband's death in 1919 she found herself destitute and made her way from Petersburg to join her son in Odessa. On the road she was reduced to begging, to eating corn gathered from the wayside, and, by the time she reached Odessa, she was half-crazed and dying. The doctor in charge of her case in the local hospital recognized the name, and read her the poems which, he said afterwards, moved her to tears. After her death in 1925, it was found that, through all her tribulations, Kseniya Mikhailovna had carried Blok's letters, tied with red ribbon.[4]

trees, the vegetation looks miserable, they hardly even try to grow flowers. The Gothic in their cathedrals—even in Milan, Pisa, and Orvieto—is something they play at, like children who have not fully grasped the object of the game.

The birthplace of the Gothic is Germany alone, the country most nearly akin to Russia and an eternal reproach to her. Oh, if only the Germans would take Russia under their protection!... Here I would not be ashamed or hesitate to find a job and would be prepared to work in any office. To be a civil servant in Germany is to stand guard.[5]

Like all Blok's outbursts of enthusiasm or ill-temper, this paean of praise for Germany and diatribe against Italy was the emotional expression of a passing mood. He could be equally scathing about his wife or about the Russian 'common people' (both of whom he not only loved but reverenced), about the bourgeoisie, Europe-in-general, Russia-in-general, English tourists, or Jews, of whose omnipresence at Bad Nauheim and pervasive influence in Russian literature he had several unprintable remarks to make that very week.[h] After this holiday, he always loved Italy and often dreamt of returning. As to his admiration for the German genius, this was modified that very day by a continued reading of *War and Peace*:

(25 June)
Bad Nauheim

Today I wrote to Mama: Oh, if only the Germans would take over Russia. But now, under the influence of Pierre's dream, ... there is one other way out. The same way—'the people'—'they' (in Pierre's dream and in waking; perhaps Russia is the triumph of the 'inward man', a constant reproach to the 'outward man').

(Z.K. 149)

Perhaps the most important event during Blok's stay at Nauheim was his attendance, evidently in a singularly receptive mood, at a concert. With Wagner's music, heard in the Gothic cool which at once refreshed his nerves and set his imagination soaring, he coupled that Platonic anamnesis which had remained a key concept for his own understanding of art, life, and religion. It was immediately after listening to this concert that Blok jotted down a rough outline of

[h] In *Pis'ma k rodnym*, as in all publications of Blok's notebooks and diaries, the barrack-room word '*zhid*' is consistently omitted. This word, in a country where State-organized pogroms were not yet a memory and Jews were still legally discriminated against, was and is considered improper usage for a member of the intelligentsia. Blok used a great many expressions not consonant with his liberal and genteel upbringing. He was not free from prejudice, but his record with regard to official anti-Semitism was irreproachable (see chapters IV–VI), and he had many Jewish friends.

his thoughts on music which was—like the people and the intelligentsia, Russia and the 'element'—a symbolic concept that became increasingly fundamental to his understanding of creative work in general and, in particular, of poetry:

Music is the most perfect of the arts because it is the most perfect expression and reflection of the plan of the Architect. Its immaterial, infinitely tiny atoms are points *whirling* about a centre. For this reason, every orchestral moment is as it were the image of a system of galaxies—in all their simultaneous variety and mutability. There is no 'present' in music—it shows more clearly than anything else, that the present in general is a purely conventional term defining the boundary line between the past and the future. The musical atom is the most perfect—and the only truly existent—atom, because it is creative.

Music creates the world. . . . It is only possible to listen to music with your eyes closed and your face shielded with your hands . . . i.e. by inducing nocturnal silence and darkness—'pre-world' conditions. In these conditions of nocturnal non-being, that which has hitherto been formless and non-existent, chaos, begins to flow in and take shape. . . . If poetry be extended to its final limit it will probably drown in music.

Music was before all things which it conditions. The more my own apparatus is perfected, the more selective I become and finally I shall inevitably *become absolutely deaf* to everything that is not accompanied by music (that is all contemporary life, politics and such-like).

(Z.K. 150–1)

Here, for the first time, we find Blok thinking of himself as a medium; not even, as he called himself elsewhere, a servant of art, a man in bondage (v. 404), but as an instrument, an 'apparatus'. The idea had always been inherent in his thinking about his vocation, but now that it had become 'remorselessly clear' that ordinary personal life had passed him by (III. 74), the idea came to possess him altogether. This was the secret of his remarkable power over his contemporaries. The poet Aleksandr Blok continued to use the body of Sasha Blok, to live in his house, to burn with his passions and to ail with his sicknesses, but already he was, in a sense, as Aleksey Remizov said, 'not a human being at all'.[6]

Meanwhile, Blok and Lyubov' left Bad Nauheim and travelled up the Rhine to Cologne, and from thence, via Berlin, to Petersburg. They crossed the border and were passed through the customs at dead of night, went back to sleep and woke up—in the depths of Russia:

A light rain, ploughed fields, scrubby bushes. A solitary keeper with a gun slung over his shoulder rides about the plough land. Circles around. The striped poles marking the versts—whole books of poetry.... It's a long way to Rezhitsa—and what is there in that Rezhitsa? The same wet platform, unbroken grey clouds, two telegraph officials and a peasant woman shouting against the wind. And that is the white day of Russia after the repulsive Italian day (everything rotting), after the matutinal transparency and Gothic of the German towns and machines. Comfortable, quiet, slow slush. But such a desire for life (*Three Sisters*), and for some reason you look forward impatiently to the evening, to Petersburg? And what is there in that Petersburg? Just the same large, wet, homely Rezhitsa....

And Lyuba is sleeping there before me covered by my coat. Above her dangles her worn little girl's sun hat....

Pity—that's what you feel whenever a human being appears;

When a bewildered German, in Russia for the first time, with eczema on his face, looks on at a slanging-match between his porter and somebody else's;

When the customs official who has spent a lifetime watching other people go abroad or arrive from abroad but has never been out of the country himself asks politely and condescendingly whether you have anything to declare and whither you are bound....

(*Z.K.* 151–2)

And so Blok returned to Russia with the very thoughts he had taken away: reverence for the mysterious and sappy youth of his country and the memory of *Three Sisters*. What he had gained in these two months abroad was a sense of distance, of personal freedom, of choice; and, springing directly from these, an agonizing, compassionate affection for his huge native land and those millions of its inhabitants who had been nowhere and seen nothing; and a renewed, intensely chivalrous, albeit occasionally resentful dedication:

> Russia, my life, must we toil on together now?
> Tsar and Siberia, Yermak and gaol!
> Is it not time to take leave of each other now...
> Must my free heart for your darkness go bail?

(III. 259)

So Blok experienced Russia as he returned from his brief love affair with Venice, his laborious pilgrimage into the far past of Europe, his refreshing stroll through the 'eternal morning' of the German Gothic: '... my own unhappy Russia, befouled by civil servants, dirty, battered, dribbling, the laughing-stock of the world. Hail, mother!' (v. 404).

3

Before going down to Shakhmatovo, Blok paused in Petersburg to stock up with books on the art and culture of Renaissance Italy.[i] He was determined to fulfil his plan of living quietly, reading and studying, seeing fewer people. Apart from the books, he and Lyuba also planned to take with them (in a wicker basket) Aunt Maria's cat, which had been found forgotten in the concierge's larder.

For the next three months they lived, companionably and peaceably if not happily, at Shakhmatovo. Blok read, worked in the garden, built fences, scythed weeds and long grass 'till his hands shook', studied German with Lyuba, mulled over the impressions of their trip abroad, took stock of what was happening in Russia and prepared himself for the coming season in Petersburg. Outwardly, the summer was disturbed only by Lyuba's sudden flare-up of tonsilitis which necessitated a trip to Petersburg for a minor operation towards the end of July.

There were, however, various disturbing undercurrents. While Lyuba and Blok had been recovering abroad, Aleksandra Andreyevna and Maria Andreyevna had plucked up courage to dismiss Martyn, their Latvian agent, whom they had come to dislike and distrust. Unable to manage the estate themselves, they had entrusted the farming to a Russian tenant, retaining house and garden for their own use. To begin with this seemed an excellent solution and for the first time they felt free in their own home, both from the tiresome duties of an active landlord and from the petty despotism of the agent; but it soon became clear that the tenant, too, was a far from ideal solution.

The other Kublitskys, the family of Blok's Aunt Sofia, had bought a much grander house at Safonovo, some twenty versts from Shakhmatovo; it was not yet ready, but this was the last summer Sofia Andreyevna and her family were to spend at their old home. Blok and his cousin Ferol had grown up to be very different kinds of people and the poet wrote to Zhenya Ivanov of daily disagreements with the Kublitskys and 'strained relations which of course affect Mama worse than anybody else' (VIII. 291). Even in the country, Ferol and his brother Andrey wore stiff town suits; they were cosmopolitan, correct, conventional. Ferol was always rather sceptical of

---

[i] These included Goethe's *Journey to Italy*; V. Rozanov's *Impressions of Italy*; P. Pertsov's *Venice*; Chateaubriand's *Journey through America, France and Italy*; Renan's *Historical and Religious Studies*; Walter Pater's *The Renaissance*; J. Burckhardt's *Italian Culture in the Age of the Renaissance*.

Galla Placidia Imperatrice: the fifth-century empress who captured Blok's imagination at Ravenna.

N. K. Roehrich's drawing for Blok's *Italian Verses* in *Apollon*; the artist presented Blok with the original, which he kept always.

Christ in the Garden, a panel from SS. Annunziata, Florence. In the works of Fra Angelico Blok found the landscape of his soul. (Alinari)

Blok's vocation and thought his 'Beketov' attitude to Shakhmatovo as a refuge for relaxation and study rather than a prestigious residence to which to invite one's friends and relations was a symptom of arrogance. The premonition of catastrophe and the genuine horror of social life which Blok shared with his mother may well have seemed to the prosperous Kublitskys nothing but an excuse for their chronic inability to conform. Ferol's father, Adam Feliksovich, can hardly have found Aleksandra Andreyevna the ideal wife for his hard-working brother Frants; and Blok's disruptive and vigorously expressed opinions and scandalous private life were a source of embarrassment to his respectable cousins.

The poet himself had studiously avoided all conventional family ties since the summer of 1906, always excepting his relationships with his wife, mother, and, to a lesser degree, Aunt Maria. He even resented Lyuba's visits to her own family at Boblovo: she came back 'as ever, estranged and looking plainer' (Z.K. 153). What annoyed him still more was to hear of a society party being organized at her old home. 'The Russian revolution is over,' he noted, but:

All Nature has become spellbound again, immediately after the spell has been lifted from people. The Soul of the World is sad and yearning, again, again. From behind the crosses of the fir trees terrible faces look down from the leaden, creeping clouds. All the old faces, and others, new ones, the faces of those who have suffered injustice, execution, deprivation, the faces of great lovers—Galla, Isotta[j]—and others who are especially mine.

The leaden clouds creep across the sky, the wind is sharp. The peasants bow just as they used to do, the village girls fear the lady of the house, Petersburg is meekly being eaten up by cholera, the concierge kisses our hands—but the Soul of the World will avenge herself on us for every one of them. 'Return'.[k] ... Everything, everything will return....

Much is still to come. But You—come back, come back, come back at the end of the trials appointed for us. We will pray to You amidst the fear and passions which are our destiny. Again I shall wait—always Your slave, having betrayed You but again, again—returning.

Leave me my poignant recollection, as now. Do not lull my acute unease. Do not interrupt my torments. Let me see Your dawn. Come back.

(Z.K. 153–4, entry for 8 July 1909)

Blok's Most Beautiful Lady again came very close to him in this quietest, slowest summer. His thoughts on Russia, now perceived

---

[j] i.e. Galla Placidia (cf. above) and Isotta degli Alti, wife of Sigismondo Malatesta, Duke of Rimini in the fifteenth century. At the end of 1919, when setting out plans for a 'Scenes from History' series, Blok made a few sketchy notes for a possible play about Isotta (cf. IV. 548).

[k] 'Return' was the title of Andrey Bely's 'Third Symphony', written in 1905.

more distinctly after the previous autumn's rereading of the Russian
classics and his present absorption in Europe and the great epochs
of the fall of Rome and the Renaissance, took on a new precision.
Still very much 'a soldier of the reserve', quite incapable of action
in face of the all-pervading apathy, Blok at least knew what he did
not want for his country:

I (we) are not for those who are for the Old Russia (the Union of the
Russian People to which Rozanov has such leanings!), not with those who
are for Europeanization (socialists, Kadets, Vengerov, for instance), but for
some kind of *new Russia* or 'none at all'. Either she will never be, or she
will take quite a different road to Europe—we cannot wait for *culture*.

                                                                    (*Z.K.* 154)

This thought troubled him, for he had begun to be keenly aware
of himself as a bearer of culture. Yet the experience of Italy, where
he had constantly felt that there was *only* art, no life, and above all
no organic tie between art and life, made him acutely aware of the
danger of overestimating culture *per se:*

Culture should be loved in such a way that its destruction should not seem
terrible (that is, it is among those things most worthy of love). This is the
attitude of a man frightened by his times, but that is something I can't
help!

                                                                    (*Z.K.* 155)

That August, Blok read Ruskin's *Art and Reality*, in the 1902 translation by his Aunt Olga Solov'eva, and made copious notes, finding
much confirmation of his own ideas on art and nature, decadence
and progress and the nature of genius. For himself, he was writing
little: polishing the Italian poems and producing the occasional lyric,
including the ballad-like 'Smoke from the fire—a blue-grey ribbon'
(III. 258), which embodies many of the sentiments and impressions
of the summer and, for the first time, introduces the expression 'the
terrible world' (*strashniy mir*), contrasted here with the peace and
'heavenly depths' of Shakhmatovo.

With the poem 'All that has been, has been, has been' (III. 131),
however, he seems to have choked on thoughts of eternal repetition
which underlined the necessity of self-renewal: 'I can't write. Perhaps I should not. Something is struggling against my former
"romanticism" (always leaving something unsaid etc.), and can't
break surface but just keeps putting spokes in the wheels' (*Z.K.* 159).

It was Zhenya Ivanov, returning in a long friendly letter to his
bête noire, The Song of Fate, who had brought Blok a step nearer to

understanding the nature of this new crisis in his own work. On 13 July Zhenya had written:

One profound theme runs right through the play. That is the agonizing desire for incarnation: the words and dramatis personae are avid to take on flesh and blood, to become incarnate. In this there is a kind of reaching out on the part of the author himself to the first commandment of being, to the 'I am'.

It's something like that question of yours—do you remember? 'Do I exist or not?'[1]

Zhenya pointed out that the element of mysticism in *The Song of Fate* was closely bound up with the theme of ecstasy induced by drunkenness—the hero, standing lost in the snow, is taken for a saint by a wandering pedlar, and Zhenya reminded Blok of the working-man's expression, 'he's enlisted with the saints', meaning: 'he's taken to drink'. The intoxication of the last act of *The Song of Fate* and the ecstatic state of communion with sky and snowbound wastes was not, Zhenya said firmly, where the poet would find his higher identity, his own 'I am'. Neither would he find it in communion with the people, symbolized at the end of the play by the pedlar who appears to guide the hero on his way. Even Dostoyevsky's devil in *The Brothers Karamazov*, Zhenya continued, wanted to 'take on flesh':

And the devil will whisper in your ear: 'I would like to take on flesh—finally and for real—in a 250 lb. merchant's wife', or, if not in a 250 lb. merchant's wife, then in a 150–180 lb. pedlar.

Germann, having almost enlisted with the saints, gives up this way of mystic anarchism as not leading to 'I am' and pins his hopes on the reality of a pedlar, wandering along without a fixed road because the road of Fate sings within him. But that can't last long either. He'll drop in to a tavern on the road and most likely begin to curse the Yids—but at that point the threads get all tangled....[7]

To this letter, which he did not get around to answering until 9 August, Blok had responded with relaxed affection:

Dear Zhenya, I have neither written nor answered your letter for the simple reason that I am a lazy hog. None the less, your letter about *The Song of*

---

[1] 'Do I exist?' Blok had once asked Zhenya, who replied solemnly in the Old Church Slavonic '*Ty esi*' ('Thou art'). 'I am' is of course the secret name of the God of the Old Testament, and there is a legend, later used in the poem 'Man' by Vyacheslav Ivanov, according to which God recognizes the absolute being of all His creatures by the gift of a diamond on which are carved the words 'I am'. From this gift stemmed the fall of Lucifer, but from this also stemmed the redemption of man through Jesus Christ.

Fate I have taken to heart. I think from the mystical point of view your criticism very probably says all there is to say. To everything that you write I say 'yes' and from that it follows that to *The Song of Fate* itself, after all my excuses for it, I say 'no'. *Nu, i Bog s ney.*[m]

(VIII. 290)

It was not until September 1909 that Blok took the next step away from mystic anarchism and mystic populism towards formulating his new thoughts about art as 'music', as something 'strictly mathematical'. He confided these thoughts to Zhenya in a letter of 3 September (VIII. 292–3), and two days later, set them down for himself:

The form of art is generative spirit, creative order.... (There is no such thing as formless art, whereas art without content—as a result of the absence of the world of the soul and the body—is possible.) However much Tolstoy and Dostoyevsky may heap chaos upon chaos I *prefer* great chaos in nature. The *good artist*, as I see it, is of necessity the one ... who creates a cosmos.

(*Z.K.* 160)

4

So Blok emerged from his long summer holiday[n] with a new, more humble attitude to life and to art and a lively desire to keep the two separate. Yet the chaos from which his cosmos was to be created was growing ever darker:

The nocturnal feeling of the irremediability of everything begins to creep up on me in the daytime also. Let them all turn away and wash their hands of me—let them: I had my youth. I am afraid of death and afraid of life, dearest of all to me is the past, the holy place of my soul is—Lyuba. She helps, I don't know how, possibly by that which she took away?

(*Z.K.* 160, entry for 22–3 September 1909)

Blok, however, now saw his duty as a poet not simply to mirror this nocturnal chaos, but to detach himself from it and to create his own ordered world, to show at least the glimpse of green garden at the end of the dark corridor.

To do this, he had somehow to dissociate himself from his own darkness and it was not fortuitous that, early that autumn, he

---

[m] Following a well-tried precept for translating Russian into English, according to which one always translates God by the devil, heaven by hell, and vice versa, one is tempted to render this last phrase: 'Well, and to hell with it anyway!' But the Russian 'And God be with it' is undoubtedly gentler and more deprecating, although the implication is still, 'because I certainly can't do anything more about it!'

[n] He and Lyuba did not return to Petersburg until 30 September 1909.

returned to the 'double' theme. Again, as in 'Smoke from the Fire', Blok used the form of the song, the romance, yet this in no way detracted from the eerie solemnity and moral significance of this confrontation of self with self:[°]

As I strolled through the mist one October
I strove to recall a refrain
(O, innocent joy of the moment
O, kisses not bartered for gain).
Then, through the blind murk of October,
Arose the forgotten refrain.

Of my first youth the tune set me dreaming
And of Thee, ah, so clearly, of Thee ...
And the darkness, the bitter rain teeming,
And the wind were as nothing to me.
(So youth returns sometimes in dreaming,
But Thee—shall I ever find Thee?)

All at once, from the murk of the evening
There steps forth and reels up to me
A youth, somewhat aged. (Half-believing
That face, once familiar, I see.)
He steps out from the murk of the evening
Unsteadily—straight up to me.

'I am weary of roving,' he whispers,
'And of breathing this shivering mist,
And of looking in other men's mirrors
And of other men's women I've kissed.'
And the thought struck me then with a shiver
That I'd meet him again in the mist.

A knowing smile flashed, supercilious,
And then—I was left by myself.
The fellow had seemed so familiar,
As though we had met somewhere else.
Or was it, perhaps, just myself
Escaped from the smooth-surfaced mirror?

(October 1909; III. 13–14)

[°] D. E. Maksimov in his article 'A. Blok. Dvoynik'[8] examines the significance of this poem for Blok and the general significance of the 'double' theme in Russian literature. Illuminating and erudite, this definitive analysis of a single poem tells us more of Blok's *mirovozreniye* (personal philosophy) than do many studies of the whole *œuvre*, for its author, himself a subtle poet and something of a 'Petersburg mystic', writes with more than academic sympathy.

This is not to say that Blok in any way reformed his private life. Rather the contrary. But he had at last clearly perceived that the bottom of a glass was no place to seek transcendental values. In the poetry of *The Terrible World*, debauch and drunkenness are not aestheticized but are shown, increasingly, as anti-life, as aspects of hell. In one of the first poems of the winter season, 'On the Islands' (III. 20–1), the poet depicts the game of passion played coldly and impersonally, without pretty words or sentiments, setting the ritual sleigh ride and embraces in the very heart-country of 'The Stranger', the Elagin Bridge and the Islands, as if to mock the now suspect mystical intoxication of the preceding years.

Blok himself said repeatedly that it is the artist's obligation to 'show and not to prove'. The admission, in poetry, that 'Art is Hell', and the effort to avoid 'the confusion of art and life, while remaining, in life, an ordinary man', preceded the prose formulation of the same ideas later that winter.[9]

The thought of 'the ordinary man', outcast as Adam, sleeping off a wild binge during which he has lost his way and his vocation, is central to perhaps the most perfect poem of this autumn:

> In the late autumn, from their anchorage
> At the quayside deep in snow
> Upon their pre-determined passages
> Heavy ships prepare to go.
>
> Against the black sky, outlined distantly,
> Above the water rears a crane.
> A single harbour light, insistently,
> Winks out from the snowy shore.
>
> A single sailor, lurching drunkenly,
> Left stranded by his ship, in vain,
> Now all is lost, all drunk, comes stumblingly
> And falls. Enough! I can—no more.
>
> And there, beside the empty anchorage,
> First snow lies light upon the ground.
> In that soft shroud, that shroud immaculate,
> Sailor—are you sleeping sound?

14 November 1909
(III. 19)

Yet even as the poet looked fixedly into the heart of nightmare, and tried to find form to tell of what he saw, the literary figure Aleksandr Blok plunged once again into the hurly-burly of the Petersburg season.

The season opened with a success as indisputable as that of 'The Stranger', with Blok's reading of his *Italian Verses* to members of the *Apollon* 'Academy' (more properly known as the 'Society of Lovers of the Artistic Word'). Sergey Makovsky, who to judge from his reminiscences was out of sympathy with Blok and did not consider him a great poet, nevertheless described it as 'a minor occasion':

There he was on his feet, erect and still, then he walked unhurriedly across to the corner of the room and rested his hands on the back of a chair. He was not wearing the shirt with the wide collar as in so many portraits but the most ordinary littérateur's dinner jacket; the black bow tie showed off the even, ruddy colour of his face (his face was remarkable for the evenness of its colour, without the least rosiness in the cheeks); when he threw back his head a little you could see the handsome, full neck. He looked straight in front of him, above the heads of his audience, tense, but trying to appear calm and 'simple'.

He remained silent for a few seconds, then, in his hollow voice, began to drop line after line, deliberately, monotonously, making almost no concession to the sense, accentuating only the rhyming word.... He recited at length; six or seven poems from the still unpublished 'Italian' suite. One after the other, with brief pauses (it was not customary to interrupt a recitation with applause).

He fell silent. And everyone else kept silent. How clearly it was to be felt in that first silence that Blok's declamation had cast a spell over his listeners! There was something extraordinarily impressive about his reciting. It was as if the verses spoke convincingly for themselves quite apart from the actual words.

After this our chairman Vyacheslav Ivanov pronounced a laudatory speech. Immediately I asked Blok for some of the poems he had just read for *Apollon*. He agreed.[10]

The artist Roehrich asked *Apollon* to let him contribute a half-title for their selection from Blok's *Italian Verses*. This pleased the poet, and he later had Roehrich's drawing (an elegant view of a tiny mountain city) framed, and kept it always in his study.

Makovsky, it is true, was to prove a troublesome editor, making several schoolmasterly attempts to introduce pedantic corrections in the Italian poems.[11] Gone were the days, however, when Aleksandr Blok had sat down meekly to rewrite his verse at an editor's bidding. He refused, point-blank and on principle, to alter anything whatsoever:

For me this is the way things are: any grammatical slip in these poems is *not fortuitous*, there is something behind it which I inwardly cannot sacrifice; in other words this is the way 'it sings itself' to me....

This is the reason for my answer—almost the feeling of a young mother when she is told that her child is suffering from this, that, or the other albeit quite minor imperfection; an almost physiological vexation: 'all right, I know, but all the same he's fine as he is, uniquely fine, even, and I wouldn't have him any different ON PRINCIPLE'. . . .

(VIII. 301–2, letter of
29 December 1909)

5

To begin with, Blok and Lyuba were well content to be back at their old flat in Galernaya Street. There was a new maid, Pasha, to cook their dinner, which again created that illusion of domestic well-being Blok found it so difficult to do without. It was pleasant, too, to see old friends—Chulkov, Verigina, Meyerhold—however much one might have inveighed against the social round and the 'hysterical laughter' which had been associated with precisely these three.

Verigina, in Petersburg for a month before the opening of the season in Moscow, spent almost every evening with Blok and Lyuba, vicariously reliving their Italian journey through Blok's poetry and the postcards and photographs they had brought back. In search of light relief, she recalled, the three of them would go to the cinema:

Sometimes Aleksandr Aleksandrovich would be in the mood for fun. His model at that particular time was Nat Pinkerton.[P] For instance, when inviting Lyubov' Dmitriyevna and me to the cinema on the Petrogradskaya Storona he would say: 'Let us cross the Thames to the City' and once, when the three of us were crossing 'the Thames' and found ourselves walking behind a drunken, tattered individual who could scarcely keep his feet, Blok turned his head to me and asked in a voice implying some discovery of the utmost significance: 'Have you not the impression that there is a strong odour of *whisky* about that gentleman?' In the cinema Aleksandr Aleksandrovich continued to chatter on in the same spirit and we laughed so much we paid virtually no attention to what was going on on the screen. . . .

On the whole, however, the time of the 'merry, unreal masks' was over and the three of them were already 'people on a serious

---

[P] Korney Chukovsky, who went to the cinema in the hope of cultural stimulus, not, like Blok, in search of relaxation, wrote a series of articles about the new vogue for escapist entertainment in which he was particularly scathing about comedy movies and 'Nat Pinkerton', the hero of a series of cheap detective stories, compared with whom, he claimed, Sherlock Holmes was a miracle of refinement.[12] But then Blok had always had a pronounced taste for Sherlock Holmes.

plane in real life'. Lyubov' Dmitriyevna had renounced the stage, clearly in response to Blok's wishes, and was, as usual, hating being 'the poet's wife' and nothing more. Her apathy, indeed, worried Verigina:

To my question as to what she was doing she replied: 'Nothing really. Just reading books.' This doing nothing was a bad sign. Usually, Lyuba was full of interests. Now she was studying the architecture of old St. Petersburg, now antique porcelain, now lace, now she would be looking up old magazines and all this would be undertaken thoroughly and seriously. You could tell she came from a scholarly family.[13]

Verigina was not the only person to be worried about Lyuba. Her mother, Anna Ivanovna, had become a frequent visitor to the young couple's home.

For Blok himself, however, the most pressing anxiety of this winter was the health of his own mother. On her return to Revel after the summer at Shakhmatovo, Aleksandra Andreyevna had fallen into a deep clinical depression, sitting motionless all day while her husband was out about his duties, unable to speak or to smile or react in any way when he came home in the evening.[14] She was again troubled by epileptoid fits. Blok's letters to her throughout this winter are full of care and anxiety; he was in constant touch with Frants Feliksovich and spent much time making enquiries about possible cures, doctors, and sanatoria.

In his letters, Blok was never guilty of jollying his mother along, yet he wrote at length and amusingly of any little thing that might conceivably give her pleasure or make her smile. At the same time, without in any way implying that she was 'abnormal', he constantly urged her to seek medical advice. In a sense he identified with her alienation. In a letter of 24 October, for instance, he wrote:

I am saved from the condition you are in now by a great number of people, relationships, and things to do. Everything has started up again at full pressure because the *Italian Verses* seem somehow to have made my reputation all over again. I have been elected a member of the presidium of the 'Society of Lovers of the Artistic Word' (attached to *Apollon*) as one of six: Makovsky, Vyach. Ivanov, In. F. Annensky, Val. Bryusov, Kuzmin, and me. And I am invited to contribute to *Apollon* (the Italian poems). If you can I would advise you to subscribe. At least there will be one avant-garde artistic periodical in Russia (*Vesy* and *Zolotoye Runo* are closing down), in spite of the heterogeneous quality of the contributors—rather in the style of *Mir Iskusstva*. You will find all the 'names' there. . . . Tomorrow we meet in honour of Makovsky at Pivato's[q] on the occasion of the publication of the first number of *Apollon*.

He went on to tell her more about his literary affairs; he was receiving honorariums from various magazines and newspapers, including *Rech'* and the popular *Novyy Zhurnal dlya Vsekh*:

They treat me as an established literary figure. I've written an extremely long autobiographical note for a collection published by Fidler for charity.[15] When it comes out you'll be interested to read it—there's a lot about you.... I am so glad you are trying a cure. Of course, a sanatorium in Revel is not to be thought of.[r] But do write me if only a word or two whenever you can, because I always begin to feel anxious whenever I don't get letters.[16]

A few days later, however, Blok himself fell ill with a slight but persistent fever, swollen glands, and a sore mouth and gums. His lips were dry and cracked and he was in considerable pain. Dr. Belogolovy was called in, diagnosed a mild form of scurvy (a strange disease for a young man returned to Petersburg only a month before from the autumnal plenty of the Russian countryside), and recommended a vegetable diet and rest. Bored but docile, Blok kept the house for almost three weeks, entertaining his friends (when not in too great discomfort), playing draughts and chess with his wife, writing regularly to his mother, inveighing against *Apollon*, the first number of which did not come up to expectation, finishing off his albums of postcards and writing the fine prose *Lightnings of Art*, unfinished impressions of that summer not destined to be published until after his death.[17]

It was during this period of enforced inactivity that he wrote 'The Song of Hell' (III. 15–18), an attempt at a modern *Inferno* in which the poet pictures himself as a lonely pilgrim who has lost his Beatrice. In Hell, he again meets his double, condemned to eternal torment for his dissolute life on earth. Blok handled the *terza rima* with assurance, but only 'fairly liked' (VIII. 296) the result—and that because there was something from 'the holy past' in it rather than for its immediate lyric impact. Indeed, the vampire motif in this poem, particularly the pointed amethyst ring, is in the kind of lush bad taste to which European modernism as a whole only too frequently succumbed.[s] The exploitation of the 'double' theme, too,

[q] A restaurant in the centre of St. Petersburg. Blok enjoyed the evening, which he described as comparatively sober, with some excellent poetry.

[r] Aleksandra Andreyevna blamed her condition largely on her enforced sojourn in Revel and would undoubtedly have felt isolated and unhappy in a sanatorium there.

[s] This notwithstanding the fact that the amethyst ring had a purely autobiographical

is literary and unconvincing compared to the elusive double met by chance on the wet streets of Petersburg earlier that October.

Deprived of outward distractions, Blok began to feel the familiar tentacles of depression, and confided to his mother:

The only 'comfort' is the general state of horror wherever you look. All people living in Russia are leading it and themselves to inevitable ruin. Now, finally and decisively, the 'rule of order' has been firmly re-established, which means that the inhabitants of Russia are now bound firmly hand and foot, to themselves and one another. Any active movement (in any sphere whatsoever) leads only to the likelihood of causing pain to a neighbour, who is trussed up exactly as I am. Such are the conditions of our social, civic, and personal life. I advise you, while not forgetting your illness, nevertheless always to take into account that you are neither better nor worse off than all other *thinking* people living in Russia. For this reason, one can only feel *tolerably well* in moments of *forgetfulness*.... In order to forget about the pathetic state you are in together with me and all the other inhabitants of Russia one has to have an idea 'under the skin', or a dream which pulsates in the blood, now calmly, now stormily, now consciously, now subconsciously. You have such an idea, and so do I, therefore it is still possible to go on living....

(VIII. 296–7)

Yet when his physical indisposition relented a little and he again felt fit enough to walk abroad and take a more active part in literary life, Blok still had sufficient resilience to enjoy the first, fresh snow—and his own fresh fame.

Of the theatrical events of the season he was most deeply moved by Wagner's *Tristan und Isolde*: 'Every time I hear him', he wrote to his mother, 'I am more excited, music is the most influential and dangerous thing.'[18] Mostly, however, his engagements were of a literary character and he would return home in the small hours, tense and overstimulated by conversation or reading and discussion of poems, and be unable to sleep until 4 or 5 a.m., after which he would not get up until one o'clock in the afternoon. This was quite a usual timetable for literary circles in Petersburg, but the perpetual 'night shift' lent its own frenetic quality to all life and thought—particularly as, in mid-winter in Petersburg, there are only a few hours' daylight anyway.

Lyuba still had some of her inheritance from her father and Blok himself had collected 200 roubles owing to him from various publishers at the beginning of the season, so he was able to let his

significance, having been presented to Blok by Sadovskaya. His father, too, always wore such a ring, a gift from the poet's mother.

intention of seeking a way to earn a living outside literature go by
default. What he might eventually have done about this is empty
speculation, for on 18 November he received news from his father's
pupil Spektorsky that Aleksandr L'vovich was dying of tuberculosis
and a heart condition.

Immediately, Blok contacted his father's second wife, now living
in Petersburg with Angelina, her daughter by Aleksandr L'vovich,
in the flat of her brother, an artillery officer. Maria Timofeyevna
left for Warsaw, taking Angelina with her, but Blok hesitated. His
relations with his father had been complex and cool. He had never
been to see him in Warsaw. To arrive at the hospital, Blok thought,
would be tantamount to informing his parent that he was dying.
The round of literary engagements, too, held him firmly.

He hesitated for almost a fortnight, then, on the night of 30
November, in response to an urgent letter from Maria Timofeyevna,
left for Warsaw:

... The long corridor of the train—at the end a candle burning. By morning
it will have burnt itself out and the soul will be full of unimportant plans.
But now—now it is just that I can't sleep, just as I couldn't sleep in my own
bed in Petersburg. . . .

My father lies in the Valley of Roses and raves in agony, breathes with
difficulty.' And I—I am in the long, hot corridor of the train, and sparks
light up the snow. The old man in his underpants doesn't worry me—I'm
alone. I want nothing. Everything this miserable life has to offer I have
taken, I hadn't the strength to take more from heaven. I am an outcast—
here on the way to Warsaw just as in Petersburg. Only She is not here
with me to be childishly bored, shake her head, sleep, get up to mischief,
laugh. . . .

We are coming into Warsaw. As usual, I am miserable without Lyuba,
I can't be parted from her. And she? Amongst the scattered sparks—a few
stars. The candle is guttering. They've taken the tickets.—For a quarter
of an hour the glow in the sky above Warsaw has been visible, the accursed
accompaniment of big towns.

(*Z.K.* 161–2, entry for
30 November–1 December 1909)

Then: 'Mama, I arrived this evening to find Father already dead.
He died at five in the afternoon.'[19]

' These lines, which in Russian are very rhythmical ('—'—'—'—'—|'—'—'—'—'),
foreshadow the iambs of the long poem *Retribution*, into which they were later incorporated. The 'Alley' (not the 'Valley') of Roses, improbable though it sounds, was the
address of the hospital.

CHAPTER III

Taking Stock

(December 1909 – December 1910)

> ... the present position of Russian literature shows quite
> clearly that we, the Russian Symbolists, have traversed a dis-
> tinct lap of our journey and are now faced with new tasks;
> in cases when the moment of transition is so clearly marked
> as in our day we call upon the help of memory and, guided
> by its thread, we seek to establish and to point out—per-
> haps more for ourselves than for others—our origins, that
> country from which we have come....
>
> (v. 425)

1

Professor Aleksandr L'vovich Blok had made a good end. Having
been reconciled with his second wife, Maria Timofeyevna, and received the full rites of the Church, his last words were for his Maker:
'Let us glorify the Lord'.[1] His son arrived in time to see the peace
in the dead face.[2]

Blok's coming gave coherence to a scene that had lost its central
figure. He took solemn leave of his father and removed, with some
difficulty, his mother's ring—the cabochon amethyst so like his
own—from the dead hand. Touched by the stillness of the face and
by the evident emotion of his stepmother and his father's pupil Spektorsky, Blok recalled how he and Lyuba had felt unusually attracted
to Aleksandr L'vovich on his last visit to Petersburg the preceding
Easter. It seemed to him, in retrospect, that his father had even then
been aware of many things not revealed to those who are still in
the midst of life,[3] though at the time he had merely noted: 'Al. L'v.
came to see us and pleased us both by his cleverness, wit, and resemblance to one of the Nibelung dwarfs'.[4]

Now, in a strange city, surrounded by strange people whose lives scarcely touched on his own, Blok felt suddenly very close to the dead man. He wanted to find out more about him, went meekly with Maria Timofeyevna to make the acquaintance of her military relatives stationed in Warsaw, and then spent half the night wandering about the city with Spektorsky.

The following morning, Blok supervised the removal of the body from the hospital to lie till burial in an open coffin in the flat where Professor Blok had lived since his second marriage. The next two days, passed in hushed solemnity, were a time to reach out in imagination towards his father: not the minatory, sarcastic, remote parent, but the man himself. Blok disliked conventional mourning as much as he disliked official religion, but he was at ease with the dead and the private ceremonies decreed by the Church from ancient times. The rites of the *panikhida*, the lighting of candles and the reading of Psalms, had been dear to him since the death of his grandparents. True, the mourning for his father fell somewhere between the private and the official. There were too many uniforms and medals, too much sense of the mourners being representatives of an occupying power in a hostile city for Blok's liking. Nevertheless, during these two timeless, sometimes boring days, he loved his father (III. 435).

On Friday 4 December, Blok attended the funeral. Pyëtr L'vovich came from Petersburg, there was a kinsman from Warsaw, Meinander, and an impressive contingent from the University. On the day of the burial, Blok wrote to Aleksandra Andreyevna:

Mama, today was the funeral, very solemn, like the *panikhidi*. From everything that I see here and from dozens of different people with whom I have been talking all the time, Father's character is becoming much clearer to me: —in many ways it is a revelation. Everything bears witness to the nobility and loftiness of his character, to a most unusual solitariness and to a quite outstanding nature. I feel a real affection for Spektorsky, who has also somehow shown himself in quite a new way.[a] Death, as always, has explained much, made many things seem better and eliminated much that was superfluous. . . .[5]

At Warsaw University, Aleksandr L'vovich had occupied the chair of State Law for thirty-one years and, over this period, had acquired all the usual academic honours, enjoying not only the respect but the devoted admiration of many of his students. For the

[a] Blok had met Spektorsky when he visited Petersburg with Aleksandr L'vovich over Easter 1908 though at the time the poet had been too disturbed in his own mind to improve on the acquaintance and had avoided a second meeting (cf. vol. I, p. 325).

last two years of his life he had served as dean of his faculty, an elected office. He had been an upholder of the Russian presence in Poland, an outspoken advocate of imperial law and order, and a candidate to join the notorious Union of the Russian People.[b] Nevertheless, as the obituaries in the more liberal newspapers showed, he had commanded a certain respect even amongst his political enemies thanks to the consistent and disinterested quality of his conservatism.[6] The picture of his father that Blok was now gathering from Spektorsky and others who had known him as a professional was very different from his own recollection of the rather seedy and pedantic person whose formal calls in Petersburg he had always dreaded.

Through Spektorsky, who was preparing a biography, Blok now, for the first time, obtained some insight into his father's mind: fastidious, ironic, and fiercely realistic. In his book, Spektorsky was to speak of the 'elegance of perfectly formulated nuance' which characterized his teacher's exposition of his own subject, of his passion for facts, however seemingly contradictory and apparently mutually exclusive, and of 'his profound, ruthless irony.... At the basis of this irony is what Friedrich Schlegel defined as "a clear awareness of infinite chaos" and, one assumes, of the inevitable lack of correspondence between ideal and reality.'[7] It was this 'awareness of infinite chaos' underlying not only the world as a philosophic concept but also the perfectly real and apparently rigid forms of Russian autocracy, that confirmed Aleksandr L'vovich in his harshly conservative opinions—opinions which could not but fill his son with shocked dismay.

Accepting many Marxist and neo-Marxist tenets on the ineradicability of conflicting interests, Blok's father had favoured an enlightened despotism which would control these from above, rather than a 'bourgeois', limited constitution which would put power into the hands of the merely wealthy, or a free democracy which would give it—in the last analysis—to the merely numerous. The bourgeoisie he disliked. The 'masses' he considered barbarous and irresponsible. Compromise in the Western European mould, with a little of everything for everybody in reasonable measure, he despised as 'petty-bourgeois'.

Blok, of course, was the more shocked precisely because he *shared* both his father's political prejudices and his political realism. Painfully, almost obsessively aware of the serious and terrifying tensions between educated and uneducated Russians, between the people and

[b] An ultra-conservative nationalist organization whose 'strong arm' was the Jew-baiting Black Hundreds.

the intelligentsia, he utterly rejected the 'demonic' idea that the superior individual has the right to seek inspiration in the pursuit of truth, beauty, and even goodness while relegating the rest of the world to the role of political animals. He shared his father's vision of a society in which irreconcilable forces were moving towards a fatal clash, but he would not admit this to be a reason for clamping down upon all movement.

Yet it was no accident that, of all his son's poetry, Aleksandr L'vovich had most appreciated the verses about Russia. The two men had shared a contradictory combination of intuitive faith in Russia's greatness and clear-sighted perception of her faults. When writing of Russia, father and son, quite independently of one another, often hit upon the same quotations from Lermontov and Tyutchev to express their feelings.[8]

Spektorsky also told Blok about his father's unfinished book *Politics in the Sphere of the Sciences*, an attempt to locate jurisprudence in relation to all other scholarly disciplines and to establish the superiority of the humanities over the natural sciences.[c] The story of this unfinished book combined with accounts of his father's exceptional musical talent fascinated Blok. Yet the very fact that Aleksandr L'vovich had been endowed with such profound feeling for 'music', both in the direct sense of the word, and in Blok's own, symbolic sense, made his advocacy of the forcible containment of the element of creative chaos in political life all the more unacceptable.

Two years later, when Blok had had time to think over all he had learnt in Warsaw, he was still to find his father's views profoundly repellent:

My father is the heir of Lermontov, Griboyedov, Chadayev, of course. He demonstrated this *demonically* in his remarkable 'classification of the sciences'. The shining heights do exist (truth, beauty, and goodness), but you, people, are swine, and all that is quite beyond your range, and you will do much better to base any action you may undertake in your *primarily political life* (the extreme of cruelty and irony) on remote ideals ... of a juridical nature. Is that not *demonism*? You are blind, you are unhappy, go on and wallow in your politics (the caressing melancholy of the Demon) and don't raise your snouts to the shining summits (that supraterrestrial smile

[c] It is a measure of Aleksandr L'vovich's devotion to learning that he undertook to educate himself in the latter in order to write this book. Attempting to model his style on Flaubert, he had, by constant revision, finally succeeded in reducing the text to such esoteric and paradoxical brevity that only his most devoted pupils could understand it, yet the legend of a brilliant work lost to mankind by the wilfulness of its author persisted among them.

of contempt—the Demon *himself* elected to lie up in the mountains and there is no way for 'people' to come there). All that in the unhappy exterior envelope of A. L. Blok, very sinful and lustful.

(VII. 112, 26 December 1911)

For Blok, there could be no 'lying up in the mountains', except as a prelude to return, to incarnation and self-immolation; yet for him, too, there was a dangerous closeness between the images of perdition and salvation, of the Demon who rejects the world and the Christ-figure or 'genius' who would save it,[d] for the 'genius', too, in that search for the promised land which is his calling, tends 'to go further and further away until we get left behind and lose him from view' (V. 423).

A figure which seemed to Blok to unite the qualities of the genius and the Demon in irreconcilable duality was Ibsen's Brand,[10] who turns his back upon the meanness and ugliness of human life to search in the mountains for that God of Love Whom he fails to find on earth or in his own heart. Blok's autobiographical poem *Retribution*, first conceived during this fortnight in Warsaw, was to break off with an affirmation of faith in which he evoked the only charm he knew against this arid male dualism: the image of the Most Beautiful Lady, albeit in a new hypostasis. It is the Eternal Mother who, in this poem, absolves the poet from the cold, irreconcilable contradictions of 'will'. When he wakens her image in his own heart,

> Then, in that moment past compare
> The frost-ferns on the street lamp's glass,
> The frost that turns your blood to ice,
> The love that in your heart grows cold,
> Will flare and blaze and, thankful, you
> Will bless all things again, aware
> That life is infinitely richer
> Than Brand's determined *quantum satis*,
> And that the world is beautiful.[e]

(III. 343)

These lines point to the basic difference between son and father. Discord had been the very stuff of the father's being. The son walked

---

[d] I use the word Christ-figure rather than Christ because of Blok's insistence that he never knew Christ. He told Pyast he had only 'felt Him once' and then 'very superficially. Hardly at all ... Neither Christ nor Anti-Christ'.[9] Nevertheless the persistent idea of 'in-carnation', of 'taking on flesh', of 'humanization' and of 'coming down from the mountains' all reach beyond the concept of human martyrdom into the realm of pure spirit and divine kenosis, reverently and profoundly understood.

[e] Aleksandra Andreyevna kept a copy of this passage, written out for her in Blok's hand, in her writing desk to her dying day.

Blok's doodle about his late father, done in 1910: a sketch of Aleksandr L'vovich, entitled 'The Prisoner at the Bar', and some lines about him. (Reproduced in F. D. Reeve, *Aleksandr Blok: Between Image and Idea* (1962), from a manuscript page of *Retribution*.)

throughout his grown-up life in the sphere of discord, but his first foundation was in harmony and the ideal towards which he strove (and which, to use his own language, he always 'remembered') was as sunny, catholic, and all-embracing as his father's was stormy, individualistic, and exclusive. Aleksandr L'vovich, Blok thought, by the time he volunteered for the Black Hundreds had *'forgotten everything'* (III. 339).

Nevertheless, there was something about this strange man that fascinated and drew him and it was here in Warsaw, literally over his father's dead body, that Blok at last fully realized his sonship, and with it a kind of responsibility for Aleksandr L'vovich.

2

The extent of Professor Blok's eccentricity only became really clear after the funeral when people stopped pronouncing the usual panegyrics and the relatives (Blok, Pyëtr L'vovich, Maria Timofeyevna, and Angelina) embarked upon the herculean task of clearing out his flat. Aleksandr L'vovich had apparently never thrown anything away. Angelina's cot stood where it had been when she was taken from her father at the age of four—under a thick layer of dust, like everything else in this extraordinary dwelling. The Professor had been not only too mean to keep a servant, he had denied himself the comfort of lighting the stove for several winters, sitting huddled at his desk in his worn winter coat. The mania for saving had even extended to economy of movement: all the things he used regularly in his everyday life were so placed that they could be reached from where he usually sat, so that he could make himself a cup of tea or shave without taking an unnecessary step.

Blok, revolted but fascinated, came—amidst piles of dirty linen and mouldering crusts—upon heaps of photographs of his mother and her old letters ('Naturally, I did not read the letters, I think that would have been disagreeable for you').[11] There were other things, too, which he preferred not to mention; and there were great wads of money hidden, as a woman might hide her jewels, amongst the household linen and his father's clothes.

In general, there was much more money than anybody had expected. Aleksandr Blok had for long paid out regular alimony to Aleksandra Andreyevna and Maria Timofeyevna, had helped his children through their education, and bailed out his son from time to time with small loans or gifts of money: all this, as far as his family knew, on his comparatively modest professor's salary. He had continued till his last illness to eat in cheap restaurants and for many years had spent the barest minimum on his house or his person. Now it transpired that he had died intestate, leaving a considerable fortune inherited from his mother almost intact. After three gruelling days sorting out his father's papers and belongings, Blok spent much of 8 and 10 December with his family and lawyers arranging what he refers to as 'money matters'. These were regulated with the utmost decency and the minimum fuss, Maria Timofeyevna and Angelina insisting that Blok, as the eldest child and the only son, should take the lion's share which was his legal due,*f* and Blok himself gallantly advocating an equal division. He had his way about the money, but since his stepmother and sister had no home of their own was happy to take his pick of the furniture from his father's flat. The necessity of having this packed up and dispatched to Petersburg kept him in Warsaw for a further week because of the intervention of the 'Polish' Christmas on 12/25 December.

The money, of course, could not have come at a more opportune moment. It made it possible for Blok to put into practice his summer's resolution to devote himself to art and eschew literary hack work—without taking on regular work of an extra-literary character. He could also pay off the mortgage on Shakhmatovo and buy out Aunt Sofia, which settled a problem that had been getting quite out of hand since the dismissal of the agent Martyn. Now there would be sufficient capital for the family to reinvest in the estate, which had been quietly running down over the last few years, and to reassume responsibility as landlords.

Meanwhile, the poet's reaction to the unexpected windfall was a mixture of caution, incredulity, and amusement. In a long letter to his wife, he shared his impressions of Warsaw and imparted the good news of the legacy with almost mischievous one-upmanship:

Lyuba, my darling, I miss you terribly. It takes me by the heart all the time. All the same, it looks as though I am going to have to stay on here for not less than a week. There are a great many things to be seen to and business to be done. Most of the time goes on sorting and packing up the flat.... I am bringing a whole lot of things and in January I think we will have to move to a decent flat. I am bringing some delightful old things for you and for me. My sister and her mother are so nice I even feel a closeness to them both. Angelina is interesting and original and very chaste, but

f Under the law Blok should have received five-eighths, Angelina three-eighths of the inheritance.

still a child in spite of her seventeen years. Maria Timofeyevna is surprisingly straightforward and kind. I wouldn't mind keeping up the acquaintance. And you?—and I am living somehow in quite a different way, seeing a lot of 'ordinary' people and—surprisingly—finding them most interesting. For the most part I feel young. . . .

(VIII. 299–300, letter of 9 December 1909)

To his mother, also, Blok wrote of his pleasure in the discovery of a sister. He was charmed by Angelina's tremulous austerity, nervous, delicate mind, and strong religious faith. And they could laugh together:

My sister and her mother are very sympathetic to me, so that I have even made friends with them. My sister is interesting and original and pure, we have many characteristics in common (irony, for instance), but in something very important there is a basic difference, I think in that she is not rebellious; her mother is infinitely kind, tired, and 'wouldn't say boo to a goose'[g] but with a will of her own. I'll bring their photographs. I would like not only to keep up the acquaintance, but to introduce you and Lyuba to them. Though I don't know, for that matter, whether they would like that—or you? I am often at the house of the young Belayevs who live here and stay to dine with them, very typical military people and, to my surprise, this does not only not oppress me, but rather the other way about. I feel for the most part as if I were young again, spend hours discussing the regimental holiday and the dog they brought back from China with them— charmingly and pleasantly. I am considered a man of the world. I have given quite a few interviews and the general attitude is as to a person who may 'have his little ways', but is something of a celebrity. . . .[12]

All his life, Blok was subject to these brief crazes for non-literary company, but he usually paid dearly for them. He could not communicate with people without spending himself, and attempts to do so over any length of time left him drained of charity and full of spleen. The Belayevs, a nice family with radical political interests into which they evidently felt it neither expedient nor tactful to introduce so ethereal a being as a Symbolist poet,[13] were soon to be dismissed by that poet as 'those mounted and foot artillerymen for whom I can feel nothing but the most profound contempt, all those "good", "polite", "decent", "nice" and so forth people . . . who have tortured me with their hospitality and their modesty', people whom, on his return to Petersburg, he was terrified of meeting, obviously wanting neither to perpetuate the acquaintance nor to hurt their feelings by his most unfair (and entirely inwardly motivated) volte-face. As he wrote a few weeks after his return from Poland to Aleksandra

[g] The Russian here is *bezotvetnaya*, literally one 'who never answers back'.

Andreyevna, who in spite of her depression was still struggling gamely to reassume her social duties whenever she felt slightly better:

As to your paying calls and Frants's allowing you to do so, I'm simply cross with you both. *Every* person has to be, at least to a certain MINIMUM, himself, and there are certain borderlines that *should not be crossed.* Such a borderline *for you and me* (both to an absolutely equal extent) is our attitude to 'ordinary' people, and extraneous 'neighbours' [*postoronnym 'blizhnym'*].

I know for certain that if I once begin to 'fulfil obligations' as you do (even if only to Maria Timofeyevna Blok's relations, or to my own) I should not last long. Because whether I like it or not (as in obligation to myself) I am bound to spend myself economically—and not for anything would I give away one particle of my soul (or my 'leisure', or my time) to such extraneous people. If I should do so I might easily go mad without any exaggeration whatsoever....[14]

Blok also later became estranged from Maria Timofeyevna. While in Warsaw, however, he genuinely liked both her and her family.

Even so, the strain of acting up to the conventional demands made upon his time and attention during the week immediately after his father's death led to the usual reaction. On Tuesday 8 December he had a night out and was feeling much too like the morning after to attend the last solemn service in his father's memory on the following day. Instead, he wandered about Warsaw alone and, by the next evening, had found a 'simple Polish girl' who took him in for the night. It pleased his imagination to believe she might have conceived and borne him a son,[h] but there is no evidence that he ever saw or heard of her again. These excesses, probably combined with the perennial torment of the great Christian feasts, led to an attack of black depression on Christmas Eve (11 December, according to the Russian reckoning). From then on he seems to have divided his time fairly equally between the restaurant Aquarium—he could now afford champagne rather than the old, cheap red wine—duty visits to professors and distant relatives, and the sorting and packing of the contents of his father's flat.

Wandering alone about the Polish capital in slush, rain, and wind, as he so often now wandered alone about Petersburg, Blok became increasingly aware of the characteristics he had inherited from Aleksandr L'vovich. He was, he later stressed, a stranger to his father in every way 'except, perhaps, in the most secret' (III. 437).

Their minds worked in the same way. The poet had inherited his father's predisposition to realism, his love of 'facts', and his rejection of tidy theory in favour of 'the elemental nature of being'. The diaries and notebooks which Blok kept throughout his life are a chaotic

[h] Cf. the rough draft of the poem *Retribution* (III. 472–3).

record of the 'facts', real and emotional, of his everyday life.[i] He knew that every now and again they would cohere and form a pattern: 'I always write down the trivial alongside the significant with this sole purpose' (VII. 109). In a sense, he worked with these facts as a child works with a kaleidoscope, shifting them this way and that until, all of a sudden, they formed a pattern, a poem. Blok's life work was to 'programme his kaleidoscope', observing intensely, collecting carefully, throwing in the occasional 'given' word or phrase. When the patterns came, they came easily, as if given from without. Yet they were paid for by a life of unremitting creative concentration.

In Blok, as in his father, the jangling discordancy of 'facts' aroused irony and an acute sense of underlying chaos. As with the father, discordancy had entered deep into the son's flesh and blood, distorting what might have been a healthy masculine temperament into a predatory, 'demonic' sexuality. Blok's father appears to have accepted that love and his own particular brand of proprietary cruelty and lust were part and parcel of the same emotion: inextricably mingled. For the son, brought up in the chivalrous ideals and gentle atmosphere of a very different family and taught from boyhood to reverence nature and all natural processes, this 'sinful and lustful' temperament was something unnatural, an aspect of nocturnal chaos which quailed and faded before women who inspired real love; to which he could give full rein only in drink and dreams and chance meetings with prostitutes. The record of his worldly love affairs, his seductions in the *demi-monde* and in the realm of art and literature, was a series of Don Juan-like disappointments: the excitement of the chase, the triumph of conquest, then boredom, a sense of let-down, of cold, cruel sobriety. 'Vampire passions' and 'black blood' broke over him in waves, and the debauch he now embarked on in Poland was to continue, off and on, throughout that winter.

A month after his return he wrote to his mother: 'My father's darkness is still here on this earth and wreathes about me. This man needs to be exorcised.'[j] Six weeks later, he was writing in his notebook:

... And then there came such a whirlwind that now, on the following day, I am still shaking, although I've already taken a steam bath. I remember their sidelong glances, enquiring and scared—I even seduce them into

[i] As the critic A. Selivanovsky tartly remarked after their first publication: 'the "inexpressible" cohabits with "what's-for-lunch"' (*Na Literaturnom postu* (Moscow), no. 1 (January) 1929, 48).

[j] The word translated as 'exorcised' is *zamalyvat'*, meaning literally 'prayed away' and usually used of sins rather than people.

things which are sweet and agonizing to them themselves. 'God knows how far you'll go.' 'I'm afraid of you.' My sins are so burdensome that in the morning the thought of confession came to me. When I die—all this will come to an end. One of them: 'You'll come to a bad end,' she said. 'There's nothing you wouldn't do.' So be it. 'I'm afraid of you.'

(Z.K. 166, 2 March 1910)

On 13 March 1910, he wrote the poem which concludes the cycle 'Black Blood' and ends with the evocation of a man deserted by the woman he had seduced and struck 'with a stick', hearkening to a wild inner music which tells him that he is now free, that he has exchanged 'a better lot for low passion' (III. 59). It was indeed almost as though, in those dark Warsaw nights, he finally gave house-room to some demon that was to remain with him for the rest of his life and, eventually, to kill the body he had abandoned to its gruesome attentions. Even now, he was not at all sure that the sudden illness he had suffered that autumn was, as the doctors had told him, merely a product of nerves and incorrect diet.

In all this alien world of official visits and murky debauch, there was one person who constantly reminded him of his 'promised land': Angelina.

> By light of day, as I recall,
> I was 'a poet', but by night:
> Delirium, darkness over all,
> The Vistula ran dark, no light...
> Only your deep anxiety told
> Of truths forgotten or defaced:
> That this world is God's dwelling-place;
> That there is fire—and bitter cold.
>
> (III. 436)[15]

All her short life, Angelina was to be one of the people Blok 'listened to'. Originally, he had meant to dedicate *Retribution* to her. In it, he calls her his sister 'appointed by fate' and recalls his own 'sickness' at the time of their meeting, and his 'rusty soul'. Eventually, however, the poem extended to embrace the whole period from the end of the Russo-Turkish War and became a chronicle of the times and of both sides of his family. So, more appropriately, he dedicated *Iambs*[k] to Angelina. The epitaph Blok chose for these militant, classic poems was from Juvenal: '*indignatio fecit versum*', and even those that were written before they met might have been designed to imbue

---

[k] Verses written between 1907 and 1914, many of which were in fact extracts from the first draft of *Retribution*.

his sister's gentler spirit with that rebellious fire which, almost from their first meeting, he had felt she lacked:

> In fire and cold of troubled thought
> Life passes by. Let us remember
> That in a wholesome hour God brought
> Us two—before the dead—together.
>
> And I believe: a new age springs
> From such unhappy generations.
> For each in their own time have hymned
> The murdered Genius of salvation.
>
> And even as He, all are offended
> Deep in their souls, their singing souls.
> The sword of war gleams bright and splendid
> Where the remorseless storm-cloud rolls.
>
> And though the day's not yet at hand
> We pass the word to youths and maidens;
> Contempt matures as anger—and
> The fruit of anger is—rebellion.
>
> Play out your life, a hand at cards:
> But poets' hearts are tense and listening.
> And in their dark unease—a glistening
> Bright core of freedom, diamond-hard,
>
> Sleeps like black diamonds, buried under,
> A strange and breathless, spellbound slumber,
> Deep in the earth's dark womb—until
> The pick breaks silence in the hill.

> 1910–6 February 1914
> (III, 96)

On Friday 18 December, Blok accompanied Angelina and her mother back to Petersburg.

3

On his arrival home, Blok promptly retired to bed again, this time with bronchitis. He had no wish to see anyone but his wife and the faithful Zhenya, who came to visit him at their flat. The impressions of Warsaw were too important to be pushed to the back of his mind by the usual literary round. Also, there were several highly disturbing letters from his mother and from Frants Feliksovich. He had to renounce his plan of spending Christmas with Aleksandra Andreyevna because of his own indisposition, but the 30 December saw him on his way to Revel, followed the next morning by Lyuba so that the whole family might be together for the New Year.

Although Maria Beketova tells us that Aleksandra Andreyevna's state was so serious that she scarcely benefited from her son's presence, his visit undoubtedly gave her pleasure. He and Lyuba stayed for over a week and on 9 January Aleksandra Andreyevna wrote to Maria Pavlovna, Zhenya Ivanov's elder sister, who had become one of her closest friends:

Yesterday the children left after spending ten days. It was a very happy time, those ten days. For three months I have not talked about anything important. But now Sasha and I have said everything to one another that it is at all possible to put into words.[16]

Indeed, Blok's letters to her throughout this difficult time are so matter-of-fact, concerned, and understanding that it seems impossible he should not have had a soothing influence. To some extent, she was indeed on her guard (as unselfish parents tend to be) against relying on him too much, holding out against his suggestion that she should come to live with him and Lyuba while deciding on a suitable sanatorium. She wrote to Maria Pavlovna: 'All that you write about my relations with Sasha is probably quite right. My sin is that all my world is in him.'[17]

On the very day after his return from Revel, Blok went to see the Merezhkovskys, and Filosofov recommended a well-known doctor for chest and nervous diseases, Chigayev. 'He looks after the Diaghilevs and the Filosofovs et al.,' Blok informed his mother, 'and has been consulted by the royal family, has been Z. N. [Zinaida Nikolayevna Hippius]'s doctor for twenty years, was once in love with her, and is a good friend of the whole Merezhkovsky household and a regular visitor.'[18] Armed with an introduction from Filosofov, Blok went on 15 January to consult Doctor Chigayev, arranged an appointment for his mother as soon as she could be persuaded to come to Petersburg, and took the address of two possible sanatoriums.

By 8 February he had Aleksandra Andreyevna's promise to come. He and Lyuba had taken the next-door flat and had a door knocked through the wall into their own. A few days after his mother's arrival, however, apparently out of a clear sky, the latent hostility between the two women began to create an intolerable atmosphere. Lyuba's position was awkward enough without having to endure the benevolent but intense attention of her mother-in-law. She was fighting her own battle for the health of her husband's body and soul, and she felt the presence of this sick, unhappy woman exacerbated his own melancholy. The situation was indeed thoroughly irksome and Lyubov', whose family background had not, like her husband's, been free of petty intrigue and practical scheming, was evidently visited by unworthy thoughts and said some unworthy things, provoking Blok to one of his almost pathological outbursts of anger:

Lyuba has reduced Mama to this sickness. Lyuba has alienated me from people, Lyuba has created all the unbearable and exhausting complexity in our relationships as they now stand. Lyuba thrusts away from herself and from me all the best people including my mother, that is, my conscience. Lyuba has spoilt so many years of my life, exhausted me and reduced me to what I am now. Lyuba, as soon as she touches on life, becomes just as bad a person as her father, mother, and brothers. Worse than bad—a terrible, grim, low being with a taste for intrigue, like all her Popov[1] family. Lyuba on earth is something terrible, sent to torture and destroy earthly values. But 1898–1902 have made things so that I can't be separated from her and love her.

(Z.K. 166, entry for 18 February 1910)

As in Blok's other diatribes—against Florence, against Russia, for instance—his hatred is directed against the evil in the object he is castigating, not the object itself. Lyubov', in her memoirs, justifies her attitude by saying she was trying to defend her husband against the 'abnormality' in his own family. A more subtle if somewhat incoherent analysis of the situation between the two women was left by Zhenya Ivanov, probably the only person who knew the torment the situation caused Blok: 'In the mother', Zhenya wrote, 'was night and darkness ... that swallowed up the light of day', but this, as in Blok himself, was only one of her 'doubles':

In the wife was something different, of the day, elementally opposed to the glooms of night: Something of the dawn of their first love. And in her soul she wanted to tear the mother away from the son like a weed, as the root of the inborn dark double that was growing within him.

Both mother and son, Zhenya goes on, were aware of what Lyuba was trying to do and even saw some reason in it; Aleksandra Andreyevna, particularly, did not wish to burden her son with her own gloom. On the other hand, neither wanted to become estranged from the other, and Blok regarded his mother's disinterested pain for all the apparently irreparable dreadfulness of the world as something

[1] Lyubov' Dmitriyevna's mother's maiden name was Popov.

sacred which it was his duty to share. His wife, he maintained, was half-asleep, or she would have realized the impossibility of personal happiness in the world as it was.

To Zhenya, this long drama, solved only by his friend's death, was no mere domestic disagreement but something in the nature of an ancient tragedy:

When at Shakhmatovo in 1910 he spoke to me about what was going on in his home, and that 'Mama' had already attempted suicide (and that his wife was unjust), I asked who was at fault and he answered without hesitation 'It must be myself—I am.' He added the 'I am' as if to emphasize his own guilt ... and I could not help him.... [19]

Zhenya goes on to liken Blok's relationship with his mother to that of two people wandering hand in hand through a dark labyrinth looking for light at the end of the way and Eternal Youth. In the verses dedicated to Aleksandra Andreyevna, Blok often reasons and argues with her but always in the tone of a loving fellow spirit. Certainly it was he who supported her rather than the other way about and this is the secret of his dependence on and exasperation with Lyuba. Aleksandra Andreyevna, who was nothing if not generous, paid her daughter-in-law the ultimate tribute of writing—again to Maria Pavlovna: 'If only you knew, Maria my dear, how well, how selflessly Lyuba loves Sasha! I could not love like that. Only mothers can. There is such a profound spiritual beauty in her feeling.' [20]

The situation that winter was solved by Frants Feliksovich who, after much hesitation, agreed to place Aleksandra Andreyevna in a sanatorium in Sokol'niki on the outskirts of Moscow, where she remained from the end of March until the beginning of July. Blok wrote to her every few days, perhaps a little more bracingly than earlier that winter but always of things that interested her: his own life and what she should read (both were absorbed in Andrey Bely's novel *The Silver Dove*, which was being serialized in *Vesy*), and his plans for Shakhmatovo.

4

These domestic anxieties had not, of course, absorbed Blok completely. On his return from Revel after the New Year, he had been drawn back almost immediately into the cultural life of the capital. He had to finish a survey of recent literature which he had been planning when he left Petersburg for Warsaw. [21] Entitled 'Contradictions' (v. 406–14), this survey had been promised to the liberal *Rech'* for a February number and he approached it with a sense of responsibility now increased by the knowledge that his critical writing was no longer essential to his livelihood. Over the years, however, the regular writing of surveys for *Zolotoye Runo* had developed the poet's critical faculties and he was becoming increasingly equitable in judgement, at once more compassionate and more unapproachable. Less well-established writers had begun to appeal to him for help in getting their work published or, if published, noticed in his reviews.

Only that January, he had been approached by Pimen Karpov, a representative of those Sectarians who hung about the fringes of Merezhkovsky's Religious-Philosophical Society and who had shown such interest in Blok's 1908 paper on 'The People and the Intelligentsia'. Karpov, evidently thinking to play upon Blok's social conscience as his colleague Kluyev had done the previous winter, asked the poet to review his book *Govor Zor* (The Voice of the Dawns), admonishing him that the intelligentsia would never appreciate the anguish of the peasantry until, as he put it, they ceased from vain imaginings and took to the plough. 'Why?' Blok replied bleakly.

Just imagine all the monstrous absurdity of what you suggest: some wretched man with flabby muscles weaving his way along a furrow. He wouldn't get the whole field ploughed and he'd rupture himself. Why has he developed strength of mind at the expense of strength of body? Is it not, in the last analysis, to *overcome falsehood*?

(VIII. 303–4)

To overcome falsehood required more than integrity of thought. It required mastery of form—and this was something of which Karpov and his like were simply not aware. So Blok, albeit with due respect for the experience they were attempting to communicate, denied them any place in literature. 'Their books', he wrote, 'are at best clumsily expressed, but true martyrs more often express themselves clumsily than with eloquence' (v. 439). In another context, he compared Karpov's mind to a wounded bird fluttering blindly about a smoky, windowless *izba* (v. 659) and, while acknowledging the sociological significance of what he wrote, maintained that, as art, it simply did not exist.^m

In his reviews, Blok's voice had acquired a note of unpretentious authority enhanced by the tone, always that of one seeking the truth rather than laying down the law. At twenty-nine, he was a mature poet with his youth behind him and, as the winter drew to an end,

---

^m Cf. Blok's 1913 review of Karpov's sensational book *Plamya* (Flame) (v. 483–6) and his 1917 assessment of his play *Tri Chuda* (Three Miracles) (v. 658–9).

this fact was emphasized by two more deaths: not, this time, people of his father's generation such as Innokentiy Annensky, who had died unexpectedly of a heart attack while Blok was in Warsaw, but two fellow spirits: Vera Kommissarzhevskaya and the painter Mikhail Vrubel. Kommissarzhevskaya died of smallpox on 7 February, while on tour in the provinces, and Blok wrote a poem to her memory—a poem full of spring and nostalgia and Pre-Raphaelite elegance." There was, however, a more than theatrical aftermath to this 'agonizing, but young, but pre-spring death' (v. 415). There was the hushed meeting with old friends at an evening in Kommissarzhevskaya's memory on 7 March 1910 and, in Blok's memorial speech on this occasion, a new perspective on the art of his time.

In death, the great actress was more vividly present and significant to him than she had ever been in the two years he had spent in the wings of her theatre. How false the sensational aspects of the 'mystic anarchism' of that period had been, and how insignificant now seemed the academic disputes which so absorbed *Apollon* and its 'Academy',° how needlessly rowdy the assertive advent of such new trends as Futurism and Ego-Futurism. 'Now', Blok said in his speech, 'it pleases many people to ask the idle question: what was V. F. Kommissarzhevskaya's attitude to the "new art"? The answer is simple: It was the attitude of any artist to art in general. There is no such thing as art that is not new' (v. 417–18). For, he continued, 'There is no art in our day outside symbolism. Symbolist is a synonym for artist.'

By symbolism, Blok meant not only the particular school to which he belonged by an accident of birth and timing. He meant that the artist does more than describe what is perceptible to the five senses, that he is more than a craftsman: 'The artist is someone for whom the world is transparent, who has the eye of the child, but in whose eyes yet shines the light of mature understanding ...' (v. 418).

Vrubel had been such an artist. He died—stark, staring mad—less than two months after Kommissarzhevskaya. Blok had never met him but was fascinated by all that he had heard of him. Telling his mother of how he came to speak at the painter's funeral, he wrote:

I saw him for the first time in his coffin. He has a small face, all screwed up with suffering—eyes tightly shut and the mouth too under a blond moustache. Over the last months he reduced himself to a state of complete exhaustion because he had made up his mind that if he could remain standing for 17 days, God would give him emerald eyes.

" Ruined by an unfortunate pun on her name, Vera (Faith), in the last verse.
° See pp. 88–90 for the dispute between Symbolists and 'clarists' (later Acmeists).

Before one of the *panikhidi* Ge[P] came up to me and asked me on behalf of his mother to speak at the graveside. I did and it was the only speech— you will probably read it in the papers. The artists didn't speak, mainly because they don't know how, but they were all there.[22]

Blok was not happy with his speech about Vrubel. Moreover, he was sick of writing articles.[23] 'I want to be an artist,' he complained, 'not a mystic giver of talks and writer of feuilletons....'[24] He had come to the conclusion that the very words 'to explain art' were a contradiction in terms, for the essence of art was that it expressed that which is beyond explanation.

Nevertheless, he could not refuse the request to speak about the artist whose picture of the fallen Demon lying with crushed wings and broken body at the foot of the mountains reminded him so strongly of the spirit of his dead father. In his oration, Blok retold 'a page from the Vrubel legend' which could not but recall Aleksandr L'vovich's unfinished book:

... they say that he [Vrubel] painted over the head of his Demon as many as forty times; once, someone who chanced to call in while he was working saw a head of unheard-of beauty. Afterwards, Vrubel destroyed the head and painted it over again—*spoilt* it, as the language of legend has it; this language forces us to bear witness that the work of art we can see now in the Tret'yakov Gallery is only a faint memory of the one that was actually made for one brief moment and preserved in the memory of one man.

The *result* is lost—no more.... But who sets more store by the fact that a marble Venus has been *found* than by the fact that her statue *exists*? Creative work would be barren if the final aim of art were at the mercy of Barbarian-Time or Barbarian-man.

(v. 422)

5

Although Blok had not sought the honour of speaking at Vrubel's funeral, the impression of the artist's work, of his life, madness, and death, went so deep that, in his next public lecture, he described a whole period of his own development—the period of the 'antithesis', the 1905 revolution and 'The Stranger'—in terms of Vrubel's colour imagery.[q] He even went so far as to suggest that the concept of his

[P] Nikolay Petrovich Ge, the art critic, a friend of Blok and E. P. Ivanov. His mother was Vrubel's sister-in-law.

[q] Elsewhere, Blok speaks specifically of the link between 'music, painting, architecture,

Stranger and those of Vrubel's and Lermontov's Demon were inter-related, almost interchangeable.

This next lecture, too, was virtually imposed on him. On 26 March Blok attended a meeting of the *Apollon* 'Academy' at which Vyaches-lav Ivanov produced a polished, dialectical defence of Symbolism against the 'Parnassians' or, as Bryusov called them, the 'clarists'. This defence moved Blok, who disliked the militant aestheticism of the younger generation and felt strongly in sympathy with Ivanov's idea that the aim of the artist was to uncover the true 'canonic' reality behind the seeming: a *realibus ad realiora*, a task of objective, not merely individual, significance.

Blok listened absorbed, hearing his one-time friend and mentor trace the development of Symbolism as a whole and recognizing, in what he heard, the history of his own experience. He only dis-agreed with Ivanov on one point: the older poet's belief in theurgic art. He voiced his doubts there and then, speaking of the black back-ground of Leonardo's pictures (necessary to show the brightness of his saints and madonnas), of the 'Prince of this World', and of Vrubel. Still, he felt very much more in accord with Vyacheslav Ivanov than with his opponents, and said as much. The advocates of art for art's sake such as the rising young poet Nikolay Gumilev were utterly alien to him. His strong sense of sin recoiled from their conception of man 'as a kind of "primeval Adam"' (III. 296), and he felt that their insistence on 'craftsmanship' implied too irresponsible an atti-tude towards the artist's calling.

From this public expression of solidarity with Vyacheslav Ivanov, it was only a step to allowing himself to be persuaded to 'support' the older poet's speech. Nevertheless, the paper he then sat down to prepare on Symbolism was undertaken reluctantly and never in-tended for publication.[26] Indeed, after the wider perspective on art he had gained in Italy and under the impression of the recent deaths, he was especially reluctant to identify himself with any particular school or faction. So it was on the understanding that he was speaking only for his fellow poets and not for the wider public that Blok con-sented to read a paper entitled 'On the Present State of Russian Sym-bolism' (v. 425–36) before the 'Academy' on 12 April 1910.

For this paper, Blok, taking Ivanov's dialectical formula of thesis,

---

and art' (VIII. 344). M. Elik has compiled a whole book devoted to Blok and music and there are a number of articles on the relationship of his work to the visual arts,[25] while at the Third Conference on Light and Music held, however improbably, at the Kazan Institute of Aviation in 1975, one contributor, I. Blinov, was even moved to read a paper on 'Audio-visual Synaesthesia in the Poetry of A. Blok'.

Blok's half-sister Angelina as a schoolgirl, at the age she first met Blok.

Blok at the funeral of Mikhail
Vrubel, in the spring of 1910.
(From the collection of N. P.
Il'in)

Vera Kommissarzhevskaya, at
whose memorial evening Blok
spoke in the spring of 1910.
(From the collection of N. P.
Il'in)

antithesis, and synthesis as a compass, sought to map out the route he himself had already travelled. The language he used was metaphorical, as esoteric as the verses themselves, but this, within the narrow circle of the 'Academy', would have mattered little. The image suggested is that of a man who, having groped his way blindly across a great valley full of smoky cities and misty marshes, has been trudging steadily uphill for some time, and now, pausing at last to look back, finds that he can again descry the summits of the Delectable Mountains from which he set forth. In his paper, Blok made it quite clear that it was in these mountains, where once he had sung of the Most Beautiful Lady, and not in the dangerous shifting world of 'The Stranger' and *The Puppet Booth*, that he saw the mainspring of his poetry.

The journey, however, had been essential. There was no note of regret or repentance, no wish to return to the state of primal innocence, only a firm resolve to go on. 'My conclusion is this', Blok said:

the way to the accomplishment of the task that is laid upon us by our calling is first and foremost apprenticeship, *recollection*,' steadiness of watch and spiritual diet. It is necessary to begin again, to learn of the world and of that little child who still lives in our burnt-out souls.

The artist must be reverent in boldness itself, knowing the cost of confusing art with life and remaining, in life, an ordinary man.

(v. 436)

Only remembering Blok's arrogance, that contempt for the 'mob' that runs right through his life from the schoolboy bravado of his answers to the Bad Nauheim questionnaire to the last great speech, 'On the Calling of the Poet', is it possible fully to appreciate the humility of his final words: 'We should remember and value the pilgrimage of Signorelli who, coming at the end of his years to the steep, alien town of Orvieto, humbly begged permission of its citizens to paint the frescoes in their new capella' (v. 436).

When he had finished, Vyacheslav Ivanov stepped forward and, taking Blok's hand, drew him to himself and kissed him long and earnestly full upon the lips.

Blok himself was not pleased. Not only had he allowed himself to be talked into trying to explain his poetry in prose, but he had done precisely what he had refused to do when, only three and a half years earlier, Bely had persuaded him to write a public disclaimer

---

' The Russian word is *samouglubleniye*: to retire into the depths of self in order to make that self more profound.

of mystic anarchism; he had aligned himself with a literary group, declaring for one school in preference to another. Once again, he found himself 'in the same cage' as Vyacheslav Ivanov, a position which, much as he respected the older man, he foresaw would prove untenable. What he did not realize until he saw his speech in print was that he had come very near to formulating his whole poetical credo.[5] At the time he assessed it with considerable irritation: 'I read my paper in the "Academy" for which I was praised and Vyacheslav kissed me, but this paper, too, is bad and wordy. From words, in which I have finally got all tied up and contorted by falsity, I am running away to Shakhmatovo as if from the plague.'[28]

6

At Shakhmatovo the poet was confronted with a quite unprecedented accumulation of practical business. He had planned much-needed repairs which were already under way when he arrived and, by the middle of May, there were thirty men working on the house. The existing foundations and walls had been strengthened. New tiled stoves were to be put in, old ones repaired. A new two-storey wing was to be built on to the main house as an alternative to repairing the old annexe. Upstairs was a large, light room for Blok with its own way out into the garden down an outside flight of steps. Downstairs were Lyuba's rather dimmer apartments, with a French window leading out past a great bush of red roses which glowed like embers in the evening light. The veranda had already been entirely rebuilt before their arrival and the whole house was to be repapered inside and repainted from top to bottom.

More urgent than the work on the house was the problem of Yegor, the tenant-manager installed by Aleksandra and Maria the previous summer, who greeted his landlords effusively and promised to do everything just as they wished. Obviously, however, he had to go. The animals had been so neglected that the one remaining horse had not strength to stand and had to be raised in a sling. Yegor, moreover, had sold the other horse and a cow, besides much of the harness and agricultural implements, almost as soon as he had felt

---

[5] It was a fine instinct that made Sir Cecil Kisch, the author of the first book about Blok in English, give an extremely detailed paraphrase of this article.[27] The existence of this, and the fact that I have had occasion to quote frequently from the paper in order to explain or illustrate various aspects of Blok's poetry, permit me not to dwell on it at greater length in the context.

himself free of supervision the previous autumn. New evidence of dishonesty and neglect came to light every day. He was not easy to get rid of, as Blok, in a tone of rueful good humour, wrote to his mother on 11 May:

We are edging Yegorka[1] out by fair words and foul—he has now promised to have all his stuff out of the way by Sunday (not the first deadline) and to hand over 'everything' (although, of course, lots of things simply aren't there). However, the main things have not been touched—the logs for the building, the firewood (which he has taken only from the corner pit), the trap, the grey horse, the machines.[29]

Blok was sorry for Yegor who, like Chekhov's three sisters, like the whole of his 'vast, wet, homely Russia' 'wanted so much to live'. Who was he, Aleksandr Blok, to make life more difficult for him? Only the day before he had written, in the last poem of that spring:

> How hard it is to walk with other men
> And to pretend to them you are not dead.
> And passion's tragic play to tell again
> To those for whom all life yet lies ahead ...

(III. 27)

On the night of 11–12 May he got up to observe the approach of Halley's Comet which, according to the astronomers, was due to hurtle by so close that the earth would, on 18–19 May, actually pass through its tail. Rumour had been rife in Petersburg that this tail was of pale blue carbon dioxide and Blok, with his usual love of catastrophe, had been enchanted by the (consciously whimsical) notion that all mankind might quietly pass into sleep and death after an exquisite moment of universal reconciliation. True, he had some time since lost faith in the comet 'and its tail', but he was still interested enough to leave his warm bed at four o'clock in the morning to see if he could get a sight of it.

I did not see the comet but I did see how Yegor, having risen together with his pregnant wife, hurriedly and thievishly trussed a load of straw and carried it off to his croft; how his sheep came out and flung themselves unshepherded on our clover, how his unfed chickens tottered out and ran on to the new-sown oats, how three miserable calves emerged and pregnant Olga went hobbling about with a bucket.... Hunching up against the morning cold I am angry with Yegorka, feeling that it is *my own clover* his sheep have trampled, etc. I just happen to have got up quite by chance to take an idle look at a star of heaven, and the carpenters, the masons, the stove-makers, the batman, the odd-job man—all those we have

---

[1] Contemptuously familiar form for Yegor.

gathered together here to build our sick lives—are still asleep, and only Yegorka is out working early in the morning, patching up his poor croft, stealthily weaving his children a nest from the straw that he should have put on our manure this winter.

We are moneyed people and childless. And that thievish Yegorka shears the wool from his sheep for his children, uses the straw to warm his children, gives the eggs from his underfed chickens to his children. . . .

(Z.K. 171, entry for 11–12 May 1910)

Having at last with, as he wrote to his mother, all the stringency of which he was capable, sent Yegorka packing to his own home at Tarakanovo, Blok and Lyuba settled down for the first time as master and mistress in their own home. They diverted Aunt Maria and her tyrannical Annushka to stay with Aunt Sofia at Safonovo and, to begin with, enjoyed themselves immensely. At last there was an outlet for Lyubov's energy. She supervised all the working of the estate, tended the animals and the staff, sang with the peasant girls and even helped milk the cows. Cheerful, stately, aglow with health and her own ample, very Russian beauty, she was popular with the villagers, and it was generally felt that the young couple's decision to take the running of the estate into their own hands was the beginning of better days.

Blok was worried about his mother, but it was a relief to have escaped from the capital and he was happy to be involved with simple yet colourful people, with animals, growing things, paint, stone and wood:

On the 9th Lyuba and Nikolay" went to the market at Rogachevo and bought two horses: a black for 127 roubles and Malchik (a dapple grey) for 90 roubles. They are both five years old, frisky, particularly the black, very strong, well-fed, big and beautiful (particularly the black). Old Seriy has got back into condition and is quite fat and the dogs are in condition again. . . . We are going to buy a little cart (a *tarantas*) for going to the station, to Boblovo, just out for rides, etc. . . . There are a lot of us here on the estate, including the workmen, and it's fun. We've sown two *desyatina* with oats, the potatoes are going in tomorrow, the tanner is mending the harness, we are going to buy a new water barrel and have repaired the stables. . . . [31]

" The new odd-job man, Nikolay Lapin. On 4 May Blok wrote to his mother: 'Today we engaged Nikolay, Efim's cousin, he will come on Saturday and live here without his wife until 1 June. We took him on (with his wife) for 20 roubles, his own food except what comes from our fields (i.e. meat and cereals). I like him. Before him we interviewed Platon, whom Lyuba liked but I didn't—he's got quite a reputation and was a bit too keen to be taken on. Nikolay has more dignity and his way of speaking and manners are like Efim's, only he's skinnier. Never mind—we'll feed him up.'[30] Efim was Frants Feliksovich's batman so Lapin was not a native of Shakhmatovo.

One of the new horses turned out to have thrush and one of the carpenters cut his finger. Lyubov', in her element, tended them both every evening. In May, she made the journey to Moscow to visit her mother-in-law at her sanatorium, 'so kind and nice', as Aleksandra Andreyevna gladly informed Maria Pavlovna.[32] The letter Blok wrote to his mother towards the end of the month was still full of enthusiasm:

I spend all my time on the building site. I like all the workmen very much, they are all highly individual and each is cleverer, healthier, and better-looking than almost any member of the intelligentsia. We talk a great deal. One thing spoils them—drink: understandable, of course. The senior stove-builder speaks of 'the soul of the stove', his junior is a lyrical type, he sings very well. One of the painters is the image of Filippo Lippi, face, hat, interests and all: his favourite topic of conversation is boxing. The masons from Tver are great observers of nature....[33]

But as the days passed, and then the weeks, the demands of overseeing so large an undertaking became more and more exhausting. The workmen were quarrelling among themselves, some of the more enterprising had begun to wheedle tips and then disappear for days at a time, and they all grumbled to Blok about the foreman who, they complained, was not seeing they were properly fed. The weather grew hotter and drier, Blok thinner and more irritable. He was beginning to lose his sense of identity as a poet and to feel 'like a squeezed-out lemon' (VIII. 313). Depression crept back.

During the Trinity respite, when the workmen went back to their own homes for almost a week, Blok walked off by himself and sat for a long time on a stone overlooking the neighbouring village of Rudnovo. A terrible poem came to him, a vision of a spring that failed and a sun that would not rise. It began to form itself in heavy, stumbling, inevitable words: 'O children, if you only knew the cold and dark of days to come'. But he fought it off: 'I want that the heart should be merry'; 'I was born winged and merry'; 'it is only now ... Only until the time is fulfilled that the entrance is blocked by a heavy stone and my spirit is in the tomb' (III. 515). He did not complete the poem until February 1914, when he gave it the curious title 'A Voice from the Chorus'.

Everything was proving more expensive than he had calculated and on 14 June he had to go Petersburg for more money. From the heat and thundery atmosphere of Shakhmatovo he was suddenly plunged into raw cold and even his plan to rout out Zhenya Ivanov from his place of work faded in sheer apathy. A fortnight later he wrote his friend to explain:

... I didn't have the energy. It was very dull and cold, there were even a few snowflakes falling. I sat alone in a second-class sleeping car (this last by my own stupidity—I have completely given up counting money, it doesn't really seem to be doing us any good).

(VIII. 313, letter of 29 June 1910)

He was sleeping badly and it was about this time that he had one of those vivid dreams, fraught with a crushing sense of responsibility for his wife and mother yet touching on mysteries of a more universal nature, which were to haunt him from now on. He considered such dreams important and would write them down in his notebooks, but of this one he made a poem and dedicated it to Aleksandra Andreyevna (III. 134). It is called simply 'A Dream' and tells how he awoke in an ancient tomb; shades of Tuscany and Umbria, perhaps, but also of the utter despair that had attacked him on Trinity Sunday and of the memory of his father's coffin being sealed with lead 'so that, having been resurrected, he should not rise from the tomb'. In his dream he lay in this sepulchre listening to the sound of an approaching host proclaiming the Resurrection, led by Christ and His angels 'just as we read in books, bored and unbelieving'. His wife slept on peacefully, not wishing for resurrection. His mother, wide awake, anxiously implored her son to raise the stone. 'No, Mother,' he replied. 'I have been stifled in this grave and my strength is gone. Pray, both of you, that an angel should come and roll away the stone.'

7

Meanwhile, work on the house dragged on. On 22 June Blok had written to Aleksandra Andreyevna, who was feeling deceptively better after three quiet months in her sanatorium:

Mama, you will have to stay on for a week after the 29th, there's nothing else for it. The carpenters will have finished, but not the painters. There are 22 carpenters" on the job now.... I am sick to death of all this work on the house and making every effort to get it all over and done with.[34]

The results, however, were most agreeable, as Maria Beketova, who came over from Safonovo, recorded:

  " 'Carpenters' is perhaps a misleading translation. The house being made of wood, these men were in fact builders.

I arrived a few days before my sister. The children were still putting the finishing touches to their mother's room before her arrival and in the dining room Sasha hung a big, bright lamp he had bought in St. Petersburg ... our sister Sofia Andreyevna, I, Anna Ivanovna Mendeleyeva, and Aunt Sonya who came to stay for a few days were all most enthusiastic about the renewed Shakhmatovo, how well-thought-out it all was by the master and in what good taste.... Sasha had his grandfather's old writing-desk, made on their estate by serfs, put in his new room. This desk had come to him from his father. There were all sorts of secret drawers, where he kept his wife's letters, her portraits, some manuscripts and, amongst other things, the diary Lyubov' Dmitriyevna had kept before her marriage.

As to the house itself, it was a pleasure to behold: 'It all shone with fresh paint, all grey and white with its green roof, but the old-fashioned homeliness had not been destroyed, all the alterations had been carried out in the traditional style.'[35]

It was the second week of July before Lyubov' Dmitriyevna was able to go to Moscow to fetch Blok's mother. Everyone so far had been delighted by the alterations. Not so Aleksandra Andreyevna: the changes, the new servants engaged that spring in her absence, the presence of the painters, all cowed and startled her, and she seemed to shrink into herself, saying almost nothing but looking about her with scared eyes.

Lyubov', who had put heart and soul into making her Sasha's house a place of joy and comfort, was irritated beyond measure and Blok himself, though at first happy to have his mother back from the sanatorium, was disappointed. He had hoped that she would share the general pleasure in the new prosperity of their home and had clung to the illusion that she would emerge from the sanatorium fully cured.

Within a week or so, Aleksandra Andreyevna had herself sufficiently in hand to approve all that had been done, but with the best will in the world she could not forbear offering Lyuba advice on the running of the estate—obviously with the silent approval of her sister. Lyubov', to her own shame and dismay, tended to react with almost hysterical sharpness. It seemed to her that the older woman was actually intriguing against her, working on her son's affection and exploiting her own ill health to get her way over various purely practical matters. She must have felt as if she would never have her husband to herself, never be given a free hand to create that cheerful domesticity which he demanded of her and of which—without really considering it an aim in itself—she yet knew herself to be amply capable. Why should she—an intellectual, perhaps, after all, a great actress—waste her time trying to make people happy when all she undertook appeared to be having the opposite effect? The peasants shook their heads and reckoned the old *barynya* and the young *barynya* each wanted to run things her own way. Sympathy was all on the side of Lyubov' Dmitriyevna, and Aleksandra Andreyevna was blamed for spoiling her son's marriage.[36]

Of course, it was all infinitely more complicated, but the fact remained that this summer, which had begun with such promise, was one of the unhappiest ever spent at Shakhmatovo. The two months Blok had given to supervising his 'thirty grown-up children', as he had called the builders in a final, exasperated letter to his mother,[37] were all wasted energy: vanity of vanities. Even for himself, he could not be a 'builder of life'. As he had half foreseen as he watched Yegor's morning pilfering, all the effort and expense had gone merely to create a comfortable summer home for two lonely ageing women and a childless couple who could scarcely be said to form a family. True, they did all genuinely love country life and this particular corner of Russia, and this, for the time being, was enough to keep them together, but Lyuba alone was gifted with the kind of vitality needed to make a home—and even this was becoming more and more turned in against itself.

It is no wonder that the poems Blok wrote that summer reflect the general gloom. 'The iron yearning of the road' rasps through them all (III. 27–30, 195–6, 260–1) and the image of the woman who commits suicide because the happiness for which she has waited all her life never comes gives the keynote to other poems besides the supremely successful 'On the Railway Line'.[w] The poem recalled Blok's own thoughts as he had sat in the train travelling back from Petersburg to Shakhmatovo that June:

... so it is always—life 'passes through to its next destination' like a train; in the windows are all sorts of faces: sleepy, drunk, cheerful, and bored, and I yawn and watch them go by from my 'wet platform'. Or—people still wait for happiness, just as they wait for trains at night on an open platform all drifted up with snow.

(VIII. 313)

The image of people waiting on a frozen railway platform for a train that never comes was to haunt Blok all his life, and to recur with devastating effect in 1917.

[w] This near-ballad, dedicated to Zhenya's sister Maria Pavlovna Ivanova, was in part an echo, recognized only *post factum*, of an incident in Tolstoy's *Resurrection* in which the peasant heroine, waiting on a dark, open platform, catches a glimpse of her princely lover riding by in a brightly lit first-class carriage.

8

Towards the end of August, Blok and Lyubov' made up their minds
to stay on alone together at Shakhmatovo after the departure of their
relatives and friends (Frants Feliksovich had joined the unhappy
party and so had Alya Mazurova, the daughter of a friend of Aunt
Maria's). As usual, it fell to Lyuba to make the practical arrangements; she went up to Petersburg, vacated the flat on Galernaya
Street, and stored their furniture. It was decided they should try to
winter in the country and make no definite plans for the future.

Before the older people left, however, a visit from Zhenya Ivanov
brought a brief respite from the growing tension and misunderstanding. Blok, having informed his friend jokingly that people who
turned up on foot like tramps were 'not received' at Shakhmatovo,
took the new *tarantas* to the station himself, twenty-six versts over
a rough road in a cold wind, and the two drove happily back
together, Zhenya jumping down to walk then climbing on to the
cart again, revelling in the whole experience, his active imagination
peopling the golden woods with Tartars and Muscovites and invad-
ing French armies. At the house, he listened to everybody's troubles
and, if the situation was, in a sense, past mending, at least all of them
felt there must be some hope and goodness in a world that contained
the Ivanovs: and in them themselves, since Zhenya so patently
understood, loved, and reverenced each individual member of the
family. He stayed to celebrate Lyuba's name day on 17 September
and left the following day, to be followed a little over a fortnight
later by Aunt Maria and Aleksandra Andreyevna, on her way to
resume a quiet invalid existence with her husband in Revel.

As soon as the others were gone, Lyuba and Blok retreated into
their own new wing of the house and set about preparing for the
winter, pasting over cracks, putting in double windows, securing
shutters: and only just in time, for within three or four days the
weather broke, the house was shaken by driving winds, and snow
and sleet appeared to be trying to penetrate every cranny.

Left alone, Blok and Lyuba were faced again with the 'impossible'
tenderness of their relationship. They were not yet thirty, yet Blok,
at least, knew that ideal love was no longer possible for him: the
more idyllic the setting, the more intolerable the pain of this knowledge. Somewhere, there had been a cruel mistake that was still be-
devilling their whole lives. Perhaps, he thought, the root of it all was
the old self-deception about Lyubov' being his first love. He had
felt things for Sadovskaya and given her words which should have

been given to one woman only, and when, that spring, he had heard
a false rumour that his first love was dead, it had touched him more
deeply than he would have believed possible. Now, however, in the
stillness of autumn, he realized that Sadovskaya must be an old
woman.

To add to the confusion, that spring in Petersburg Blok had
become involved with a married woman, a *jolie laide* with 'wild,
weak hands' and an eager, incoherent voice 'like strings of pearls'
(*Z.K.* 172–3): Valentina Andreyevna Shchëgoleva. It was in part to
this infatuation that Blok owed the final realization of his inability
to form any further profound ties with a woman, and the crystalliza-
tion of the theme of retribution[x] which enabled him to write the
superb but baleful 'Steps of the Commendatore' (III. 80–1). The
doom of betrayal was bound up with the sight of a passing car and
the sound of a motor horn in the night: these themes first figure
in two poems of 11 February 1910—brief, poignant lyrics—but in
September the thought of Valentina brought back the memory of
the sound and with it the associations of hopelessness and betrayal.
Objectivizing his own experience, Blok rewrote, in a poem of ten
short stanzas, the last scene of *Don Juan*, when the horn—'triumphant
and amorous'—announces the arrival of the Commendatore, driven
from the grave to the door of his residence in a quiet car with powerful headlights.

So Blok contemplated the hopeless tangle of his love life, read
Nietzsche, and worked away copying out and correcting last
winter's poems for the Moscow publishing house Musaget. As he
worked, the blustering wind and sleet turned to soft-falling snow
which, overnight, enveloped the whole countryside in a deep and
holy calm.

It was too quiet. He could not stay here and flirt with the idea
of an earthly paradise. His body, nerves, temperament were no
longer fitted for simple happiness. He was bored, because his experience and needs were quite other than those of the child Sasha who,
on the first morning of the snow, ran out gladly with Lyuba to build
a snowman. Aleksandr Blok had long ago abandoned his 'quiet white
house' and he could not now return, other than momentarily, to
laugh at himself and Lyuba staggering through the fresh drifts in
clumsy felt boots, to take a brief delight in toboggans and skis. Yet,
in these last days at Shakhmatovo, it was as if the dream of first
love visited him once more. From the depths of the snowy stillness,

---

[x] In his personal life, not in history, as depicted in the cycle of poems called 'Retribution'
(III. 516–20), not the long poem.

a voice came to him and a familiar form seemed to bend over his pillow in the sleepless nights.

But, in the poem for two voices which he made of this 'Visitation' (III. 262–3), the past is acknowledged to have gone beyond recall and he dares not meet the tender concern in the ageing face of his love, nor respond to the startled recollection in her eyes. Whether the voice that came to trouble him in the long October nights was Sadovskaya's or whether it was Lyuba's—still, in his poetry, his bride, eternally crowned for him alone—or whether it was that of the Beautiful Lady Herself,[y] Blok repulsed it, and with it all whole and tender earthly love.

To his mother he wrote merely: 'But it's impossible to spend the winter here—deadly boredom and depression. Even the peasants say so' (VIII. 319, letter of 22 October 1910). On 1 November, struggling through miles of mud and churning water, Blok and Lyuba left Shakhmatovo, defeated.

9

A telegram from Moscow, 'MUSAGET, ALCION, LOGOS[z] WELCOME, LOVE, EXPECT BLOK', decided the direction Blok was to take. He caught the train to Moscow while Lyubov' Dmitriyevna went straight to Petersburg to see about a new flat.

That September, the publication of 'On the Present State of Russian Symbolism'—against which Blok had protested so vigorously after the reading to the 'Academy' only a few short months before—had brought him a letter from Bely containing an unconditional apology for anything that might have been his fault in the events leading up to their last quarrel in the spring of 1908. Blok, wrote Bely, had

[y] Z. G. Mints, in a close textual study of the poetry of Blok's maturity,[38] defines a 'land of First Love' which is connected with the mythical prototype of Paradise Lost and with the Rousseauesque-Tolstoyan concept of lost natural innocence. This, she maintains, is a 'country' that exists in the poetry, not in the world, and the 'She' who inhabits this land, while usually inspired by either Sadovskaya or Lyubov' Dmitriyevna, is essentially a persona of the poetry. L. V. Zharova[39] quotes Maria Beketova as saying that the first voice in this poem is Sadovskaya's. Certainly, in the notebooks, the poem runs on from the entry about Sadovskaya's presumed death and 'the wife' who, although 'he' called her so, was not 'his first love', but this suggests a confusion of the two images. Certainly the earliest variants of 'The Visitation' (begun in August 1909 and temporarily abandoned) were written at the same time as others from the cycle to Sadovskaya 'Twelve Years Later', but among the many rejected variants of October 1910 is the line, pronounced by the 'Second Voice': 'Ne pomnyu, chy golos zvenit' ('I do not remember whose voice rings out').

[z] Alcion was the musical section of the primarily literary publishing house Musaget, Logos a philosophical journal.

spoken for all true Symbolists, and he intended to side with him against Bryusov, in the polemics still continuing in *Apollon.*[aa]

Coming after so long a silence, this letter confirmed Blok's own impression that he had managed to state his credo far more effectively than he had thought at the time (v. 758; VIII. 315). He was also very glad to be on good terms again with Bely whose *Silver Dove* had affected him deeply and of whom he still often thought as of someone 'far more significant' than himself (*Z.K.* 172, entry for September 1910). 'Your letter', he had answered Bely's by return of post, 'is profoundly dear and important to me.'

Blok agreed to publish some recent poems in Musaget's almanac and to give them a collection, *The Night Watches*, on which he was then working,[bb] but did have qualms when Bely asked him to read a 'programmatic' lecture in Moscow. He felt it his duty to explain in painstaking detail that 'On the Present State of Russian Symbolism' had not been, in any sense of the word, an act of contrition, and that while he now wished to continue on a different, more sober road and saw many things more clearly, he was still and would always remain the author of *The Puppet Booth* and 'The Stranger'. If Bely wanted him as an ally, he wrote, he must accept him as he was, not as a penitent but as a lover of 'perdition':[cc]

Have you really taken into account that *I love perdition*, have loved it from the beginning and do not renounce this love? I insist that *I have never contradicted myself in what is most important* ... although I *love and understand,* perhaps above anything else in the world, those people who have 'gathered their own dust' in an 'urn' so that it should not keep the light from their living 'I' (you, Nietzsche)—I myself remain in the shade, in the dust, loving perdition.

(VIII. 316–17, letter of 22 October 1910)

Bely took some time to reply to this letter. It was not what he had hoped for, but he had grown wiser and more tolerant:

... whoever you are, I accept you; if you want perdition for yourself, or if perdition is the dominant element in your soul, I can tenderly regret that your soul is still in 'ashes'.... If you had wished perdition for all men, if

---

[aa] Bryusov's pro-Parnassian article, published in *Apollon,* no. 9, 1910, elicited a reply from Andrey Bely in no. 11, 1910. Blok refused to be drawn into further printed polemics, although he had written to Bryusov on 3 September that he could have answered the criticism of his own position on all points (VIII. 313).

[bb] It was Andrey Bely who had put Blok directly in touch with Musaget, sending his first letter through their secretary A. M. Kozhebatkin.

[cc] The Russian word is *gibelv'* which can mean 'final destruction' (as of Atlantis, for instance) or 'death' as well as 'perdition'. James Forsyth in a recent article felicitously suggests that the concept implied is best rendered by the German word *Untergang.*[40]

your activity had had its origin in destruction and sown death, then I would have felt that intuitively and would not be writing you letters. More than that, you would not write what you are writing, for your article in *Apollon* I understand and accept *to the end*.[41]

So Bely allayed his old friend's fear that he might compromise the 'cause' of Symbolism understood as religious art. Nevertheless, this alliance with Bely and Vyacheslav Ivanov, who since the previous winter had been working steadily to affect a reconciliation between the two younger poets, was little more than a temporary *rapprochement*, for Blok's feet were now irrevocably set upon his own road. He was pleased to have Bely—and Seryëzha Solov'ev who had also written to congratulate him on the appearance of his article—restored to him as friends, for, as he had written Bely long ago, people meant more to him than ideas; but the fact that they approved some of his poems and rejected others prevented any real closeness. When Seryëzha, for instance, remonstrated with him for the blasphemous motifs in the *Italian Verses*, he answered stubbornly: 'I have to do it like that. If I had not written 'The Stranger' and *The Puppet Booth, On the Field of Kulikovo* would never have been written either.'[42] Yet Bely was right about Blok not wishing perdition for others. In letters to young poets, he warned always against 'the poisons of decadence'.

As it happened, Blok did not have to read a paper in Moscow after all. Instead, he heard Bely speak on Dostoyevsky and met a number of old friends whom he had seen only at rare intervals since his and Lyuba's triumphant visit to the old capital in January 1904. He was also introduced to the Turgenev sisters, to one of whom Bely was now engaged, but was not sure whether or not he approved as he never made out which of them was Bely's fiancée. He found the Muscovites impressively hard-working, impressively serious, and they, for their part, took him to their hearts—all over again.

Here in Moscow, the retrospective pathos which had dominated the whole year now took on a purely practical dimension. Musaget wanted to obtain that perspective on Blok—as one faithful through all betrayals and falls to the 'true Covenant' of which he had sung in his early verse—which had been suggested by 'On the Present State of Russian Symbolism'. It was clear, both to him and to them, that the time had come to reissue his earlier poetry and to publish his *Collected Poems*. There was talk even of a Collected Works, but Blok himself decided against this, for it still seemed to him that most of his prose was purely ephemeral in character and not worth reprinting.

So, when Blok rejoined Lyubov' Dmitriyevna in Petersburg five days later, it was with a commission from Musaget that was to keep him busy revising and rereading his early poetry for the rest of that winter.

10

Not all the reactions to 'On the Present State of Russian Symbolism' were so favourable as Bely's, or so correct as Bryusov's. Merezhkovsky attacked the article in the liberal newspaper *Russkoye Slovo*.[43] Blok, in Shakhmatovo, could not immediately come by a copy of the article, offensively entitled 'The Puppet Booth and Tragedy', but Andrey Bely lost no time in informing him that it was 'a provocation, a scandal and a dirty trick'.[44] Even this, however, had not altogether prepared Blok for the virulent tone which Merezhkovsky (a dear friend and admirer!) had seen fit to adopt. Blok, in his article, had identified his own subjective experience with that of Russia as a whole—a clear proof of megalomania, wrote Merezhkovsky. Blok, who still felt he had been talked into making public a very personal statement of faith, was utterly vulnerable and really hurt:

... they are petty people who are too fond of words and prepared to sacrifice live people to them, people who are engrossed in real work; they mix everything together in a heap (religion, art, politics, etc., etc.) and abandon themselves to pure hysteria.
     I have had to write Merezhkovsky a real scold,

(VIII. 321)

he wrote to Aleksandra Andreyevna after his return to Petersburg. Merezhkovsky, who was in France again, humbly turned the other cheek, ascribing the misunderstanding to his own 'stupidity of heart'; so self-consciously 'Christian' was his reply that Blok could not resist a follow-up in the form of a still more incisively worded second letter. At the same time he drafted an open letter to Merezhkovsky in which he reformulated the idea of the poet's identification with his country, refuting the accusation of megalomania:

But in fact what is so very self-confident in the idea that a writer who believes in his calling, irrespective of his actual stature as a writer, should measure himself against his motherland, assuming that he is sick with her sicknesses, suffers with her pain, is crucified together with her and, in those moments when they leave off torturing her tormented body, albeit for a moment, feels that he is at rest together with her.
     The more you feel the tie with your homeland, the more vividly and

easily you see her as a living organism; we have the right to this, because *we writers are obliged to look life in the eye as steadily as possible ; we are not scholars, we have our own methods for the classification of phenomena, and it is not our task to systematize our findings. Neither are we statesmen and we are free of the burdensome obligation of trying to trammel the wild animal which has just broken loose and is trying to kick over the traces of all legal restraint in an iron net of juridical theories.*[dd] We are just human beings, human beings by profession, and that means that we are obliged first and foremost to capture the breath of life.... We writers, free from all obligations but those incumbent upon our humanity, ... are not her [the motherland's] blind instincts, but her heart's sorrows, her meditations and thoughts, the impulses of her will.

(v. 443–4)

During the revolution, Blok maintained, writers had been as 'sick and crazed' as the country herself, but now that Russia was beginning to emerge from the shock of defeat and revolution and new impulses of growth were to be felt, it was foolish to continue to scream and rave, lest, like Leonid Andreyev, one should appear in the 'comical guise of a drummer who, having deafened himself with his own noise, goes on drumming after the orchestra which he was accompanying has fallen silent' (v. 444).

Having thus reformulated, more or less to his own satisfaction, what he had been struggling to say about the artist's relationship to the historical moment and to his mother country in 'On the Present State of Russian Symbolism', Blok yielded to Zhenya Ivanov's persuasions and refrained from embarking on printed polemics with Merezhkovsky.[ee] 'It's too late', he wrote to Aleksandra Andreyevna at the end of November. 'And anyway Zhenya's been talking me out of it.'[46,ff] By 9 January 1911 the last sparks of animosity had faded. 'I'm reading Z. N. Hippius's new story in *Russkaya Mysl*',' he informed his mother. 'I dreamt about her last night and decided to write to Merezhkovsky and make peace.'[47]

[dd] The italics are mine, the imagery obviously suggested by Blok's thoughts about his father.

[ee] That October, when Blok was still in Shakhmatovo writing round angrily to try to find out exactly what Merezhkovsky had said about him in the offending feuilleton, Zhenya had written humorously, ascribing the older author's hostility to jealousy of Blok's new *rapprochement* with Bely and Ivanov. 'What on earth do you want to keep going into battle for, snapping back at people left, right, and centre, instead of keeping straight along your own road? I've been meaning to write to you for ages (since 20 September) to ask why the devil you had to write the Merezhkovskys that you'd made it up with Bely: I'd have thought it was obvious you could write anybody at all about that, only not them....'[45]

[ff] The 'Answer to Merezhkovsky' was first published posthumously in *Russkiy Sovremennik*, no. 3, 1924, and was reprinted from manuscript in S.S., v, 442–5.

11

The new flat which Lyuba had found was eminently suitable to one intending to make a new beginning: situated on the Peterburgskaya Storona where Blok had spent his youth, Malaya Monetnaya Street, No. 9, it comprised four bright rooms on the top floor of a brand-new building. The flat commanded a fine view and Blok, rather surprisingly considering his marked preference for old furniture and old buildings, took to it at once. It seemed to him not so much new as 'young'.

On leaving Shakhmatovo for Moscow, Blok had sent his mother the first newspaper cutting about Tolstoy's sensational flight from his home.[gg] In Petersburg, he heard of the last death to affect him deeply in the twelve-month span which had already seen that of his own father, of Innokentiy Annensky, Kommissarzhevskaya, and Vrubel; the death, as he later wrote, of 'humane gentleness' and 'wise humanity' (III. 295–6).

Blok was not present at the Religious-Philosophical Society's meeting in memory of Tolstoy because of his quarrel with Merezh-kovsky, who he had thought to be still in Petersburg. Instead, he paid his last tribute to Tolstoy in a speech at another memorial evening in honour of his first teacher, Vladimir Solov'ev. Apropos the last three years of Solov'ev's life Blok recalled the ancient law by which, 'albeit weakened by the falls and betrayals of life, old age remembers youth ... a sign that the circle is about to be full drawn, that the *end* is near but not perdition, dormition but not death' (v. 447). Society, he said, had deliberately turned a blind eye to the solemnity of Tolstoy's 'dormition' because it offended the worldly that the genius who wrote *War and Peace* should, at the last, have turned his back on fame and all other worldly business and made off like a young boy, without even the blessing of the established Church,[hh] to seek 'another country'.

[gg] Aleksandra Andreyevna, shocked at Tolstoy's family's desire to recall him, wrote to Maria Pavlovna: 'Surely it is not impossible, while dearly loving one's own people, one's wife, family, children, and friends, yet to long with every fibre of one's being to get away from home, ... and, even if it means riding roughshod over those you love, to seek the ascetic feat, the spiritual freedom that has burnt in your heart all your life long?'[48] Sofia Andreyevna, Tolstoy's widow, she declared to be the happiest of women, an opinion to which she had every right, for her attitude to her own son was consistently sacrificial.

[hh] Tolstoy was making for the Optyno-Pustyn' monastery to consult the elders there when death overtook him at a provincial railway station. These 'elders' were men of great wisdom and sanctity and the desire to consult them would not necessarily have indicated a desire to do penance before the official Church, which had put itself in the terrible position of having excommunicated Tolstoy and which was, after his death, to offend its own

By the gallantry of his death, Tolstoy had reminded Blok of that lost harmony and innocence which he and his country had somehow to reconquer. Here again, it seemed, the way was shown by the genius dying on the borders of 'the promised land'. Only that spring, Blok had likened his own poetry to an out-of-tune violin sawing and wailing against the mounting harmony of the world orchestra (III. 192). This year of looking back and taking stock, beginning with his father's death and ending with Lev Tolstoy's, had helped him to realize that he must find new rhythms and abandon, for the time being at least, the harps and violins of his lyrical poetry, in order to bear a more disciplined part in a greater symphony.

---

adherents by consigning this man, whom many looked on as a near-saint, to anathema. The wording of the anathema deeply distressed Blok's mother; he told her he did not intend even to read it.

CHAPTER IV

The Search for Form (1) — *Retribution*

(January 1911–December 1911)

> I feel that, in the thirty-first year of my life, I have at last
> entered irrevocably on a very important new stage, which
> makes itself felt through my long poem and in my feeling
> for the world. I think that the last shadow of 'decadence'
> has withdrawn. I definitely want to live and I see ahead all
> kinds of simple, good, and attractive possibilities—and,
> what is more, I see them there where before I saw no such
> possibilities.... From now on, I shall not dare to grow
> proud as I once did when, as an inexperienced youth, I
> thought to disturb dark forces and brought them down
> about my own head. Because, from now on, *I am no longer
> a lyric poet....*
>
> (VIII. 331, 344)

1

Throughout 1911, Blok wrote virtually no lyric poetry—five or six
poems in all and most of these towards the end of the year. January
and February he devoted entirely to the long poem which he had
had in mind ever since his father's death: *Retribution*.

Working on the poem involved more than just writing. It involved putting into practice what the poet had learnt from his visit
to Europe: listening to the 'sounds of history', struggling to 'give
form and flesh to that profound, elusive content which fills every
Russian soul' (VIII. 331) and becoming 'a "social" man, an artist, who
looks the world courageously in the face and has won for himself
the right to study form, to make controlled tests of suitable and

unsuitable material, to look into the contours of "Good" and "Evil" at the price of losing a part of his soul' (VIII, 333).

As Blok wrote to his mother on 21 February 1911, he felt an urge to *widen* the circle of his life which, up till then, had been *'deepened at the expense of the needful widening'*. Now, after the long pause to look back which had occupied so much of the previous year, his life does indeed appear to have flowed on again only to broaden out like a lake upon whose deceptively still waters the poet sits with oars shipped, watching and listening, borne on only by the powerful, scarcely perceptible undertow of history.

In his preface to *Retribution* (III. 295–7) Blok gives his own assessment of the year 1911, using his father's method of juxtaposing apparently unrelated facts. He wrote of his own discovery of Strindberg; of the smell of 'burning, iron, and blood' that presaged the First World War; of Milyukov's lecture on 'The Armed Peace and Armaments Reduction'; of strikes in London and troubles in the Mediterranean; of rumours of impending war between Russia and China.[a] Amidst war and rumours of war, armies marshalling to the east and to the west, Russia herself was stirring uneasily in an ever-thickening murk of real foreboding and unreal internal crisis.

Society split, as in France over Dreyfus, over the *cause célèbre* of the Jewish workman, Beylis, who in the autumn of 1911 was brought to trial for ritual murder. A wave of anti-Semitism, marked, as so often in Russia, by a virulent increase in anti-liberal, obscurantist sentiment, poisoned public opinion for the duration of the case—until the eve of the Great War. In this year, too, Stolypin, the minister whose 'nervous aristocratic hand' had, according to Blok (VII. 9), 'twisted tight the noose' by which Witte and Durnovo had thrown and tamed the 1905 revolution, was shot at the Opera House in Kiev by a member of the Social Revolutionary party in the service of the Secret Police. For Blok, this lurid assassination marked 'the final transfer of the government of our country from semi-aristocratic, semi-bureaucratic hands into the hands of the police department' (III. 297). Under Stolypin, although liberal opinion had been gagged and the new organ of representative government, the Duma, rendered ineffective, a vigorously conducted and in many ways liberally conceived economic policy had cleared the way for healthy growth and there had been talk of intended reform from above. Now power

---

[a] Apropos these rumours, Blok wrote Andrey Bely who, having married Asya Turgeneva, was at that time on honeymoon, contemplating the pyramids in North Africa: 'Come back to Russia, all the same. It may well be that there is not much time left to see her *as she is now*' (VIII. 334, letter of 3 March 1911).

passed to time-servers and sycophants and, while the rest of the world mustered armies and forged weapons, the Empire of All the Russias grew steadily softer at the top.

At the same time, the body of the country, grateful for a few years of peace and order, was healing with the rapidity of youth. Industry was expanding; schools and hospitals were being built; a class of yeomen farmers, helped by Stolypin's efforts to provide opportunity for the capable and ambitious, was beginning to make better use of the land; the settlement of Siberia was proceeding apace and the mineral wealth of the Urals being more and more effectively exploited. The theme of this growing prosperity throbbed insistently through the poet's awareness of the world about him and directed his thoughts towards the need for a new type of artist with a range of interests equal to that of the great men of the Renaissance.

In the course of 1911, he withdrew somewhat from established literary circles and spent a great deal of time with his friend Vladimir Pyast, who shared his absorption in the political and economic development of Russia, and with a new circle of acquaintances from what can only be described as the technological intelligentsia: mathematicians, physicists, engineers,[b] and one astronomer,[c] whom Blok used to visit at his place of work in the Petersburg Observatory. In this company, the talk was less of literature and philosophy than of Russia: her present state and her destiny in the world. On long walks with Pyast through the outskirts of Petersburg, Blok would pour out his thoughts on the economic development of Russia—in despite, as it were, of political reaction—and of how 'If a foreigner who had visited us in 1903 were to return to us now, eight years later, he would see before him quite a different country'.[1 d]

The currents of energy generated by these beginnings of an economic renaissance at home and by the muster of men and weapons abroad penetrated Blok's private life through the microcosm of his

[b] N. I. Idel'son, mathematician and lawyer, and V. I. Yegorov, an engineer, were friends of Pyast. N. P. Bychkov, an engineer, had married Valentina Verigina, who came back to live in Petersburg in the spring of 1911 and resumed a close friendship with Lyubov' Dmitriyevna. B. P. Gushchin, a physicist, was an old friend of the family of whom Blok saw a good deal at this time.

[c] This man wrote symbolist verse under the pretentious pseudonym Graal Arel'sky, but Blok liked him better as the professional astronomer Stephan Stepanovich Petrov.

[d] Pyast did not have Bely's gift for catching his friend's hesitant, allusive speech, but the thoughts he records undoubtedly formed the subsoil of Blok's poetry throughout the years leading up to the 1914 war. Lyubov' Dmitriyevna when asked how Blok would have reacted to the Soviet Thirties, is said to have replied hesitantly: 'I don't know. Perhaps he would have got enthusiastic about "Socialist Construction"' (D.E. Maksimov, oral communication).

own interests, his own body. That winter, he became an *aficionado*
of two forms of sport: wrestling (in the circuses of Petersburg) and
aviation. This was the time when crowds of smartly-dressed men
and women would turn out as to the races to watch some brave man
take up a flimsy plane to 'loop the loop' and, occasionally, to see
one crash to his death.' The propeller, Blok told Pyast, had introduced 'a new sound into the world'.² As he listened to this sound
at Kolymyagi, the thoughts it brought him were of death and dyna-
mite (III. 33, 197), yet the 'idea' of flight delighted him, as one of
mankind's oldest dreams, a predestined stage on man's road to the
stars, to the time when he would abandon the mother country, 'when
frontiers will be erased and the whole earth will become our motherland, and then not the earth only, but the endless universe ...' (v.
444).

   Blok did not confine himself to the part of spectator. He became,
more than ever, an enthusiast for exercise: bathing, riding, cycling,
walking ... walking for hours on end. That winter his doctor, finding him nervously debilitated and in need of 'toning-up', prescribed
a course of systematic physical exercises and Swedish massage,
together with the 'spermin' injections fashionable at that time ('*all*
they do is to improve the circulation', Blok assured his mother,
though the newspaper advertisements hinted at other, more sensational, benefits). Blok had always been strong. Now he became
fascinated by the whole process of building up not only calves and
biceps but the finer muscles of chest and back. The time, as he felt
it, was a time of preparation, 'of profound, manly tension and
expectation' (III. 296). It seemed to him that

... the most direct expression of the rhythm of that time when the world,
preparing itself for unknown events, was making such concentrated and
deliberate efforts to develop its physical, political, and military muscles, was
the iamb. Probably that was why I, long driven about the world under
the lashes of that iamb, was drawn to commit myself to its bracing swell
for a longer period of time.

                                                        (III. 297)

The iamb was the metre of *Retribution*.

' Blok's poem 'The Aviator' (III. 33, 1910–12), inspired by the Russian airman Shmit
who crashed to his death before the poet's eyes at the Kolymyagi aerodrome in May 1911,
is comparable—except that thoughts of war are replaced by social satire—with Yeats's
'Death of an Irish Airman'. The feeling for the lonely ecstasy of flight, for which a man
may willingly risk life itself, is remarkably similar.

2

Blok had begun work on his 'Warsaw Poem', as the first draft of *Retribution* was finally subtitled, at Shakhmatovo in June 1910. By 2 January 1911 he had completed the first version of the part devoted to his father's death (later Chapter 3).*f* It was, however, clear to him that he needed to place this incident in a wider historical setting. Much of the spring of 1911 was spent in gathering materials about Poland: Polish Messianism, history, legends, the family history of the Polish family of Pestovsky (his friend Pyast). The summer and autumn he devoted to researching the European scene and Russian social history.

Even as his own development naturally followed a spiral course, so Blok conceived the movement of history: not, as his grandparents had done, as a majestic forward march, but rather as repeated, though never identical, spirals of infancy and childhood, youth and maturity, decline, senility, and death. Blok's classical education had conditioned him to accept this cyclic view of mortality and his own experience of life had confirmed it: 'What happens beyond all this? I do not know, and I have never known; I can only say that this whole conception*g* arose under the pressure of my ever-growing hatred for every conceivable theory of progress' (VII. 298).

So Blok wrote in the final introduction to *Retribution*, dated 12 July 1919. Yet the intense care for what would happen 'beyond all this' is implicit in this long historical poem, as in his lyric verse. Painfully aware that all things come to an end only to pass on into a new cycle of being, he would not knuckle under to the threat of everlasting repetition, but sought always the point of transfiguration at which things become other than they seem, the 'end' or 'dormition' as he had said of Tolstoy, rather than biological death. Hope in the ultimate 'beyond all this' was the *source* of Blok's poetry, yet he differed from Vyacheslav Ivanov and the theurgists in that he faced up squarely to the fact that such hope could not be its *subject*. Art, he still maintained, involved self-limitation, and his energy

---

f The first draft entitled *Retribution (A Warsaw Poem)*, dedicated to Angelina and containing several lyrical digressions later incorporated as separate poems into Iambs: *Contemporary Verses (1907–1914)*, is printed as an appendix to Blok's *Third Volume* of verse in the eight-volume Collected Works (III. 434–44). The poem was first entitled '1 December 1909', then 'Father'. This movement from the particular to the general (a date, a man, a city, an abstract concept) is typical of the development of all Blok's poetry: *from* the moment, intensely experienced, *to* the universal.

g i.e., the conception of the poem *Retribution*, the story of a declining family in a changing world.

was now bent on confining his own art to the cycles of mortal life.

Sometimes, these essentially pagan cycles were full of beauty and enchantment. More often, they bore more resemblance to the circles of Dante's Inferno.[h] So, in January 1911, we find the poet contemplating his father's last, half-crazy years and searching for some link with the life of his times which might have made sense of them. Somehow, the sullen, 'mole-like' image of his father, turning his back on all joy and light to 'bury his soul in the earth', led on to an image of Poland, on the one hand oppressed, driven underground, secretly plotting vengeance; on the other collaborating with the Imperial occupying power.

As he tried to determine his father's place in the history of his time, so Blok sought to determine his own in the history of his family. In the notes on his own life which, in the poem, was to be the subject of Chapter 2 and to lead up to the moment when he took the train to Warsaw to be at his father's deathbed, he wrote:

Against the background of each family arises its own rebellious offspring— as a reproach, a ferment, a revolt. Possibly, they are worse than the others, possibly they themselves are doomed to perish, they perturb and destroy their own kin, but they are *justified* by virtue of newness. They help man to evolve. Usually, they themselves are barren. They are—the last. Everything fuses in them, a closed circuit. For them, there is no way out of their own rebelliousness—neither in love, nor in children, nor in the founding of new families.

Although they break away from their families, by doing so they also break up the family they leave behind. They are the favourites, the spoilt children—if not of fate, then of the family. They are always 'demonic'. They are ruthless and challenging. They throw down the glove at fate. They are the caustic salt of the earth. *And they herald a turn for the better.*

(III. 464)

The question of his own unfitness to continue his line, to found a new family, appears to have nagged at Blok again that year as it had not done since his marriage. Yet he freely allowed that other men were eminently suited to become fathers and found families and this, in others, he found 'good and beautiful'. 'How nice Seryëzha is, a brilliant man, a future scholar of language and literature, my brother in spirit and by blood, a magnificent patriarch, a carrier-

[h] It is one of many *correspondances* between Blok and Zinaida Hippius that whem, in old age, Hippius attempted a poem on the subject of the *Divine Comedy*, she wrote: 'The *modern* Dante enters the deepest circle of Hell, and there he finds people whom he had once known. At the end he goes to Paradise. But I stopped here, for what do we know about Paradise?'[3]

on of his line, whereas I am a disintegrator ...,'[4] Blok wrote to Bely on 6 June 1911, two months after his cousin Sergey Solov'ev's first visit in six years to his home in Petersburg.[5] Later that year, on being introduced to Zhenya Ivanov's fiancée, his reaction was similar: 'Yes, Zhenya may be a good family man, according to my weak, indefinite, and abstract understanding, it is all right for him to marry. He is capable of making something beautiful out of family life. And in that tender, chaste young girl there is both blossom and fruit' (VII. 74, entry for 19 October 1911).

This from a man who, four years later, was to write of himself: 'I would be afraid if I had children.... Let one of the Blok lines at least end with me—there is little good in them.'[6]

He did not get far with the chapter about himself, which in the published version of *Retribution* survives only as an introduction, intended to set the scene for an autobiographical *Bildungsroman* which Blok never wrote. As it stands, this introduction is uneven. It never quite finds its own style or gets to grips with its autobiographical subject, but grows from a kind of invocation, in which long vowels and soft labials are marvellously deployed to suggest the hushed, enchanted sleep of Pobedonostev's Russia, into an impressionistic description of Alexander III's Petersburg: a phantasmagoric, amorous city, where the cab horses greet one another in the frost 'with a scarcely audible snicker' and the fares in the cabs are no more than 'a black moustache, all mixed with fur, that tickles lips and eyes'.

With a sudden change of tempo, the light running of the sleighs passes into an elephantine march as the poet—in a basso profundo of rounded *o*s and *oo*s and weighty *g*s—brings Alexander III himself, accompanied by all the royal family, rolling forth from the palace gates, to a loyal roar of 'hurrah!' From this it is scarcely a step to a satirical picture of the miseries of Lent—the season which Blok invariably associated with his school days; in the streets, alternate thaw and frost and, in men's hearts, unremitting spleen:

> And when you look a passer-by
> Full in the face, you'd take good aim
> And spit—had you not caught his eye
> And read his wish to do the same.
>
> (III. 330)

But winter passes and the prosaic slushy streets take on a new poetry from the white nights; Petersburg, again mysterious and unfathomable, appears to be hovering weightless above its marshy foundations. A great fleet comes quietly sailing past the sphinxes to the steps of the old Admiralty with Peter himself, dread founder of a doomed capital, at the helm of the leading frigate. In the foaming wakes of the ships a red dawn is reflected, a dawn sanguine with the menace of Tsushima, Port Arthur, the 9th of January....

3

To concentrate on a major poem was not easy. 'Modern life is very kaleidoscopic and shifts constantly before my eyes,' Blok complained. This was not only due to outward circumstances. The nucleus of his life—his relationship with his wife and mother—was now so damaged that the dancing particles all about seemed in danger of flying apart: inchoate and senseless.

The precipitous evacuation of Shakhmatova had made this terribly clear; he had no home. The bright new flat was simply a place where he and Lyuba happened to be living. It was not until much later that Lyuba began to understand Blok's sexual inhibitions and to make allowances for him and herself. Now, she blamed everything on Aleksandra Andreyevna and was resentful and uncooperative. Blok, fatally accustomed to subtle feminine sympathy and support, sought comfort in a series of infatuations which, in their turn, increased his estrangement from his wife.

Almost immediately after their return to Petersburg in the late autumn of 1910, the Bloks had attended a charity evening organized by the Chulkovs, at which the poet again met the Valentina who had haunted his thoughts that autumn. Her husband, Pavel Shchëgolev, a distinguished historian and Pushkin specialist, was serving a three-year sentence in a Petersburg prison for the publication of seditious material in his journal *Byloye*. At the Chulkovs' evening, organized to raise money for political prisoners and exiles, Valentina, a professional actress, gave an inspired recital of Vyacheslav Ivanov's 'Menada'.[i] Blok took her home after the reading, and for a short time they seem to have been on the verge of a serious romance. He talked of his youth and of himself, identifying his own fate with the fate of Russia, perhaps trying out the truth of the words he used in the unpublished answer to Merezhkovsky which he was turning over in his mind at the time. Valentina Shchëgoleva was a sympathetic,

---

[i] Vyacheslav Ivanov, in his diary for the summer of 1910, mentions appreciatively how he met and liked Shchëgoleva at the prison where he was visiting Professor Anichkov (released that autumn) and she her husband (released in early 1911 after pressure had been brought to bear on his behalf by the Academy of Sciences).

intelligent woman who accepted the poet's admiration with excitement and a sense of wonder. For a time, Blok sought her company. It was this autumn that, to her intense delight, he sent her the romantic cycle of poems: 'Three Letters' (III. 162–3).[j]

This new affair did not help to mend his relationship with his wife. She could not even bring herself to write to Aleksandra Andreyevna: 'Lyuba has written you a letter but she won't send it, says it's false, and wants to write another,'[7] Blok informed his mother on 3 December. Two days later the notebooks contain an unexplained entry—since he and Lyuba were undoubtedly living in the same flat—about an ever-growing temptation 'not to be alone': 'What am I to do and how am I to go on living? I still don't know. Never have I experienced such humiliation, terrible, irremediable, pitiable' (Z.K. 175).

Lyuba refused point-blank to go to Revel, so Blok went to spend Christmas with his mother, then hastened back to Petersburg to see in the New Year with his wife. They spent the day bogged down in 'very painful talk' but, in the evening, Zhenya Ivanov came and, after he left them at eleven o'clock, they felt able to face 1912 together in peace. Eventually, they agreed on a temporary separation. They would spend the following summer apart so as to give themselves time and not to make their disagreements public.

The rest of the winter season, however, was not easy. Blok's mother was in despair, as she wrote in February to Maria Pavlovna:

Should I tell you what torments me so, my dear good friend—it is all my relationship with Lyuba ... she did not even come to visit us in Revel, she herself refused. And what went on at Shakhmatovo, if only you knew— And now she simply will not commit herself to live with me this summer and it may well be will go off somewhere just in order not to be with me. Perhaps you think I exaggerate? No, all this is now said straight out in so many words.... When Lyuba is with him, she influences Sasha, and he begins to say God knows what to me.... He changes towards me and makes the most lethal accusations. I say lethal because I really have more than once decided to die after such accusations, and not because life is unbearable, but because I have been pronounced an absolutely repellent and harmful person. My attempts at suicide were serious enough, but they didn't come off....[8]

These letters were written at a time when Blok was writing to

---

[j] This account of Blok's relationship with Valentina Andreyevna Shchëgoleva is taken largely from an unpublished memoir by N. G. Chulkova (the wife of Georgiy Chulkov) in the possession of the late N. P. Il'in in Moscow. With the memoir go two notes from Blok himself, both urgently demanding rendezvous with Shchëgoleva.

his mother regularly and affectionately twice a week, though possibly with superfluous frankness:

... I couldn't go to sleep for hours and was in a black depression such as
I haven't had for a long time (from three to five in the morning of the
night of 12–13 February. Were you feeling bad then?). In the morning
it had all worn off, but suddenly I made up my mind to find a separate
flat (Lyuba and I have been discussing this possibility for quite a time). I
went and actually found one straight away on the 8th Line (the corner of
the Embankment) directly opposite my masseur: three furnished rooms
with bath and telephone. Rather dirty. The landlady is an old merchant's
wife. They bring up food from the restaurant in the same building. I decided
to put off the decision until the following day. Went home to dinner. Verkhovsky[k] turned up and invited me to take part in a court of honour between
him and Count A. N. Tolstoy. It is an old and unsavoury story, there are
many writers involved (it's *a secret*, by the way!). But we are only supposed
to be going into one aspect, the incident with the perfectly innocent Verkhovsky. I said I would. Verkhovsky had not yet gone when Meyerhold
appeared with Syunnenberg.[l] We had a very lively conversation late into
the night and ate pancakes. This morning I was at the bank with Angelina,
organizing our affairs. We've at last got all the money (a further 31,000
or so). This time we divided it according to the law, at the insistence of
Angelina and Maria Timofeyevna: five-eighths to me. i.e. 19,500. As a
result, I again have over 30,000. I came home—and am not going to leave.
I decided to stay. The sun's shining, it's spring, though frosty.—All my
abortive idea of leaving sprang from agonizing thoughts during the night
and day before yesterday, all to do with Lyuba's attitude to you, which
is a constant torment to me (we hardly ever speak about it). But to leave
will settle nothing. Sometimes I think it will all settle itself when the time
comes. And what do you think? In Lyuba there is more light these last
few days. The crisis with my leaving is over, perhaps that helps....

(VIII. 329–30, letter of 14 February 1911)

It was not easy to live like this—stripping oneself and others of
all self-delusion, constantly striving after a kind of total integrity.
Neither did Blok help himself or Lyuba by continuing to grasp at
the occasional moment of sympathy, or 'magic' that arose between
him and other women. This winter he fell half in love with Anna
Gorodetskaya, the wife of his old friend the poet Sergey Gorodetsky,
and a complicated relationship ensued which dragged on for over
a year, with Gorodetsky playing the gentlemanly role that Blok, in

[k] Yu. N. Verkhovsky (1878–1956), poet and critic.
[l] Konstantin Aleksandrovich Syunnenberg (pseud. K. Erberg), a minor poet of Left
Social Revolutionary affiliations who later worked with Blok in Narkompros (see below,
p. 331) and was one of the founders of Volfil (the Free Philosophical Academy). Blok
uses both his name and pseudonym in his diaries and notebooks.

his time, had played with Lyubov' and Andrey Bely: 'putting all
the responsibility on to me, as I once did on to Andrey Bely, oh
my God' (VII. 109), Blok noted bitterly. The Gorodetskys even came
together to consult him as to whether or not they should divorce.

Then, in the spring of 1911, a young girl, Natal'ya Nikolayevna
Skvortsova, who had fallen in love with Blok's poetry, came all the
way from Moscow to win the poet for herself:

Mama, yesterday I had a visit from Gilda. I was not at home when a young
girl arrived from Moscow and left a message that I was to meet her at a
place appointed by herself. I went feeling bored, but excited as well. We
spent all yesterday evening together and all today. She is twenty years old,
very vivid, beautiful (without and within) and natural. In everything down
to the last detail, including her costume, she resembles Gilda and says all
the things Gilda ought to say.''' We went for a sleigh-ride, walked about
the town and in the suburbs, sat at railway stations and in a café. Today
she went back to Moscow.

                         (VIII. 333, letter of 28 February–1 March 1911)

Of course, 'Gilda' fell head over heels in love, and this was the beginning of a long romance by correspondence.

The pattern of these and other, more fleeting affairs was basically
the same. Paradoxically, Blok's striving to live honestly, in harmony
with the given moment rather than according to any fixed moral
code, was always involving him in false situations. Acting on the
principle that what is beautiful cannot be evil, he would pursue, again
and again, the magic of some momentary infatuation, only to find
himself confronted with angry, demanding women who wanted to
leave their husbands for him or insisted that he dedicate to them and
them alone 'all his verse'. Feeling no response in himself to such radical demands, he would begin to back out, suffering for all concerned,
often inflicting cruel wounds yet, miraculously, making no lasting
enemies. 'Blok', wrote Valentina Shchëgoleva to Nadezhda Chulkova after the poet's death, 'is the vindication of our times. Not of
the present time, but of *our* time, the pre-revolutionary period!'[9]

Perhaps it was better when his romances remained nothing but
might-have-beens, an unforgettable yet half-imagined glimpse of a
lovely face, as on that April evening of 1910 when he had stared
steadily at a young girl at a neighbouring table in a restaurant and
sent her 'a black rose in a beaker of champagne as gold as the sky'
(III. 25). 'This I found most impertinent, so I got up and left,' Maria
Dmitriyevna Nelidova commented thirty-eight years after the

''' Gilda, as Blok called Natal'ya Skvortsova, was the youthful heroine of Ibsen's *The
Master Builder* who appears to the ageing Solness in the guise of Retribution.

event, adding that she did eventually meet Blok properly when they were both visiting Aleksey Remizov: ' "A-a, the Stranger," he said. "Why did you run away that evening?" We introduced ourselves. He recited the verses "I sat at the window. The room of the restaurant was crowded." We met again....' And, the story ends decorously, 'At his request, I translated Péladan's *Oedipus and the Sphinx* from the French. Blok liked my translation and promised to turn it into hexameters' (III. 504).

Yet now, in his maturity, Blok met with few such setbacks. His 'piercing, inhuman beauty',[n] his magnetism, even his dangerous reputation, even the demonic cruelty of his poetry, merely made him the more irresistible. And so the pattern repeated itself:

I see that the blood flows evenly, calmly and merrily beneath the skin of your cheeks and in the supple muscles of your arms. And my blood grows young in answer, so that our fingers are drawn towards one another with inexplicable tenderness and intertwine as it were without our volition. It is still difficult for them to meet, because it seems to me that you are sitting on a high ladder leant up against the white wall of a house and the sky above you is already light, whereas I am down at the bottom on the very lowest rungs, where it is still misty and dark. Soon the wind of my hands scorching itself on you and growing hot, tears you down from your high place and already our lips can meet, because you are on a level with me. Then in my ears sounds the whistling and ringing of the violas, and my eyes, sunk in your merry, wide-open eyes, are already looking down into yours. I become vast, and you quite small; I, like a great cloud, envelop you with ease, a white bird diving into the heart of the cloud and crying in ecstasy....

(VII. 86)

"But, good God, my dear', he wrote a few days later in an unsent letter to 'Gilda', 'that is not what you want, nor I neither' (VII. 90). Yet: 'No, it is not in my power to release you. This is very necessary to me.' And so, out of the romance or non-romance with 'Gilda', came, most surprisingly, the darkly sensual cycle 'Black Blood' (III. 54–9) with its leitmotiv: 'Ah no, I do not wish that you and I should fall' (III. 55).[o]

Also 'Gilda's', although it is about a Petersburg brothel and not in the least about the proud young girl from another city, is the poem

[n] The expression is that of the composer Yuriy Shaporin, who met Blok when writing the music for a cantata on the theme of *On the Field of Kulikovo*.

[o] At least, this cycle could not have been written without 'Gilda', though there are many other moments, many other women involved.

'Humiliation' (III. 31–2), written in December 1911, the notorious poem that ends:

> You are bold! Cast aside every fear, then!
> Neither husband, nor friend I—so deal
> Me my death-blow, my yesterday's angel,
> Through the heart with your pointed French heel!

The hopeless yellow sunset, the pictures of the brothel ('is it a house indeed?') and of humiliation through passion ('was it *this* we called love?') are all taken from the same unsent letter to N. N. Skvortsova, the train of associations having been set in motion by a phrase in one of her letters to him using the word 'humiliation' in connection with her love for him (*Z.K.* 90–1, entry for 15 November 1911).

Blok was experienced enough not to send his letter. 'It was written more for me than for you,' he said in a second attempt. The third version, which he did send, was merely an elegant riposte in the duel of dalliance which, not surprisingly, enraged the recipient. It was Blok's habit to demand an impossible understanding of women. The amazing thing was that he so often got it.

Like most successful Don Juans, he genuinely liked feminine company for its own sake, and perhaps his happiest relationships with women were those not complicated by romance. Just a friend, for instance, and a very good and loyal friend, was the ever-lively Verigina, who 'tells stories very well and in such good Russian—in general, there is much of the sweet Russian woman in her. The slipperiness has gone' (VIII. 333). Very different was Zhenya Ivanov's deeply religious sister Maria Pavlovna, close friend of Aleksandra Andreyevna and, like her brother, a tower of strength to the whole Blok family. Maria Pavlovna, it is said, took Blok's letters with her to her grave, but she was older than he, self-controlled and tactful, and their relationship was one of spiritual friendship. 'I always learn from you' (VIII. 330), Blok wrote her on one occasion and, to a friend, of the whole Ivanov family: 'Simply knowing there are such people in the world makes it easier to live; in them there is—support.'[10]

Then there was Elizaveta Yur'evna Kuzmina-Karavayeva, now an aspiring poet married to 'a decadent Bolshevik lawyer', but still at heart that same Liza Pilenko who had 'stood on his path' at the age of fifteen. On 14 December 1910, she reappeared in Blok's life on the evening when he had spoken to an indifferent and unresponsive public on the tenth anniversary of the death of Vladimir Solov'ev. Her husband was acquainted with Blok and offered to introduce them, but Elizaveta Yur'evna, overcome by belated shyness, declined. Blok, however, had already recognized her across the room, and the next thing she knew she was being introduced to an amused and rather superior Lyubov' Dmitriyevna who invited her and her husband to dinner. 'We met like acquaintances, like well-brought-up people in polite society. Not like the first time when I had burst into his flat out of the mists of Petersburg, straight from the street.'[11] The dinner had passed in reminiscences of the revolution. After this, Elizaveta Yur'evna and Blok met often, for they now moved in the same world, but the relationship partook of the artificiality of Petersburg literary society. He discouraged her from printing her poetry, considering it was essentially 'not for publication' (VIII. 431). For her part, she had as yet found neither herself nor her God. Her living tie with Blok was their unspoken awareness of a larger world outside their own brilliant but enclosed society, an awareness that brought with it a sense of profound foreboding and of lively shame. Of this she wrote:

We lived in the midst of a vast country as if on an uninhabited island. Russia could neither read nor write—in our circle we concentrated the whole of world culture.... It was Rome at the time of the decline. We did not live ourselves, we contemplated all the extreme refinements of life, we feared no words and, in the sphere of the spirit, we were cynical and unchaste, in life lethargic and inactive. In some sense we were, of course, a revolution before the revolution, so deeply, ruthlessly, and destructively did we turn over the soil of tradition, so bold were the bridges we flung out towards the future. Yet, at the same time, this profundity and boldness was combined with ineradicable decay, with a spirit that was moribund, phantasmagoric, ephemeral. We were the last act of the tragedy of estrangement between the people and the intelligentsia....

At Vyacheslav Ivanov's 'tower', which Blok also frequented, Elizaveta Yur'evna would listen till the small hours to the talk of Christ, the revolution, and the Second Coming. 'In the morning they bring a fresh samovar and fried eggs. Time to go home. Along the sleepy street the cab horse jogs steadily. There is a sort of sickness in the soul. Drunkenness without wine, food that does not satisfy.'[12]

Sickened by shrill discussions of redeeming suffering 'at the tops of our voices ... until the fried eggs', Elizaveta Yur'evna began to feel an ever-increasing, protective sympathy for the genuinely stricken: for 'the revolutionaries because they are laying down their lives and all we can do is to talk cleverly and loftily about their dying'; for Christ (she did not at that time believe in God), 'Who also died, sweated blood, was tortured to death'; for the silent Russian people; and, for some reason she herself did not fully understand, for Blok.

Unconventional, practical, impatient for 'real work' of some sort, Elizaveta Yur'evna eventually, at the beginning of 1912, after two years of the 'tower' and the 'Poet's Workshop',[p] made up her mind to break away from St. Petersburg and to go back to live on her estate, amongst her own people in the South. The first person she told of this decision—indeed, the decision took her by surprise even as she told him—was Blok: ' "Aleksandr Aleksandrovich, I've decided to get away from here. The only thing left to do here is to lie down and die. But I've still got some fight left in me." Seriously, conspiratorially, he answered: "Yes, yes, it's time. Soon you won't be able to any more. You must hurry." '[13]

4

If there was in all these intense relationships some element of romantic love, there was one young woman with whom Blok could communicate freely, unhampered by romance: his half-sister Angelina. She and her mother, having taken a holiday in Germany in the summer of 1910, had brought him back a book for his thirtieth birthday: the *Nibelungenlied*. After the long summer and autumn separation, this well-chosen present confirmed Blok in his good opinion of his newly acquired relatives and reminded him of Wagner's *Siegfried*, inspiring the superb lines on the forging of the sword in the prologue to *Retribution* (III. 301).

During the winter of 1910–11, he saw a good deal of Angelina. Gradually, the full extent of her mother's conservatism was borne in upon him, and his initial respect for Maria Timofeyevna turned to irritation. She was strongly opposed to Angelina's attending the Religious-Philosophical Society, which she considered a hotbed of dissent, and dismissed Merezhkovsky's Christianity as 'a subtle kind of Khlystovstvo'.[q] Although Blok did not always agree with the 'New Christianity' and did not set himself up as an authority on Ortho-

---

[p] *Tsekh poetov*, the name taken by the future Acmeists, comprising, amongst others, Gorodetsky, Gumilev, Akhmatova, Mandelstam, Makovsky, and, peripherally, von Guenther. Elizaveta Yur'evna does not accuse them of the 'spiritual immodesty' of the Tower, but describes their gatherings as 'earnest, like at school, a little bit dull and mannered'.

[q] A Russian sect; cf. vol. I, p. 105n.

doxy, this overprotective attitude offended his own questing spirit and his respect for Merezhkovsky.'

Blok's work on *Retribution* kept Angelina constantly in his mind. What would her life be like? Would she become febrile, destructive, passionate, like so many of the 'decadent' women? Or would she knuckle under to her mother's milieu and become a pious little oyster, sheltering behind the hard shell of established custom? He wanted her to become a 'real person', as he wished to be himself, and advised her to read medicine at the Bestuzhev Courses. This would, he thought, at least provide a draughty, disinfected antidote to the mother-of-pearl enclosure of her schoolgirl years. On 1–2 March 1911, Blok completed the Prologue to his poem and almost succeeded in giving artistic expression to that faith in an ultimate purpose which, as a mere man, he found it so impossible to communicate to her:

> Life is without beginning, without end,
> And each of us is subject to blind chance.
> Above us lowers the everlasting dark,
> Or shines the radiance of the face of God.
> But you, the artist, steadfastly believe
> In ends and in beginnings. You must know,
> Where Heaven watches over us—where Hell.
> With a fair judgement it is given you
> To measure all things that you here may see.
> But let your eye be single, firm, and clear.
> Eliminate the aimless strokes of chance,
> And you will see: the world is beautiful.
> Learn where to look for light, and you will learn
> Where darkness is. And let all holy things
> And all things sinful filter slowly through
> The fever of the heart, the cold of mind.

(III. 301)

Yet what right had he to introduce Angelina to the Hell he had elected to traverse for the sake of his poetry? She was not a strong,

'In January 1911 Blok had made his peace with Merezhkovsky as well as with Zinaida Hippius.[14] In November 1912 Knyazhnin poured out his heart to Blok in a scathing criticism of Petersburg literary personalities. Blok went home, thought it over, and decided Knyazhnin must be called to order. Among others, he took Merezhkovsky unequivocally under his protection: '"Merezhkovsky at the Rel. Phil. meetings boasts that we, as he puts it, have spoken with God",' Blok recorded Knyazhnin as saying and repeated in a letter: 'Excuse me, but that, if I may say so, is sheer philistinism. And the only answer is this: "Yes, Merezhkovsky, who has lived a long and tormenting life and who has written what he has written, *has spoken with God*". Merezhkovsky is more alone than anyone else, to this day, and we all know the burden he has carried, and carried successfully, on his own shoulders ...' (VIII. 404–5).

serene character like Zhenya Ivanov, capable of playing Dante to his Virgil and emerging unscathed and even enriched. Perhaps, he thought, it would be better not to tamper with her beliefs at all. But one day at the end of the spring of 1911, Angelina came to him full of praise for a book published by a firm that bore the odious name of K. P. Pobedonostsev. Blok tried to convince himself that it was none of his business:

I am *weak* to lead Angelina out of the darkness with which she is surrounded. What is needed is to find even one man in all the world who *honestly and religiously* believes in the future of humanity—without conservatism, without tearfulness, without parasitism. But is there such a person in the world?

(*Z.K.* 179, entry for 6 May 1911)

Yet after writing this he devoted the following day to reading the offending book, 'a sentimental English story, tenderly caressing to the soul, comfortably ordinary', fit only to uphold the obscurantist opinions of 'people of low calling (such as all kinds of governesses without name or family)'[5] who would use it 'to crush those great spiritual, intellectual, and, in the last analysis, even political movements without which our country would long since have stifled to death'. Blok saw his stepmother as an incarnation of the obscure multitude who formed 'the background against which *we* act' and who were more reactionary than any government.

Should Angelina be rescued, or not? And who is there to rescue her? Or maybe it would be better for her to live out her life knowing *nothing* either of God, or of the world, or of love, or of freedom?
      Soon after this Angelina came to see me with her mother—so tender, so sensitive, nervous, and believing that—she must not be left that way.

(*Z.K.* 180–1)

How these private considerations about individual people nourished the poet's work and how his thoughts when writing

---

[5] Blok was thinking of Maria Timofeyevna, who came in fact of a well-established, part-Scottish military family whose history was similar to that of the Bloks, though they had lacked the ambition, and possibly the ability, to climb so high in the social scale. Neither Maria Timofeyevna nor the Belayevs had anything to do with the English 'governesses' and 'tutors' of Blok's imagination, but after her divorce she had been forced to earn her living and had taken the only post for which the liberal education of a young lady of that time really qualified her: that of a teacher in a young ladies' seminary. Blok's impatience, as so often in his notebooks and diaries, is ill considered, and one can only suppose that he kept it in check when he and Maria Timofeyevna met, since they remained, outwardly at least, on tolerably good terms until she fades from his story after Angelina's death in 1918.[15]

affected his relationships with people can be clearly seen from the way Blok followed up this line of thought on the very next day in a letter to Andrey Bely, weaving it back into his meditations about his father's negative attitude to contemporary life in the poem *Retribution*:

The whole question is, is there now in Russia *one single person* who believes sanely, honestly, and in godly fashion (i.e. having in the depth of his soul a hidden but sincere 'yes') who is capable of saying 'No' to all contemporary life? Anyway, I have begun (though now I shall give it up for a time) working at the unravelling of this thread which I have been brooding over all winter and which nothing will now induce me to abandon. I am writing and want to write about it, only not in letters....[16]

Indeed, Blok had done no more work on *Retribution* after completing the Prologue at the beginning of March. Here, he had made an explicit lyrical statement embodying, in so far as he was able, the dichotomy he wrote about to Bely and felt so acutely in his dealings with Angelina. But now the effort to find an objective narrative form that would appear to speak for itself whilst somehow conveying that same overt 'No' and implying—most difficult of all—the 'hidden but sincere "yes"', was getting him nowhere. By Easter, he had decided to put the poem to one side until he had achieved a clearer vision.

5

Lent had done nothing to ease the strain between Blok's mother and his wife. Frants Feliksovich's posting in Esthonia was at an end and he had been reappointed to Poltava. The Kublitsky-Piottukhs intended making a short stay in Petersburg on their way south; he to take up his new command and she, as usual, to spend the summer at Shakhmatovo with her sister Maria. Blok was asked to find them a temporary flat. He was worried—both at the thought of the two elderly ladies alone together in the country ('you must get the batman to come and sleep in the house,' he counselled anxiously) and still more at the possible effect of a further stretch of provincial military life on his mother's mental health. Lyuba, however, was insistent that he might do as he liked but she was not going back into the claustrophobic atmosphere of Shakhmatovo as it had been the previous year. She would go abroad, and he might join her later if he wished to do so.

Towards Easter, as usual, everything came to a head—not, this time, in poetry but in a dream. After attending the Good Friday service with Pyast Blok came home and fell asleep. He found himself back in the side street near the Barracks where the factory with 'yellow windows' was.' He had found his mother a flat, but she would not go in, sitting disconsolately on the steps before the front door. Then all the lights went out. Blok, desperately fumbling with matches, was trying to re-illumine one street lamp.

I realize they have laid off work at the gas factory because of the midnight service. But why is it only here in this side street that there are no lights? At the same time I am acutely aware that if the gas did catch light from my match it would burn my hands and face.

(Z.K. 177, entry for 9 April 1911)

There follows a nightmare chase through the factory, running along pipes, ducking under working machinery. Just as he reaches sanctuary—his own flat—he realizes that it is divided into two: 'our half' and 'the Mendeleyevs''. The Mendeleyevs' flat, opulent and comfortable, is all decorated with slender sprays of flowers—by Lyuba, Blok realizes, because their 'half' has similar sprays, but arranged with less love. And as he stands hesitating in the hall he hears his wife and her mother moving towards him through the 'Mendeleyev' rooms, the mother-in-law hesitating 'as ladies of leisure do, so that you can't tell when they're going to move on'. Terrified of being apprehended, he flings himself into his own 'half' and escapes down the back stairs ... out into the dark again.

Such was Blok's state of mind by the end of the 1910–11 season: Easter over, the Kublitsky-Piottukhs actually installed in the flat he had found them and the weather improving, he managed to soldier on into the spring, though the month was barren of poetry. On 17 May Lyuba left, as they had agreed, for Berlin and Blok to join his mother, who had already gone down to Shakhmatovo. Before they parted, he and Lyuba went together to see the flying at Kolymyagi aerodrome:

People, aviation, Sestroretsk, a sleepless night, a dusty, hot spring.... Through everything—sadness and a feeling of bewilderment at the thought of parting from Lyuba for the summer. And—within me—a kind of gnawing apathy and inertia.

(Z.K. 181)

' See vol. I, p. 146.

6

At Shakhmatovo, Blok supervised the rebuilding of the byres
and read Strindberg, to whose work he had recently been introduced by Pyast, and, for light relief, Carlyle, whose *History of
the French Revolution* he found 'inexpressibly cleansing to the soul'
(VIII. 347).

The friendship with Pyast, whom Blok had known since his
student days, had only become really close since the previous
autumn. Pyast wrote both prose and poetry but the subject of their
conversations was not 'literature' but Russia, a never-ending debate
like a game of chess which somehow never quite came to the point
and sent 'little Lyuba' off to sleep before their eyes. All through the
winter they had talked of founding a journal with Vyacheslav Ivanov
and Professor Anichkov. Andrey Bely was also to be invited to contribute. Blok wanted the journal to provide individual authors with
an opportunity for almost informal self-expression and to reaffirm
the indivisibility of culture: of literature, life, philosophy, and religion. Where *Apollon* offered elegant distraction, their journal was
to convey a tragic sense of urgency and to teach courage. Of the
various names they had discussed for it the one which appealed to
them most was Sagittarius, the Archer: *Strelets*.

Neither Blok nor Pyast, however, had the organizational ability
to bring the project off. Anichkov, Blok soon realized, though a
charming host and a delightful personality, was too self-satisfied for
their purposes. Vyacheslav Ivanov was not keen, and Blok felt that
his own bond with Pyast was 'not of a journalistic nature'. Meanwhile, however, the two men had continued to see a lot of one
another throughout the winter and Pyast had introduced Blok to
two pleasures which were to become all-absorbing crazes: reading
Strindberg and tobogganing in the Finnish hills north of Petersburg; in the summer he found an excellent substitute for the latter
in the roller-coaster at Petersburg's Luna Park.

At Shakhmatovo, lonely and unable to settle down without
Lyuba, Blok invited Pyast to come to stay in the uselessly enlarged
house.

Here, as always, you are immediately cut off from the world. Letters and
newspapers reach us twice a week. Do you know what? Couldn't you perhaps come for a few days? There's lots of room, quiet, sweet air. I think
you would be interested to see this Russia and ought to see it: only 60
versts from Moscow yet it might be 1,000: a sweet-scented wilderness and,
in this earthly paradise:—twisted, unhappy, and browbeaten people with

ideas and beliefs from before the flood, people who have forgotten even themselves.

(VIII. 337, letter of 24 May 1911)

But Pyast, convinced, in spite of his doctor's assurance to the contrary, that he was suffering from mumps, rightly assumed that Blok—who clung to the idea of joining Lyuba abroad as soon as possible after midsummer—would not want to run the risk of infection. So, since he had, over the winter, developed 'a constant need' to inform his friend of every revolution of 'the cogs of his brain', Blok was reduced to writing him letters.

Writing to Pyast from Shakhmatovo helped the poet to look at his home from that detached historical, sociological standpoint which they had together been cultivating throughout the winter. The maddening delays in repairing the house the previous year, the abortive effort to dig a new well, the peccadilloes of the feckless Yegorka, and the unaccustomed direct involvement of the family in the management of the estate had all added a painfully acquired personal insight into the ways of the Russian countryside. It seemed to him, as he wandered about field and forest, that every sociologically-minded Russian owed it to himself to get to know the life of the villages. Pyast, as a representative of 'demonic' Europeanism, needed, he thought, to experience at first hand the vast inertia of the countryside which, as he told him in a letter, must either sap the will to reform altogether, 'making a man Russian in the Chekhov sense', or temper it to a driving force of tenfold, 'super-European' power.

'More and more often,' he wrote to his friend,

I find myself believing that the mistakes of the Social Democrats in the recent past stemmed from their not knowing and not wishing to know the country; not even to know, perhaps (I say this because it may be *that for us it is already impossible to know it*, and the split into opposing camps which began under Peter and Catherine must inevitably lead to a terrible confrontation), but, if not to know, then *at least* to see with your own eyes, even if you hate what you see. . . .

(VIII. 346, letter of 6 June 1911)

Blok had hoped to continue *Retribution* once he had recovered from the staleness of the winter, but this year he could not settle and did only mechanical work, preparing the second and third volumes of his *Collected Poems* for Musaget.[a] Musaget had already brought

---

[a] The plan of these three volumes was different from that of Blok's later *Collected Poems*. Volume I comprised the *Verses about the Most Beautiful Lady* but contained almost three times as many poems as those in the original edition published by Grif. Volume II was

out Volume I, a revised and greatly expanded edition of the *Verses about the Most Beautiful Lady* with a brief author's preface (I. 559) which Valeriy Bryusov had found 'most interesting' and 'full of matter' (VIII. 605). It was pleasant to receive appreciative letters (and there were many) about this first volume, but the revision of his more recent poetry bored him, and when a group of new poems appeared in Musaget's almanac he wrote to Andrey Bely:

I received Musaget's 'Anthology'. *Why did we do it?* The time for almanacs is over; it seems to me that this is an unnecessary book. The *talented* movement called 'the new art' is finished; i.e. the minor tributaries have emptied themselves into the great eternal stream, giving it their all. Now there is only good and bad, art and non-art.

(VIII. 344, letter of 6 June 1911)

As for his own 'trilogy of humanization', as he called it in the same letter to Bely, he was heartily sick of it: 'Another set of proofs of *Night Watches* has arrived. My one wish is to get through them as soon as possible and finish off the *Collected Poems*—and then not to write any more lyrical poetry till old age' (*Z.K.* 182, entry for 4 June 1911).

The persistent discomfort caused by a recurrence of the illness he still referred to as 'scurvy' and treated by 'eating masses of eggs and milk' (VIII. 399) and eschewing meat, made the two months in the country exceptionally burdensome. Blok was bored and miserable. Every evening he would wander disconsolately downstairs into Lyuba's room. Two portraits of her stood by his bedside: 'the one where you are little and sly (at the age of seventeen or so), and the other taken when we were engaged' (VIII. 342). He had, he informed Lyuba, also received a large photograph of Natal'ya Nikolayevna Skvortsova, the girl he called Gilda:

Now there is a girl with whom I might have become most 'uniquely' involved, had I not already given everything I had to give to you. This I understood quite distinctly only yesterday. Of course, I did not know it before, but human relationships, like all works of art, require 'a last finishing touch'.

This letter is dated 30 May 1911, the Feast of All Souls (a feast which Blok's mother had brought him up to see as the most 'human'

---

only the first part of the canonic *Second Volume* and consisted largely of poems from Blok's second book *Joy Unhoped-for*. Volume III comprised *The Snow Mask, The Earth in Snow,* and *Faina* (all now included in the *Second Volume*), as well as *The Night Watches* which had been published as a separate collection by Musaget that winter and which was composed of poems later included in the canonic *Third Volume*. Although Blok was writing no new poetry, this stream of publications—including much hitherto unpublished work from an earlier period—explains the steady growth of his reputation over this period.

in the calendar[17]), and the train of thought that led to this 'finishing touch' had been set in motion when Blok had drifted, on the eve of Trinity, into the little church where he had been married, to find it all decorated with pungent, fresh-cut birch boughs and with lush, flowery grass from the water meadows scattered over the floor. The next day, 'very wide-awake and clear-headed', he had suddenly understood much in his relationships

... with a number of people. First of all, with you.... What I wanted to write you is that everything unique in myself I have already given to you and cannot now give to anybody else even when, at times, I have wished to do so. All I have left for others is, first and foremost, my mind and the sentiment of friendship, which is distinguished from love only in that it is pluralistic and loses nothing by being so, otherwise I have only—demonic feelings, or indefinite infatuations (more and more seldom) or, finally, low instincts.

(VIII. 341)

Lyuba's letters from Berlin—about picture galleries and Max Reinhardt's production of *Hamlet*—pleased and interested him. In Paris, however, she met up with the Remizovs and her old admirer Chulkov. To make matters worse, she went into ecstasies over the shops and was incautious enough to try to share her delight with her husband. Blok's pride rebelled at the thought that she was gadding about the world while he was sitting at home in the country: the other way round, he pointed out with uninhibited masculine logic, would have been much more natural. Still more annoying was the fact that she was seen by their Petersburg acquaintances to be so gadding: the Bloks kept almost everyone but the Ivanov family at more than arm's length as far as their relationship with one another was concerned. To add to Blok's irritation, the letters he had sent to Germany were all returned to him, with the exception of the 'really important one' of 30 May. On 7 June he sent Lyuba a devastating scold, followed three days later by a second letter, somewhat mollified by having received an interesting account of Versailles 'without Remizov and Chulkov'! Even this, however, contained a remnant of disapproval:

Write to me when you can bring yourself to leave the shops in peace. Try, once and for all, to understand one simple thing: all objects of contemporary manufacture are vulgar trash and not worth a brass farthing, and for this reason the only things worth buying are books and practical things one can't do without.

(VIII. 347)

On 13 June, brooding over Chulkov with his handsome, ironic face and his talent for double entendre, Blok sent a third, still harsher dressing-down, the gist of which was that Lyubov' and Paris did not mix and the sooner she was out of the big city the better he would be pleased. There he was sitting in Shakhmatovo thinking beautiful thoughts about her, and there was she fluttering about Europe and making no effort to find herself. 'Go away to the ocean,' he ordered. 'Swim, look at the water, and think.'

Meanwhile Lyuba, virtuously on her own again in Aber-wrach, a charming fishing village in Finistère where she had decided to bathe and wait for Blok to join her, was rejoicing over her husband's confession of his unique feelings for her and writing happy letters: she couldn't wait to see him and he was not to forget his black bathing costume and his cool white suit. As always when in affectionate mood she called him 'Lala' and 'Lalalka'. His angry letters descended on her with all the added weight of distance, eliciting what can only be described as a spontaneous yelp of pain, immediately controlled and contained by understanding. She knew, wrote Lyubov', that his assessment of her as a 'third-rate person who had lost her spiritual significance' was dictated more by the state of his nerves than by his real feelings towards her, so, although it was difficult, she was going to go on writing to the man she knew, the one who had sent the kind letter, not to somebody brandishing a knout 1,000 versts away. After this she maintained a steady flow of affectionate correspondence, urging him to see a doctor, telling him the small news of her quiet village. He responded warmly enough, though not neglecting to remark how much nicer her letters had become since leaving Paris. 'We ought to go to live in Paris together for a while sometime and find—under all the accumulated rubbish of the present—the ancient, holy city and the city of the Revolution. I am sure that this must be possible.'[18]

On 14 June Blok went to Moscow for two days to see Kozhebatkin of Musaget and to deliver the last two volumes of his *Collected Poems*. This left him free to leave, yet he remained another fortnight at Shakhmatovo, drained of all energy, of all desire to go anywhere at all. Aunt Maria says discreetly that he had to oversee the building of a house for their general factotum Nikolay, but on 24 June Aleksandra Andreyevna wrote to Maria Pavlovna:

We are here just the three of us and we are so gloomy and sad for whole weeks on end: both I and my Detochka" are afflicted by attacks of an illness

" Detochka ('little child') or Dushen'ka ('little soul') were Aleksandra Andreyevna's usual form of address for her son: naturally, she would only use them of him to very close friends.

which the doctors call 'cyclotilia.' It occurs periodically, in some kind of cycle. In my case it is accompanied by a seizure rather like epilepsy ... and I always know that it *has begun*. But his reaction is different. Now, for instance, the position is this. He should be already on his way to bathe in the sea, and meet up with Lyuba whom he is obviously missing, and he was getting ready to go the other day, but now, all of a sudden, *he doesn't want to do anything*. I wish with all my heart that he would see a good doctor, take a proper course of treatment, go to the seaside as soon as possible, for it was on the doctor's advice that he was to go in the first place. Before it is too late he ought to look after his nerves. Now is the dead season. There aren't even any doctors in Petersburg. I don't know to whom to send him.

Lyuba is in Brittany, bathing in the sea, she's taken rooms in some little village. That's all right for her, but he needs more comfort and to be under the observation of a doctor. It is my opinion that he and Lyuba should be together.[19]

It was not until nearly the end of July (Russian style) that Blok overcame his apathy and left his mother and aunt at Shakhmatovo to their dull strolls (Aleksandra Andreyevna's heart condition did not permit her to go far from the house) and their tremulous awaiting of his letters. It was a bad summer for Aunt Maria, for Aleksandra Andreyevna, always insistent on the utmost cleanliness in the house, now settled down to find fault with the servants and to wage war on the dogs—whom Blok had succeeded in smuggling one by one into the rooms and had ended by permitting to romp all over the furniture! Without him, Shakhmatovo grew very dull, and even Maria Andreyevna's patient efforts to start her sister reading again met with little success:

Our conversations always circled about the same themes and I reduced my sister to despair by my placid attitude to life and my opinions, which to her were quite unacceptable. In many ways we differed from one another by our very natures, and she could not make me share her philosophy of life, which irritated her beyond all measure. It seemed to her that an impassable gulf had opened between us, that we had nothing more in common, but, of course, she was mistaken: in spite of our many differences we were alike in many ways, and close, and in the most important thing of all, that is in our attitude to Sasha, we were always at one....[20]

Uncertainty as to her own future was undoubtedly at the bottom of Aleksandra Andreyevna's inability to overcome her depression. That spring she had had a meeting with Lyuba and they had had quite a good talk, but had parted dryly, without one word of affection. She was too sensitive to impose herself on Blok and Lyuba in

Petersburg, but she dreaded Poltava. Revel at least had been a capital, however small; it was European, pretty, polite. The old Cossack centre of Poltava offered a kind of *Three Sisters* background and was much further from Petersburg. Mercifully, this dilemma was solved towards the end of the summer by Frants Feliksovich obtaining a transfer to the capital, which gave Aleksandra Andreyevna the opportunity to set up an independent establishment in the same town as her son, and ushered in a rather happier period in all their relationships.

7

In Petersburg, Blok determined to follow Lyuba by the quickest route through Berlin and Paris—he had had some hazy idea of travelling via Scandinavia but was suddenly all impatience to rejoin his wife. The arrangements for the journey delayed him for several days and he visited the Ivanovs in Tsarskoye Selo and went cycling with Zhenya. He also called on Pyast who lived out to the north of Petersburg in Pargolovo and walked with him about the Shuvalovsky Park. On his way out for a second visit he noticed, in his old haunt of Ozerki, a poster advertising gipsy singers at the circus. He wrote his excuse:

Feeling that this was Fate—and that it was already too late to go and drag you along to the concert with me, I remained at Ozerki. And so it was: they sang God knows what, tearing the heartstrings; and that night in Petersburg under the teeming rain on the railway platform the gipsy who was at the root of the matter gave me her hand to kiss, tanned with long fingers—all armoured with spiky rings. Then I wandered about the streets and finally I drifted into the sopping Aquarium where they had gone on to sing, looked into the gipsy's eyes and dragged myself off home. . . .

(VIII. 350, letter to Pyast of 3 July 1911)

He also went to see a doctor, who made a thorough examination, advised daily bathing 'for not more than a quarter of an hour a day', three months on the water-wagon, and soothing pills containing bromide.

Blok, having decided against breaking his journey in Berlin, travelled on to Cologne in an express train which occasionally touched on '100 kilometres an hour'—so exhilarated by this unprecedented speed that he only just had time to recollect how he loved Germany before he found himself in Paris:

Mama, yesterday morning I was on Unter den Linden, and that evening stood on the Hohenzollern bridge over the Rhine and in Cologne cathedral, and now I have just emerged from Notre Dame and am sitting in a café on the corner of the rue de Rivoli opposite the Hotel de Ville drinking *citronade* [in French in the original]. The train hurtled along even quicker than through Germany, there's a heat wave, probably about 40°, the air quivers over the awning, the wind is hot, Paris is all blue-grey and mysterious, but I'm not tired, on the contrary, I feel dreadfully exhilarated. Paris pleases me extraordinarily, it is narrower somehow and not so big as I expected, and for that reason one feels at home in the crowd.

Everything is within arm's reach and very clear and simple, simpler even than Cologne, or, for that matter, than any Germanic complexity. It's tremendous fun—a great din and shouting all around and I'm sitting almost out on the road....

France is really *la belle France*, there are great open stretches of country such as you don't see in Germany, and it's not so tidy.

Just now they're wheeling a load of roses past me....

(III. 352–3, letter of 8/21 July 1911)

But not even the enchantment of this first glimpse of Paris could delay Blok now. All he writes of the journey breathes the excitement of new places and a tempestuous impatience to reach Lyuba:

When I left Paris it was about 30°, everyone was drooping in the carriage, my head was just a muddle of impressions; so it was till the evening. Suddenly, the train flew through two short tunnels—and everything changed, as in a fairy story: an austere country of rocks, scattered thorn trees, bracken and thick mists. That is the influence of the ocean, a whole hour before you get to Brest. In Brest the harbour was full of warships. I had second thoughts and suddenly decided to go on by car, not to spend the night at a hotel. We went tearing along at 36 kilometres an hour. Very eerie. The night coming on, the fog getting thicker, and the big car with its headlights speeding along the hard, white road, scattering everyone before it in all directions. And the black silhouettes of the churches.—At last, lighthouses began to appear and we, having lost our way for a while in the fog, found the hotel and drove into the courtyard. Lyuba had just fallen asleep....

(VIII. 353, letter to his mother of 24 July [n.s.] 1911)

Lyuba had hoped much from this meeting in the far country of Tristan and Isolde.[21] Yet again, however, Blok's love for her seems to have reached its peak in separation. The jealous letters, the loving letters, the wild journey through mist and darkness and the long-

awaited, beloved husband coming in haste from the other end of
Europe to wake her from her first sleep: all culminated in a quiet,
affectionate reunion with a man whose heart was altogether in the
power of poetry. As Blok depicted the Breton minstrel Gaetan in
the play *The Rose and the Cross* (the only lasting result of their stay
in Aber-wrach), so he had become: a wanderer, untouched by ordinary love, a voice without substance, a call to no known goal.

Lyubov' was a strong-minded woman and an optimist. This man
'who stole the scent from the living flower' and who had once
written her that she was all his earthly being was her fate, her doom,
perhaps, and once again she shouldered the easy burden of responsibility and companionship.

There were many compensations. The Hotel des Anges where
they were staying was a converted seventeenth-century monastery.
An old fig tree grew in the courtyard. Their windows looked west-
ward over the edge of the Old World and great ships from many
countries—a Japanese squadron out of Cherbourg, giant liners plying
between Hamburg and America—went dipping past them like so
many toys. Fishing boats sailed from their own quiet bay and signal
lights flashed all night. Blok collected legends of olden times and
of yesterday. He was particularly struck by the story of a lighthouse
keeper's wife who, with the help of two small children, had kept
the light flashing all night by hand after the sudden death of her husband. Such sombre tales of duty done and watch well kept he found
'nourishing', and nourishment was what he now, more and more,
required of art.

At first Blok was delighted with everything and in good humour,
though he soon began to find the regular holiday regime rather dull.
There was good, plenteous food at the hotel with an abundance of
shellfish and artichokes, raspberries and pears. Lyuba took him bathing beyond the dunes in green, shallow water—strangely, he had
never learnt to swim. They boated and rode and walked together,
and together they sought out old books and immersed themselves
in the history of Finistère. Blok borrowed a collection of Lives of
the Breton Saints from the local doctor. He was again busy copying
out Latin inscriptions—not, this time, of the Renaissance or antiquity, but of the Celtic Christian tradition where holiness, history,
and poetry are as indistinguishable one from the other as spray and
salt fret and low, scurrying cloud.

The modern world, however, pleased him little:

In general, of course, life is as it is everywhere, poor and pitiable in inverse
proportion to the splendour one can put into describing and drawing it

... of course, there is nothing approaching our poverty, yet all the people around us are working in sweat and despair.... To make up for this it is very quiet here; and it is very pleasant to give a month of one's life to this poor and charming Brittany. In the evenings, the ocean sings very loud and clear, and in the daytime all your sight is filled by foam breaking among the rocks....

(VIII. 357, letter to his mother of 2 August [n.s.] 1911)[22]

It took only two weeks, however, for a complete revulsion of feeling to set in. Everything began to get on his nerves: the boredom; the French women with their 'faultless figures' and 'cold, appraising, sensuous eyes'; and, most particularly, the dirt:

... Even dogs are never quite so dirty as in France. When the puppy Fellow is given a bath he immediately goes running off to sleep on the compost heap, lovingly sprayed with liquid manure by the master of the house, then, in half an hour's time, he does me the honour of coming to sit on my knee.

(VIII. 360)

He alleviated his boredom by comparing the local people to characters out of Chekhov. As always, his most sympathetic portraits are of animals (the unquenchable Fellow) and of children. The landlady, he noted, was horrid to '... her little stepson, who is always sad and pale. At night he cries in the dark corridor from fright at being made to go off to bed all alone'(VIII. 360).

Other guests at the hotel were an English family with whom the Bloks spent much of their time. The father was the representative of an Argentinian news agency and Blok was fascinated by the mechanics of his work: the impressive technical facilities for conveying various pieces of news such as the results of the test match or 'a conference on the Hapsburg jawbone' to the other side of the Atlantic so that, thanks to the time lag and the miraculous underwater cable across the ocean bed, 'the New World will know $2\frac{1}{2}$ hours in advance what is going on in the Old' (VIII. 360).

On 15 August (n.s.) they left, with a feeling of relief, for Quimper. Here Blok spent almost a week in his hotel bedroom nursing a sore throat, watching a fair which occupied the square below his window for the Feast of the Assumption, and observing the colourful international jostle in the street below.

He devoured newspapers, actually getting through up to fifteen a day:

... Europe and the pulse of the world is to be felt far more strongly ... here than in Russia, partly thanks to the talent, the sure aim and the quantity of the newspapers (together with freedom of the press), and partly thanks to the fact that in every corner of Europe mankind now dangles over the very edge of the abyss ('and gathers samphire: dreadful trade', as Edgar says as he leads blind Gloucester about the flat field!) and is living feverishly and intensely 'by the sweat of his brow'. ... Here one clearly perceives all the monstrous absurdity to which civilization has been reduced, it is brought into high relief by the tense faces of rich and poor, the dodging crowd of cars quite devoid of all inner purpose, and the press—venal, talented, free and raucous.

(VIII. 365)

Everywhere—in the papers, in the sight of the great naval port, and in conversation with English, Americans, and French—he read the signs of war:

Wilhelm is looking for a fight and by all the signs he *will get his war*.... All this together reminds me of the deafening and exhausting fairground that I'm looking out on just now. All Europe grinds and whirls and secretly there is no reason for such activity, because everything is over already.

(VIII. 366)

Like other Russians, before and since, coming fresh from a country where educated people looked upon Western Europe as a second homeland and her cultural heritage as their own, Blok was struck by Europe's indifference to Russia:

In all this it is interesting that everything in Europe seems to be the concern of everybody else. The newspapers are not only interested in the 'great powers', they write also of Italy and Spain, the most remote parts of the world are on the tip of everybody's tongue. They all have colonies in Africa, money in America. Less often is there talk of Asia, Europe seems cool towards her; but less than any of these, by far, do they think and speak of Russia, or perhaps it would be fairer to say of the Slavs in general. The Slavonic element never became integrated in this civilization and, what is most significant, went sailing through Catholic culture like some kind of alien astral body. This interests me very much. I hope to observe the secret inroads of Slavonic pathos (those aspects of it which mean so much to me just now[w]) in a certain corner of Paris: behind Notre Dame, behind the morgue, there is a little island which was the home of Baudelaire and Théophile Gautier; there, in an old house, there is now a Polish library and a little Mickiewicz museum (he lectured in Paris in the '40s). In other words, on this little island, thinly populated and quiet although in the very centre of Paris, it is as if a sign had been set: it is one of the fermenting agents of the future—a magic mirror in which one can conjure the spirits of Byron, Mickiewicz, the French Revolution and the Slavonic, etc, etc.

(VIII. 366–7)

---

[w] Blok is referring to his interest in Poland in connection with his work on *Retribution*.

After an enforced stay of over a week in Quimper, Blok and Lyuba went to Paris. Here they stayed at a small hotel in the Latin Quarter. Blok, however, could recapture nothing of the joyful excitement of his first impressions. His illness had left him tired and sightseeing exhausted him. The summer had been very hot and the city looked parched.

Paris is a Sahara of yellow boxes among which, like dead oases, rise the greyish-black immensities of dead churches and palaces. A dead Notre Dame, a dead Louvre. Inside the Louvre, everything is terribly neglected ... threadbare sofas, dirty floors and dull, dark walls on which gleam grey Dianas, Apollos, Caesars, Alexanders, and the Venus de Milo with a nasty smirk on her face (due to soot in the right nostril) and, upstairs, Raphaels, Mantegnas, Rembrandts, and four nails where, only a week ago, the Gioconda was still hanging.[x] ... The Tuileries is an arid desert where they feed sparrows and photograph the bourgeoisie. The Esplanade des Invalides— the same. Only the tomb of Napoleon is splendid—there is a blue light there and a reverent silence.

(VIII. 369)

It is almost possible to feel the poet's nerves relaxing as he escapes from the noise and glare into the cool of Napoleon's tomb, or as he climbs out into the fresh air before Sacré Coeur. Looking out over Paris from Montmartre, however, he could not resist contrasting the French capital, most unfavourably, with Moscow:

Paris is not as Moscow seen from the Sparrow Hills. Paris from Montmartre is a picture of a thousand years of senselessness, majestic, fiery and soulless. Here, there neither is nor could be an equivalent to the Novo-Devichiy Monastery, which is the first thing that meets the eye, the first bastion of Moscow; and there is not one flake of Moscow gold or warm brick-red, just a greyish-black sea—constantly and senselessly roaring ... at times the heat and senselessness achieve the intensity of genius.

(VIII. 370–1)

Blok's austere Nordic spirit found nothing for itself in France, no mysterious 'memories' of the world's youth such as had come crowding about him in Venice, Florence, and in Germany: 'I never was in France, have no sense of loss here, she is profoundly alien to me—Paris no less than the provinces ...' (VIII. 370). Not even the children comforted him: 'In the scorched squares there are a mass of children, pale, with the English sickness. All the faces are either

---

[x] Blok's stay in Quimper had coincided with the sensational theft of the *Mona Lisa* from the Louvre.

horrifying—the bourgeois—or heart-rending in their tenseness and weariness....' Not even art:

I tried in vain to visit the Louvre a second time: in these befouled royal barns you get exhausted from the sheer distances you have to walk, and it is impossible really to see a single picture—to such an extent have the French stamped out the very spirit of art.

As for the night-life of Paris, the fabled Gay Paree:

The usual blasphemy, pornography calculated to impress III- to IV-form schoolboys. Occasionally, a very witty vaudeville, or suddenly—an astonishing song, always old (Provençale, for example) or heard already a thousand times (one of Yvette Guilbert's, for instance ...).

(VIII. 371)

And so, leaving Lyuba in Paris to return independently to Petersburg, he set off for home on 5 September (n.s.), via Belgium where he had, he informed Aleksandra Andreyevna, an overwhelming impulse to see the eighteen hippopotami in the zoo at Antwerp.

Alone in Antwerp he wandered about the city like a man released from nightmare: '... The Scheld is huge, like the Neva, clouds of ships, docks, cranes, scaffolded distances, the smell of the sea, a mass of churches, old houses, fountains, towers. The Museum is so delightful that not even Rubens is altogether repulsive ...' (VIII. 371–2).

The Low Countries pleased him well enough, but he felt most of the things he really liked—primitive paintings, Quentin Massys, Gothic architecture—to be somehow unconnected with the present, something in the nature of stage decorations: 'Somehow you don't quite believe in it all because the foundation of their world no longer rests on the Middle Ages or the Memlings ...' (VIII. 372). His final verdict on Holland—after a round trip in a slow train through Zeeland—was lukewarm: 'There is not much fun to Holland after all—nice, tidy and watery, nothing to take exception to' (VIII. 372–3).

In Amsterdam, on 12 September, Blok received the good news about Frants Feliksovich's transfer to Petersburg. The next day he went on to Berlin, where he had a tentative arrangement to meet up with Lyuba. She, however, had gone straight on to Petersburg to look for a new flat, and he settled down alone to enjoy German cleanliness and to tramp round the Berlin museums. He also went to the operetta, the circus, and the theatre—to see Goethe's *Faust* and the Reinhardt production of *Hamlet* to which he had been looking forward ever since Lyuba had written him about it that spring. His letter to Aleksandra Andreyevna about *Hamlet* is in his old vein of blasé schoolboy humour. The Claudius, he said, was the best he had seen, the image of their ex-agent Martyn. Hamlet, of course, like all Russian and English heroes, talked too much and made liberal-minded remarks to curry favour with the public. 'I am very ashamed', he went on,

that I am not bringing back one single present. I wandered in vain through all the shops of Paris and Berlin and in all the big towns, but I firmly believe that in Europe they sell only the most tasteless nonsense or else useful and hard-wearing underpants, suppositories, and other things that it is not customary to give as presents.

Hamlet presented Ophelia with such awful trash (an album with views of Elsinore, I dare say) that he had to pretend he never gave her anything.

(VIII. 376)

In Berlin, he heard the news of Stolypin's assassination. The Russia to which he returned a few days later was already set upon a different, finally catastrophic course.

8

On 7 September (once again by the Russian calendar), Blok rejoined his wife in Petersburg. They decided to have their old flat repapered and disinfected—Lyuba had come home to an invasion of bedbugs and cockroaches from the neighbouring apartments— and to remain there for another season: 'It's sunny here, Gorchakov's garden[y] is very beautiful, and it's dry, clean and cosy.'[23]

Blok was glad to be back. Petersburg, he discovered, was still 'the most terrible, the most fascinating, the most rejuvenating for the blood of all European cities' (VII. 72) and Russia had made herself felt immediately after the border 'in one of those interesting and dreadfully tragic conversations that nobody abroad seems to go in for'.[24]

Such conversations set the tone for the whole of that autumn and, by Christmas, Blok was thoroughly tired of them:

All these dear, good Russian people with no idea of times or seasons, they drop in for a chat and 'enjoy going into something rather deep' . . . it is a terrible evil because, to no good purpose and with the best possible intentions, you waste your last strength, your last nerves and capacity to work.

.(VII. 109)

Almost before the fresh paint was dry in the flat on Monetnaya

[y] The flat enjoyed a pleasant view over the private gardens of Prince Gorchakov.

Ulitsa, the visitors began: 'Zhenya, incomprehensible to me as he was this summer, but dear and beloved' (VII. 69); Pyast, over-worked, angry, cohabiting uneasily with his heavily pregnant, men-tally unbalanced wife in inconvenient quarters; Gorodetsky, who had written a touching article about Blok's early poetry—quieter than before;[25] Dmitriy Kuzmin-Karavayev, 'half-mad', talking wildly of the future and dangerously of the past;[z] the genial Anich-kov; the peasant poet Nikolay Kluyev, whose first-ever visit, inter-rupted by Kuzmin-Karavayev and a violent scene 'offstage' between Tanya the cook and her drunken husband, was a social disaster.

Kluyev, however, came again. Both he and Blok appear to have been bristling with social inhibitions, but Kluyev had been Blok's first reader 'from the people' and his personality in the flesh was quiet and colourless enough not to break the powerful enchantment of his letters. Blok told him that he did not consciously write for other people but, as he noted in his diary, was touched and comforted to hear

... how they sing my poetry in the Olonetsk province and how (or so I understood) those who read *Joy Unhoped-for* ... are proof against every-thing half-said, everything sinful. I did not, maybe, have the right (the faith) to say what I did say in *Joy Unhoped-for*, but they permitted me to say it: speak on! And for the first time in my life I understood quite clearly and simply how it is that L. D. Semyënov and even A. M. Dobrolyubov are living as they do.

(VII. 71)

Kluyev brought Blok the blessing of the Russian backwoods upon his life and his poetry: about Dobrolyubov and Semyënov, he explained that there were many people who had to choose the 'ancient way' upon which these poets had embarked, the way of renouncing the world and going to the people, but that it was not necessarily the best. Those who remained in the world had more 'influence'. 'I love your voice and the way you dress,' Kluyev reassured Blok, who, fresh from Europe, was paralysed by the thought that he must seem a la-di-da semi-foreigner to this 'man of the people' in his high boots and belted Russian shirt.

These meetings with Kluyev confirmed Blok's growing sense of mission. More than ever, he now wanted to be 'alone', to avoid literary cliques. The men of literature who had been closest to him in the autumn of the previous year—Andrey Bely and Vyacheslav Ivanov—were drifting out of his orbit. On his return to Petersburg,

---

[z] Blok was working on the assassination of Alexander II, which he considered the begin-ning of modern Russia, and Kuzmin-Karavayev was talking regicide.

Blok had found a letter from Bely taking up an idea of his and Pyast's about a periodical publication of 'poets' diaries' and proposing a counter-plan for a bi-monthly journal, *Dela i Dni Musageta* (The Works and Days of Musaget). This journal, which was to unite the mystics of 'Orfey'*aa* and the philosophers of *Logos* with Ivanov and Blok, was to serve, like all Bely's projects, as a spearhead in the battle for 'culture' as understood by Bely himself. The idea may have influenced Blok in his resolve to keep a diary—which he began on 11 October 1911 and kept conscientiously until the spring of 1913—but his correspondence with Bely was hampered by the fact that Bely was living outside Moscow and did not always get his letters.

In addition to this, Blok no longer wanted a triple alliance with Vyacheslav Ivanov.

If you want to preserve him—there is no other way than to keep your distance. He has shaved his beard and an indescribably horrific line cuts deep into his chin. Inside Goethe is howling, 'classicism' (keep calm, keep calm). He says hurtful things, pricks, hisses, wags his tail, provokes one to play along with him. He is of considerable stature but less than he *should* (or could) be. The daughter is thin, pale, tired, sad.
Literary circles in Petersburg have reached the last stages of putrefaction. They are beginning to stink.

(VII. 72)

Blok, as one of his friends politely put it, was 'no rigourist',[26] but found it hard to stomach Vyacheslav Ivanov's marriage to his step-daughter Vera—apparently on the express instructions of the spirit of her mother, his own late and deeply-loved wife, Lydia Zinov'eva-Annibal.[27]

Bely, being bogged down in work on his new novel *Petersburg* and in grave financial difficulties, was in no state to bring the two men together. The first number of the new periodical, which had been envisaged for November 1911, was not in fact published until the following spring, and even then no real, vital cohesion had been established between the three supposed principal contributors, Blok remaining very much on the periphery. He did, however, help Bely over his financial crisis with two considerable loans and the two men, both scrupulous and disinterested as far as money was concerned, emerged from this transaction with increased mutual respect.

So it was that, over the 1911–12 season, Blok finally managed to disentangle himself from the literary movement or 'camp' which had been laying claim to his allegiance ever since 'On the Present State

aa 'Orfey' (Orpheus) was a mystical series published by Musaget, mainly under the aegis of Vyacheslav Ivanov.

of Russian Symbolism', and this he did quite deliberately. When the first number of *Trudy i Dni* (as it was eventually called) came out the following spring he wrote to Bely:

The first number is geared from the start to speak of art and of a school of art, not of human beings and artists. This we owe to Vyacheslav Ivanov. . . .

After all, it is to 'become human' that we are co-operating in *Trudy i Dni*; yet all the first section might just as well have been printed in *Apollon*. . . .

(VII. 387–8, letter of 16 April 1912)

Blok objected to Vyacheslav Ivanov's honeyed classicism, his use of the word 'catharsis' when writing of the fresh wounds and insoluble agonies of 'sorrowful and ragged Russia'. Two days after this letter to Bely, Blok wrote his 'farewell' poem to Vyacheslav Ivanov, which commemorates their brief 'romance' during the heyday of Revolution, but passes into a solemn valediction:

> But now the storm is past and over
> And these years in a bitter line
> Have ploughed across my heart. No brother
> Do I perceive in you as then. . . .

(III. 142)

Nevertheless, Blok continued, throughout the autumn of 1911, to frequent Ivanov's Tower. Here and elsewhere in Petersburg there was a whole crop of new authors: the strident voice of Kamensky, to whom Blok took an instant dislike; Igor Severyanin, a kind of poetic pop star famous for the manner in which he chanted his poetry before an audience of near-hysterical young girls; Aleksey Tolstoy, already holding the floor at literary evenings with descriptions of 'who came to blows with whom in Paris' (VII. 75); and representatives of Nikolay Gumilev's 'Poets' Workshop'.

Amongst this babel of new voices, Blok quickly distinguished the laconic sublimity of Anna Akhmatova. At the Tower, it was customary to put poets 'on trial' and, after one of Akhmatova's first readings, Vyacheslav Ivanov offered himself for the defence and suggested that Blok take the part of the prosecution. Blok refused. Ivanov offered to reverse the roles. Blok refused again. But Vyacheslav Ivanov was determined: just in a few words—what did Blok think of the new poet?

Blok blushed—he had an astonishing capacity to blush when embarrassed—looked seriously about him and said:

'She writes verses as if standing before a man and it is necessary to write as if standing before God.'

There was a silence. Then the next poet began his recital.[28]

This same season, however, we find the entry in his diary, 'Anna Akhmatova read her verses—already moving me. The further, the better' (VII. 83).

9

In spite of all these distractions, Blok did manage to return to work on *Retribution*. He revised the third (Warsaw) chapter and completed the first, which he envisaged as an attempt to give a broad, panoramic picture of the 1870s into which he would introduce the themes of his own family—the Beketovs—and of his father in the guise of demon-suitor.

This chapter led him to intensify his historical reading and he spent much time at second-hand bookshops, searching out the books on his country's revolutionary past that were beginning to emerge again 'from under the counter' for the first time since the onset of reaction. Such reading, however, tended to draw him too deeply into the past. 'One should not read too much and, most important, one should read creatively,' he admonished himself. 'In addition, it is necessary to read "for the work in hand" with careful thought and a plan.'

By November 1911 he was not much nearer to the creation of a cogent whole, and though he completed the first version of Chapter I that autumn, he was not satisfied with it. In his search for objectivity, he had bypassed the romantic narrative poem, and had taken as his models Pushkin's 'realistic' 'novel in verse' *Yevgeniy Onegin* and Nekrasov's civic poem *Who Lives Well in Russia?* Yet Blok had not, could not have Pushkin's grace. Pushkin wrote *Yevgeniy Onegin* as he wrote his letters and love poems for a small circle of people with cultivated tastes. It is the measure of his genius that his readers, of whatever social background, time, or country, can enter with delight and without conscious effort into this intimate, sheltered world; but it is one thing to enter a world ready-made, quite another to recreate such a world in different circumstances. On the other hand, Blok had not the self-confidence of a Nekrasov, who wielded his verse like the singing whip of an expert ringmaster, providing a rich and varied spectacle for a loose-knit democratic audience.

If the twentieth-century poet could not count on a select group of readers 'of his own circle', neither could he count on the status of preacher and teacher which Russia had accorded her 'civic' poets in the second half of the nineteenth century. It was too late to preach. The only way Blok could hope to command the attention of his audience was the way of the pelican: by offering them his own inner truth, his living experience. Now, in attempting to sustain this lyrical intensity, he had overreached himself and was approaching breaking point: 'If only I knew how to pray for form' (VII. 77), he noted on 25 October 1911, and, a month later: 'The poem is no good at all. It needs a plan, and a subject' (VII. 96).

On 3 December, Aleksandra Andreyevna suggested that the poem should end with the hero's death 'on the barricades'. The impossibility of writing in circumstantial detail of one's own death, especially in so romantic and out-of-date a fashion, may well have been one reason why the fourth chapter never did get written, but at the time the suggestion gave the poem direction and Blok was pleased with it.

The plan, as he envisaged it in the autumn of 1911, was: Chapter I (on which he was then working), 'The Demon'. Chapter 2 (to which he had written an introduction that spring and to which he was to return only in the year of his death), 'Childhood'. Chapter 3 (the first to be written, now revised), 'The Father's Death'. Chapter 4, 'War and Revolution—the Son's Death' (never written).

Blok read the first chapter to the *Apollon* 'Academy'. Gorodetsky, who was present, recorded that it produced a profound impression.

> The Nineteenth Century—in truth
> A cruel age, an age of iron!
> .   .   .   .   .
> The age of foreheads beating walls,
> Of economic doctrines, banks
> And congresses and federations,
> *Bons mots* and after-dinner speeches,
> Shares, dividends, and government bonds,
> And all-too-passive, sluggish minds,
> And talents meted out by halves
> (To 'go a fair half' is but just!).
> Salons give way to drawing rooms
> And Récamier—to hostesses
> Of less repute ... and bourgeois wealth
> Grows ever—an invidious ill
> Beneath the signs of 'brotherhood',
> 'Equality' ... dark deeds matured ...
>
> And what of Man?—From day to day
> Life bore him on. Not man was master but
> Machines and towns ... his mind was drained by 'Life'
> So painlessly he did not feel

His spirit's anguish as before.
But he who moves the marionettes
And orders every country's weal
Sent down a mist of humanism—
Full well aware of what he did—
And there, in the grey, putrid fog
The flesh grew soft, the spirit quailed,
And even the angel of just wars,
It seemed had taken wing and flown....

(III. 304–5)

The younger poets thrilled to Blok's voice, hollow and uncertain as ever, as if talking to himself, pondering the origins of their own time, putting the one pertinent question in that age of extreme individualism: 'And what of Man?' For the literary arbiters of Symbolism, however, the context of the question was altogether too down-to-earth and the narrative part of the poem unforgivably straightforward. Vyacheslav Ivanov tore it to pieces: it was a backsliding into realism; a betrayal of Symbolism and of the theurgic principle....

Blok, never good at defending himself, appeared crushed.[29] He felt Ivanov's criticism to be unanswerable, not because he agreed with its substance but rather because he was acutely aware of the poem's failure to enchant, to *disarm* all criticism. He referred to the occasion as 'my flop' and afterward suffered an unaccustomed attack of stage-fright before taking the chair at the 'Academy' on 3 December (VII. 99).

What Blok did not fully realize at the time was that, in his efforts to break away from pure lyricism and to write a modern narrative poem, he had adumbrated a general tendency which Vyacheslav Ivanov himself was soon to follow.[30] Although Blok was disappointed by the reception of *Retribution*, it was not so much criticism from without as the strain of sustaining a long historical poem on a level of absolute lyrical intensity that led him to yield, more and more often as the winter deepened, to the temptation of the shorter, 'inspirational' poem—and eventually to embark with relief upon an entirely new, and less demanding, major project.

CHAPTER V

The Search for Form (2) —
The Rose and the Cross
(Autumn 1911 – Spring 1913)

No, in my present state (cruelty, angularity, maturity, sickness) I cannot and I have no right to speak of *more* than the human. The 'Cross and the Rose'—that is beyond my scope. Let it be the fate of a man, a failure, and if I can 'humble myself' before art it may be that through my theme people will perceive—something more. That is: self-discipline and an all-out effort to be 'modest' may help the play to become a work of art, and a work of art is a developing entity and not a motionless corpse.

(VII. 186, entry for December 1912)

1

Surprisingly, it is not to Visha Grek, Chulkov, Sapunov, or any 'boon companions' that we owe the most poignant sidelight on Blok's night life, but to Maksim Gorky, who at this time hardly knew him, and to a little prostitute off the Nevsky Prospect who told the story:

... 'It was autumn, very late, slushy and misty, almost midnight by the Duma clock, and I was terribly tired and about to go home when suddenly on the corner of the Italyanskaya he came up to me, well-dressed, good-looking, and such a proud face, I even thought at first he was a foreigner. We went on foot—just round the corner, really, Karavannaya, no. 10, there's rooms there. Well, we went along and I chatted away and he said nothing, I was even a bit vexed, unusual, you know, and I do like people to be polite. When we got there I said could I have a cup of tea; he rang and the waiter didn't come and didn't come, so he went out into the corridor and I was tired, you know, and so cold, and I went off to sleep, just sitting there on the sofa. Then suddenly I woke up and saw him sitting

there opposite me with his head in his hands, looking at me so sternly—
dreadful eyes! But I was so ashamed I took no notice, just thought: "Oh,
my God, he must be a musician!" Curly hair, you know. "Oh, I *am* sorry,"
I said, "I'll get undressed right away."

'But then he smiled politely and said: "No, no, don't bother." And he
sat down next me on the sofa and took me on his knees and said, stroking
my hair: "That's all right, sleep a little." And can you imagine—disgraceful
really—I went to sleep again! Of course I knew I shouldn't but—I couldn't
help it. He rocked me so tenderly and I felt so at ease with him and every
now and again I'd open my eyes and smile and he'd smile. And it seemed
as though I'd hardly slept at all when he shook me gently and said: "Well,
good-bye now. I must go." And he put twenty-five roubles on the table.
"Here," I said. "What's that for?" Well, of course, I was most embarrassed,
I kept on apologizing, it was all so queer, somehow. And he laughed—
quiet-like, gave my hand a squeeze and even kissed it! He went and when
I went out the waiter said: "D'you know who that was with you? That
was Blok the poet—look." And he showed me a photograph in the paper
and I saw there was no mistake—it really was him. "Oh dear," I thought.
"What a stupid thing to happen." '[1]

When Blok returned from his holiday in Europe in the autumn
of 1911, the desolation and elemental gipsy excitement of Petersburg
night life had threatened to engulf him completely. Ecstasy alternates
with apathy in his diary and the thought of death was very present:
'If I should die now a lot of young people would follow my coffin
...,' he noted with genuine satifaction apropos of several visits from
aspiring poets, a category of visitors whom, though he usually discouraged them, he took very seriously.

Ecstasy haunted his waking hours:

I begin this diary ... tired from several days (or weeks) of extreme tension
and *ecstasy*.

(vii. 69, 17 October 1911)

The air these days is like water: the city—the silent ocean bed. Something
is going on. Madness, madness and ecstasy ...

(vii. 84, 8 November 1911)

and his dreams:

a gathering of people, a room. I was given a large, handsome tablecloth
and, a winged demon, I began to circle the floor, learning to fly. There
was ecstasy in my breast, I came to a halt in my sliding around the floor
(same movements as in skating); Zhenya asked where we should fly to and,
'stretching out my arms', I pointed out of the window: There! It was not
funny....

(vii. 84, 9 November 1911)

The continual debauch was physically exhausting, his nerves were taut to breaking-point, and his mind, at times, ominously clouded:

The Variety Show. The acrobat comes out, I implore her to go with me. We fly, the night yawns. I am absolutely beside myself.... I tear her laces and satins, in these coarse hands and stiletto heels there is a kind of power and mystery. The hours with her are a torment, barren. I take her home. There is an almost sacred feeling, as though she were a daughter, a child. She disappears down a side street, familiar yet unknown. It is cold, sharp, all the tributaries of the Neva are full, night everywhere, the same at six o'clock in the evening as at six o'clock in the morning when I return home.

No work today, of course. A walk, a bath, something painful in the breast, you want to groan aloud, because this eternal night cradles and increases tenfold one and the same sensation—to the point of madness....

Mama came to lunch. A good talk with her after lunch. Saw her off on the tram. Again night—the sparks from the tram. The evening and the morning are an end and a beginning. In our November there are neither ends nor beginnings—just one ever-growing, ungovernable, penetrating needling of infatuation, madness, groanings, ecstasy.

(VII. 85, 10 November 1911).

And so it goes on: 'I slept after lunch and then I went—where did I go?' (VII. 86)—and in a few days' time: 'In the evening, as always after "only books"—"only flesh"' (VII. 96). Then, in December: 'At night bad dreams again, new ecstasy, new despair' (VII. 100).

Gradually Blok became alarmed at the extent of his own weariness. 'There is so much of the winter still to go. I should give up drinking ...' (VII. 108), he noted on Christmas Eve. On 12 January 1912 he felt so ill he consulted a doctor and on 20 January the nature of the disease was confirmed. Syphilis was feared and discussed, but the doctor tactfully gave it another name and it seems doubtful whether Blok was fully aware, at least at the time, of his own danger.[a]

2

In a sense, even disease was grist to the mill of Blok's poetry. It almost certainly intensified his premonitions, aggravating the natural disgusts of a fastidious nature to an almost pathological degree.

[a] Blok was treated as for syphilis and on the evidence of his own diary, largely expunged for publication, it is a fair medical assumption that he was suffering from some form of this disease. After this severe attack in January–February 1912, he had three further courses of treatment (August–September 1912, January 1913, and May 1913) and continued Wassermann tests for over a year.

The certainty of war, the probabilty of revolution, the growing conviction of the decadence of his own cultural tradition, led to a shuddering awareness, in part through his own vices, of the vices of society. Rightly or wrongly, Blok, following the tradition of Vladimir Solov'ev, associated the corruption of this society with the East. In common with Solov'ev, Merezhkovsky, and Bely, he saw the Orient as the spiritual purveyor of negation, passivity, Nirvana.[2] As his device against compromise and spiritual surrender, Blok took Tyutchev's poem 'Two Voices', in which he perceived 'a Hellenic, pre-Christian sense of destiny' (VII. 99, entry for 3 December 1911):

> Take courage, oh friends, ply your weapons unyielding
> Though hopeless the struggle, the battle unequal![b]

Strindberg, with his unflinching Nordic spirit, was an ally in the same battle, and it was Tyutchev's 'Two Voices' that Blok was to ask Lyuba to read at a memorial performance of the Swedish playwright's Guilty—Not Guilty the following summer. He owed the poem, however, to Zhenya Ivanov, who had quoted it to him a year earlier.

Meanwhile, Blok felt himself beset by signs and portents. Many of these were of a purely private nature. In Moscow, for instance, Sergey Solov'ev had attempted suicide and Bely, who had visited him at the mental home to which he was temporarily consigned, wrote Blok that one of his cousin's obsessions was 'the Oriental face'. Bely himself, absorbed in his novel Petersburg which is shot through with a febrile awareness of the 'yellow peril', hinted at similar thoughts of his own: '... everything tentatively suggested in your letters is more than familiar to me: the yellow prelest'.[c]

Blok noted these and other disjointed 'facts' which confirmed him in the idea that Russia was, spiritually at least, selling out to the East. The revolution in China reminded him of 1905 and, when he first read about it, he quoted grimly from his beloved Macbeth:

> Two truths are told
> As happy prologues to the swelling act
> Of the Imperial theme.

Yet the 'yellow peril' in Blok's symbolic system was not connected with the positive aspects and hopes of revolution, only with the

---

[b] Blok quoted the poem in full or in part more than once in letters and wrote it out in his diary that autumn of 14 November (VIII. 397; VII. 88; etc.).

[c] Bely here uses the word prelest in the sense not of 'charm' but of 'spiritual temptation'. It is an ascetic term usually left in the original in translations of Orthodox—particularly hesiachist—literature.

threat to European culture inherent in any great upheavals such as, in his opinion, were being constantly provoked by the torpid conservatism and corruption of his own government and by Europe's suicidal preoccupation with the arms race. The cynical inertia of the old world he felt as a personal threat:

... From every side a frightful, bestial face materializes that seems to be trying to say: 'Aaa—so that's the sort of man you are, is it? Why are you so tense, why do you think, act, construct—why?' ... And so, yawning a little, we speak of the 'yellow peril': Anichkov once said to me goodnaturedly (this summer): 'You don't take a broad enough view. Tsushima was not an important event. It was not Russia that fought Japan, but Europe.'
So think all the officers, right up to the first Officer[d]—drinking with his bodyguard as though he had not a care in the world.
Where do all these 'Persian lamb' coats and valuables that we see on all the gentlemen and ladies on the Nevsky Prospect come from? Behind every single Persian lamb coat is a bribe. ...[e]
Everything is coming undone at the seams, the threads are rotting (falling apart) inside, and only the outside is left. It would be enough just to give a slight tug and all the Persian lamb coats would fall apart to expose the filthy, dirty, animal face, the tormented, bloodless, violated body.
And so we, too, yawn over the yellow peril but China is already within us.... There remains a brief last act: the physical occupation of Europe. It will happen quietly and sweetly, to judge by outward appearances.... That will be the moment when we shall have to unseal all the mysterious renaissances of the New World (Poe) and of the Slavonic World (Pushkin, Russian history, Polish, 'Messianism', Mickiewicz's island in Paris, all that sleeps in Ravenna, awake Galla). ... *The sense of tragedy is in the hopelessness of the conflict; but there is no despair, no flabbiness, no folding of the hands. A high dedication is essential.*

(VII. 87–9, entry for 14 November 1911)

Everything not conducive to spiritual struggle Blok now saw clearly as a betrayal of the old, Christian-humanist tradition.

From Theodosius of the Caves to Tolstoy and Dostoyevsky, the great theme of Russian culture has been religious. In our day, society has taken to 'aesthetic idealism' (that is, by my definition, their blood is turning yellow).

(VII. 95, entry for 21 November 1911)

Yet the poet was well aware of his own inadequacy to uphold this active, religious tradition: 'What am I as yet? It is only that I have

[d] Tsar Nicholas II.
[e] This remark probably explains the malicious lines about the 'lady in a Persian lamb coat' in *The Twelve*. Bribery—in those days of China's decadence—was very widely associated with the Orient, especially on the grand, governmental scale.

been vouchsafed a glimpse—in dreams and awake—of something which others have not yet seen' (VII. 89). This 'glimpse' had to be pondered, understood, and conveyed to others, and in this he now saw his vocation as an artist.

The only right Blok felt he had to the private means inherited from his father was that he lived 'in a state of tension, not forgetting all obligations' (VII. 79). Awareness of his sickness—and of its origins—oppressed him with a kind of shame that exacerbated his vulnerability:

In the afternoon I sat at home, sticking in pictures. Lyuba was not at home and, as always when she is out, there were voices from the kitchen the tone of which, the insistent tone of which is enough to make you want to sink through the floor and puts in doubt every value in the world. It was stupid women talking, our cook and the cooks from the next-door, petty-bourgeois flats, but *how* they talk, such words (only occasionally audible), that the blood runs cold from shame and despair. Emptiness, blindness, poverty, resentment. The only salvation would be a hermitage; a gentleman's flat with thick, well-fitting doors would be still worse. There you might hear something just once by mistake and never forget it, ever.

*Of course, I react like this because my conscience is not clear because of debauch.*ʃ
(VII. 98)

There were days, and in January and February 1912 whole weeks, when he could not bring himself to see anyone, disconnected the telephone and refused to answer the door. Petersburg whispered that he had turned misanthrope, that he was drinking.

More and more, as the nightmares closed in, his world began to centre around Lyuba. 'Today I played chess with little Bu on the big sofa....,' he would note comfortably. Then ...'Lyuba will come home and come into my room—and make a fuss of me' (VII. 77). 'Coming up three in the morning (again!) and I'm making this entry hurriedly. It's time to sleep, to go and tuck up little Bu ...' (VII. 78). On 9 January, when Lyubov' had a chill: 'Yesterday is as though it had not been. There was only the evening and a few looks at little Lyuba. To make her well again, cosset her, see that she is comfortable' (VII. 120).

Then, at the height of his illness, confined to the house and beset by 'wild and terrible dreams': 'Yesterday morning—a talk with Lyuba to the effect that she cannot go on living *like this* for long (not a bad talk) ...' (VII. 126, entry for 25 January 1912). Lyuba, indeed, wanted to help, but even her sanguine spirits were oppressed by Blok's sickness and the darkness of his mood. She 'has the right

ʃ My italics. A. P.

ideas', he noted tenderly. 'It's just that she needs to amuse herself sometimes.'

While he still felt unable to face the world she sat at home and played children's games with him: occasionally when he was rather better, they would slip out together to the circus or the cinema or just for a walk. Blok enjoyed popular entertainment and invariably preferred the flea-pits where the audience booed and hissed to the sophisticated cinemas of the Nevsky Prospect.

Realizing their Sasha was really ill and needed them both, his wife and mother managed throughout that winter to effect a real improvement in their relationship. Lyuba had made an effort to be agreeable after attending the funeral of the last of the Beketovs, Blok's Uncle Nikolay, who died at the end of November, and Aleksandra Andreyevna was profoundly touched by her daughter-in-law's care for her husband, and also by the stormy tears Lyuba had shed as she watched Mussorgsky's opera *Khovanshchina*, identifying totally and tragically with the heroine:

Lyuba's sorrow at the *panikhidi* touched me so much because I knew it was not caused by the *panikhidi*. And how the tears poured down her face watching *Khovanshchina* when, before the Sectarians set themselves on fire, Marfa sings the hymn for the departing over the man she loves, walking round him three times with a candle and singing 'Alleluia!' Then the Elder Dosifey tells her: 'Have patience, little dove, love as you have loved and all that you have passed through will pass by.' Lyuba cried and cried, hiding away in the back of her box....[84]

During Blok's illness, the great world dwindled to a microcosm: to these two women for whom he felt responsible and whom he loved. 'Were my wife and my mother not with me in this world, there would be nothing for me to do here' (VII. 150), he wrote in his diary.

Other women, though he was never to be free of them till the end of his days, were for a time put out of his mind:

... it is time to break off all *such ties*. Everything happens precisely as one expects, it's all a bore and quite unnecessary to either side. They fall in love or even come to love one, hence letters, heaps of letters, demands, endlessly turning up at the wrong moment: she imagines (or rather they all invariably imagine) that I *want* to reattune my soul 'to suit her'. Then, after a certain time—reproaches. All women are the same, whether a sixteen-year-old girl

---

8 The box was not the Bloks' own but one put at their disposal for the evening by the Anichkovs.

or a thirty-year-old lady. Misogyny[h] comes over me every now and again—and now is one of those periods.

(VII. 123, entry for 13 January 1912)

That winter, perhaps because life was so very ominous, he turned to prayer. 'Mama says she prays constantly aloud and that there is no salvation outside prayer,' he noted in the autumn of 1911. Then, on 30 October, 'In the night, fear came on me. I woke up, I'm writing—thank God, it's quiet. I am getting calmer, I shall pray' (VII. 79). Exclamatory prayers occur in his diary:

> Lord, bless.
> Lord, bless.
> Lord, bless and preserve
> (VII. 97, 27 November 1911)
> Lord, help me to be better
> (VII. 114, 29 December 1911)
> God, grant me to live—noticeably.
> (VII. 116, New Year 1912)

At the beginning of Lent (1912), he noted that his mother was thinking of attending seances[i] and that he had advised her rather to fast through Lent under the direction of Ageyev, one of the more liberal priests who attended the Religious-Philosophical Society.

Essentially, Blok was a spiritually sober man. The more religious was his own mood, the more he distrusted fashionable 'mysticism'.

---

[h] Blok's misogyny' was not unconnected with his passion for Strindberg, a response of something in the blueprint of his own nature to a theme more definitely expressed in the works of another artist. In the first draft of his obituary article on Strindberg, Blok wrote: 'Deformities, unavoidable during the evolution of a new type, have left their imprint on all the European literature of our century: all our "pornography", all our uncertainties and doubts, which produce neither anger nor violent breaks but rather lackadaisical betrayals, hole-and-corner apostasy, is the result ... of the fact that the soul of the new man is wavering between the male and the female principles.' Strindberg, he wrote, was justified in his misogyny, because '... it was not the "feminine", but only the "female" that he hated ...'.[5]

[i] The only record of Blok's attendance at a seance—an extremely popular pastime at this period, much cultivated by Valeriy Bryusov—is Pyast's account of such an entertainment arranged for New Years's Day 1913 at the home of Professor Anichkov. Pyast, who appears to have taken the whole thing rather seriously, attributes the remarkable success of this occasion to Blok's 'mediumistic' gifts. Blok's own account is more sceptical: 'We sat three times and the third time I nearly dropped off to sleep, absolutely endless. ... Guzik [The medium. A. P.] has a headache, the veins stand out on his forehead and everyone treats him like a lackey. ... The first time I had to sit with my little finger crooked round the little finger of a fat, hoarse old lady as tall as a grenadier. ... The next two times I sat between my darling and Pyast. ... We ... left at three o'clock in the morning, in a taxi again, of course. Pointless pastimes lead to pointless expenditure' (VII. 202–3, January 1913).

Shakhmatovo from the front, after the alterations to the house in 1910. (From the collection of N. P. Il'in)

Safonovo, the new country residence of Adam Feliksovich and Sofia Andreyevna Kublitsky-Piottukh.

Lyubov' Dmitriyevna at
Shakhmatovo in the summer
of 1909.

Blok at Shakhmatovo with
his favourite dog, Diana, in
1909.

Often, it is apparent that he was drawn towards the Church.[j] At this moment of history, however, the official Church presented a less than edifying spectacle. Rasputin's influence was all-powerful at court and, through his nominees, in the Synod, and the only two ecclesiastics outspoken enough to oppose him, Bishop Germogen and Father Iliador, were in extreme disfavour. Blok was rather well informed about the situation because a friend of Angelina's had cast herself at the feet of the Tsar to plead for Germogen and was now sleeping on the floor at Maria Timofeyevna's flat (as an act of asceticism, not for lack of beds) and inviting people to hear Father Iliodor denounce Rasputin—actually in their home. Angelina revered Germogen and was convinced that if only the Church could obtain a restoration of its autonomy (under a Patriarch rather than under the government-appointed Holy Synod)—all would be well. Blok's first reaction was that the state must indeed be on the verge of collapse if such traditionalists as Maria Timofeyevna were harbouring rebels. On second thoughts, however, he felt that the whole idea was no more than an attempt at the artificial reanimation of an essentially seventeenth-century institution:

... Better all the cruelty of civilization, all the 'godlessness' of 'economic culture', than the horror of ghosts of times past; the best of men may fall before an invincible phantom, whereas he might survive the horror and monstrosity of *reality*. We need reality, there is nothing in the whole world more terrible than mysticism. ... But possibly it is a *matter of indifference* whether or not 1912 is stalking up to the restoration of the Patriarchate? God is there no longer, even as He is no longer in the Synodal Church. He is in *the still, small voice*.

(VII. 134, entry for 19 March 1912)

Now, through all his ecstasies and illness, Blok was straining every nerve to hear and understand the promptings of this 'still, small voice'. A shadow of falsehood, he felt, had fallen over the whole of life and literature. 'It is *our duty*', he noted in his diary, 'to bring back that integrity which has disappeared from Russian life' (VII. 103).

---

[j] Two devout women, Elizaveta Yur'evna Kuzmina-Karavayeva in her reminiscences written after taking the veil, and Nadezhda Aleksandrovna Pavlovich, unhesitatingly maintain that Blok was too 'spiritually healthy' a person to go in for the anthroposophy or theosophy which attracted so many of his contemporaries. Had he been able to accept Christ, Pavlovich maintains, he would have opted for the Orthodox Church.

3

All through the winter of 1911–12, making full use of the period of retirement from mid-January to early March, Blok was reviewing his course in literature and society, almost as though he had been a young man faced for the first time with a choice of ways. There were several people only too anxious to direct him. Kluyev, after his visit that autumn, had written a minatory letter:

... Now I see your really fateful position, because you stand with one foot in Paris and the other 'on the wild banks of the Irtysh'.... It is clear to me that such people as myself can only be raw material for you, models for your literary operations, or at least that in no circumstances can we be close, brothers.

Then there's another thing: things that move me so deeply that I have to put on a stretched smile to hide my tears met with irony, even, from you, with complete distrust. (Do you remember at dinner I spoke of Forgiveness and you laughed in answer?) All that revealed to me that you are in peril, that your work is religious and therefore of the people only in as far as you hold aloof from all those Parises and Germanys and so on. ... I repeat, all my speech with you was one long struggle against the foreigner in you....

In this present evening hour I am quietly praying that you should be delivered from death and that the cult—not of Beauty alone which has a heart of ice—but of Suffering also might be revealed to you....[6]

Blok, still deeply impressed by Kluyev's 'tenderness' and his 'blessing', ignored the deplorable pseudo-fairy-tale language in which the peasant poet had couched this homily, and noted, genuinely conscience-stricken: 'I know what should be done. I should give up my dinner jacket, and my books ... but I can't, I don't want to' (VII. 101, entry for 6 December 1911).

As usual when in doubt, he had sought the opinion of others. The Merezhkovskys, who had some experience of people of Kluyev's type, were indignant that the peasant poet should have taken it upon himself to lecture Blok—or that he should have so misjudged him. Blok, always ready to condemn himself, did not feel particularly misjudged, but he did feel that his 'Europeanism' was necessary to his poetry, and was rather grateful to his friends for their support. He even went so far as to copy out Maria Pavlovna Ivanova's opinion of Kluyev's letter from one of hers to his mother:

... You can see he loves Aleksandr Aleksandrovich, but he does take an awful lot on himself, offering such accusations, threats, almost invocations.

Whither is he calling? To give up everything and to follow him[k]—and to do what? To serve Russia? But it's not even Russia he's talking about, only his own *wild pine forest*. Surely truth is not only to be found there? ... He was offended at A. A.'s laughing with a certain irony and distrust at things that are dear to him; but it seems to me that was laughter to cover up bitterness and dissatisfaction with himself. I think and hope that God, Who bears the definite Name of Our Saviour and Who gave A. A. talent, will eventually help him to find the true road to salvation for *himself* and *others* because A. A. does *not* understand only beauty but suffering as well.[l] ... Zhenya read the letter, and he didn't like it either....

'I shall take all this to heart', Blok wrote after copying out this letter (VII. 106–7, entry for 23 December 1911).

Another volunteer to guide Blok on his way through life and literature was Andrey Bely, who came to Petersburg for January and February 1912 to make further arrangements about the Musaget journal *Trudy i Dni*. This was precisely the time when Blok was seeing no one. He wrote to Bely, who was staying with Vyacheslav Ivanov, begging him to talk to Pyast (who, he felt, was better acquainted with his own present state of mind than Ivanov) rather than to his host about his plans for the journal. Through Pyast, Bely eventually, on 24 February, arranged a meeting with Blok in a dingy, out-of-the way restaurant:

He was thinner, paler, all worked up somehow ... something had changed in him; all that was fully as it had been were the eyes (humble, resigned, clear, kind).... He began to tell me that lately he had been taken ill with a sudden weakness he had not understood at first; had even suspected that he had become infected by a certain unpleasant disease; the doctors, suspecting this disease, had given him injections; only later it had turned out that the illness was something quite different (basically nervous) and he had been reassured....

'So from what I've told you, you can imagine the kind of life I'm leading. ...' And again he looked at me questioningly, sadly. Shaking his head, he reached out for a glass of wine.... Then he began to tell me of the character of his life and the causes which at times pushed him into that sort of life, which might sometimes seem purposeless and debauched; he spoke of 'gipsy life' as an element of the soul; and behind all his words, in all the excitement which was so uncharacteristic of him, you could see a deep sadness.... From everything he said, a suppressed cry seemed to be trying to escape: 'How can one seek one's own salvation, look after oneself, when

[k] Blok noted: 'That is how I understood him—*that* is the honest way to understand him.'
[l] 'That is true,' Blok noted. 'The Merezhkovskys also say that Kluyev doesn't understand me. "Surely you don't love only Beauty!" Merezhkovsky exclaimed.'

all around—people are perishing! When this sort of thing is going on all about you....'[7]

That winter Blok had taken to lonely walks about the town and he may well have unburdened himself to Bely, recalling their walking the back streets together in 1905, about those places where, as he wrote in his diary within a few days of their meeting,

... hooligans break the street lamps, a small puppy attaches himself to you, there are dirty windows with scant curtains. A small girl is walking along—you can hear from quite a long way off that she's breathing heavily like a horse; obviously consumption; she is gasping for breath from the hollow cough, bending right forward every few steps ... terrible world.

(VII. 130, entry for 28 February 1912)

So black was the night about Blok at this time, that he felt 'a kind of magnificence in the blackness', not to be alleviated by individual virtue. He would quote Leonid Andreyev on the shame of being good[m] and maintained that, since one could not help everyone, one might as well spend money on self-destructive debauch.

Bely, whom Blok *had* helped and always would, not for sentimental reasons but because he believed in his genius and really did regard him as a 'brother', now tried, in his turn, to help Blok. All that day, he poured out his discovery of Steiner's anthroposophy and told Blok how he was determined to devote his life to studying and furthering this marvellous creed. Bely had an overwhelming personality and Blok—just emerging from two months' seclusion, not sure of anything—was impressed by his fire and conviction. Only later, after much thought and consultation with those of their mutual friends who had met Steiner,[8] did he realize the dangers of Bely's impressionability. At the time he merely noted, '24th spent all day with Borya (at Leyner's). Borya's personality, the impression from him and his words. He had something very important to say' (VII. 129).

Bely, knowing he was going abroad for a long time, took leave of Blok outside the restaurant in the freezing fog:

... I remember A. A.'s black, broad-brimmed hat (he waved it at me), disappearing into the thick of the fog and suddenly turning around again; for some reason, I remember his hand in a brown kid glove; and the kind smile in the unkind February fog; I looked after him; his straight back going away; now he ducked under the raised umbrella of a passer-by; and—instead of Blok—out of the darkness of the damp evening came trotting towards me: a rascally nonentity with a little beard, a cap and shiny

[m] The words are from '*T'ma*' (Darkness), a short story.

galoshes; the people in the street bustled on, there were prostitutes standing;
I thought 'Perhaps that one will go up to him....'⁹

And so Blok continued on his way—alone. In so far as he can be
said to have reached any conclusion that winter about his own
'course', that conclusion is best expressed by the dour optimism of
his answer to an admiring young Georgian poet, written shortly after
his meeting with Bely:

You say: 'There is a sweet melancholy in poetry.' 'Without poetry, life
is nothing but misery, simply muck.' I answer: I understand you, but this
is something *that I do not want to know*. We are not here either to be melancholy or to take our ease. That wonderful admixture of contradictory feelings, thoughts and impulses which bears the name of the 'human soul'
is called by that *glad name* (yes, glad, in spite of all the 'muck' we're sitting
in) because its face is set more towards the future than towards the past:
towards the past, also—in so far as the future is built into the past. Man
is *the future*. ... I am speaking to you from my own experience—I am afraid
of all *my own* subtle, sweet, beloved, slow-working poisons. I am afraid
and, with an effort, I make myself go back all the time to simpler, more
democratic fare. ... My last request to you! If you love my verses, overcome their poison, read in them about the future.

(VIII. 385–6)

4

Paradoxically, at this moment of intense uncertainty, when for a
whole year he had done nothing but struggle with a poem that he
could not bring to a satisfactory conclusion, Blok found himself in
demand as never before: and not so much as a poet, but as a literary
journalist, a moulder of public opinion with his own vision of
Russia's place in the modern world. On 30 December 1911, one of
the editors of the liberal newspaper *Russkoye Slovo*, Arkadiy
Rumanov, had launched a personal campaign to groom Blok for
this part, a campaign in which he was to persist for close on a year.

To Blok, with his new-found social and economic interests, the
prospect of having his own column and of sharing his thoughts with
a readership of 2,500,000 scattered between Moscow and Vladivos-
tok was not unattractive. Rumanov, moreover, always had the latest
inside story of what was going on at court or in politics and Blok
enjoyed being in the know as much as anybody else. Their constant
meetings, now at Blok's flat, now at expensive restaurants about the

town, were only interrupted by Blok's illness. Rumanov was convinced that Blok—potentially, at least—was a journalist of the calibre of Katkov," but he had reckoned without two things: opposition to Blok's appointment from the secretary to the editors of his paper in Moscow;° and the fact that his potential star prose-writer was primarily a poet. Sociological and historical insight Blok had, but it was intuitive and inspirational rather than analytical and sustained. It seems unlikely, also, that Rumanov understood the sacrificial intensity of Blok's love for 'the future'. *Russkoye Slovo* was careful to disassociate itself from the openly conservative *Novoye Vremya*, but its programme most certainly did not comprise social upheaval. It required Blok's patriotism and the flair for making practical issues exciting which he had, to some extent, from his father, not the uncompromising radicalism that was his heritage from the Beketovs.

In the end, it got neither. Rumanov did, however, arrange for it to publish some splendid verses including 'The New America' (III. 268–70), one of Blok's few poems about his country written in a sustained major key.

For himself, Blok simply decided that poetry and politics did not mix: 'the worlds of art', he stated in another context, 'relate to politics in much the same way as the sea relates to a ship' (v. 475). Having seriously considered the possibility of writing regularly about art for the national press, he let the opportunity slip from him:

The ceremonial side of our attitude to art should be solemn, unhurried, without vanity or advertisement. This is how we should speak of art and, if our speech is conducted in any other tone, then sooner or later those who have introduced the element of vanity will be punished, on their heads will fall a slow nemesis more terrible than any of the swift penalties exacted by man. Art avenges itself like an ancient deity or like the soul of the people, reducing to ashes, wiping off the face of the earth all things on which there is any trace of vanity, all things that attempt to drown out, with their petty, hasty, breathless rhythms, its own unique and measured tact.

Newspapers, by their very nature, are hasty and uproarious, the faster the beat of life, the more furious is the clamour of politics....

(v. 474–5)

" Mikhail Nikiforovich Katkov (1818–87), editor and publisher of *Moskovskiye Vedomosti* and *Russkiy Vestnik*, extremely influential organs of enlightened conservative opinion, has been called 'a reactionary liberal'.[10]

° N. V. Vol'sky's account of his opposition to Rumanov's plan (of which he says Blok knew nothing) gives the quite unjustified impression—corrected by his editor Gleb Struve—that Blok's primary interest was to get himself on to *Russkoye Slovo*'s payroll.[11]

5

Rumanov, however, was not the only 'entrepreneur' now anxious to harness Blok's talent, and the commission that the poet accepted after emerging from his incarceration at home in the spring of 1912 was far removed indeed from the vanities of politics. An admirer of his poetry, Mikhail Tereshchenko, millionaire, aesthete, and rising star in the official cultural hierarchy, who occupied an unspecified position attached to the Director of the Imperial Theatres, approached Blok with a commission to write the scenario of a ballet for the composer A. K. Glazunov.

Blok was first introduced to the twenty-eight-year-old Tereshchenko by Aleksey Remizov after a performance of Tolstoy's *Living Corpse* by the Moscow Art Theatre during its 1912 Easter season in Petersburg. He was immediately fascinated by the idea of the scenario, which was to be about medieval Provençal troubadours, a welcome escape from the intractable contemporaneiety of *Retribution*—and began work the very next day. After his illness and half-acknowledged failure to complete his long poem, this outside stimulus was most important to him. Knyazhnin, indeed, records a conversation with Blok, who told him:

'I owe a great deal to Tereshchenko. He made me finish *The Rose and the Cross*.'
'Made you?'
A smile, a nod of the head.
'Made me. I went and read him every single act, over and over again, until I got it right.' After a brief silence, naïvely and modestly: 'Otherwise I never would have finished it....'[12]

In spite of the poet's commitment to the future, it was a refreshment to his spirit to turn back to the morning of Europe, to the 'country' he had come to love so much in the paintings of Fra Angelico, Bellini, and Signorelli. 'I feel', he wrote to Andrey Bely, recalling the end of his article 'On the Present State of Russian Symbolism', '... as though I had been given a little chapel to decorate with frescoes, and so everything smells of the twelfth century, of spring and almond trees in bloom somewhere in the mountains' (VIII. 388).

This was an exact description of what *The Rose and the Cross* meant to him. His prayer had been granted: he had been presented with a ready-made 'form' and, as he had suspected for some time, the 'form' turned out to be European. Into this European mould, however, this mannered 'ballet-cum-opera-cum-drama' of medieval

France, Blok was to pour the sorrowful poetry and formless anxieties of his own life and his own land: 'In order to take part in the "creation of life", it is necessary to take on flesh, to show one's sad, human face. And not the pseudo-face of a nonexistent school. We are all—Russian' (VII. 140).

And so it was through his impressions of Brittany and France, which he peopled with archetypal characters from his own experience, that Blok came to tell once again the story of Lyubov' and her search for love and life against the background of poetry, inevitability, tragic loyalties, and thoughtless merriment that made up his own life. Yet *The Rose and the Cross* is no allegory. Blok created his own historical world, carefully researched in every detail.[13] He was himself a man 'of medieval soul' and his imagination had long dwelt in castles, lingering in closed gardens and familiar with the slow-flowing lives of holy monks and of ladies awaiting the return of their lords from far campaigns. Yet he saw the twelfth century in Europe, like his own time in Russia, as a transitional period. Violence and revolution, usually offstage in the play as in his own life, formed the true backdrop to both.

For the first time, that spring, Blok had had a dream in which his wife and his mother were one person (VII. 145) and the heroine of *The Rose and the Cross*, Izora, with her all-too-earthly yet divine discontent, is to some extent inspired by both. The 'husband', Count Archimbaut, is one-dimensional reality, that inescapable 'realism' so detested by Dmitriy Karamazov, that common sense that crushes life and growth with dead wealth and brute force, square, heavy forms, stone and iron and prison bars. Yet, in a sense, Blok loved Archimbaut, for there is still a faint aura of true aristocracy about him. He is tragic in his stupidity, his inability to perceive the subtle tendrils of change that will leave not stone upon stone of his bluff, square castle. Bertrand, the faithful 'knight of sorrows' devoted to Izora but unnoticed by her, 'the unhappy guardian of this pompous castle', has much of Blok himself, but much also of one of the dimmest, saddest figures in his own story: the long-suffering colonel with the tragic eyes and old-fashioned loyalties: Frants Feliksovich.[p]

[p] I owe this insight to A. M. Turkov's *Aleksandr Blok* (Moscow, 1969) in the series 'Zhizni zamechatel'nykh lyudey'. To test his intuition that Bertrand is, in part at least, based upon the character of Blok's stepfather, one has to go no further than the dialogue between Gaetan and Bertrand beginning 'It's all right for you—you are not bound by service' (IV. 201). On the other hand, there is certainly something of the author in all the three principal male characters of the play (the Count, Bertrand, Gaetan), and Bertrand is no more a straightforward portrait of Frants Feliksovich than are any of the other characters portraits of living people.

ДѢЙСТВЇЕ I

СЦЕНЯ I

ДВОРЪ ЗАМКА . СУМЕРКИ .

БЕРТРАНЪ глухо поетъ

«ВСЮДУ БѢДА И УТРАТЫ, .
ЧТО ТЕБЯ ЖДЕТЪ ВПЕРЕДИ?
СТАВЬ ЖЕ СВОЙ ПАРУСЬ КОСМАТЫЙ
МѢТЬ СВОИ КРѢПКІЯ ЛАТЫ
ЗНАКОМЪ КРЕСТА НА ГРУДИ"—
СТРАННАЯ ПѢСНЯ О МОРѢ
И О КРЕСТѢ, ГОРЯЩЕМЪ НАДЪ ВЬЮГОЙ
СМЫСЛА ЕЯ НЕ ПОСТИГНЕТЪ

The first page of *The Rose and the Cross*, in the illustrated manuscript copy made by M. N. Kupreyanov, 1915. (From the collection of N. P. Il'in.)

Gradually, Bertrand—'an ordinary man, a failure'—was to become the central figure of the drama.

At the beginning of the ballet, the low-born[q] chatelaine of the castle, the young and vital Izora, has fallen into a melancholy induced by a haunting, half-remembered Breton song about joy and suffering and eternal conflict. When Bertrand is sent to the north of France on his lord's business, she enjoins him to seek out the singer. But the minstrel Gaetan whom Bertrand eventually brings back from Brittany is old and fey, no more to be possessed or loved than the spindrift off his native coast. Gaetan consents to sing at Izora's court, but it is the bright page Aliskan—out for nothing but a lark and a kick—who finally gains her bedchamber, literally over the shoulders of the mortally-wounded Bertrand.

It was the character of Bertrand that finally 'outgrew' the forms of ballet and opera which Blok and Tereshchenko had originally envisaged. This, as it transpired, did not matter, for Glazunov proved an unenthusiastic collaborator and, by the time it became clear to Blok that he was writing a play, not a scenario, he and Tereshchenko had become friends.

6

The first act of *The Rose and the Cross* was written during the summer of 1912, which Blok spent largely in Petersburg. Reluctantly, in gratitude and humility, he had ceased to oppose his wife's nostalgia for the stage. She had attempted to make a comeback in the spring— without success—but now, together with Verigina, Meyerhold, and others, she was planning to spend the summer staging studio productions in Terioki,[r] a forest resort on the shores of the Gulf of Finland about an hour's train journey to the north of Petersburg.

Blok was at first quite well disposed to the project as such. He thought it would help Lyuba to find her feet in the theatre, to test her own gifts. He was, however, somewhat riled by the pre-publicity, which described her as 'the wife of the poet' and made out that he himself was one of the moving spirits of the group.

When it came to the point, he hated her going. She was leaving

[q] Blok never fully explained, but always insisted upon, the 'low birth' of Izora. Certainly, it serves to put her right outside the 'square' feudal system of ready-made loyalties. She is an aspect of the 'Eternal Feminine' and thus of life itself; 'beyond good and evil', admitting no law but its own necessity, and thus she is linked with the popular element and, potentially, with revolution.

[r] Now called Zelenogorsk.

him 'between flats' and with a new maid whose face, in his present
state of almost pathological sensitivity, struck him as inexpressibly
terrible: '... a mixture of the human race with some *unknown* lower
species.... My wife, the actress, does not understand this or want
to know about it' (VII. 144–5).

By the time Lyuba finally departed for Terioki, he was regretting
not having made more effort to nip the whole project in the bud:

It seems to me that there has been a considerable change in the spirit of
the enterprise. At first they all wanted a really important work with ideas
behind it, to study etc. But they weren't sure what they did want, were
feeling their way in the dark. Then, gradually, several enterprising modern-
ists came in on it and showed talent and initiative, as they do everywhere
these days, and so quickly took things into their own hands, and ... instead
of a BIG, *traditional* undertaking, which is beyond them, there has sprung
up a SMALL, talented, decadent undertaking.... There was much said about
Shakespeare and ideas, but what they are actually *doing*—to begin with,
anyway—are Meyerhold's pantomimes; ... how it will all turn out I don't
know. I must try not to condemn it in advance.

(VII. 146, entry for 28 May 1912)

What he did know was that he hated seeing Lyuba off and return-
ing to an empty flat: '... The little white dog with red eyes on the
table is absolutely miserable. I am afraid of life, the street, everything.
It is terrifying to remain alone, and Mama, too, is going away'
(VII. 146). Two days later, he saw Aleksandra Andreyevna off to
Shakhmatovo ('May God look after her') and went down to
Tsarskoye Selo to seek comfort of his friends Zhenya Ivanov and
Pyast.

To begin with, it seemed as though summer alone in Petersburg
would not be so bad after all. Within a week he had finished the
first act of *The Rose and the Cross*. He had little time to feel lonely
when not working, being almost constantly in the company of Pyast,
Remizov, Gorodetsky, or the ever-energetic Rumanov. He visited
Lyuba in Terioki and brought her back for the night. Then he began
seeing a lot of the artist Sapunov, another lonely, talented man
leading a wild and dissolute life. This, on the night of 6 June, led
to 'one of the most dreadful nights of my life', in company with
the artist and, by chance, Leonid Andreyev. By 11 June Blok had
still not recaptured his working rhythm.

A visit to Terioki to see Lyuba act was inconclusive and, after the
performance, he walked with her along the misty beach beneath a
red sliver of moon, feeling suddenly lonely again and miserably

depressed. She must have sensed this because next day she paid him a surprise visit in Petersburg:

Out of the blue my darling came, it was so good to see her. Frants paid us a visit and sat for a while. I saw my darling off at the station, I love her to the point of tears.

Perhaps this foul, stinking stretch of life will soon pass and another will come. I am afraid of life.

(VII. 149)

He could neither work nor sleep and was distressed at the direction Lyuba's theatre appeared to be taking. Moreover, Sapunov and Kuzmin were now trying to talk him into attending a St. Peter's Day 'Carnival' at Terioki. Meyerhold's particular atmosphere of elegant play was one Blok had long since outgrown, and he was worried as to how it would effect Lyuba. He did not go to the carnival, but Sapunov did, and was drowned. Lyuba wrote that she had already gone to bed on the night of the carnival when she had been woken by cries coming from the sea, but had thought all had ended happily as these so soon ceased; Sapunov, however, who could not swim, had simply failed to surface when the boat he was in capsized. Blok went to Terioki on the following day, 17 July. He watched Lyuba play an old lady in 'a very vulgar comedy by Oscar Wilde', frustrated by people crowding round to talk to him when he had wanted to concentrate on her acting, and came away with a gnawing feeling that the whole project was pointless. A short walk with Lyuba 'along the shore of the sea in which Sapunov's body was lying' only served to emphasize the feeling of unreality.

Exhausted by the animation at Terioki and by the hot city summer, Blok again began to withdraw from people. He had to see to various matters connected with moving to a more comfortable apartment in an old house on the other side of the town, No. 57 Offitserskaya Street,[5] flat 21. When not busy with practical arrangements, he would walk alone through the outskirts of the town, still sick in body and mind, feeling, in his self-imposed loneliness, totally exposed. One day, he drifted into the Zoo:

... and having looked at various delightful little animals I sat down to listen to the utterly outmoded *Orpheus in the Underworld* ... but fate decreed otherwise—a drunken army colonel came and sat down next to me, probably kind, unfortunate, penniless and lonely. And immediately in his drunken talk—distrust, contempt for the civilian ('Are you a man or

[5] Now Ulitsa Dekabristov.

a woman in disguise', 'nice to be a rich man', 'If I had money I'd——
all these women', 'you're blasé, can't carry corn' etc. etc.)—i.e. *yet another
especially sent to persecute me.*

   According to the old way of thinking, the colonel is perfectly right, but
then there are millions of colonels in this world and I am *almost* alone; what
can I do but quietly take refuge in my secluded corner, so long as I have
one; and I still do have one. *Only here* and *from here* can I *do* anything. Is
that not so?

   They're after you, put your feelers out, be your own keeper, don't drink,
a happier day will come.

(VII. 152)

   That same day, he had been expecting Lyuba. She came later than
arranged and this in itself was a torment. A telegram informed him
that she would arrive on the last train and, late that evening, he was
preparing to go to the station to meet her when

suddenly, from the balcony, I see a tattered man walking along,
stealthily, obviously not wishing anyone to see, stooping all the time towards the ground. Then, suddenly, he stretched out full length over some
hollow in the road and, as far as I could see, raised the grating over the
drain, *drank the water*, wiped his mouth, and went cautiously on. *A man.*

(VII. 153)

This incident is the key to the appearance of the beggar-double in
the poem 'The Life of a Friend of Mine' (III. 47–53) who, demanding
'frankness' and 'humility', forces the poet to turn out his own pockets
and find them—empty; to look into his own heart—and to weep.

   Lyuba came, but left again the next day. It was becoming increasingly obvious that she grudged every moment away from the
theatre.

   Unable to concentrate on his work, Blok noted miserably on 26
July:

Something infinitely hard to bear is happening in my life. Lyuba is deceiv-
ing me again. On the basis of my letter written on 23 June and of what
she herself said I had every reason to expect either her or a telegram from
her today. . . . And now it is getting on for three o'clock, the day is wasted,
all the morning I've been tensed up waiting for her which is of course a
bad preparation for a meeting. Perhaps she won't come at all today. . . .

That time, however, it was all right:

Bu came just as I was writing that. She had tea and we went to look at
the flat, chose the wallpaper and, in the evening before her bath, I read her
my opera, she liked it. She said it was not a play but an opera, that for

a play it was too much of a mosaic. That is true. I was led astray by my unhappy Bertrand. In his character there is something that has outgrown opera.

(VII. 153–4)

Blok's suspicions of Lyuba though not unfounded, were premature. For the moment, however, he still had hopes that she might have a serious vocation. While acutely aware of her weaknesses, most of which he ascribed to lack of experience ('trying to grab hold of art, a kind of cramp, whereas art requires to be approached smoothly and boldly, without fear of burning oneself on its flame', VII. 154), he still looked forward to seeing her in a serious part.

This was granted him. On 15 July, the Terioki studio staged a memorial performance of Strindberg's *Guilty—Not Guilty*: a suggestion which had emanated from Blok in the first place.[1] Strindberg's daughter, who was married to a Russian professor in Helsingfors, came down to watch, and Pyast gave an introductory talk. The production was a triumph for Meyerhold, who was well served by the artist Yuriy Bondi. The action took place against dark blue-black curtains through which there were glimpses of flame and silhouettes of things going on 'offstage'. Lyubov', in the part of Janna, rose to the occasion:

... All the first act Lyuba never left the stage and for the first time I really approved her as an actress: she played with great power. The action takes place in a church. Janna stands in the centre of the church with a baby in her arms and pronounces words full of terrible foreboding (the play was written at the same time as *Inferno*); Lyuba at last spoke in her own voice, very strong in sound and expression, which went well with Strindberg's language. It was the first time I had heard this language from the stage, and I was very struck; simplicity taken to the point of terror: the life of the soul translated into mathematical formulae, and these formulae in their turn expressed through specific signs reminiscent of zigzags of lightning against a very black cloud; in those years, Strindberg spoke only in the language of lightning....

(VIII. 398)

So Blok described the play to his mother, with whom he had just spent a restful week at Shakhmatovo, working in the garden, eating strawberries, and relaxing among the roses and the lilies and the usual atmosphere of general adoration.

---

[1] In April 1912 Blok had written an article on Ibsen and Strindberg for Bely's *Trudy i Dni* (no. 2, May 1912) and an obituary on Strindberg for the journal *Sovremennik* (no. 5, 1912) which he reworked for *Trudy i Dni* that August.

It was hot in Petersburg, and after the Strindberg play, Blok spent much time out of town, walking and bathing. On 24 July, at the height of the heat wave, Lyuba took time off from the theatre to help move flats:

Mama, we made the move yesterday! I am writing you absolutely wet through, having been all day unpacking and arranging books, outside it is hell. This is a pleasant flat. Lyuba left yesterday evening, terribly busy this week (five performances). Look here! I suggested to Lyuba that, at the end of the plays, we might come to Shakhmatovo for a week or two and she would like to very much. What do you think? Couldn't they wait to paint the floors till after we've gone? We would come then; I, perhaps, before Lyuba, as soon as I get things straight here. There's a lot of work to do with the carpenter etc. [14]

In spite of the heat, he seems to have been happy alone in the new flat. It was the time of the state visit of Poincaré and Blok at once appreciated the nearness of the harbour. From his windows he could catch occasional glimpses of the masts and flags of the French ships at anchor downriver.

His first visitor was, as he informed his mother, a very strange one.

The day after the move I was sorting out books, all covered in dust, when suddenly Doctor Skvortsov, the father of Natal'ya Nikolayevna Skvortsova, appeared to ask me what he should do about his daughter (she is ill), to find out about her love for me and whether I am really married (for some reason she doubts this), bringing a letter from her in which she definitely proposes that I should marry her. We sat together for about three hours ... it ended with me writing a brief note and giving it to him to give to his daughter (the gist of it being that 'I love only my wife'). Odd. [15]

During the ensuing days Blok did not go once to Terioki. 'I feel embarrassed, somehow,' he wrote to his mother. He preferred to wait for Lyuba to rejoin him, as she had promised to do after the end of the season on 11 August, at Shakhmatovo. He himself went there on the 8th. On the 13th he visited his publishers in Moscow and the next day Lyubov' came from Petersburg, not for the promised fortnight but for three days, as a gracious visitor. On their wedding anniversary, 17 August, they returned to Petersburg by the same train they had taken nine years before.

Lyubov', however, went back to Terioki, and Blok again found himself alone in the new flat.

7

One of the first demands upon Blok's time in this 1912–13 season came from the New Peasant Sectarian group. This group had founded a publishing house, Novaya Zemlya (The New Earth), and I. P. Brikhnichev," one of the editors, asked Blok to give his opinion of the programme of their journal, *Novoye Vino* (The New Wine). It is evident from Blok's answer that Brikhnichev, like Kluyev, whose poetry he asked Blok to review for their journal, was attempting to proselytize by stressing the religious significance of his verse and his potential as a 'popular' poet. Blok declined the invitation. 'I am no enemy of yours but neither am I one of you,' he answered:

... I am engaged in trying more and more to consolidate artistic form, because for me (for my 'ego') it is the only defence. You, on the other hand (that is all Novaya Zemlya), neglect form, or so it seems to me, as though you hoped that the souls of those who accept your content will themselves become the form to contain it.... My conclusion: it is on the way of the artist, or so it seems to me, that I can do most. I have not the voice to be a preacher. That is why I am alone. But, believe me, it is with neither pride nor despair that I tell you this.

(VIII. 400–2, letter of 29 August 1912)

Nevertheless, Blok *was* alone, in his private life as in his work, as he had not been since his student days before his engagement to Lyuba. He was undergoing an intensive course of treatment (the first of three series of injections and tests) and had been told he must face up to a radical change in his way of life. 'Wine and prostitutes have long since lost their charm for me,' he added after recording his doctor's instructions.

On his return from the country he had engaged a new servant to look after him but, after his mother's return to Petersburg, he went more and more often to dine with her. Every day he waited, in mounting anxiety, for news of Lyuba. She had promised to rejoin him in their new flat on 3 September but did not. In answer to two urgent telegrams, she eventually came on the 8th.

The joy of her return was short-lived. She was always out, 'at her teacher Meyerhold's', as Blok noted jealously. She was in demand. Flowers and chocolates showered in on her name day.

'Sasha is gloomy—says terrible things,'[16] his mother noted anxiously. One evening he came to her and found her alone: '"Let her go," he said quietly, quietly. "She has her own life to live. I don't

---

" Brikhnichev was an ex-priest who had abandoned his sacerdotal office for literature and journalism.

mind now because I've faced up to it." "[17] He was noticeably thinner
and spoke of Lyuba tenderly, with lowered eyes. His diary for this
period is full of guilt and compassion.

Lyuba's constant escort, Konstantin Kuzmin-Karavayev,[v] at first
failed to make much impression on him, but when, after his departure
for the provinces, Lyuba had her photograph taken 'especially for
him', Blok wrote possessively: 'It will be a rare portrait (in one
copy) but I have a rarer and a better' (VIII. 170, entry for 27 October
1912). This photograph, indeed, served as a catalyst. Blok could no
longer allow himself to believe that his 'darling' (milaya), as he still
called her, was unhappy because her summer's acting had brought
her no autumn engagement, or that their disagreements were purely
theoretical, stemming from his argument that all the work of Meyerhold and his group amounted to nothing but 'talented squiggles
round an empty space' (VII. 164). His wife was in love with another
man.

16 October. At night—an acute feeling for my darling, poor little unfortunate. She doesn't go to her cellar,[w] does not see her comrades—who seem
rather a doubtful lot to me—and is turning pale, letting herself go, lies
late in bed in the mornings, it's dull and hard for her to live. It's boring
for her with me, too. I am busy with myself and my thoughts, I can't 'give'
her anything.

(VII. 65)

Perhaps only I alone love my darling but I don't know how to love her
and don't know how to help her.

(VII. 169)

After the incident with the photograph, Blok decided to bring the
situation to a head:

Over evening tea I raised the question (not for the first time) that the situation was not natural and to drag it out was to take refuge in sleep. It is
quite clear that the 'theatre' in her life has become nothing more than an
appendage to that love which I can see is developing every day, whether
real or temporary; she should not deceive herself; lessons with Panchenko
and Meyerhold in the basement of the Brodyachaya Sobaka and other
places with people who may be very nice but who can give 'neither milk
nor wool' cannot be considered 'work', nor can they form the content of
life. The days are passing, whichever way you look at it, in thoughts of
another man; whenever you come into her room she's reading his letters

[v] Not the husband of Elizaveta Yur'evna, but a young actor with the same surname.
[w] The bohemian restaurant known as the Brodyachaya Sobaka (The Wandering Dog),
of which Blok disapproved and which at that time he never visited.

or writing to him or sitting dreaming. The obvious thing to do now is for her to go Zhitomir[x] and after that things will clarify themselves ... on that I broke off my harangue and went to my own room and my darling went to hers having, I think, really taken notice of what I had been saying.

It will be worse for both of us if we go dragging on like this. This lack of clarity and her seeming attitude to me is worse than anything. The Lord be with you, my dearest.

The most agonizing is all the 'outward' side: how, what, where, when, to see her off, to say goodbye, to part, for long, for a little time, order cabs, make phone calls, people, luggage, the days before she goes.

Or is that the real *retribution* which has come and which it is my duty to accept?

Well, what of it? I shall write down in black and white the whole story that I always hide within me.

The answer to my own unceasing transgressions was: first A. Bely, whom I, *most probably*, hate. Then—Messrs. Chulkov and some absolute nonentities (Ausländer[y])—who at the moment just make me feel sick. Then the 'hooligan from Tmutarakan'—the main one.[z] And now—I know not who.

(VII. 170)

By this Blok meant, of course, not that he did not know the identity of his wife's lover, but that he had no idea what he was really like.

'I shall look in quietly on Lyuba, she's asleep. My little one is asleep and mutters something welcoming at me through her sleep' (VII. 171), he noted in the night following their explanation. It was arranged that Lyuba was to rejoin Kuzmin-Karavayev in the provinces for a time. The affair was patently not going to last:

At dinner she cried: He is a boy, 'good' (twenty-two years old), pure, 'knows what her life has been', 'loves' her. On 7 November ('exactly 10 years'),[aa] probably she will go to Zhitomir. Now, for the moment, we both think: just temporarily. The future will be made clear in time.

(VII. 171)

Throughout these painful weeks, Blok had been struggling to finish *The Rose and the Cross*, for Tereshchenko was holding him to a deadline. The evening of Lyuba's departure Blok spent with Tereshchenko, and read him all that he had written so far. It was clear that the play had not yet found its final form and Tereshchenko, though impressed, suggested alterations.

---

[x] A town in the south of Russia where Kuzmin-Karavayev was acting that winter.

[y] A minor poet, the nephew of Milhail Kuzmin. His role in Lyubov' Dmitriyevna's life must have been transitory and Blok's relationship with him was outwardly correct.

[z] The father of Lyuba's son Dmitriy.

[aa] From the date when Lyubov' Dmitriyevna accepted Blok's proposal of marriage.

This young man from a very different world was unhappy in his private life, self-critical and uncertain, a state of mind Blok found appealing. A few weeks earlier they had had a conversation about art and religion which the poet had found so important that he had written it down in unusual detail:

Tereshchenko says that he has never been religious and that everything he thinks religion can give he has received from art (two or three moments in life, chiefly—musical). In answer I began to develop my *invariable thought*: that in art there is *infinity*, we know not what, transcending all things, but empty, leading perhaps to perdition, *whereas* in religion there is *the end*, we know what, plenitude, salvation (I said less? but even so it was a schema and therefore involuntarily false). And about art: would I want to repeat or bring back those minutes when art has opened up infinity to me? No, I can't wish for that, even if I had the power to bring them back. What is behind all that cannot be loved (Loved with a capital letter).

That evening of 7 November, Blok went on to read Tereshchenko his poetry: 'The Steps of the Commendatore'[bb] and 'The Dance of Death'. But all the time his mind ran on Lyuba, chugging along in the train to meet her 'pure', 'good' boy. 'She will arrive tomorrow. Promised to send a wire. The Lord keep her' (VIII. 173).

After Tereshchenko had gone, Blok's feelings found release in poetry. Poe, Goethe, and Dostoyevsky are all present in this poem, but Blok makes them his own through experienced suffering:

> One autumn night, beneath the raindrops' glassy patter,
> I sought the old, hard mystery to unseal,
> When, to my study, dim-lit, vast and lofty,
> Came that same gentleman—a rough cur at his heel.
>
> And wearily the guest sat down beside the fireplace,
> Upon the hearthrug—at his feet—the cur.
> He said politely: 'Surely that's enough now?
> It's high time to accept your Fate, good sir.'[cc]
>
> 'But in old age—youth will return, and ardour ...'
> So I began ... he interrupted: 'Nay!
> She will be just the same. Mad Edgar's poor Lenore.
> There is no going back.—Not yet? I've had my say.'
>
> How strange: life once was ecstasy, hell, thunder,
> But here—with that strange man, alone at this late hour,
> Beneath his businesslike, long since indifferent gaze, I
> Must confess it seemed far simpler than before.

[bb] Final version completed during his illness the previous winter.
[cc] 'Sir' in English in the original.

The gentleman is gone. But always at my side now,
A comforting companion—lives the cur.
When life turns sour—a hard paw scrapes my knee, and
The kind eyes say: 'Time to accept things, sir.'

(VII. 42)

But he would *not* accept things. On 7 November, remembering the suicide note in his pocket when he had proposed to Lyubov' ten years before, he wrote:

She is my link with the world, the affirmation of the world's inexpressible content (*neskazannost'*). If this inexpressible content *is*, then I will bear much, everything that is required of me. If it is not, if it breaks off, deceives, is forgotten—no, that I 'cannot accept', 'with all due respect, I return my ticket'.[dd]

(VII. 176)

Lyubov's first letter from Zhitomir said that she had not yet decided what to do. Perhaps she would spend the whole winter there, but she could not face a final break with Blok because she still felt more than affection for him: even that they might fall in love again ('*Vstretit'sya serdtsem*'). He replied at once, demanding her return:

What you are doing now is the final moment of somnambulism, which must lead to a catastrophe or to the destruction of that original and unique harmony, the meaning of life, once found but not yet justified, not given form.

Translating that into your language, you may call that catastrophe a new awakening, the establishment of a new harmony (for yourself and a third person). I do not believe in this new harmony, I *curse* it in advance not only personally, but also objectively. It is of a lower sort than that which was once achieved and that this is so I am prepared to swear by all that was and is dear to me.

If you have doubts about that, I have none. If you believe in the establishment of a new harmony for yourself I am prepared to remove myself from your path, much more decisively than on 7 November 1902. Believe me, this is neither threat nor anger, but a clear, *religious* conclusion, a definite refusal of all compromise.

Your letter is only slightly clearer than the previous ones. It is essential to be more definite, because now each new day is an *action*, which leads us nearer to the one or the other conclusion.

Be so good as not to address me any more in intimate language. Wake up—or another will awake for you. God bless you and help you to become not a destroyer-woman, but a creator.

ALEKSANDR BLOK

[dd] The words in which Ivan Karamazov, in conversation with his brother, the novice Alyësha, rejects the concept of a paradise founded on the suffering of even one small child.

From this letter, Lyuba understood one thing: that her husband might take his own life. She sent a telegram at once: 'Your letter received and understood. Coming 19th'.

On 20 November, early in the morning, she arrived at the flat in Offitserskaya Street direct from the station, and remained with Blok in Petersburg—for just over three weeks. This act of consideration, however, was enough to put him back on his feet and, although Lyubov' left him again, returning for the New Year and remaining with him this time for over a month, until 7 February, she was able at these times to give him enough of herself to keep him from total despair.

8

Indeed, Blok had for some time now been learning to live with unhappiness:

> And you'll recall from time to time
> With just a smile of tenderness
> The fond, elusive, childhood dream
> We used to know as—happiness.

19 June 1912
(III. 144)

Now he was after something greater. He had begun to judge works of art by their 'universal significance'. Valentina Verigina, finding this altogether too solemn, objected that since she herself was not of 'universal significance' she was no doubt scarcely worth talking to. Blok laughed and took her roller-coaster riding. Nevertheless, he insisted that, in *art*, no other criterion was possible. As usual, he was headed full into the wind, *against* the spirit of the times. In these days when, in his poetry, Blok was walking the circles of Hell, listening to the sound of 'bone scraping against bone' (III. 37), and the shining silences of space and non-being (III. 203), the world around him grew ever more frivolous:

Before the war of 1914 a kind of indefinable triviality entered into people of the art world.... Like a statue of ice to which no vulgarity could stick, Blok stood amidst the many-coloured, bright-feathered flocks of artists, writers, and poets. He always remained 'himself'. To the least suggestion of philistinism he reacted with painful nervosity...,[18]

wrote Verigina, who this season saw much of Blok and of his mother, at whose flat she and a group of friends began to meet regularly for 'serious discussions' from January 1913.[ee] Yet she was taken by surprise when, years after his death, she came to read Blok's diary and to understand the intensity of his gloom. She remembered him, in spite of his withdrawal from the blatant frivolity of the period, as a still merry companion with a young laugh, always ready to pay her back in her own coin of light banter. Puzzling over this, she wrote many years later: 'I think that these dark moods must have over-taken him all of a sudden, causing him to set no store by all the amus-ing and good things that had happened to him during the day.'[19] In this, Verigina's evidence accords absolutely with Maria Beke-tova's, who recalls Blok reducing the whole family at Shakhmatovo to helpless laughter on some of the very days he wrote his grimmest poetry.[20]

The poetry he wrote that autumn was grim indeed. His night walks about Petersburg still took him back to the Peterburgskaya Storona, the island where he had lived throughout his school and university days. Taking care to avoid his old school which, as Zhenya Ivanov later told D. S. Likhachev,[21] filled him with a sense of horror, he would return to the little restaurant with the pattern of ships on the wallpaper and to the wooden bridge to the tragic Krestovsky Island on which he had set the second act of The Stranger. On the corner by the bridge, its gleaming red, yellow, green, and blue jars reflected in the waters of the Malaya Nevka like a symbol of eternal return, stood a chemist's shop:

> Night, the street, a lamp, the chemist's:
> A dim and apathetic light.
> Though you lived on a quarter-century—
> Nothing would change. There's no way out.
>
> And if you die—it's but beginning
> Over again. All things repeat.
> The night. The river's frozen ripple.
> The chemist's shop. The lamp. The street.[ff]

(VII. 37)

The weariness in this poem seems absolute. Yet Blok was writing with a quiet power and a mastery of form and rhythm such as he had never until now achieved. This was the autumn of 'The Dance

---

[ee] At their first meeting were the artists Y. M. and S. M. Bondi, Zhenya Ivanov, Pyast, B. N. Solov'ev, Verigina, her husband N. P. Bychkov, and Lyubov' Dmitriyevna—but not Blok, who was obviously considered rather above such an amateur debating society.

[ff] Just a quarter-century later, this poem elicited Anna Akhmatova's magnificent re-sponse: 'He's right. Again the lamp, the chemist's ...'.

of Death' (III. 36–8), but also of the idyllic 'Dreams' (III. 226–7)[gg] and a variety of other poems.

It was on 29 December 1912 that Blok wrote the important poem 'To the Muse' (*K muze*, III. 7–8) with which he eventually chose to open the *Third Volume* of his collected verse. This poem has frequently been cited to demonstrate the demonic, deeply amoral source of his inspiration,[23] yet, in the context of the poet's life, it rather confirms what he had tried to tell Tereshchenko about art and religion earlier that same autumn. It celebrated the creative act as a moment of passion, briefer than gipsy love, and began:

> There is warning of doom and perdition
>   In the depths of your secret refrains
> And the curse of commandments most sacred
>   And of joy—set at naught and made vain.
>
> And so powerful a spell of seduction ...
>   I have heard, and I would not deny,
> That your beauty brought down the great angels
>   To serve you from out of the sky.
>
> Are you evil, or good? All—from yonder,
>   Far beyond every bound I can tell:
> But for some   you are Muse, inspiration.
>   And for me—you are torment and hell....
>
> (III. 7–8)

Blok's mother was so affected by her son's unhappiness and Lyuba's determined pursuit of her own interests, that she actually thought this poem was about her 'elemental' daughter-in-law—one of Aleksandra Andreyevna's rare misjudgements. The poem is about poetry, not about a woman. Lyuba, moreover, figures in Blok's verse as a human being or as a religious force ('the inexpressible'). She is never 'demonic'—never altogether confined to the 'country' of his art. Having been a near-incarnation, she had become a comrade:

> Look at me. I am not turning
> To hide my face from you in shame;
> I stand amidst the burnt-out wreckage
> All scorched by the eternal burning
> Of the infernal flame.
>
> But where are you? Ah—do not tarry
> For you no star now shines ahead

[gg] See vol. I, 143n.[22]

Nor yet for me. Come soon, then, comrade,
Fellow pilgrim through this valley
Of bitter toil that we must tread.

(III. 84)

Lyubov', however, was not ready to resign herself to the role of comrade. It was a grief to him that she could not or would not any longer share his 'complex and rich life' but still longed for some fulfilment of her own. She was bored living in his shadow, bored by his 'rejection' of a world she still found full of promise. Blok saw there were flowers in her room whenever she returned, made the sign of the cross over her bed every night while she was away, wrote letters that would have melted the heart of the Snow Queen, bought her sweet cakes and read her his poetry; but when she was with him he immediately became happily absorbed in his work and she was alone and idle again for hours at a stretch. And that winter, he was very busy, not only with himself and his art but with 'literature', no longer thought of as a means to earn a living but as a service.

9

From the friendship with Tereshchenko had sprung the idea of Sirin, a publishing house that was to be the Petersburg equivalent of Moscow's Grif, Skorpion, and Musaget. Tereshchenko and his sisters had the money, vitality, and enthusiasm. Blok and Remizov agreed to provide the inside knowledge of the literary scene. To bear the brunt of the work and to balance the 'aesthetes', the literary critic and sociologist Ivanov-Razumnik, author of a solid multi-volume *History of Russian Social Thought*, was invited to act as secretary to the editors. Blok spent several hours a day with Razumnik and Remizov talking over practical plans and more abstract questions such as the relationship of decadence to Symbolism, of individualism to objective truth.

Another time-consuming but for a short while absorbing project, involving a rather wider group of literati, was the new liberal (Kadet) newspaper *Russkaya Molva*. Ariadna Tyrkova-Williams[hh] was the moving spirit, and she asked Blok to prepare a report on 'Art and the Newspaper' (v. 473–9, 763) as a guide-line to the paper's policy on art criticism and to help select correspondents. At the first editorial meeting, at eleven o'clock in the evening of 21 November 1912, Blok read his report in the presence of a congenial gathering:

[hh] Parliamentary correspondent of the Kadet party.

Ariadna and her husband, the Englishman Harold Williams; Remi-zov; A. P. Ivanov (Zhenya's brother, the art critic); Knyazhnin; Pyast; N. P. Ge; and the poet-critic B. A. Sadovskoy. Rather to his surprise, Blok found himself 'turning into some sort of leader'.

To both the Williamses, Blok stood out among his colleagues as a man exceptionally dedicated and assured,[24] but his 'report' con-fronted them with a dilemma. While the reflections on art and the newspaper were unexceptional, there was a subsection of quite con-siderable length in which the poet specifically attacked the largely Jewish 'Odessa' school of literary journalism. Blok considered the Odessa critics—even Korney Chukovsky whom he later came to value—as slick in their judgements, 'yellow' in their morality, and inveterate misusers of the Russian language. Taken to task for anti-Semitism, Blok argued with a virulent acumen worthy of his father that Russians had no sense of self-preservation and that the news-papers and periodical press were becoming increasingly dominated by non-Russian elements. Blok's point of view did not accord with the liberal principles of *Russkaya Molva* and the editors persuaded him to omit the anti-Odessa section when they printed his article.[ii] His feelings were ruffled and the incident served to confirm him in the conviction that it was not his calling to express himself through newspapers or in conjunction with any political party. But the prob-lem of how to reach and touch a wider readership remained.

To Lyuba, Sirin and *Russkaya Molva* represented dry-as-dust committee work. Her thoughts were elsewhere, even when she was with him in Petersburg, and this Blok resented, almost as intensely as her physical absences: 'And through all this—all day long—exasperation with my darling, she does not listen, does not hear, can-not help and doesn't want to and, it seems, is not thinking about me at all, or about what is mine, or what is Ours' (VII. 188). It was her 'last infatuation', Lyuba pleaded. Blok had himself been the one to suggest she should go to live with Kuzmin-Karavayev in the first place. She must be allowed to get it out of her system, to live for some time and to rest with her lover (VII. 189, entry for 2 December 1912). How well she had assimilated Blok's teaching on the tem-porary nature of passion, its comparative unimportance! She did not want to leave her husband altogether, for was not love some-thing quite different from such temporary aberrations of the flesh?

[ii] Reading the original text in full in the Collected Works one rather wonders what all the fuss was about, for any direct offence to Jewish opinion could have been removed by deleting one sentence (v. 478).

Towards evening my darling told me: 'If you abandon me, I shall perish there (with that man, in that milieu). If you renounce me, my life will be broken. This phase of my love for you is demanding. Help me—and that man.'

All this was tender as the downy, snowy day today and the snowy evening. . . .

(VII. 211, entry for 22 January 1913)

Though indifferent to her husband's civic commitments, Lyubov' was still keenly interested in his art, and particularly in *The Rose and the Cross*[ii] which, on her first return in November, Blok had decided to rework completely, breaking the original unity of place 'which will tighten up the action and differentiate between the individual scenes' (VII. 181). The play was becoming more and more centred on the unhappy Bertrand, and Lyuba suggested that, at the end, he might build a chapel dedicated to the Mystic Rose. Blok considered the suggestion but rejected it as 'too pretty'.

Tereshchenko was upset when he heard Blok was to rework the play and, on leaving for abroad, instructed him to telegraph him as soon as the new version was completed. A week after Lyuba's second return, on 7 January, Blok wrote:

A miserable day—ill. Have been writing almost all day. Quarrelled with Lyuba. Now it's all finished. Only one or two more 'strokes of the brush' and Izora's monologue with the ghost. Last thing at night I read it all to Lyuba, she is pleased with it and so am I. Reconciliation.

(VII. 205)

Into the lines which he gave to the dying Bertrand, the poet had written a benediction, saved from over-sweetness by the doom-laden counterpoint of premonition:

> Be happy, Izora:
> A beautiful boy is
> Better than cloudy and terrible dreams:
> May your heart find
> Sweetness and calm
> From its storms!
> O, how far from you, Izora,
> Is the gift of the fairy
> That faded cross!—
> Flower, then, rose

[ii] The story of the writing of *The Rose and the Cross* has been tactfully and feelingly told by R. D. B. Thompson in his article 'The Non-literary Sources of *The Rose and the Cross*'.[25] Only the fact that he did not have access to all the letters which passed between Blok and his wife at this time has made it worth retelling at length.

In the promised garden,
Scent the air of the world while
The sacred spring flows over it!
Keep, Izora,
Your young soul
Against dark days....
I hear, I hear,
How the waves clamour,
The ocean roars,
The cross burns high above the storm,
A summons to brave the snowy night.

(IV. 242)

Two days later, the promised telegram was dispatched to Tereshchenko and, on 19 January 1913, the play was really finished.

In February, Lyubov' left for Zhitomir again and Blok remained
in Petersburg 'with some kind of firm ground under my feet in the
thought that we shall go quietly away together this summer to have
a holiday abroad' (VII. 230). In the interim, she wrote from a pension
(suitably called The Lull [*Zatishiye*]) in Zhitomir. The first letter of
17 February was reassuring: '... I love you, Lala, I wish that fate
would stop playing with me soon, I want to be with you and not
to be parted.' But gradually, a warm, lazy content suffused the dull
pink paper, the round, firm hand, the gentle, affectionate words. She
hopes he is walking in the sun, that his work is going as he likes;
she is taking slimming baths, wearing her new spring suits, looking
at the early blossom of the South, reading French novels (letters of
1 and 8 March).

Lalka my dearest, I got your letter, you write you are sad. Darling, darling,
Lala, I so want you not to be sad because of me, to think lightly of my
absence. You know that I will come back and that we'll spend the summer
together, as comrades. I think of you all the time; this morning I read *The
Night Watches* and, of course, wept my heart out. My Lala, but I won't
come back yet. I keep meaning to write little letters, but there's no calendar,
no newspapers, and I don't notice how more days slip by than I had intended....

she wrote to him on the 20th.

Blok hated these letters. It seemed to him that she was 'forgetting
everything in the world', asleep, even dead.... He wrote and told
her so, but she answered only:

... I think that, in essence, you understand how I am here and why and
that you wrote about 'forgetting all the world and death' because you were
feeling very miserable yourself at that particular moment. You know that

A. M. Remizov's view of Blok (*above*) and Andrey Bely, in drawings made after their deaths.

if I felt it was my *duty* to be with you, I could break up everything of my own and come to you because I love you and I can forget myself for your sake. But you love me too and you yourself gave me leave to come here and I am so 'grateful' (stupid word, but I feel it with all my heart).... It is not oblivion, nor death, nor, in the very least, is it a betrayal of you, because it is something good in itself and I feel closer to you here than in all the last years I have been with you all the time.[26]

In the face of a storm of arguments and reproaches, she insisted on her right to remain in Zhitomir until they were to go abroad together in May. It must be said, however, that by this time she knew Blok very well. When he was really desperate, she had come; when he could not do without her, she was there. Throughout this winter, however, he had been steadily regaining his physical health and mental equilibrium. Love letters and flowers rained down upon the new flat and Blok was—in spite of his complaints of loneliness—surrounded by friends, extremely busy, and writing superb poetry.

10

Above all, however, he was absorbed in testing out people's reactions to his play. The first reading, to his mother, aunt, and a friend, met with general approval, although Aleksandra Andreyevna was shocked at her son's leaving Izora 'to the mercy of the page'.[27]

The Tereshchenkos, Mikhail Ivanovich and his sisters, were so complimentary that Blok noted gratefully: 'God knows what they didn't say to me. They liked it very much and you could tell it was genuine' (VII. 212, entry for 29 January 1913).

On 31 January, he risked a reading to a wider circle in the flat of Aleksey Remizov,[kk] who kept saying 'Very sad, very sad'; then, on 3 February, he assembled quite a company in his own home. Aleksandra Chebotarevskaya, Sologub's sister-in-law and a distant rela-

---

[kk] The hunch-backed, half-blind, poverty-stricken, and utterly genuine Remizov (cf. vol. I, pp. 196 ff.) was one of the few writers of stature of whom Blok was consistently and evenly fond. From the spring of 1912 they had spent much time together, co-operating on various literary projects, and Blok was always struck by his colleague's extraordinary defencelessness. On Holy Saturday 1912, he saw people tormenting a blinded rat and, remembering Remizov's story of how he had rescued his little daughter, now living with relatives in the country, from a fire at night, Blok wrote: 'Remizov is sometimes like that rat. He was like him, most probably, when he had to carry Natasha in his arms half the night, rocking her to sleep, and then ran out from the fire in nothing but his underclothes and the sewing woman threw a silk jacket round his shoulders (in 22 degrees of frost at night in the provinces).... All that is all one, all one: paschal, "Holy Easter", oh my God!' (VII. 136–7).

tive of Lunacharsky's, declared the play 'a contribution to Russian literature'; Meyerhold said Blok had never before written anything for the stage with such command of his medium; Zhenya Ivanov was so moved he had to go behind the curtain to recover.... 'Again it produced a powerful impression—A good evening' (VII. 214), Blok noted and, immediately after the reading, 'At last I have the impression I have written something genuine' (VII. 213).

There was no more talk of opera or ballet, but opinions differed as to whether or not the play should be staged. Verigina, identifying Gaetan's marvellous songs with the hollow ring of Blok's own voice, thought it should not. Meyerhold wanted it for the Aleksandriynsky Theatre; another producer, A. P. Zonov, for a new enterprise of his own: 'Our Theatre'. Later, Blok was to receive offers from Vakhtangov, then on the threshold of his career, and from other Moscow theatres. As with *The Song of Fate*, however, he wanted only one producer: Stanislavsky. And he wanted to see Stanislavsky in the part of Bertrand.

Before submitting the play to the Moscow Art Theatre, he tried it out once more at a public reading before seventy-odd 'cold subscribers to *Novoye Vremya*'. 'Inwardly I fought hard and I think I won,' he wrote to Lyubov', stimulated and triumphant. 'I think that yesterday I was a living man among the dead. Yes, for the moment I am still on the right track' (VIII. 414, letter of 5 April 1913). Aleksandra Andreyevna, whose presence, he said, helped him considerably, described the occasion to Maria Pavlovna:

Sasha's reading took place in an atmosphere of patent leather slippers, white carnations, and all the dreadful hallmarks of sophisticated dissipation. Painted women's faces, evening dresses, smiles. We simple people who look for the resurrection of the dead[ll] shrank together in misery.

I was full of doubts, and Remizov, too, I think. Sasha cut right through that contaminated atmosphere with his verses about the cross blazing above the whirlwind, about joy that is suffering....[28]

This was probably the last moment of pure satisfaction Blok obtained from *The Rose and the Cross*.

When Stanislavsky brought his theatre to Petersburg for the Easter season, Blok invited him to hear his play in the presence of Aleksey Remizov 'and no one else' (VIII. 415, letter of 19 April 1913). Stanislavsky put him off at the last moment—he had a cold—then kept him on tenterhooks for several days, with the result that, when he came, Blok read badly. The reading was over by about six o'clock

---

[ll] Deliberate quotation from the Creed.

on the afternoon of 27 April and Remizov left shortly after, abandoning the poet and the producer to a nightmare discussion which lasted until nearly midnight.

... the whole action had seemed monotonous and grey to him, he had lost the thread. When I began to tell him everything in detail (in much simpler, coarser words) he at once understood. The conversation went like this. First I began to tell him that Bertrand is 'a man', Gaetan 'a genius', what Izora is really like (why she is a 'seamstress'). Then he gave me a detailed account of the basis of the courses he was conducting in his studio in order to approach the play from that angle.

Stanislavsky told Blok all about his theory of relaxed muscles within a circle, which reminded the poet of nothing so much as theosophical exercises, and of the way he trained his actors to observe the psychological reactions of chance-met people in the street. None of this seemed to have much to do with *The Rose and the Cross*. Blok, in his turn, launched into a detailed explanation of the development of Bertrand's psychology. Stanislavsky, constantly apologizing for the coarseness of his imagination, took fire from the poet's hesitant description, 'and here,' Blok wrote wryly,

is what the two of us worked out together.

Once upon a time there lived Bertrand, *a man brought low* by circumstance. This we should show at once by having Alissa ordering him to throw out the slops, almost a chamber pot. A *knight* lays down his sword and shield and carries out a bucket. 'Give me that, as an actor, give me a scene like that,' Stanislavsky kept on repeating at such moments.

After a number of suggestions in a similar vein ('That's what the public pay their money for, that's the way you'll really get them'), Stanislavsky concluded: 'You ... hide the most effective moments from the spectator (and the actor), the parts where Bertrand can be shown at his full stature, where Bertrand becomes a *part*, even a plum part like Hamlet or Don Quixote. ...' After this extraordinary conversation, Stanislavsky took his leave, murmuring that he feared his advice might do more harm than good, and that it was time 'for us producers to learn how to talk to authors'.

Blok remained unshaken in his desire for the Moscow Art Theatre or nothing, but for the present he decided to settle for publishing rather than staging the play:

I doubt if I could make concessions to all these 'theatrical' (actor's and public's) demands as they are put by Stanislavsky. I doubt now, too, whether one *should* 'popularize', say things right out, dot the i's. Perhaps it is not I who write in a way so hard to understand, but the theatre and

the spectator who are not yet ready for my 'laconism'? I'll think about
it. . . .

(VII. 240–5, entry for 27 April 1913)

Tereshchenko, who took the fate of the play very much to heart
and wanted to see it on the stage, had been dialling Blok's number,
6–12–00, all that evening, but the poet had disconnected his telephone.

After Stanislavsky left I rang him and told him as best I could what had
happened, very tired. He was most indignant.

True, Stanislavsky did say himself that he had become slow and stiff on
the uptake. I had the impression that he had aged a great deal, that he was
tired. . . . Still, all this is sad. I've been writing for a year, living in and for
the play, it has integrity. Then along came a sensitive man in whom I have
faith, who has done great things (Chekhov in the Art Theatre) and *understood nothing, 'accepted' nothing and felt nothing*. Once more, this means I
must go on writing 'in seclusion'. . . .

(VII. 245–6)

II

In a review of *The Rose and the Cross*, Blok's colleague Ivanov-
Razumnik called him an eternal outsider 'in a glassy desert', and with
the failure of his play to please Stanislavsky, it did indeed seem that
both his attempts to find objective form and to reach a wider
public—*Retribution* and *The Rose and the Cross*—had proved stillborn.

True, Blok's lyric poetry was more and more popular and people
wrote to him for advice—other writers and readers; often people
in despair. Such letters he would answer conscientiously and
thoughtfully, sometimes even succeeding in cheering himself.

True again, his position *vis-à-vis* Sirin was an enviable one. Not
only had they promised to republish his own Collected Works as
soon as the Musaget three-volume edition was sold out,[mm] plus a
fourth volume of plays,[nn] but he had persuaded Tereshchenko to put
out Andrey Bely's *Travel Notes* (*Putëvye Zametki*), and his *Petersburg*
(which Tereshchenko himself did not particularly like), as well as
the collected works of Bryusov, Sologub, Remizov, Rozanov, and
Balmont.

[mm] Blok had received *carte blanche* to transfer publication of his works to Sirin from
Metner, who had replaced Kozhebatkin as secretary to Musaget.

[nn] These projects did not come off because Sirin closed down at the beginning of the
1914 war.

Blok's drawing of the Brittany coast, with lighthouses, 1911.

мое окно и мой балкон
столовая окно.

The hotel where Blok and his wife stayed at Guéthary, on the Basque coast, in 1913.
Blok has marked his and Lyubov' Dmitriyevna's windows.

Nikolay Alekseyevich Kluyev.

Blok in 1913.

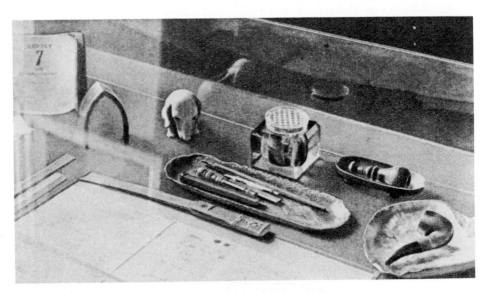

Objects on Blok's writing desk.

Yet, Blok still felt isolated. The old alliances lay in ruins all about him. What was left of *Mir Iskusstva*, in whose eclectic pages he had first read Merezhkovsky, and first heard and recognized the apocalyptic voice of Andrey Bely, had now become the Ballets Russes. Tereshchenko, who had met Diaghilev while abroad, told Blok things that scared him:

Diaghilev's cynicism and his strength. There is something frightening about him, he does not *walk alone*: art, he says, is a stimulus to sensuality; there are two geniuses: Nijinsky and Stravinsky. He asked Mikhail Ivanovich about my play.—A very black impression, a terrible epoch, reality has far outstripped imagination. Dostoyevsky's, for instance. Svidrigaylov is an innocent child. Everything about Diaghilev is terrible and significant, including his 'active homosexuality'.

(VII. 230, entry for 12 March 1913)

The *Novyy Put'* group (the Merezhkovskys and Filosofov) now interested Blok more as people than as writers. Their passionate concern for what was going on in Russia and the rest of the world commanded his sympathy and respect, yet they had found his article for *Russkaya Molva* anti-democratic whereas it had been aimed not against democracy, but against vulgarity. Vyacheslav Ivanov, whom he had studiously avoided all the preceding winter, had now gone to live in Moscow. Bely was abroad, absorbed in Steiner's anthroposophy. Chulkov Blok seldom saw; Zhenya Ivanov, 'the best of men', was not a creative artist and, moreover, was inclining to theosophy; Meyerhold, in spite of several serious talks, Blok persisted in regarding with deep suspicion; Sergey Gorodetsky had gone over to the Poets' Workshop group, who were now known as 'Adamists' or 'Acmeists', and this same Acmeism was a barrier between Blok and the increasingly influential Nikolay Gumilev, whose theories he regarded with scepticism, considering him not a true innovator but very much of the old school, overburdened with good taste and culture 'from Shakespeare—to Théophile Gautier'.

As to the Futurists, they were openly hostile. Led by David Burliuk and Mayakovsky, they demanded, as Blok himself carefully noted, 'the emancipation of Russian literature from the muck in which she has been left sitting by Andreyev, Sologub, Blok, etc....' (VII. 233, entry for 25 March 1913). In spite of their aggressive manners, however, Blok preferred them to the Acmeists, finding them 'more earthy and alive'. Khlebnikov, he suspected, was a poet of significance. Igor Severyanin, 'God preserve him', had a 'real, fresh, childish talent' but lacked 'a theme'. Burliuk had 'a fist' (VII. 232).

Mayakovsky he was beginning to take very seriously. But to these younger poets Blok was not a fellow artist searching, as they were themselves, for forms adequate to express twentieth-century life, but rather an established idol it was their vocation to topple.

As for the two writers with whom the Futurists had so cavalierly coupled him, Leonid Andreyev and Fyëdor Sologub, Blok had little in common with either. Andreyev he had admired during his own 'mystic anarchist' phase, but now that writer's strident pessimism struck him as self-indulgent and rather foolish, almost a caricature of that unbridled chaos which he was struggling to exorcise from his own poetry. Sologub, to whom Blok had also been closest in the period of *The Snow Mask*, had 'married and shaved his beard' and lost his old mordant hatred of life. At a moment when Blok was buckling himself into heavy armour, Sologub had become muted and sad, softened by late and short-lived happiness.

The course to which he had held since the autumn of 1911 was proving lonely and unrewarding, but Blok found his isolation bracing:

It is time to untie my hands, I am not a schoolboy any longer. No more symbolisms—I am alone, I answer for myself, *alone*—and I still have it in me to be younger than a great many 'middle-aged' young poets, weighed down by progeny and acmeism.... The longer I live, the more I 'establish myself' 'as an artist'. There is an instrument inside me, a good piano, the strings are taut ... the thing is that a *very* good instrument (an artist) is *hard-wearing*, and a few hard kicks only go to strengthen the strings.
                    (VII. 216–17, entries for 10 and 11 February 1913)

His powers were at their height, and he knew it. He was making simple and staggering discoveries which he was too sophisticated to publish abroad: that art is bound up with *morality*, for instance (VII. 224, entry for 23 February 1913), but that it was art critics, not artists themselves, who had thought up the concept of satire, of 'flaying' the vices of society: 'To *depict* a man, you have to come to love (i.e. get to know) him. Griboyedov loved Famusov, I'm quite sure, and more sometimes than he loved Chatsky. Gogol loved Khlestakov and Chichikov; Chichikov—most especially' (VII. 218, entry for 11 February 1913).

These were new truths for Russian modernism, which had made its début as a reaction against too much morality in literature, and which had from the beginning shown a marked tendency to exclude sentiment of any kind, but Blok had returned to the concepts of good and evil, love and hatred, via his own discovery. He hated the Ter-

rible World all right, but he loved it too, as he loved Count Archimbaut in *The Rose and the Cross*, as he loved the drunken colonel who
had pestered him in the park, as he had—on occasion—loved his own
father. People all around him were talking of a revival of democracy,
but Blok perceived only a lowering of standards, a growing vulgarity.

People are no longer even pretending they understand symbolism, or enjoy
it. Soon they will stop pretending they like art. Art and religion are dying
in the world, we are on our way down to the catacombs, held in utter
contempt. The most cruel kind of persecution is complete indifference.
But—thank God—there will be fewer of us as a result, and our quality will
improve.

(VII. 231, entry for 22 March 1913)

Nevertheless, the last two years had brought him much pain and
many disappointments. As always at the end of the winter season,
he was tired and stale. He spent the month of May riding the roller-
coaster ('I stayed till it closed down. 21 trips in one day') (VII. 249),
brooding over Stanislavsky, undergoing a third course of treatment
and injections—and waiting for Lyuba. By the time she came, on
26 May, he was too apathetic to care and on 29 May he gave up
keeping a regular diary.

On 12 June they left for Paris and remained abroad until the beginning of August.

CHAPTER VI

The Nightingale Garden

(Summer 1913 – Summer 1914)

> Oh Lord, I humbly accept this love also, the second and the
> last—for her and for me—which Thou hast given ...
>   (Note in Blok's hand, written 4–5 January 1921[a])

1

It was an unhappy, disunited couple that arrived in Paris. Blok took
a disgruntled look round the Louvre, tried the Parisian roller-coaster
(which he found rather tame after the Petersburg variety), mooched
about the city for almost a week, and, sipping milk and enveloped
in a powerful aroma of incense, contemplated a pleasing, misty Paris
from his favourite vantage-point outside Sacré Coeur. 'Paris', he informed Pyast, 'is indeed unique in all the world; I would say that
nowhere have I seen human beings so desperate, so like beasts at bay;
because of this all people seem better, somehow, and you can live
as you like, simply and splendidly, philistinely and not philistinely—
whatever you do, no one will take any notice' (VIII. 424).

The doctor had again recommended sea bathing and Blok decided
to take Lyuba on to the Pyrenees. After a wretched journey—they
balked at the price of a first-class sleeper and at that time you had
to sit up all night if you travelled second class on the Chemin de
fer de l'Est—they installed themselves at Guéthary in a decent pension with windows on the sea, eight miles or so from Biarritz.

There was some pleasure in the sight and smell of the ocean, but
it was several days before it was warm enough to bathe and their
own relationship was still stiff and strange. Divorce was in both their

---

[a] This note was preserved among Lyubov' Aleksandrovna Del'mas's papers. It was sent
to her by the poet's mother after his death.

minds, but they did not speak of it. It was not until they had been
ten days at the Hotel de la Plage that the storm broke in a long morning talk 'to the point of tears'. Nothing was decided, but they both
began to feel more comfortable together again and, in the evening,
Blok bought Lyuba a gift of roses.

They passed the time 'like other bourgeois' (Z.K. 195), eating and
sleeping, swimming and walking, watching the local carnivals and
the *guignol*, going for expeditions up into the hills, across the border
into Spain, on horseback to the mouth of the Adour. The bathing
was a little spoilt by the comic-postcard seaside atmosphere; hideous
men and women in pre-1914 bathing gear; having to change in wet,
sandy bathing huts. However, the Atlantic surf rolling straight in
from the open ocean was a new and exhilarating sensation. Blok also
enjoyed looking for shells and starfish and playing with crabs among
the rock pools, feeding them cigarette ends. On their way back to
the hotel from the beach, they toiled uphill past a villa standing in
its own garden down whose high stone walls cascaded roses and other
flowering plants. The narrow gate was always locked and the place
caught Blok's imagination. In the evening, Lyuba went early to bed
and Blok waded through Balzac's *Séraphita*, of which he enjoyed
only the first chapter, and reread *Coriolanus*.

His letters and notebooks give the impression that only a small
part of him was alive. He even had to pretend to himself, to while
away the dull meals at the pension, that he was interested in a beautiful Spanish lady he had nicknamed Perla del Oceano—but was too
honest to keep it up. He wrote more letters than usual when on holiday, waited impatiently for news from his mother, wrote often that
he wished he were at Shakhmatovo, ostentatiously reckoned the days
by the Russian Orthodox calendar: 'The Transfiguration', 'Elijah's
day', etc. Yet he was reluctant to leave the sea, 'as though a whole
great stretch of life were disappearing beyond return' (Z.K. 194).

Before they left Biarritz, the old impression that Europe had long
since forgotten her past glories was confirmed by an expedition to
the Pas de Roland 'which the French translate as "The Steps of
Roland" and I as "No Roland here" '.[1] Yet from Paris he wrote:
'We were very sorry to leave Biarritz.... The last day the sea was
cold, the waves were so rough you could neither swim nor keep
your feet standing. All that Spanish-French coast is a beautiful
"country".'[2]

In Paris, the Bloks—uncharacteristically—decided to refurbish
their wardrobes and went on a concentrated spending spree. 'I am
running round with my tongue hanging out buying trousers of every

sort and such-like trinkets..., ' Blok informed his mother.[3] They had one Sunday for sight-seeing and went to Versailles:

Everything about the eighteenth century, beginning with the proportions, is revolting to me, and so I found Versailles even more hideous than Tsarskoye Selo. We went back through the Bois de Boulogne, which was all trampled underfoot, for in democratic republics the bourgeois is allowed to graze and to dirty the ground where he will.

(VIII. 426)

Aleksandr L'vovich Blok, no doubt, would have heartily endorsed his son's valedictory assessment of the 'bourgeois freedoms' of Western Europe.

2

On their return to Russia, Lyubov' met up with her Terioki friends and plunged happily into the pre-season bustle of the last peacetime winter of theatrical St. Petersburg. Blok went down to Shakhmatovo—feeling, after all, much fitter for his holiday—to play charades with his aunt,[4] correct the proofs of *The Rose and the Cross* for Sirin, and to continue, half-heartedly, affectionately, and for the most part good-naturedly, his campaign to wean his wife from her devotion to the stage. Without success. Valya Verigina had plans to make a film with Lyuba ('I hope', Blok wrote minatorily from Shakhmatovo, 'that if you are asked to act anything indecent you will refuse', VIII. 427), and Meyerhold persuaded her to ask Blok for permission to stage his play:

Meyerhold begs and begs *The Rose and the Cross* for the Aleksandriynsky Theatre; both when we meet and on the telephone, hurrying me.... I don't know whether or not I should plead his cause with you, remembering the Aleksandriynka actors. But Meyerhold produces an excellent impression on me and on Valya: his stay in Paris has given him a new lease of youth and inspired him. He himself has begun to organize the studio that we were trying to get under way last year and has already found premises [at the Tenishev School] that we can have for nothing.... Lalalka—after all—let them put on *The Rose and the Cross*—it would be so good to see it on the stage. You'll never get a perfect production.[5]

Blok was unimpressed. 'I simply do not feel his existence as an artist,' he wrote of Meyerhold:

Don't think I'm writing with malice. No, it is just that my mind is waking up and many things are coming back into my head, only what does not

come back in the very least are all those old ideas about a 'new theatre'
or a crisis in the old theatre, that is the so-called difference between the
ideas of various fashionable producers, etc., etc. It's as if I'd seen all that
in my dreams when I was a child; first it was charming nonsense with mystic
overtones, then it was just plain nonsense, then all the producers wrote
books about it, which soon became thoroughly tiresome, and then—
honestly, all that is over and done with, the books and the 'experiments'
and the 'studios', and all that remains is the old division of people into those
with a head and a heart and without heart or head.

(VIII. 427, letter of 21–22 August 1913)

It seems more than probable that Blok's stubborn inability to 'see'
Meyerhold as an artist was bound up with his resentment of the great
director's influence on his wife. The men who had loved her—with
the exception of Andrey Bely ('whom I most probably hate')—he
did not recognize as rivals. But Meyerhold—without intending to,
without effort—was taking Lyuba away from Blok far more effectively than any Kuzmin-Karavayev, drawing her into a world of
sparkling make-believe and calculated effect that really was deeply
alien to her husband, whose whole being was now concentrated on
'restoring integrity to Russian life', on the problem of how to restate
simple ethical truths in a way so new, so exquisite, and so indirect
that people would feel they had rediscovered them for themselves.

It may be that I shall return to Petersburg quite soon after all. I don't feel
altogether easy in my mind. And you, that's the main thing, with your
Berdichevs[b] and your cinematographs; childish nonsense. I am afraid that
you're just drifting with the wind....

If you only knew how quiet and good it is here you would come. After
abroad one appreciates the genuineness of everything quite particularly.
I do not see the winter. I am afraid; the first thing to crop up when I come
back will be this question of Meyerhold and *The Rose and the Cross*; there
is no such question, it does not *exist*, there's the pity of it! And I'll have
to decide 'yes' or 'no' about something which is—a smoke and a phantom.
And so it is all the time with *town* life; stupid, wearisome, unanswerable,
exhausting and ... in the last analysis very, very unpleasant. What do you
think about it? But you won't understand anyway, your little head is full
of Berdichev and Valya....

So he ended the letter—crossly and rather unfairly—but added a
P.S. the following day: 'It's a rainy day today and all the trees are loving

[b] Blok uses Berdichev—a town in southern Russia—as an insulting synonym for Zhitomir. It was considered an archetype of Russo-Jewish provincialism and Chekhov makes
play with it in *Three Sisters*, when the drunken Chebutykin keeps on reading out
from the local newspaper—'And Balzac has got married in Berdichev'.

it. The Lord be with you, little Bu. If there are any letters (important ones) send them on. Better still, come yourself . . .' (VIII. 428).

Lyubov' yielded and came. She had made her film—one of the first attempts in Russia to shoot scenes for a non-documentary film outside the studio—but for technical reasons it was never screened. By 1 September, however, she was back again in Petersburg, busy with plans for the studio. A week later, Blok followed her.

3

The 1913–14 season began very much under the sign of Lyuba's studio. She and Blok quarrelled about it incessantly. Eventually he was, in part at least, disarmed by the unrelenting admiration of her friends. They persuaded him to take over editing the poetry section of their journal *Lyubov' k trëm apelsinam* (The Love of Three Oranges) which was an offshoot of this same studio, and to contribute his own poems.

The 'little labours and tiresome trifles' (III. 48) which occupied Blok's days that winter were similar to those of the previous season. Apart from the new *Lyubov' k trëm apelsinam*, he continued to be deeply involved in the affairs of Sirin and much in the company of Remizov, Ivanov-Razumnik, and the Tereshchenko family.

The season, which Blok noted was marked from the beginning by anger and mutual hostility among his own set, was shadowed by a crescendo of feeling about the Beylis case. Vasily Rozanov was banished from the Religious-Philosophical Society, after three painful sessions at the first of which he refused to resign voluntarily and at the second of which a quorum was not assembled (for the good reason that writers did not want to be placed in the position of voting either for or against his exclusion on the grounds of anti-Semitism). Blok, who had shared the general reluctance to strike a definite attitude on this issue, nevertheless now felt obliged to do so, attending both later sessions and voting for Rozanov's exclusion. The liberal intelligentsia's attitude to Rozanov, he thought, was similar to his Grandfather Beketov's to Dostoyevsky: a curious mixture of private admiration for the writer and public disapproval of the literary journalist. 'There is a whole abyss between the personal and the social,' he noted.

After this incident, a scandalous polemic broke out between Rozanov and Merezhkovsky which poisoned the literary atmosphere throughout the spring of 1914. Blok, in the general mood of irritation, discovered rather to his dismay that Merezhkovsky disliked him personally. He had always been closer to Hippius and Filosofov, with whom even now he remained on excellent terms, but had presumed himself welcome to the whole household. Yet to Merezhkovsky, who had often bored him and always been something of an enigma, he continued to listen with respect.

Throughout this uneasy season, Blok's dislike of the Acmeists increased, in inverse proportion to his admiration for Anna Akhmatova. That autumn he had met Akhmatova, at a poetry reading at the Bestuzhev Courses. Both had preferred the Courses to a far smarter gathering in honour of Paul Valéry: Blok, so he said, because he couldn't face having to make a speech in French.[c] To Akhmatova's confusion, she found she was scheduled to read her poetry immediately after Blok, who 'was already the most famous poet in Russia'.

'Aleksandr Aleksandrovich, I can't read after you.'

'Anna Andreyevna,' he replied on a note of rebuke, 'we are not tenors.'

After this incident, she called on the older poet to ask him to sign her own copies of his books. Blok was adept at true compliments. To this young—and beautiful—woman who had as yet published only one slim collection of verse,[d] he wrote simply in each volume: 'To Akhmatova—from Blok'. In the third volume he wrote the 'madrigal': 'Beauty is terrible—they'll tell you' (III. 143).[e]

Akhmatova in turn commemorated the visit in blank verse:

> I came to visit the poet
> Just at midday. On a Sunday.
> The quiet in the spacious room ...
> Beyond the windows, frost.
>
> And a raspberry sun shone
> Above the tattered, blue-grey smoke ...
> How unclouded the gaze of my silent
> Host, fixed attentively on me.
>
> He has the kind of eyes
> That everyone ought to remember
> But that for me, a cautious woman,
> It were better not to look into.

[c] He also heartily disliked the French Society which he considered a stronghold of the 'literary bureaucracy'.

[d] *Vecher* (Evening) was published in 1912.

Yet I remember the conversation.
The smoky midday on that Sunday
In the tall grey house, not far from
The sea gates of the river Neva.[7]

That same season, Anna Akhmatova presented Blok with her second collection, *Chëtki* (The Rosary), inscribed 'From you anxiety came to me/And the ability to write verses' (*Ot tebya prikhodila ko mne trevoga/I umen'e pisat' stikhi*), which confirmed him in his opinion of her quality. Aleksandra Andreyevna even hoped for a romance:

I am always hoping that Sasha might meet and fall in love with a woman of profound, unquiet spirit, and so of tenderness ... and there is a young poet, Anna Akhmatova, who is stretching out her hands to him and might be prepared to love him. He turns away from her although she is beautiful and talented; only she is sad. And he doesn't like that.[8]

Fate, as so often in Blok's own poetry personified by a train, swept Anna Akhmatova past him and out of his everyday life, though he was not quite so oblivious of her arrogant beauty as his mother had supposed. That summer, as in a vivid dream, they met again:

At the beginning of July I was returning home through Moscow. In Moscow I took the first mail train going in my direction. I was smoking on the open space at the back of the carriage. Somewhere, on an unfamiliar, empty platform, they threw out a bag of mail. Unexpectedly, Blok seemed to rise up out of the earth before my astonished eyes. I cried out 'Aleksandr Aleksandrovich'. He looked round and, since he was not only a great poet but a great master of the tactical question, asked: 'Who are you travelling with?' I just had time to answer: 'Alone'. The train moved on.[e]

4

Blok may have been 'the most famous poet in Russia' for the narrow circle grouped about the Tower, but the things he considered really important (the completion of *Retribution* and the success of *The Rose and the Cross*) continued to elude him. The publication of his play in October 1913 was an anticlimax. It aroused scarcely any comment in the press and several people whose opinion he valued (Poliksena Sergeyevna Solov'eva; Z. N. Hippius) saw no merit in it. It had

---

[e] Anna Andreyevna recorded this anecdote for television. In the voice of a dowager duchess graciously receiving a belated tribute, she continued, 'Now, fifty-one years later, I open Blok's notebook for 9 July 1914 and read: "Mama and I went to look over the sanatorium at Podsolnechnoye. My devil tempts me.—Anna Akhmatova on the mail train." '[9]

come out at an inauspicious moment when the air was already charged with rumours of war and the strident voices of the Futurists were capturing what little attention people had left for art. The public passed by Blok's delicately painted 'Twelfth-Century Chapel' without a second glance, and it may be that the play has yet to be fully appreciated, or successfully staged.

Meanwhile the Futurists, in spite of their hostility to Blok and his generation, continued to interest him. He saw *The Tragedy of Vladimir Mayakovsky* and was impressed by the democratic, urban vigour of the author's verse. Even the campaign against traditional literary values—if it did not exactly meet with his approval—at least obtained a sympathetic hearing:

But what if ... we are being taught to *love* Pushkin again *in a new way* not by Bryusov, Shchëgolev, Morozov, etc., but by the Futurists. They abuse him and in so doing they come closer to him *in a new way. I felt that while rereading* Onegin.... Abuse in the name of the new is not at all the same thing as abuse in the name of the old, even though it is not yet clear what the new will be like whereas the old is great and known. Even if only because abuse in the name of the new is more *difficult*, more of a responsibility.

(*Z.K.* 198)

Blok was even interested enough to attend a lecture by the Italian Futurist Marinetti, but made no comment on it and declined an invitation to hear him a second time.*f*

Indeed, his notebooks for the 1913–14 season are full of functions which he did not attend. 'I don't go to previews', 'I shall go another time', were his comments on invitations to two exhibitions. He drifted in and out of lectures without waiting for the end, avoided anniversaries and *jours-fixes* and jealously guarded the inward concentration that was becoming more and more essential to his art. It was in December this winter that, in one of his best-known poems, he formulated just what this concentration meant to him:

The Artist

In the heat of the summer, the blizzards of winter,
The days of your marriages, funerals, feasts,
I wait, for a faint, never-heard-before ringing
To pierce my black boredom—a sudden relief.

Hush now, it comes. And with ice-cold attention
I wait here to seize, overpower, and to slay

f Marinetti lectured on 1 and 4 February 1914 in the hall of the Kalashnikov Stock Exchange.

As—spinning out under my sharp-eyed expectance—
The tenuous thread shudders on and away....

A wind from the sea? Or fair birds of good omen
Sing in the leaves? Or time—stopped at last?
Or is it a fluttering snowstorm of blossom
Shook down from the trees? Or an angel flown past?

Hour upon hour—world significance bearing,
The sounds ever broadening, movement and light.
Past locked with the Future—eye to eye staring.
The present—as nothing. Regret—put to flight.

Then, at the last, on the brink of conception
Of forces unguessed and a world newly made—
The poet is struck by the old malediction ...
His reason intensifies—then kills it dead.

I build a cold cage to enclose in captivity
My light-feathered bird that was all joy and liberty.
The bird who was trying to draw the grave's sting,
The bird who came flying salvation to bring.

Here is my cage—see, the steel bars are heavy,
But they gleam like pure gold in the evening glow.
There in his ring sits the bird—once so merry—
And sings by the window and rocks to and fro.

The wings have been clipped and the songs sung—so often.
Does it please you to stand by the sill in the sun?
The songs give you pleasure? But I, in exhaustion,
Wait, bored as before, for a new one to come.

(III. 145–6)

Verses. Verses. *Stikhi. Stikhi.* This is a frequent entry in Blok's notebooks for 1913 and 1914. He was writing almost as freely as in his youth, but with incomparably greater art.

The theme of this poetry—whether fiercely erotic, desolate, or laden with foreboding—is a theme of loneliness. The poet is a man who walks apart and looks with tired, omniscient eyes on a crazed world; a weak man, shaken by fears and sicknesses and passions who, through no merit of his own, has been burdened with a terrible responsibility of knowledge. In his own dubious way an ascetic, who uses the word 'fasting' to convey the idea of that 'spiritual diet' he now considers essential to the serious artist and who cultivates 'wakefulness of heart'; a man almost the other side of death who retains reverence and pity for the living.

Yet Blok continued to feel that the 'secret fire' (III. 148) of his verses made him inwardly more alive than the society in which he moved. At the same time, he was aware of a similar 'secret fire' in his country, in Russia, for in her apparent changelessness lay the embryo of a future, rich and prosperous and joyful, hidden far beneath the surface of things, like the vast mineral wealth which had first captured his imagination when he read Mendeleyev at Shakhmatovo in the autumn of 1908. He considered the possibility of a play about 'a man of our time', 'a light man' with something of the gipsy about him, who finds coal on his family estate. But he could foresee no individual 'happy endings' and had laid his hero in an obscure grave 'with one woman to weep over him—and even she does not really know why she weeps' before he got beyond the sketchiest plans.[10] For Russia, however, there was more hope. In the autumn of 1913, it seemed to Blok as though her fate stood on a knife edge: between war and destruction on the one hand, unexampled growth and prosperity on the other.

In 'The New America', Blok heard and recorded, through the rising winds of war singing in her branches and the dry rustle of dead leaves about her crown, the majestic music of his country's roots: the chanting of her churches singing requiem upon requiem for the old, poverty-stricken Russia he knew and loved and, in triumphant counterpoint, the voice of her 'stone songs', the 'groaning of coal' and the 'iron ore roaring'.

But there was also another music, ancient and unwithstandable, singing in broken gusts and rushing eddies of the pity of things, of love that kills, and youth that passes, and peace eternally threatened:

> Dearest friend, even in this quiet household
>   The fever mounts apace.
> And I can find no rest in this quiet household
>   By the calm fireplace!
>
> The voices sing, the storm is calling colder,
>   I fear this cosiness ...
> And someone's eyes, dear friend, behind your shoulders,
>   Are full of watchfulness!
>
> And there behind your quiet shoulders, hazy
>   The great wings spread and thrill ...
> And fiery eyes full into my eyes blazing ...
>   The Angel of the Tempest—Azrael!
>
> (III. 286)[8]

[8] This poem is one of a cycle written in the autumn of 1913 entitled: *Of what the Wind Sings.*

5

This intense looking into the future was interrupted by the Tenishev studio's decision to stage *The Stranger* and *The Puppet Booth*. When Lyuba broke the news to him on 21 February 1914,[h] Blok's first reaction was one of irritation. The next day he wrote in his notebook:

Again I am in pain from everything to do with this *Meyerhold*, I own I can't help preferring 'healthy realism', Stanislavsky, and the Musical Drama. All that I *get* out of the theatre I get from there, whereas in Meyerholdia I strain and wither. Why do they love me? For the past and the present, I fear, not for the future, not for what I want.

(*Z.K.* 209)

Meyerhold, however, persisted in courting Blok's understanding and at last, during his work on *The Stranger*, achieved a breakthrough: 'At four o'clock Meyerhold was here—most beautiful. For the first time in my life I understood (he explained) what makes him tick' (*Z.K.* 213).

On the same day, 6 March, Lyuba, who had turned down the part of the Stranger herself on the grounds that it would not look well to have the author's wife in the leading role, was schooling the inexperienced but beautiful Ilyashenko for the part at their flat. Blok was drawn into the production in spite of himself. Yet still he resisted.

Having listed in detail the things he had disliked about Meyerhold's productions, he went on:

Contemporary naturalism is harmless, because it has *nothing to do with art*. . . . Modernism is poisonous, because it is *with art*.

A puppet theatre transferred to the stage of the Mariynsky Opera House is a *going back to the wild*, barbarity (not art).

In *Onegin* I like it when the heart is wrung by serfdom. I like the square wooden barrel to collect rainwater on the roof of the chemist's near the Plaza de Toros in Seville (Musical Drama *Carmen*). I am not distracted but helped by details. . . .

I very much like *psychology* in the theatre—and in general that things should be nourishing.

After I wrote all this down along came Meyerhold and after a boring argument suddenly found the words to tell me about himself and his work

---

[h] Cf. *Z.K.* 209. This is also the date Blok put the finishing touches to a kind of hymn of hate to Lyubov' that he had begun when she left him for the first time in 1908: 'What of it? Those delicate hands are so wearily twisted', which ends with Christ's words to Judas: 'What thou hast to do, do it quickly' (III. 46).

so that for the first time in my life I felt him as a living, feeling, loving
man....

(Z.K 214)

Possibly this relaxation of Blok's attitude to Meyerhold was made
possible by his interest in that very 'Musical Drama' which he here
mentions as an example of 'healthy realism'. He was falling in love
with 'Carmen', and was correspondingly less resentful of Lyuba's
late nights at the Brodyachaya Sobaka, of her constant absorption
in the affairs of the studio, and of those long evenings when insomnia
and loneliness drove him out into the streets of Petersburg:

> When by the throat the quiet anguish takes you;
>   No time to shout—or sigh.
> As though the night let loose on you all Hades,
>   The devil stopped your cry.
>
> You jump up and run out into the dark streets,
>   But there's no help in sight;
> Wherever you may turn, your empty eyes are darkened
>   And met and filled—by night.
>
> Above your head all night the wind goes moaning
>   High through the trolley wires;
> And, just to keep awake, the policeman hunts a frozen
>   Tramp from the roadside fire ...
>
> Then with the blanched dawn comes the longed-for tiredness
>   All things now seem the same ...
> But what of Conscience? Truth? or Life?—such trifles!
>   Come, surely—a fool's game?

(III. 48)

On 7 April, Blok attended the première of *The Stranger* at the
Tenishev studio:

At the first showing the play was not a success. Still, Blok was called out.
He forced himself to answer the call, with lowered eyes and compressed
lips, and the actors with their stuck-on noses, their exaggerated make-up,
gave him a joyous ovation, so that it seemed as though he were surrounded
by a brood of grotesque freaks. I ran into the wings and did my best not
to meet Blok again that evening.[11]

So Verigina, who was playing in *The Puppet Booth*, which formed
the second part of the programme, recalled the first night of the Blok
plays.

Quite out of keeping with Blok's hyperborean muse was Meyerhold's idea of getting a family of Chinese children to juggle with

knives in the interludes, as was the distribution of oranges by the actors during the interval. This atmosphere of Southern carnival was in complete and—at the first night—disastrous contrast to the frosty starlight of Blok's plays. There were, however, a few moments of magic: the décors for *The Stranger*, particularly the scene on the bridge and the curtain of starry snowflakes in the last act; and the work of the 'servants of the proscenium', in which Meyerhold himself took part, changing the scenery before the eyes of the public with smooth, grey stealth, like obsequious genii. There was one moment which made theatrical history, when the grey figures knelt down with lighted candles forming a line of living footlights reminiscent of the theatre of the eighteenth century.

Blok did not return to the theatre for two or three days; then one evening he came and sat quietly on the stairs between the rows of seats, side by side with the artist Yuriy Bondi. Suddenly, he too was caught by Meyerhold's theatrical wizardry, and after that he came every night. But he never agreed to Meyerhold's staging *The Rose and the Cross*.

In February 1914, Blok revised various fragments from the *Ur-Retribution*, his 'Warsaw Poem' of 1910 and 1911, making them into brief separate lyrics for the collection *Iambs* (III. 85–96). In a poem which was to become the introduction to this cycle (and his own unofficial epitaph, scribbled by an anonymous hand on the cross over his grave), he made the explicit declaration that not 'gloom' but 'light and goodness' was the secret source of his poetry. But it was another poem in this cycle which, perhaps, expressed more felicitously his feeling for life at that time:

> The earthly heart grows cold again,
> But full into the frost I fare
> To wastes unpeopled, yet preserve
> A love for people none may share.
>
> . . . . .
>
> So let them call: come, poet, turn
> Again to realms of warmth and rest
> No! Better perish in the storm.
> There is no comfort. Is no rest.
>
> (III. 95)

This, in brief, is the theme of *The Nightingale Garden*, a long poem the beginning and ending of which are set on the rocky Basque coast, the middle in the garden of the mysterious villa past which he and Lyuba had so often trudged on their way from the sea, in a fairyland of happy love where no human being may linger and expect to find his place in the world unchanged. This poem was begun in January 1914, but Blok worked on it for more than a year and it acquired, over that time, new dimensions of real experience. Now, finally committed to the unpeopled wastes and the rising storm, he was yet on the threshold of his last and happiest passion, for a woman whom it later seemed quite natural to him to describe as 'she who sings in the Nightingale Garden'.[i]

Lyubov' Dmitriyevna, in her memoirs, wrote that 'it took the sunny, dazzling *joie de vivre* of "Carmen" to overcome all the traumas and only with her did Blok discover the longed-for synthesis of the one and the other love ...'.[13]

Nothing in the poet's life was simple and uncomplicated, but this experience, long sought and perhaps no longer expected, was so vivid and summery as to make him forget—for a few short weeks— all his hard-won, tragic commitment to a wintry vocation.

> It was true, what my heart had just told me,
> And the wall was no barrier. But she
> Came, before I could knock, to set open
> The impassable gateway for me.
>
> Along the cool path, through the lilies
> The stream murmured softly of rest,
> And the nightingales' clamorous trilling
> Filled my ears. Stole the soul from my breast.
>
> And strange was the land of good fortune
> These embraces had opened to me ...
> And the clash of the gold bangles falling
> Rang more clear than I'd dreamt it could be.
>
> And drunk on a wine, full and golden,
> And caught in the flames' golden glow,
> I forgot the old road, steep and stony,
> And my poor comrade waiting below.

(III. 243)

When he shook off the enchantment—for, as Blok wrote in this same poem, it is not given to nightingale song to drown out the call of the sea—the woman whom his poet's imagination had installed as mistress of the enclosed garden followed after him: at a distance, undemanding, helpful and independent, so that, in the first week of the last year of his life, almost six years after they became lovers, he was to note wonderingly: 'Night of 4 to 5 January.

[i] Blok's inscription to Lyubov' Aleksandrovna Del'mas in her copy of the 1918 Alkonost edition of the poem. The original is lost but the inscription is well authenticated.[12]

Strange. Now she is entering into life—as though I can't *live* without her now.'[14]

<h1 style="text-align:center">6</h1>

Lyubov' Aleksandrovna Andreyeva-Del'mas was a professional singer, a fine mezzo-soprano with a scorching temperament, tawny eyes, red-gold hair and a voluptuous, graceful figure. She was mistress—on and off stage—of the now almost forgotten art of coquetry: the flashing eye, the toss of the head, the fluttering lashes. Unlike Lyubov' Dmitriyevna or Volokhova, she was emphatically not an intellectual. She kept Blok's letters until her death in 1969, resisting archivists, professors, and research students alike, and destroyed those passages which, as an old, old lady, she still considered were not for other eyes. 'You can't express yourself at all,'[15] Blok told her, and even one of his earliest love letters speaks of her 'sweet-scented letter written in ill-chosen words' ('I am a professional, can't help myself,' he apologizes).[16] In her brief unpublished reminiscences, it is not so much of Blok's personality or poetry that she writes as of the 'beautiful eyes with a blueness in them', the 'ashen curls with a touch of gold', the 'bold outline of the firmly-compressed lips', 'the determined, wise expression of the face' that was always 'penetrating, as though he saw right through to your soul'.[17]

In 1913, Del'mas, married to the successful operatic baritone P. Z. Andreyev and recently returned from an extended tour abroad, had been offered the part of Carmen at the Musical Drama Theatre, a part which she had long wanted to play and which she felt to be the final test of her abilities. Had she failed, she had been prepared to give up the stage, for her life—at the age of thirty-four—was in turmoil, her work did not satisfy her, and she was reaching out for she knew not what, 'a kind of inexplicable despair of ever finding my way'. 'Carmen was my baptism of fire,' she says of her career.

Blok saw her performance for the first time in the autumn of 1913, and was enchanted by it. On 12 January 1914, he went again, with his wife. A month later, he took his mother, expecting to see another actress in the part: 'Happily for me, Davydova was ill, and Andreyeva-Del'mas was singing. My happiness' (Z.K. 207), he noted. Astonished and excited to surprise in himself an emotional response far exceeding mere artistic admiration, he sent her roses and a letter. The long, heavy envelope impressed her before she opened it. The contents were calculated to delight and intrigue any actress:

I have now seen you play 'Carmen' for the third time, and my excitement grows each time. I know very well that I shall inevitably fall in love with you every time you appear on the stage. Not to fall in love with you—looking at your head, your face, your figure—is an impossibility. I think I might meet you, I think you might permit me to look at you, that perhaps you know my name. I am not a boy and I know this infernal torture of being in love.... I think you know this very well indeed, since you know Carmen *as you do* (I have never seen you in anything else—indeed, never seen you at all before this season). Well, and here I am buying postcards with your photograph (not in the least like you) as though I were a school-boy.... Your Carmen is quite special, very mysterious.

(VIII. 433–4)

After this he began to attend every performance—and she to expect the roses, the long envelope, the firm, black handwriting. On 2 March, Davydova, 'short-legged' and 'a slavish imitator', Blok noted sourly, was singing, but Del'mas was in the audience. Blok stared at her throughout the evening. It was a game of his to concentrate on people so that they felt his eyes on them and looked up: 'Just a game, like the games children play' (III. 43). Once or twice she turned in his direction and glowered with angry, tawny eyes 'like a lion behind bars' (III. 233). Blok lost his head completely: even the fact that she looked tired and cross and had a heavy cold only enhanced her charm for him that evening. He tried to follow her home but people gave him conflicting directions and he abandoned the pursuit. At the theatre, however, he had heard that she had played Carmen for the last time. In his next letter, he issued minute instructions in what poses from which moments of her performance she should be photographed, and signed 'Your admirer'.[18]

By coincidence, Del'mas lived in the same street as Blok, Offitser-skaya No. 53, flat 9. It did not take him many days to find out her address and telephone number and he took to haunting the pavement beneath her window. He made enquiries about her at a musical academy where she had once taught singing. One day, he saw her in the street, apparently absorbed in a hoarding. At the opera that evening—Wagner this time, not Bizet—a mutual acquaintance, at Blok's request, approached Del'mas and asked if he might introduce the poet to her. 'I was no drooping violet, but for some reason I suddenly felt shy, flapped my hands at him (as women do) and ran off, exclaiming: "No, no. I don't want to".' She left before the end of the performance.

... I had begun to wonder if it were not his steps I kept hearing behind me in the street, as though he were watching me, his wonderful eyes that were troubling me ...

Once, on my way home from the theatre, I met him again. Raising his hat, he followed me out of sight with those beautiful eyes with the blueness in them which have remained for ever in my memory.[19]

Now she knew his name she recalled having read some of his poetry and having been struck by the depths of its sadness: 'not a lucent sadness like Pushkin's', she adds penetratingly. She was flattered—and proud. On 26 March he declared himself, sending her the three volumes of his verse, accompanied by a respectful note that would have passed muster with the most jealous husband and was signed, as none of his letters heretofore had been, Aleksandr Blok.[20] The day before he had presented her anonymously with two poems from the *Carmen* cycle, the first of which, dated 4 March 1914, he had in fact almost completed after his first sight of her performance in October 1913, asking her to accept the dedication.[j] On 27 March he called and left more roses—and a polite message asking her to phone him. 'I got in very late, between one and two in the morning, and rang the number. A shy voice answered: "I want to see you, to make your acquaintance." We agreed to meet.'

They met at the opera, on 28 March, at the last performance of *Parsifal* for that season.

... Terribly nervous, all dressed up, of course, I waited for him on the staircase. I felt that this was He. Very youthfully, nervously, he ran up the stairs to me, kissed my hand and said nothing. I, too, said nothing, feeling that this was a great man. . . .

It was a wonderful, mysterious meeting. For a long time we were both shyly silent, we could not shake off our first awkwardness, it was hard to begin to talk properly, we wanted to study one another's faces down to the smallest detail. . . .[21]

There is something curiously genuine—and touching—in the awe-struck silence that fell between this bold, talented woman who had dreamt of herself as Carmen and the sophisticated, tempestuous poet who had fallen in love with her dream.

'But Sasha's fallen in love again, with Carmen,' wrote his mother in considerable exasperation in the same letter in which she sings the praises of Anna Akhmatova:

He has taken and fallen in love with her just like that, during the performances at the Musical Drama, in her part as Carmen. I saw her too. Very fine—as a singer and an actress. But now it's all sleigh-rides again, and expeditions and flowers. And whole days devoted to her. And again it is an elemental woman.[22]

---

[j] The letter, dated 22 March, was not delivered until the 25th. The poems were 'As the ocean colours change' (III. 277) and 'The angry glance of those light eyes' (III. 233).

Indeed, the cycle *Carmen* (III. 227–39) in which Blok celebrated his new passion was full of echoes of Bizet's opera. It was written between 4 and 31 March: six poems before they met; two on the day; two after. Blok was to write many other poems inspired by Del'mas,[k] but these demonic *Carmen* verses stand apart. Blok himself said that in March 1914 he had 'surrendered to the element no less blindly than in January 1907' (III. 474). The third such surrender was in 1918, when he wrote *The Twelve* and *The Scythians*.

The Carmen Blok had originally fallen in love with was not the successful singer, Lyubov' Aleksandrovna Del'mas, but the doomed gipsy woman who provokes her own death:

> The snowy spring is blowing wild.
> I look up from the book I'm reading ...
> O, dreadful moment, when she smiled
> Full into José's eyes, Zuniga's
> Hand held in hers, palm upward, and
> The flash of pearl, the mocking glance ...
> I have forgot my native land
> Drowned out in blood, for like a lance
> The low voice pierced my heart and I've
> Forgotten night, forgotten day,
> To hear her sing: *The price you'll pay*
> *To me for love shall be your life.*

> 18 March 1914
> (III. 231)

Even the rhythms are the rhythms of *Carmen*—though the 'snowy spring' is Petersburg, March 1914.

The last poem of the cycle ('important verses', Blok noted on the night of 31 March when he wrote them) is a purely demonic celebration of the Russian poet's discovery of his own feminine counterpart in the archetypal romantic figure of Mérimée's Spanish gipsy:

> No, never mine, nor anyone's, now, ever.
> That, then, has drawn me on through the abyss of days,
> Through the abyss of years, inevitable burden,
> This, then, is why I pay you court and sing your praise.

> *Here* is the fearful stamp of woman doomed and outcast,
> Behind the marvellous charm—how hard it is to see.

---

[k] Among these were 'The snowy Petersburg twilight' (III. 216); 'I remember the tenderness of your shoulders' (III. 369); 'That life is past' (III. 220); 'From one who is familiar with that clear hand' (III. 371); 'To begin with you turned all to jest' (III. 219); 'Scarcely again in deepest dreams' (III. 375); and 'Brought to Judgement' (III. 151).

There—wild alloy of worlds, ensouled creation sobbing,
Dissolving particles of starry harmony.

This is my ecstasy, my terror that dark evening!
This, my poor love, is why I fear for you!
Those are the eyes that followed me—so strangely,
Before I understood, or came to love ... or knew!

A law unto yourself—you're flying, flying by me
On to new galaxies, no orbit owned as yours ...
And this our world for you is but a fiery
Red sphere of smoke that burns and sings and calls!

And in its glow, your youth—akin to madness—
Makes happiness, betrayal nothing—when
Music and light are all, joy one with sadness ...
But so I love you: such am I—Carmen.

(III. 239)

'No one', he wrote when he sent her this poem, 'has told you this and you will not understand that it is about either you or me or recognize us in it, but it is true, none the less, I swear to you.'[23]

7

Yet the wet snow and blustering winds of March passed into the warmer days of a translucent northern spring and—to his utter astonishment—Blok came very near to happiness.

He made no attempt to hide his passion, attending performances of *The Stranger* and *The Puppet Booth* with Del'mas, introducing her to his mother and, inevitably, to his wife and all their friends of Meyerhold's studio. He even published the cycle *Carmen* in their journal *Lyubov' k trëm apelsinam*.[24] True, the extent of their intimacy was hidden from such innocents as Angelina ('I shall have to speak dryly because my sister will be there,' Blok wrote to Del'mas; 'But you, if you please, speak more tenderly'),[25] and decently veiled from Lyubov' Aleksandrovna's husband (at least Blok tried not to embarrass her by ringing her up when Andreyev was likely to answer the phone). However, the husband appears to have been complacent, if not indifferent, and the milieu was bohemian. Apart from such elementary discretion, Blok and Del'mas quite obviously liked to be seen in one another's company. In fact, they were extremely proud of one another.

There seemed no reason why that rapturous spring should not go on for ever:

... He was straightforward and would listen to all that I had to say very attentively, and I did my best to accept him straightforwardly. In our talks he would sometimes say to me: 'Take me as I am: I am complex. You—no less, only you have more control over your complexity than I.' Often he would take things too much to heart and would keep his thoughts to himself, and sometimes it was difficult to get on with him—I wanted to relieve the heaviness, the complexity of his life. I was quite different; bright, healthy. Stormy impulses were a part of my character, gloom and heaviness were incomprehensible to me. I loved the joy of life.[26]

'Everything is singing,' Blok wrote the day after they met (Z.K. 221), and, on 2 April,

Today everything is full of you, the hands that have touched you are singing.... It is as though I had been out in the open, empty sea and suddenly the warm scent of an accessible, flowering island had been wafted to my boat. But I am still in the midst of the empty sea, my feelings have become wild and I am unaccustomed to the land.[27]

And, on Easter Day, so often a day of utter discouragement: 'I don't know why, but today it seems to me that in life, in this life, there may perhaps sometimes be something utterly new. It is a long time since I have felt this so vividly.'[28]

All that April they walked and talked together. Blok was posing for Kustodiev,[1] preparing his poems and plays for Sirin, falling more and more deeply in love. The white nights came. Together, they went to visit the graves of the Beketovs and sat in the pale sunshine by the cross that marked the last resting place of Aunt Katya: 'There is beauty in her today, daring, wildness, anxiety and tenderness. "I am afraid of love." I made the sign of the cross over her. The third time since we met' (ZK. 225).

By 4 May, he was seriously thinking of separating from Lyuba, but admitted to himself, almost in the same breath, 'I am afraid, as ever. I will not be able to keep this pearl' (Z.K. 226). He wrote to Del'mas:

Before I met you, I had been aware for a long time of the growing emptiness in my life. During this month and a bit I have gradually been perceiving ever new and unexpected possibilities—that is why it seems as though literally years and years of life had gone by; and I know that, in spite of the difference between our worlds, values, tastes, life, I might still be able to see all the shimmering colours, all the rainbow, because you are like a shell

[1] For a sculptured head or bust, said to be very successful, which has been lost.

full of pearls which is found in the depths of the sea, found not by chance, found for some reason, as a reward, or a reproach, or a warning, or perhaps an omen of doom. I don't know, I only know that it is not a chance find.

All my agony and jealousy*m* and heaviness arises from the fact that perhaps it is only given to me to find, and then, like a fisherman, I don't know what to do with what I have found, and I may lose it again in this same sea where it just shone up at me, and the sea will again become empty and heavy, and I shall be left as destitute as I was before.

Yet, immediately, the fear is qualified by the voice of duty:

The important thing is that in this (which I am always afraid of) there is an element of vocation; that means, an element of truth; an element of my calling; because art is to be found where there is waning, loss, suffering, cold. This thought lies in wait for me ALWAYS and torments me ALWAYS, except for those few brief moments when I can lose myself in you and forget everything—down to the last thought. . . .[29]

On 14 May he wrote—*en passant*, as it were—one of his most remarkable poems about Russia: 'The Last Farewell' (III. 272), noting only 'I seem to be writing verse of some kind' (*ZK.* 227). The following day, he and Lyuba talked over the possibility of separation, yet the very juxtaposition of this conversation with the memory, the anamnesis of first love which imbues so many of the poems about Russia, and 'The Last Farewell' most particularly, lent their talk something of the insubstantial, unreal quality of the white nights. Indeed, in this last pre-war spring, Blok's notebooks begin to read more and more like an attempt to make sense of a dream: 'Three o'clock, a white night. The concierge slowly leads off a man who cries calmly: "Jesus, Son of God, have mercy upon me." Behind them follows a policeman with his little notebook. They disappear round the corner of Nicholas the Miracle-Worker' (*Z.K.* 228).

In accord with the eeriness of this northern solstice was the appearance, on 23 May, of Zhenya Ivanov, shaking, sick with self-reproach, twisting a woman's hat in his hands. He had come from the hospital, from the bedside of a sick girl who had 'been coming to see' him and Blok and had lost her wits at the railway station.

'The day passed as always in quiet madness,' wrote Blok the following morning, continuing the cycle 'From the Life of a Friend of Mine' (III. 47–53). He spent the afternoon with the Ivanovs, sympathizing silently with Zhenya and Maria Pavlovna but wondering

---

m Blok was jealous when Del'mas, always much courted, went into society without him. This letter was in part to thank her for being at home this particular evening when he had looked up at her window.

at their profound Christian conviction that suffering shared was in
some way suffering halved and guilt redeemed. At last, at the end
of one long day or the beginning of the next, Del'mas telephoned to
say that she now knew how her own life would end, because he *was*
the one for whom she had always waited.

So the spring—unreal, tantalizing, illumined by the lightning of
intense feeling—passed into summer and, on 8 June, Blok left with
his mother for Shakhmatovo. There he remained for over a month,
suspended between 'boredom and delight' (*Z.K.* 233). Separated
from the new love and the old (Lyuba was acting with Zonov's
troupe in Kuokkala), he wrote to both and thought of both with a kind
of hopeless tenderness.

To Del'mas he wrote:

I want to tell you again what I have said before: I cannot say that the past
is dead. The past is alive, and not only as the past, there is something pre-
sently alive in it. You understand what I am trying to tell you. Here I sometimes feel pain, sometimes sadness and light; all sorts. I just want to remind
you of what I am, there's no point in going into more detail. In a word,
it is all absolutely different, there are neither contradictions nor confusion.
It is as though *that* had been another me.

He tried to tell her what she had meant to him: the purely artistic
pleasure she had given him when he first saw her as Carmen. The
sudden awareness that he was in love. The gradual rejuvenation of
his whole self. The 'new music' behind their meetings:

and finally ... out of the *storm of music*—calm, no, not calm; *old-world
femininity*, yes, that too, but behind that—more; some depths of *fidelity*,
inherent in you; and again I am not sure if that is the right word: 'fidelity'?
Earth, nature, purity, LIFE, some TRUE aspect of life that I haven't met before;
but even that does not define it. The *possibility* of HAPPINESS, is that it? In
a word, something forgotten by people in general, and not only by me,
but by all *Christians* who put the suffering of the Cross above everything
else: something very *simple*, that cannot be explained....[30]

Yet when she wrote to him of 'seizing life in one moment' he
answered:

That is all right for a nightingale, a butterfly, a bee.
But we are human beings (or perhaps only I am?).... The Lord be with
you, red-gold head and nightingale heart.
You are better than I, anyway.[31]

8

The next day, 15 July, he wrote in his notebook: 'There is a smell of war (Austria–Serbia–Russia).'

On the 18th came a telegram from Frants Feliksovich (who was undergoing medical trement in Yalta for a chronic infection of the kidneys) that he had been recalled to Petersburg and, on the following day, Blok and his mother left Shakhmatovo. Lyuba came from Kuokkala on 21 July, went back to collect her belongings and returned to Offitserskaya Street two days later, the day England declared war on Germany.

After that things began to move very quickly. Austria declared war on Russia; the Duma was assembled so that the Russian government might, at this moment of crisis, 'hear the voice of the Russian People'. News came through on 27 July that there were already Russian wounded. Frants Feliksovich was posted to Peterhof; Mikhail Tereshchenko became head of the Red Cross in the south. Lyubov' Dmitriyevna volunteered to train as a nurse, Blok to work on a volunteer committee to help soldiers' families.

On 28 July, Del'mas, too, returned to Petersburg from her summer holiday. Blok was happy to see her but his mood was 'wide-awake and clenched teeth': 'I am ALONE, as I was before,' he wrote to her, and, on the same day, in his diary: 'My life is a series of incredibly confused human relationships, my life is a series of broken hopes' (Z.K. 235).

Lyuba's training began on 7 August. Blok, temporarily carried away by the stir and bustle of war, did not even speak to Del'mas on the telephone that evening: '... Nothing but manual labour is needed now' (Z.K. 236). Next day, however, she asked him to come and see her and was '... tender, submissive, true, we went for a walk. She was beautiful' (Z.K. 236).

Yet on 17 August, the anniversary of his marriage, miserably torn between his very real feeling for Lyuba and the mystique of his marriage on the one hand and, on the other, his still overpowering passion for Del'mas, he wrote the singer two farewell letters:"

I do not know how it happened that I found you, neither do I know why it is that I am losing you, but it is as it should be: as it should be that the months grow into years; as it should be that my heart is bleeding now

---

" The first, Del'mas destroyed, leaving only a few lines. The second she permitted to outlive her.

at this moment; as it should be that I should feel as I have never felt before—
as though, with you, I were losing the last earthly things.

Only God and I know how I love you.

A.B.

Allow me to add what you already know yourself; your victory over me
is decisive, I admit defeat, because you turned my whole life upside-down
and for a long time held me captive to a happiness that is beyond my reach.
I can hardly find the strength for the agony of parting from you, so I beg you
not to answer at all, I am hardly master of myself.

The Lord be with you.[32]

Worried by Russian losses at the front, concerned, as always, for
his wife and mother, Blok yet could not resist going back again and
again to stare up at Del'mas's window. On 20 August he dreamt
they were married. The next day he wrote: 'When will I at last be
free to put an end to myself?' (Z.K. 237). Then, on 22 August:

Lyuba has been assigned to Tereshchenko's hospital in Kiev. . . . In the evening I met Lyubov' Aleksandrovna and walked about the streets with her. . . .
Her flowers, her letters, her tears, and again my life is all in bloom and
all confused and I don't know what I should do.

(Z.K. 237)

CHAPTER VII

'The Most Prosaic War'

(Autumn 1914 – March 1917)

> If I am asked 'what I was doing during the Great War' I
> shall be able to answer that I did something worthwhile:
> edited Apollon Grigor'ev, helped to stage *The Rose and the
> Cross*, and wrote *Retribution*.
>
> (*Z.K.* 321, entry for 5 May 1917)

1

Surprisingly, over these chaotic autumn days, Blok returned to *Retribution*, writing in some fragments about his father as a young man for the first chapter. Several other poems followed, including the somehow quintessential 'The wind has fallen and the sunset's glory' (III. 271), dedicated to his mother, thinking back to their quiet month together at the beginning of the summer, and telling yet again of the call of the road: the summons on and away from retreat and recollection, on 'past the monk, the still ponds, and the stars....'.

While visiting his mother in Peterhof, Blok witnessed the solemn spectacle of a troop train setting off for the front with 'songs and hurrahs'. This resulted in a very simple, very Russian poem which might have been about 1904, or 1914, or 1941: 'The Petrograd sky was darkened by rain' (III. 275–6). The very next day, on 2 September, came the news that Blok's boyhood friend Visha Grek had been killed in action.

On 3 September he saw Lyuba off. Among the first to go, she had been duly presented to the Empress Mother Maria Fyëdorovna, after a solemn service of dedication. Blok was proud of her and his notebooks are full of affection and, again, a kind of reverence.

Ironically, Blok began to establish himself as a great patriotic poet by the publication, in Rumanov's *Russkoye Slovo*,[a] of several poems

[a] On 21 September 1914.

under the general title 'To War', which included a wildly successful love–hate poem to Russia actually written during the Christmas–New Year festivities of 1913–14.[b] The poem, which gives a vituperative portrait of a Russian merchant—a monumental incarnation of hypocritical piety, avarice, and debauch, an unappetizing, hiccuping brute who 'wallows shamelessly in sin'—ends on a note of high pathos with the declaration that, even in this form, Russia is dearer to the poet than any other land (III. 274). It corresponded precisely to the wave of 'my country right or wrong' sentiment which swept the reading public in those early days of the war, sluicing away the intelligentsia's anti-establishment attitudes, all their enlightened pacifism and internationalism, and making a virtue even of vice, so long as the vice was traditional and 'Russian'.

Any enthusiasm Blok himself had felt for the war, however, soon began to wane. Not a pacifist nor yet, as were the more extreme revolutionaries, a defeatist, he was worried from the beginning by a nagging feeling that this was the wrong war: pointless, catastrophic for the growth of the country. In the rough drafts of the poem about the departing troop train (III. 598–9) the thought is already in evidence that this war is but a prelude, and there is a suggestion[c] that Russia's historical foes lie to the East. Blok did not condemn the war as yet; but he did not understand it. It came as a clashing dissonance in that 'music of history' to which, over the last few years, he had trained himself to listen.

Aware that he needed time and quiet to readjust, Blok gradually disengaged himself from the present, slipping out of his volunteer work and burying himself in the library of the Academy of Sciences to compile an edition of the poems of Apollon Grigor'ev, a minor poet of the nineteenth century for whom he felt a great affinity. This was a scholarly labour which gave him much satisfaction.

During this autumn, the poet's bachelor existence in the capital was punctuated by frequent visits to Peterhof to see his mother. As always when living alone, he began to drink more heavily. He appears, to begin with, to have tried to see less of Del'mas, but as the winter progressed she began to come to his flat and soon they were often together until the small hours, Blok astonished still and delighted by the happy physical relationship.

None the less, he continued to write regularly to Lyuba and eagerly to await her occasional letters. These were loving and practical:

[b] Blok put the finishing touches to this poem on 26 August 1914.
[c] Removed completely from the version first published in *Russkoye Slovo*, 21 September 1914, and not restored by Blok for later editions.

she was worked off her feet and obviously took satisfaction in work well done: a filthy ward cleaned out, her patients properly washed and bandaged. At the request of Aleksandra Chebotarevskaya, Blok prepared extracts from these letters from the front for publication.[1]

One of the first things to be swept away by the war was Sirin. On 16 November Pelageya Ivanovna Tereshchenko rang Blok up to inform him personally—and before anyone else—that the family had decided to liquidate the whole concern. This involved the poet in a prolonged struggle to rescue Andrey Bely's *Petersburg*, which it had been decided to pulp as part of the war effort. He had to guarantee Bely's novel financially and it involved him in tiresome negotiations, since the censor stubbornly held out against the title, Petersburg having been renamed Petrograd at the beginning of the war to make it sound more Russian. Bely, having been caught by the war in Switzerland, building Steiner's anthroposophical temple, could be of no help.

Little by little, not only projects but people were drawn into the machine of war. Some, like Pyast, invalided out of the army with a nervous breakdown after little more than a month, it soon rejected. Frants Feliksovich, on the other hand, had left Peterhof for the front and, in his modest way, now came into his own. Blok and his mother looked anxiously for news of him in the morning papers, and he provided his stepson with a link with Lyuba (most letters and parcels were sent by hand rather than by post, both to avoid the censor and to ensure delivery), calling to see her on his way to and from the front. On 8 December he was home on leave with blood on his trenchcoat.

The war added new notes of simplicity and terror to Blok's poetry. That autumn he wrote several fine lyric poems[d] and at last made a significant addition to *Retribution*, the meditation on the twentieth century which eventually formed the second part of the introduction to Chapter 1 and which, in the broad historical context of the poem, gives a remarkable perspective on this first year of—literally—mortal combat:

> The Twentieth Century—more bleak
> And shelterless the night of life
> (And blacker looms, and vaster yet
> The shade of Lucifer's dark wing) . . .
> And smoky sunsets, red with flame

[d] Among others 'I have not betrayed the white banner' (III. 277) and 'This iron sword is raised to strike' (III. 223).

(Fell portents of this present hour)
The blue-tailed comet, threatening death,
A dreadful phantom in the sky;
Messina's end, cruel and complete
(The elements defy control),
And, inexhaustible, the roar
Of those machines that, day and night,
Forge ruin. Then, the dread surmise
That all the little thoughts and creeds
Whereby we lived were but deceit.
And then the aeroplane's first flight
Into spheres empty and unknown ...
And such revulsion from this life,
And such wild love of this same life,
And, for our country—passion, hate,
And the black blood that swells our veins
And bursts all borders ever set
With promise of unheard-of change
And unexampled mutinies.

But what of man? Beyond the roar
Of steel and fire and sulphurous smoke
What fiery distances reveal
Their secrets to your gaze? What lies
Beyond the grinding of machines?
And why does the propeller whirr
And cut the cold, the empty cloud?

(VII. 305–6)

So the year 1914 ended on a series of questions: questions about the war, Russia, mankind—and his own private life: 'Three names, Mama, poor thing, Lyuba far away, my Lyubov' Aleksandrovna. Lyuba.' (Z.K. 252).

2

Early in the New Year, Frants Feliksovich left again for the Galician front and Aleksandra Andreyevna moved back to the capital. Blok continued his lonely life as a busy man of letters. He made up an old quarrel with Merezhkovsky, who had excluded the offending article 'The Puppet Booth and Tragedy' from his new Collected Works and actually rang Blok up to apologize for the four-year-old insult. Blok was touched. He saw a good deal of Hippius at this time, accompanying her to the rehearsals of her play The Green Ring, after which, with great mutual sympathy, they discussed the agonies of the playwright in the theatre. Sometimes he would even sit and copy out her elegant, spiky verses for *Lyubov' k trëm apelsinam*.

Blok's attitude to the war at this time, one of firm but consciously temporary support for the Imperial government, was close to Leonid Andreyev's and to Sologub's, at whose home he was also a regular visitor. Indeed, the Merezhkovskys, anti-war from the first day, considered Blok to the right of their acquaintance, and Zinaida Hippius even wrote in her reminiscences of this period of his apparent 'Black Hundredism'.[2] This was a misunderstanding though the phrase was not altogether inept: Blok had not yet come round to the Merezhkovskys' way of thinking about the war, but his patriotism and strong emotional ties with the army were not so much an intellectual attitude as a kind of 'Pavlovian response' to his para-military upbringing. Intellectually, he tried to remain within the tradition of the intelligentsia while groping always towards his own, independent opinion, that inner truth to which he came through watchfulness and concentration, not via accepted criteria of the right or left. For the moment, he still 'knew nothing' (*Z.K.* 120).

Typical of this uncertainty was the incident of 'A Voice from the Chorus'.[c] When asked for some verses about Russia for *Apollon*, Blok sent them this poem. Makovsky declined to print it on the grounds that, when *Apollon* was pursuing a policy of all-out support for the government at a time of national crisis, such ominous verses would be out of place. Blok, in his reply, explained that the poem had been written before the war and was about a more distant future. As to the present, he added, he was as confident as Makovsky of Russia's ability to withstand her foes and had no wish to imply defeatism or to sap morale. But he offered no alternative and this confidence is not evident in his diary. On 28 February 1915, he noted: 'Things are bad here in Russia—drunkenness, idleness, apathy' (*Z.K.* 257).

A few days later, Blok's concentration on the situation in the country was momentarily interrupted by an unexpected literary discovery. On 9 March he was called out to the kitchen by his servant who handed him a note from a young peasant who, she said, had come to the back door straight from the country, with his suitcase. Confronted by an unknown, straw-headed nineteen-year-old, Blok, supposing it was one of the Mendeleyev tenants 'from Boblovo', ushered the youth into his study.

The lad introduced himself: Sergey Esenin, from Ryazan: straight

[c] Eventually published in *Lyubov' k trëm apel'sinam*, I, 1916.

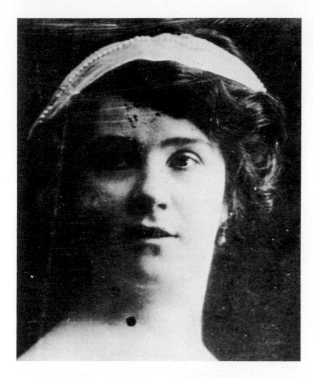

Lyubov' Aleksandrovna Del'mas, photographed in Paris a year or two before she met Blok. (From the collection of N. P. Il'in)

Blok in a Petersburg park: a photograph taken for Del'mas in the summer of 1916 before he left for war service.

Anna Akhmatova, in the painting by N. Al'tman, 1914.

from the station.*ſ* Sweat streaming down his face, he recited his verses: good poetry, inimitably spoken, remarkably free of literary influences; a supple, rich, natural talent. Blok, who almost invariably discouraged beginners, sat down then and there to give Esenin an introduction to Sergey Gorodetsky and a note to the peasant writer M. P. Murashov, recommending the bearer and his poetry. As they talked, the boy had demolished an entire loaf of white bread which happened to be on the table. Blok smiled and suggested he might also know what to do with some fried eggs. They parted in perfect charity: Esenin's meteor-rise to fame had begun.[3]

Esenin, however, was not only a 'poet by the grace of God', but a determined, not to say pushing, young man, well aware of the potential impact of a youthful peasant genius on a patriotic but effete society in time of war. He decided to improve the occasion and pursue the acquaintance, but Blok felt he had played his part and gently but firmly refused to contribute to that ruination of the young man's character in which all Petrograd—from the Countess Kleinmikhel to the Merezhkovskys—seemed so eager to participate. He declined Esenin's request for a further meeting on the grounds that he was tired, overworked, and could see no real reason to meet again so soon, adding a sober warning:

... It is difficult to look ahead, and it is even difficult for me to think of what is peculiarly yours, for we are very different; but still, I do think that the way ahead for you will probably not be short and, in order not to lose your way, you should not be hasty or nervous. For every step we take we are, sooner or later, called to account, and nowadays it is difficult to know how to set one's feet, in literature, perhaps, more than elsewhere.

I don't mean to tell you all this in order to read you a lesson, but really from my heart: I know myself how hard it is to walk in such a way that the wind should not blow you off course nor the bog suck you under.

I wish you good health and shake your hand.

ALEKSANDR BLOK
(VIII. 444–5, letter of 22 April 1915)

The plea of weariness was not a mere excuse. A constant undertow throughout that winter had been Blok's anxiety for Lyuba. 'I think of you all the time,' she had written him from the front. 'It's hard for me to tell you how—but I know that I love you more than anything in the world, wherever I may be "thrown".'[4] During the last fortnight in February, there had been some danger of her being cut off

---

*ſ*In fact, Esenin had come from the province of Ryazan via Moscow, where he had been working at various jobs off and on since 1912 and had already published some poetry in children's magazines.

by an enemy advance, a prospect she had faced with courageous equanimity, writing to her husband in a letter sent, as usual, through a friend, that he was not to worry as either the Red Cross would arrange for repatriation or she would make her own way back somehow.[5] To this letter he had replied:

You write that I shouldn't be anxious. That is just a figure of speech—anxiety. Just now everything I feel about you exceeds all anxiety; i.e. anxiety has reached its own limits and has already turned into something else, into a kind of 'fiery calm', maybe. Thank you that you go on being with me, in spite of what is yours, in spite of what is mine. It is so essential to me....

(VIII. 440, letter of 19 February 1915)

The danger passed, however, and on 16 March Lyuba was home again. Nursing, she had discovered, was not her vocation and she was eager to get back to the theatre and determined not to return to the hospitals unless there was a total emergency. In her last letter announcing her return, she had said that she was looking forward to seeing Blok 'as never before',[6] but it was not easy to resume their life together.

To Aleksandra Andreyevna, who had got used to a comparatively relaxed and animated Blok dropping in with a radiant Del'mas for evening tea, everything appeared to have become more complicated. The war which, in August, seemed to have blown away and scattered all Blok's personal problems, was now blowing them back upon him—little changed. Even Kuzmin-Karavayev was still hovering about Lyuba—with the added advantage of a uniform.

There were also financial troubles. The war was playing havoc with Blok's private income and his father's fortune was running out. Used to literary independence, he had no wish to return to writing reviews and lecturing for money—particularly in wartime:

If those who write and speak to me about the 'integrity'[8] of my poetry etc. wished to go into the matter more deeply, they would understand that: at the moment when I began to 'dry up' (about 1909), I inherited money from my father; now that is coming to an end and my position may be critical again if I cannot find some way to earn a living. For an ordinary but fastidious writer such as I to subsist on 'honest' literary earnings is almost impossible. Advise me, my dear well-wishers, how to earn money; though I am lazy I do try to carry out any task entrusted to me to the best of my ability and at least I am extremely honest.

(Z.K. 269)

[8] The word Blok uses is *blagorodstvo*, usually and more correctly rendered as 'nobility'; but here he means independent judgement fearlessly expressed, disinterestedness.

It was almost with envy that he noted on 10 June that Lyuba 'it seems, has got on to a big and useful project, whereas I ...' [h] (*Z.K.* 265). Lyuba was again absorbed in acting—this time with her husband's approval—performing for workers and soldiers with a troupe which actually visited munitions factories and local places of entertainment, bringing the theatre 'to the people'.

With his wife thus occupied and his mistress away in the country, Blok was free to postpone the question of lucrative employment by joining his mother for the summer at Shakhmatovo.

3

Before he left, Blok received the first copy of his *Poems about Russia*, collected and published as a separate book by the journal *Otechestvo* (The Fatherland). This collection, although he did not altogether approve of *Otechestvo*'s tendency to make capital out of the patriotic theme (poems like *On the Field of Kulikovo*, for instance, published without the date of writing, read very differently in 1915 than they had in 1908), 'made' and 'altered' Blok's reputation for the third time. It confirmed the impression made by the 'war poems' in *Russkoye Slovo*, setting him, finally and decisively, outside and above any particular school as a great 'national' poet. In the patriotic *Apollon*, Georgiy Ivanov wrote that these poems, though they employed no deliberate archaisms and were quite free of heavy, historical paraphernalia, yet embraced '... the Russia of the sagas and of the Tartar yoke, the Russia of Lermontov and Nekrasov, of the hermitages along the banks of the Volga and of the year 1905'.[7] The recognition of this quality in Blok's verse at that particular time was, of course, fortuitous, yet it was important in that it confirmed him, in the eyes of others besides himself, as a man who wrote about his own country rather than a Europeanized 'decadent' and, in the words of a later critic, as 'the greatest and most exact recorder of the heartbeat of his decade'.[8]

Blok's own, somewhat sceptical, reaction to the timing of the publication of his *Poems about Russia* comes out very clearly in the words he wrote in the copy he presented to Aleksandra Chebotarevskaya, who worked for the publishers: 'To Aleksandra Nikolayevna —this book, published in a non-period,[i] by no one in particular

---

[h] Blok's ellipse.

[i] The Russian *bezvremeniye* is usually translated 'a time of stagnation' or 'reaction', but the context of the 1914–18 War seemed to require something at once more literal and more energetic.

and for no good reason—with gratitude for friendship and various annoyances undergone in connection with the publication and in memory of various telephone conversations about the fatherland and "The Fatherland"'.[9]

4

That year Blok arrived at Shakhmatovo on 30 June and remained there for three months, gardening enthusiastically. Aleksandra Andreyevna, to his delight, invited Del'mas to stay with them on her way back to Petrograd via Moscow at the beginning of August. It was a strange visit. The peasants, whose opinion, naturally enough, no one thought of asking, were critical of Aleksandra Andreyevna for countenancing her son's affair with so flamboyant a creature, for in the country it was painfully clear that Del'mas was of the demimonde and could only have appeared in such unlikely company as that of the Beketov sisters and Blok himself as the *barin*'s mistress. Country memories being retentive, they wanted the legal wife whom everybody knew, the old Boblovo *barin*'s daughter Lyubov' Dmitriyevna Mendeleyeva, who had been brought up in proper ideas of country courtesy and was not above singing with the milk-maids.[10] In Petrograd, Lyuba was a not very successful character actress and her rival a star. In Shakhmatovo, on the contrary, Blok's wife was more than a dream princess, whereas Lyubov' Aleksandrovna was an unreal intruder.

Blok must have been aware of this. At the same time he had felt for a long time that Shakhmatovo itself, and the whole way of life it stood for, was receding into an unreal past. He was like a man who had woken prematurely and, having realized, in 1905–6, that all his youth and the life for which it had prepared him was but a remembered dream, had refused to go back to sleep—though the night ahead was still long and the dream might have been sweet. It is a measure of how far he had divorced himself from this dream while all about him were still asleep that he was *able* to entertain Del'mas at Shakhmatovo, to show her the actual places he had always loved almost as he might have shown her the pictures of Italy in his album, to ignore the tacit disapproval of all about him, and never for one moment to admit any comparison between her and Lyuba, as though, indeed, that had been 'a different me'.

He did, however, compare himself as he had been then with himself as he was now, and found not only that Lyuba had had the best of the bargain, but that he was no longer fitted for love or a happy private life:

> That week that you spent in the country I shall never forget. There was something very special about it for me. And that underlined all the horror of the situation still more sharply. It is more and more difficult for us to part, but we must. This feeling that never leaves me is the source of what you call 'spleen'.... My life and my soul are flawed; and all this is nothing but sparks amongst the ashes. The *real* me, at my full stature, you have never seen. It's too late.
> O, if you only knew....[11]

Blok was not the only one to whom this week in the country brought second thoughts. His mother, who had hitherto found Del'mas 'a very alien type' but, nevertheless, 'pleasant and sympathetic', was suddenly moved to make the comparison which her son would not permit himself. She told Maria Pavlovna of Del'mas's disastrous attempt to sing one of the poems to the Most Beautiful Lady:

> It ends with the words: 'Here burns the threshold bathed in light'. It is the concluding poem of the *First Volume*. The music is perfect. But it was almost unbearable to listen to. Do you remember the words? Sasha began to criticize, told her that was not the way to sing it, that it needed a cold impersonal approach. (That is something she can't manage, in everything she does there is passion and fullness of life.) It ended with him flaring up and her sulking. And thank God she didn't try to sing that again....

Before Del'mas's arrival, Aleksandra Andreyevna had dreamt of Lyuba, '... and now I know for certain that Lyuba is immeasurably the more significant and the purer ...'. There was, however, nothing she could do about the situation and she was happy that Lyuba had promised to come to Shakhmatovo in September and that Sasha still spoke of her with tenderness. '... But that other one is an enchantress. There can be no doubt of that. She sings so that I myself move about in a dream and am half in love with her....'[12]

Whether or not Lyubov' Aleksandrovna had any notion of the wall of tradition she was up against—all the broken defences of so many broken lives which yet remembered that they had once formed a part of the same structure and were overgrown with the same strong, leafy creeper, starred with the same small, secret flowers—it is hard to judge. Most probably it was her strength that she did not know it, but ascribed Blok's glooms and withdrawals to the mysterious poetic temperament which, as an artist, she revered. Also, confident of her own fascination, she rarely took offence, and was thus able to handle his moods with more thought for him than for herself. Here is her own story of her visit to Shakhmatovo:

At the station at Podsolnechnoye there were horses sent to meet me. A beautiful country road and there, in the distance, a modest wooden house.

I was nervous, I had thought so much about this journey and now here I was. On the veranda of the wooden house the whole family came out to meet me. Aleksandr Aleksandrovich in a white Russian shirt with a belt, all bathed in sunlight, and the eyes—eyes like violet cornflowers.

I was given a small separate room in an annexe where there stood an upright piano. At that time I was learning the part of Laura in *The Stone Guest*. I had the music with me. When not walking or chatting with the family I continued to work at the part. Al. Al. liked this very much. Usually he would sit on the veranda and listen to my singing or stroll about the garden paths, listening to the music. In the evenings, after tea, we would all make music together. Blok, particularly, liked to hear me singing 'For the shores of my far homeland' and 'My voice for you'.

'Go on, sing some more,' he would say. 'It feels so good—here' and he would touch his chest.

Three days flew past as in a dream, then I had to go back to the town to prepare for the new theatrical season.[13]

Del'mas went, but Lyuba did not come. Instead, Blok went up to Petrograd in August on business—to find a wounded Kuzmin-Karavayev in his flat, about to leave with Lyuba for Kuokkalla. He saw his wife for three hours only and, returning to Shakhmatovo grim and drawn, with a bad cold in the head to complete his misery, sat down to write her a letter of apology for turning up without warning.

Apart from a brief excursion to Moscow (6–8 September) to arrange for Musaget to take over the publication of the three volumes of poetry and the volume of plays he had prepared for the now defunct Sirin, Blok remained at Shakhmatovo until the end of September, working hard in the garden, clearing overgrown patches, cutting back, chopping down....

5

The 1915 autumn season in Petrograd was not, on the surface, so very different from previous peacetime years. The question of 'honest' literary earnings cropped up again with Blok's return to town and he became involved in a grandiose project of Gorky's to translate the poetry of all the peoples of the Russian Empire. He worked on translations from the Armenian, the Latvian, and the Finnish,[j] but balked at what he called the Malo-Russian, his editors the Ukrainian.

Yet, even as he laboured at these peaceful tasks, Blok was increasingly aware that the social structure of his country was beginning to disintegrate. This was no longer a vague premonition; it was the sober conclusion of his waking thought. At first, he was inclined, as ever, to welcome the idea of change. 'It must not be forgotten that, in the very near future, our children will come into ever closer contact with the people,' he wrote in response to a request from Poliksena Sergeyevna Solov'eva to give his opinion on the kind of literature that would best prepare Russian children to face the future: 'because the future of Russia lies in the still almost untapped resources of the masses of the people and in her underground riches ... the day of all kinds of cosy "privileged" institutions is over, it is too late now to think along the lines that "it'll last our time"' (Z.K. 275).

The idea of bringing up a generation of wise citizen-technicians and optimistic thoughts of 'a great renaissance that will take place under the sign of courage and will' (Z.K. 276) were, however, soon overshadowed by growing foreboding concerning the war which, rolling back and forth over the flats of Prussia and White Russia, was clearly taking so great a toll of the 'still untapped resources' of which he wrote that any renaissance promised to be stillborn.

Blok was thirty-five years old in November 1915 and there were rumours that his year might be called up before the end of the year. Aleksandra Andreyevna was deploying what influence she possessed in military circles to obtain some kind of exemption, or at least to see her son suitably placed. Blok did not, at this stage, exert himself on his own behalf, but he had no wish to fight. As Pyast later recalled:

It was not exactly that he was pro-German, or that he was a convinced pacifist. *But he was against the Allies.* He had no love for the French or for the English, either as individuals or for the national 'ideas' of the people. Belgium was comparatively dearer to him. He had travelled about the country and also about Holland, and had found the experience rewarding, an unforgettable impression had been produced on him by the forefather of the Netherlands school of painting, Quentin Massys. Yet I remember how, at the beginning of the war, I was reduced to a state of cold fury by one sentence thrown at me by Blok: 'Those toy countries of yours—Belgium and Sweden...'.[14]

---

[j] Blok did not, of course, know all these languages. The practice was to commission a line-by-line prose translation, indicate metre, rhyme scheme, and other formal qualities of the original, and then check the poet's recreation of the poem against the original. The Armenian and Finnish poetry was edited by V. Ya. Bryusov.

Never had he seen any adequate reason for this fratricidal inter-European war. As winter deepened and the Empire of All the Russias began to split and crumble before his eyes, the rot within activated by the barbarity without, his feelings became more positive. The war was not only incomprehensible. It was wrong. It had come at the wrong time, was being waged against the wrong people, had nothing to do with the 'music of history'.

Perhaps no great perspicacity was required to see this. Even Rasputin had warned the Tsar that war would mean the end of Russia as they had known it. Even Durnovo, an official of the Secret Police, had said flatly that the war would inevitably end in revolution: not a political revolution to re-establish rights granted and partially rescinded in and after 1905–6, but an elemental social upheaval. Blok was not concerned to preserve the *status quo*; yet neither was he the enemy of his own country. He did not know what to wish for and felt only a kind of dumb foreboding.

It was at this point that he found himself—for the last time—in alliance with the Merezhkovskys and completely at one with Zinaida Hippius. It was not without learning a great deal that Hippius—unfair, inaccurate, but sensitive as a frail, antennaed insect—had turned her scented drawing room into a discussion centre for the Russian intelligentsia, or had spent the years immediately after the 1905 revolution in discreet, self-imposed exile. Her acquaintance extended from churchmen to illegal revolutionaries, from respectable liberal politicians to professed terrorists, from the most refined aesthetes to visionary schismatics and peasant poets. In October 1914 she was already writing: 'No one is in any doubt at all that there will be a revolution. No one knows of what kind it will be or when it will break out and—is it not terrible?—no one is even thinking about it. We have gone numb.' A few weeks later, she added: 'I can change nothing, I only know it's GOING TO HAPPEN. But those who COULD do something don't realize for one moment that it's GOING TO HAPPEN.'[15]

Blok's immediate reaction had been less acute. Lyuba, Visha Grek, Frants Feliksovich's blood-stained trenchcoat, the soldiers singing as they steamed out from Peterhof: all these things had affected him simply and directly, so that he had even been angry with the Merezhkovskys for their defeatist attitudes. Yet his poetry, the record of that subconscious foreknowledge which always burdened him, was already echoing Hippius's diary. In a poem completed at the beginning of the war, on 8 September 1914, but begun in December 1913, a few weeks before he wrote 'The New America', Blok had looked back to 1905 and reaffirmed his faith that, if not for him, then for others, a better life would come. But then, like Hippius, he had 'gone numb' before the immensity of events and it is the inexorable advent of personal tragedy which predominates in the final version, making the hope for the future sound more like a prayer:

> If we are dumb, it is the tocsin
> Has taught us how to hold our peace.
> In hearts, once eagerly exalted,
> There is a fateful emptiness.
>
> Then let above our deathbed hover
> The crows—a raucous, swirling scum.
> They who are worthier—Father, Father,
> May they behold Thy Kingdom come.
>
> (III. 278)

These lines had been published in 1914, soon after they were completed,[k] without any dedication. It was not till the autumn of 1915, a year later, when Blok came fully to understand how similar Hippius's intuitive understanding of the contemporary situation was to his own, that he asked her to accept as hers this poem about 'the children of Russia's dreadful years' (Z.K. 279). It was Merezhkovsky himself, however, the disagreeable, pedantic Dmitriy Sergeyevich, who impressed him most by his diagnosis of events:

Odichaniye ['going savage']—that is the word; and it has been found by bookish, timid Merezhkovsky. Why was it he who found it? Because he alone has worked, whereas Andreyev and all that lot—tra-la-la—grew too pleased with themselves.

Gorky worked, but got muddled. Why? Because he hadn't the 'culture'. So, we are going savage.

Black, impenetrable slush on the streets. The street lamps—only every third one is lit. A drunken soldier being bundled into a cab (will they hang him?). The resentful, angry faces of the 'common people' (i.e. of the vrai grand monde) ...

The young are self-satisfied, 'apolitical', cheeky and vulgar. Instead of culture they have Verbitskaya and Severyanin[l] etc. No language. No love. They don't want victory, nor peace. When will the solution come—and where from?

(Z.K. 277, entry for 10 October 1915)

'Terrible country! Terrible hearts!' he quoted Pushkin after a talk with Hippius and the two Dmitriys (Merezhkovsky and Filosofov) on 27 November 1915.

---

[k] In Apollon, no. 10, 1914.   [l] Two popular poets.

Now, with every passing month, Blok became more and more sceptical about the war. On 6 March 1916, for instance, Pyast read him extracts from his own passionately patriotic day-to-day account of its early days. The artificiality of all their would-be heroic enthusiasms showed up with painful clarity and Blok wrote in his notebook:

Today I have understood that the distinguishing characteristic of this war is its *lack of greatness* ... it is nothing but one vast mobile factory.... Undoubtedly it is the most prosaic war that ever was.... That is because the world has been finally taken over by the so-called Antichrist.

This is why it is so impossible to whip up any patriotism.

(Z.K. 283)

All that a self-respecting artist could do was to maintain a lofty, apolitical attitude—however despicable this might *seem* when men were dying in their millions and the country on the verge of ruin. 'The only object worthy of enthusiasm is somewhere outside the bounds of this war; the object deserving of indignation sits behind a screen and is faceless, which prevents it receiving the slap it deserves...' (Z.K. 284), Blok noted, baffled and anxious. He was back where he had been when he wrote *On the Field of Kulikovo*: a warrior of the reserve, waiting for the call to arms. All he could *do* was to guard that passive, receptive state which, as far back as 1910, he had defined as 'spiritual diet' and 'sobriety', and which involved a deliberate retreat from 'the cares of the vain world'.[m]

The stringency with which Blok avoided such 'cares' during the winter of 1915–16 can be clearly seen in the incident of the wedding of his cousin Sofia Tutolmina (*née* Kachalova), a social occasion at which he was confronted—for the last time—with his father's family in all their worldly glory. Blok considered he had been 'had': his cousin, of whom he had been quite fond in his student days, had told him the wedding would be private and he had consented to be *schaffer* together with another cousin, a distinguished chemist, 'Niks' Kachalov. News of the marriage had, however, got about and plans were changed. Blok found himself in a brightly lit church full of relatives. Decency impelled him to last out the ceremony, but he flatly refused to attend the supper-reception afterwards. His cousins sent him flowers and verses. His reply, though gently phrased and courteous, was forbidding in the extreme and clearly defines his attitude to that Establishment of which he might so easily have become a part. Having thanked for the 'splendid flowers' and the verses, and

[m] In his speech 'On the Calling of the poet' Blok used this quotation from Pushkin in a similar context to define the first task 'laid upon the poet by his service' (VI. 163).

apologized with genuine embarrassment for upsetting Sofia, Blok went on to explain, as simply as he could, that he was not ('heaven forbid') motivated by pride:

For a thousand reasons my life has fallen out in such a way that, with a few exceptions, I find it very hard to be with people, I look on life gloomily, as they say (though I don't myself consider my attitude gloomy), and so that I have no feeling for the ties of kinship; at the same time, I know that the work I have to do (whether for good or ill—as you know I'm not in the least complacent) demands that I should be as I am and not otherwise.

You write 'brother'," and I cannot answer you as warmly and sincerely, because I do not feel this word.... What I demand of life is either the absolute, which it does not give—or nothing at all. All contemporary life is a *cold horror*, individual bright spots notwithstanding, a horror which is not going to get any better for a long time. I cannot, for instance, understand how you can say that everything is all right when our country is, perhaps, on the verge of collapse, when the social question has become so acute throughout the world, when there is no society, no state, no family, no personality where there is even comparative well-being.

(VIII. 453–5)

One person who understood and to some extent shared Blok's 'gloomy' sense of mission was Elizaveta Yur'evna Kuzmina-Karavayeva. She had returned to Petrograd from the South at the beginning of the war and they had even then embarked on one of those endless conversations that went on from meeting to meeting, speaking of 'the way' and 'the power', the 'time' and the 'season' (Z.K. 291).

From her provincial retirement among the hunters, fishermen, and peasants of the South, Elizaveta Yur'evna had brought the same conviction that the Merezhkovskys had derived from life in Paris and Petersburg and Blok from his own listening heart: that this war was the prelude to the end of Russia as they had known it. More than this, the strange pity and indignation on behalf of Christ that she had experienced in the salons of the decadent literati had become a solid and durable faith. Now, she felt Russia to be walking a knife-edge between salvation and perdition, and though Blok was no leader and she knew as well as he that he did not know 'the way' through the inevitable period of catastrophe and change to which her country was committed, she yet came to him and told him that

---

" The normal form of address to a cousin in Russian, a first cousin being a 'brother' (of the second degree), a second cousin being a brother (of the third degree), etc. Though habitual, it nevertheless sounds warmer than the remote English 'cousin', so I have let it stand in translation.

she and many others would follow him wherever he chose to go because of an instinctive feeling that he had, as it were, agreed of his own free will to bear their burdens. In her own account of their conversations she recalled saying to him:

'Before her death, Russia has concentrated all her most terrible rays on you and you are burning away for her and in her name, as her image, perhaps. What can we do? What can I do, who love you? Put out the flames— we cannot, and if we could we would not have the right. There is nothing, nothing that anyone can do to help.'

He listened in silence. Then said: 'I accept all that, because I have known it for a long time. Only give it time. It will all happen of itself.'[16]

One day in March 1916, standing in the hallway of his flat with his hands on her shoulders, Blok had accepted her participation in this vaguely defined act of coinherence and substitution. The next day, however, he hadn't wanted to talk about it. He had left her a note: 'Forgive me. I am merry at the moment and not clear in my mind. Have gone for a walk. For the time being, it is necessary to stop all this. A. B.'

Feeling something had remained unsaid, driven by a compulsion which overcame her shyness as it had on the day she gate-crashed his flat that freezing February of 1908, she had calmly sat down on the stairs to wait for him—for three solid hours. It was not until she saw his exhausted face that she was overcome with a kind of shame at her own persistence. All of a sudden, she was in a great hurry to be gone, but, as she left (at five o'clock in the morning), he asked her to walk by his window every day, to watch over him in thought: 'Just walk and look up. That's all.'[17]

Reading his notebooks, from which it is clear that Elizaveta Yur'evna's intensity wearied him—as Zhenya Ivanov's sometimes did 'almost physically' (Z.K. 203)—this last request might appear as just a kindly way of asking her not to come again. But Blok was not given to sparing people's feelings, especially those of people he respected. Once, in answer to a letter giving him an account of all she had discovered for herself after leaving Petersburg, he had written: 'I do not lie to you' (VIII. 430). Now, by asking her not to force him into overportentous discussion, he was, courteously but inexorably, as was his way, putting the relationship back where it belonged: in the realm of the 'inexpressible'.

At the same time, he did indeed find the company of intensely spiritual people irksome, particularly during this exhausting period of expectant inaction. Most of the time, he preferred Del'mas singing or bringing him roses or the joyous 'da' with which he acknowledged their passionate nights: or Lyuba to comfort him with childhood and to make him laugh with stories against herself.

6

In the oppressive atmosphere of those winter months, it had come as a welcome recall to art and to what he knew he could do well when a telegram arrived towards the end of February 1916 from Nemirovich-Danchenko, informing him that the Moscow Art Theatre did, after all, wish to stage *The Rose and the Cross* and would welcome the presence of the author for consultations. Blok left for Moscow on 29 March and stayed for just over a week—in his element. Kachalov, one of the greatest actors of the day, had been cast as Gaetan but subsequently asked for the part of Bertrand.º Of the two rival actresses who might have played Izora, Blok 'began to fall in love' with the wrong one. He agreed, however, that her voice was 'impossible' for Izora and the part was given to the younger Olga Vladimirovna Gzovskaya.[18] Blok talked to her at length and wrote her several letters about his heroine. Apart from working with the actors, which he enjoyed, Blok attended an all-night punch party with gipsy singers at Kachalov's and lunched several times with Stanislavsky.

He left reasonably well satisfied with the way things were going, though somewhat perturbed by the suddenly increased interest that Stanislavsky himself had begun to show in the production, just as the actors had been settling down to work under the direction of Nemirovich-Danchenko and Luzhsky. Nevertheless, Blok had not been disappointed by the Moscow Art Theatre at work. 'I have never seen anything like it,' he said. 'The actors come to rehearsal as if to a festival.' What he did not realize was that for them this solemnity had been induced by his own reading: the scarcely perceptible change in the expression of the face, the stance, the timbre of his voice which made him *become* each character in turn.

Blok returned to Petrograd for Easter and was almost immediately attacked by the now familiar sense of foreboding. On Easter night he walked with Del'mas to observe the celebration outside St. Isaac's Cathedral. The crowds had dwindled to less than half their pre-war numbers:

There were scarcely any illuminations. No 'solemnity' whatsoever, though neither was there the gloom and blackness of former years. All over

º At a later stage the following year he went back to Gaetan.

Falconet's statue[p] swarmed a crowd of little boys, hooligans, hanging on to the tail, sitting on the serpent, smoking under the horse's stomach. Total demoralization. Petersburg—finis.

(Z.K. 295)

After Easter, Blok's mother, who had suffered a severe inflammation of the lungs earlier that spring, had an alarming relapse. Blok and Adam Feliksovich saw off a sad and anxious Frants, who had been home on leave but had to return to the front on 15 April, and the poet was left to supervise his mother's recovery. By 4 May, however, Aleksandra Andreyevna was well enough to leave with her sister for Shakhmatovo.

On 23 May Blok was called upon to act *schaffer* at another marriage ceremony, this time a request to which he agreed willingly, for it was to Zhenya Ivanov: 'a simple, decent wedding in the sunlight', he recorded; 'I held the crown over Zhenya, changed the rings' (Z.K. 301).

He did not follow his mother to Shakhmatovo that summer because, on 27 May, he began work on *Retribution* again, straining every nerve, as he had in 1911, to break out 'from the individual to the general' (Z.K. 304), and seeking once more to put aside lyric poetry. 'I really should give up writing lyric verses, because they come too easy to me' (Z.K. 295). By 4 June he had finally finished Chapter 1 and worked in the Prologue and the introductory lines on the nineteenth and twentieth centuries. Yet it was the lyric poetry he wrote that summer, some of it very 'individual' indeed, which has preserved the flavour of the times with far greater pungency than the smooth, gently ironic saga of the Beketov family that he was so enthusiastically adding to his long 'objective' poem.

It was again Merezhkovsky's word *odichaniye*—'going savage', or 'running wild'—that provided the key to one of Blok's harshest poems, 'You say I am cold, I am dry, and reserved' (III. 156–7),[q] which he wrote the day after finishing the first chapter of *Retribution*:

.   .   .   .

It has happened. The world has run wild. Not one spark
From the lighthouse tower shines out ahead.

[p] The Bronze Horseman, the equestrian statue of Peter the Great which has come to symbolize the city itself.

[q] His mother suggested the poem should be entitled 'To a friend', but there is no evidence that it was addressed to any one particular person.

And intolerable now the encompassing dark
For those who in the stars have not read.

And the hearts of all those who know naught of the past
Or the promise beyond future night
Are clouded with weariness, vengeance—disgust
Marks each face with a cynical blight.

.   .   .   .   .

Your face mask with iron till the time be full ripe
And with reverence honour your graves . . .
Let iron be the shield of that last paradise
Where there's no place for madness—or slaves.[19]

In such a darkening world, private happiness was further from him
than ever. In harsh, tender, desolate verse, Blok had already commemorated his dismissal of this stubbornly recurrent dream.[r] Now
was the time of final self-renunciation:

Having become aware of myself as an artist I am again speaking as it were
for the community. . . .[s]
In myself there still remains very much that is personal. This transformation of life has been dragging on for years, bound up with agonizing back-
slidings. There is still ambition in me, and sensuality; that is probably the
chief thing that has remained and will last the longest.
But already in the foreground of the soul new groupings of thought are
forming, new feelings and attitudes to the world. May God help me to cross
the desert; *organically to introduce the new and the general into the organic and
individual which forms the content of my first four books.*[t]

(Z.K. 304; entry for 3 June 1916)

In this 'desert', he was again close to Lyuba, faithful 'comrade'
and unfaithful wife, who no longer offered him the least illusion of
happiness. To realize what Lyuba meant to Blok, it is necessary to
see rather than to read their letters and notes: the absurd drawings,
childish private jokes, nicknames and misspellings. Into his notebooks Blok stuck little doodles she did when answering the telephone
because they had amused him; the small doings of her workers'
theatre made him laugh ('There was only the policeman and some
children watching. All the other people were enjoying themselves
in their own way. But Lyuba shouted them all down and actually

---

[r] The poems 'Brought to Judgement' (III. 151–2; 11 October 1915) and 'To begin with
you turned all to jest' (III. 219; 29 February 1916) commemorate attempts to impose this
dismissal on Del'mas. Other poems, written after their first 'break' in August 1914, deal
with the same theme (III. 218, 220, 221).
[s] In Russian Blok uses the vivid expression *obshchim slovom*, lit. 'with everybody's word'.
[t] Italics mine. A. P.

got a special round of applause')'; 'Lyuba is again showing firmness and a sense of principle. She has refused one of the lines in Kamensky's play'" (*Z.K.* 278). 'Yesterday at their rehearsal was Grand Duke Konstantin Konstantinovich (the son of the poet). He did no one any harm but showed off in front of the soldiers, crowed like a cock and danced.... Lyuba had a lift in the Grand Duke's car—she is delighted' (*Z.K.* 303). When she had been at the front, every entry about her letters, parcels sent to her, news of her, was made in red crayon. It was for her, above all, that he laboured on, refusing to give in to life:

Bu gave me the idea.
    There once lived a husband and wife. Both were unhappy. In the end, the wife said to her husband: 'It's unbearable to go on living like this. You are stronger than I am. If you wish me well, go out into the street and find a little end of string and pull it so that all the world will change.'
    The husband felt he could not gainsay his wife. He went out into the street and was most discouraged, because he didn't know where to look for the end of string.
    Then suddenly he saw ...

                                                                (*Z.K.* 283)

That summer he found they could talk about getting old. 'Without Bu,' he wrote, 'things would be very bad' (*Z.K.* 307). Sometimes he seemed to yearn for a real reconciliation:

Night: from Lyuba's room I hear 'What pleasure do you get out of tormenting me?...' I go in, hoping that she is talking to herself about me. She was rehearsing.
    There is no way out for me. I'm tired. That'll do.

                                                                (*Z.K.* 311)

On 29 May 1916, once again on the Russian All Souls' Day," he had written: 'I have had 100 women—200—300 (or more?), but really only two: one is Lyuba; the other—all the rest ...' (*Z.K.* 303).
    He continued to see Del'mas until, on 17 June 1916, she left to holiday in Chernigov, but for the time being at least, she was only 'the most vivid, the most true, the most charming' (III. 221) amongst 'all the rest'.

" The play, as it happened, was forbidden by the censor anyway.
" It was on All Souls' Day 1913 that he had written before to Lyuba about her unique place in his affections.

7

The chief events of Blok's last few months of civilian life were wholly inward.

On 14 June, for instance, he bought the bedside book of many good Orthodox Christians, the Russian translation of the *Philokalia*, at a second-hand book stall. Brought up on 'wordly' literature, he came fresh to it, and was amazed at its relevance to his poetry. He wrote to Aleksandra Andreyevna 'about Yevgariy, a monk whose name is not even in Efron's Encyclopaedia' (*Z.K.* 307): 'What particularly interested me is that Yevgariy's attitude to demons is exactly the same as mine to doubles, in the article "On Symbolism", for instance. . . .' In Yevgariy's humanity and practical advice to novices, Blok felt something akin to Strindberg, something reassuringly 'modest', 'human', 'simple and useful', quite unlike what he called the uncompromising 'metaphysics'[w] of the Gospel:

As you know, the invariable technique of monks is to expound texts from the Holy Scriptures on the basis of their own personal experience. I retain a very strange impression from this: the texts—every single one of them— remain dead, but the experience is alive.

(VIII. 464)

'I know. I know it all', he wrote in the margin against Yevgariy's disquisition on the seductive cunning displayed by the demon that diverts men's thoughts from their true calling. But the demon of despondency, which the Abbot compares to a poison, useful in small quantities as an antidote but deadly if taken 'without measure', seemed to him one that was 'indispensable to the artist'.[20]

Over the ages, spirit spoke to spirit with great clarity and Blok, acutely 'aware of himself as an artist', was again fully alive to the *danger* of mysticism. The image of the Demon had reasserted itself in his poetry. For the past seven years, he had struggled to discipline himself, to confine his art to the purely human, to the psychological, not to force anything, not to 'let the "mysticism" break through' (*Z.K.* 285). Now, as in the cycle *Carmen*, he was feeling his wings again, and they were not angel's wings:

> Yes. I will bear you with me, onward
> Through empty flaming skies to where
> A star looms like an earth beyond us
> And earth has dwindled to a star.

---

[w] By 'metaphysics' Blok meant not so much the denial of the flesh as a complete ignoring of the requirements of the body, as though it did not really exist.

Dumbfounded then, in awed amazement,
Worlds new-created you'll perceive.
The play of my imagination
Strange visions passing all belief.

Fear and infirmity will seize you
And you will whisper: Let me be ...
My wings will open to release you
And I will smile: Fly, you are free.

Before this smile divinely gentle,
Disintegrating as you fly,
You'll sail—a far-flung, shimmering pebble—
Down through the shining, empty sky....

(III. 60)

Life, however, had now no intention of allowing him too free a flight. The time of inaction was past. Every few weeks that summer there were rumours of impending conscription. Being one of the few poets with establishment connections, military and civilian, Blok was becoming more and more involved in helping others: Remizov's brother—found not fit for active service; N. P. Ge—helped to enter the Heavy Artillery through General Belayev; Knyazhnin—proposed as an engineer to a munitions factory but turned down by the workers, who were 'fighting capitalism' (this in the early summer of 1916) and wanted their own nominee; various other quite obscure people. As V. A. Zorgenfrey[x] said, Blok was no sentimentalist and quite capable of refusing help, but when he did undertake to do anything for anybody, he saw it through. He had even—to the grateful amazement of the recipient—managed to get enough money transferred to Andrey Bely from the proceeds of *Petersburg* to enable him to return to Russia.[y]

On 28 June, having decided that it would be preferable to volunteer for the Heavy Artillery under Belayev than to wait to be called up, Blok sat down to sort out his affairs on paper and produced a most characteristic document, a strange mixture of poetry and pedantry, people and books:

My real friends: Zhenya (Ivanov), A. V. Hippius, Pyast (Pestovsky), Zorgenfrey.
  My valued acquaintances: Knyazhnin (Ivoylov); Verkhovsky, Ge.

[x] A minor poet and an admirer and imitator of Blok since 1906, Zorgenfrey had been increasingly in his company during the war years and had become a personal friend.
[y] Bely's thank-you letter,[21] in his usual stream-of-consciousness style and full of complaints about petty intrigue amongst the anthroposophists, reached Blok on 16 July, just as he was preparing to leave for the war, and rather shocked him by its impetuous immaturity.

Kindred spirits: A. Bely (Bugayev); Z. N. Hippius; P. S. Solov'eva; Aleksandra Nikolayevna Chebotarevskaya.

Remembered: Kupreyanov (will be an artist), Minich (a kindly girl).[z]

Catalogue of books (in Petersburg): have got. Some are missing (borrowed)—noted in my business notebook for this year.

In spite of the fact (or perhaps because of the fact) that I have at last 'firmly felt' myself to be *an artist,* it is seldom now that I weep over an idea (rather dully) or get drunk on harmony. The freshness has gone, is not what it was.

With 'literature' I have no connection[aa] and am proud of the fact. What I have done really worth the doing I have done *independently,* i.e. I have been dependent only on what was not fortuitous.

The best remains the *Verses about the Most Beautiful Lady.* Time should not touch them, however weak I may have been as an artist.

Of my *plays,* 'Théophile' is quite superfluous and very doubtful is *The King in the Square. The Rose and the Cross* should be published without notes.[bb]

The cycle *Carmen* should end with the poem 'Why do you drop your eyes...?'[cc]

It's not worth while to collect a volume of articles. The best article is the one 'On Symbolism'.[dd] But it is all unfinished. There is not a book to be got out of it, because the circle is not full-drawn.

The poem[ee] remains unfinished. From the technical point of view the last verses to be written mark a falling-off.

The drama about the industrial renaissance of Russia to which I have been working up for several years and which requires a great many more taking-off points (even historical) must be left to someone else—only not to a liberal or a conservative but to someone like me—uncommitted.

I am not afraid of shrapnel. But the smell of the war and of everything that goes with it is *khamstvo.*[ff] It has been lying in wait for me since my

---

[z] Two young people who had themselves sought the poet's advice on their work: N. A. Minich was a plump, good-natured girl poet and N. N. Kupreyanov, a graphic artist fourteen years Blok's junior who had written asking permission to call and show him a hand-written, illustrated copy of *The Rose and the Cross.* He first called at Blok's flat on 18 March 1915 (*Z.K.* 258). The remark 'will be an artist' was probably elicited by a rather discouraged letter of 20 May 1916 written after Kupreyanov's work had been turned down for one of the *Mir Iskusstva* exhibitions ('by Bilibin & Narbut; Benois and Petrov-Vodkin were for him,' Blok noted, *Z.K.* 301). Enclosing as a gift his engraving of King David, Kupreyanov had written that he sent it in part 'so that you should not forget that I am trying to become an artist'.[22]

[aa] By 'literature' Blok meant the same as Verlaine: 'Toute la reste est littérature'!

[bb] Blok had actually appended his sources to the text of *The Rose and the Cross,* rather in the form of a learned commentary (IV. 510–20).

[cc] This is the first line of the poem 'Brought to Judgement' (III. 151).

[dd] 'On the Present State of Russian Symbolism', 1910.

[ee] *Retribution.*

[ff] The Russian word *khamstvo*—from the biblical Ham who 'looked upon his father's nakedness'—is the antonym of all sensitivity, refinement, and true courtesy.

school days in many and varied forms, and now—it has me by the throat. The stench of a soldier's greatcoat is not to be endured. To finish the thought, this senseless war is not going to end in anything. Like all *khamstvo*, it is without end or beginning, without form or image.

(Z.K. 309–10)

These notes were written, with the obvious thought that he might not return from the front, after a talk with a volunteer to the Artillery, one Strakhov, who had called at the Belayevs' request to tell Blok what he might expect of army life. Blok had been horrified but resigned, until Lyuba, dashing out on her way to rehearsals the following morning, had informed him that, on second thoughts, she considered the Artillery too rigorous for him.

Annoyed but relieved, for she had but endorsed his own opinion, Blok wrote to Strakhov that he did not, after all, intend to volunteer, and applied to Zorgenfrey, who had a job in the Ministry of Trade, to help him escape call-up in some exempt occupation. Zorgenfrey, who hero-worshipped Blok, was shocked and informed him bluntly that it was his duty to go and get killed, scarcely believing his ears when Blok advanced such 'childish' arguments as that one might 'catch something' from eating from a communal plate.[23] The poet, however, was unabashed. The intelligentsia had *always* been against joining the army, he said, and if he hadn't gone in for active service in the cause of revolution why on earth should he do so now, for a war that was not even a cause?

Zorgenfrey relaxed his disapproval and managed, in the nick of time, to get Blok into the Organization of Zemstvos' 13th Construction Engineering Division, which was engaged in supervising the building of fortifications just behind the front line in the Pinsk marshes. His duties, Blok informed his mother (VIII. 464–5), would be to keep account of the progress of this construction. He would rank as an officer and wear 'almost an officer's uniform', and the head of his *druzhina*,[gg] an architect, was a distant acquaintance.

Even so, he had trouble with Aleksandra Andreyevna, who responded to a request for white socks and black boots by turning up in person from Shakhmatovo on 9 July ('we spent the whole day together, very badly', Z.K. 313). His nerves in tatters, he quarrelled with Lyuba but eventually managed to soothe his mother down ('She's now reconciled to everything, more or less, except the fevers from the Pinsk marshes', Z.K. 314). She persuaded him to go down to Shakhmatovo with her 'in silence in a first-class carriage' to take

gg Used originally for the bodyguard of a prince, the term later came to cover all kinds of voluntary, vigilante-type organizations.

leave of his home and his aunt. He had been wondering all summer what was going on in the garden, how his trimming and cutting back had affected the lilac, and his letters home had contained a stream of horticultural questions and instructions. Now he had two clear days in the beauty and the stillness of his home—the last.

The return journey was more cheerful (second class with a crowd of likeable officers). Del'mas was absent and Lyubov', as usual, absorbed in her career. There was something utterly flat about the last fortnight in Petrograd. On 26 July he left for Pinsk.

8

Life in the marshes was not altogether objectionable, just useless and boring. While on duty Blok, neither an absent-minded officer nor a half-hearted poet, made no attempt to write, a fact which bears out the likelihood that, had he chosen to follow a conventional career in 1906 when he wrote the dialogue 'On Love, Poetry, and the Civil Service', his gift would almost certainly have withered. Now, at thirty-six, he reverted to type. The letters he wrote to Aleksandra Andreyevna, Lyuba, and Del'mas recall now the hard efficiency of the sea-going surgeon-Bloks, now the gallantry and gaiety of the Decembrists, now the cool curiosity and vigour which helped his great-grandfather Karelin turn exile into discovery and success.

The summer months, indeed, were almost enjoyable:

I am leading an animal existence, spend half my day with my horse riding through wood and field and bog, almost unwashed; then we drink tea round the samovar, curse our superiors, doze or sleep, scribble away in the office, sometimes sit on the earth banked up round our *izba* and watch the pigs and the geese. There is much to be said for all this, but when it's over it will all seem like a dream.

(VIII. 474, letter of 21–28 August 1916)

Always methodical with any sort of paper work, Blok had had practical experience of managing men at Shakhmatovo and was a success in his duties.[hh]

Meanwhile, Lyubov' kept him in touch with what was going on in his own world. In a letter of 1 September 1916 she was able to tell him the latest developments in the staging of *The Rose and the Cross*. Stanislavsky, she wrote, now thought it essential to find a financial backer for the play and wanted to use minimal decorations

---

[hh] Indeed, at one stage—when he exposed a dastardly plot on the part of the cook-house staff to make a good thing for themselves out of catering for his workers—he seems to have had actually to dodge promotion.[24]

(all done by drapes and lighting) rather than Dobuzhinsky's designs[ii] for a massive set. She had also had a visit from Andrey Bely, back from Switzerland at last and on his way to Moscow to offer himself for call-up. 'He has grown much older, grey at the temples, thin as a stick, and much simpler, more sincere, and the "upside-down eyes", the duality have gone.'[26] At Blok's request, she had spent some time after his departure going through proofs of his new *Collected Poems* for Musaget, and had been impressed by the section 'The Motherland': 'But I just can't get over it, Lalalka,' she had written, 'what wonderful poetry you write! And how does it sometimes happen that I forget about it?'[27]

Yet when, later that autumn, he obtained leave from the *druzhina*, Lyubov' was not in Petrograd to meet him but away with a new theatre company in Orenburg. Before engaging herself in this way she had implored, but never got, Blok's approval, and now she did not encourage him to come and see her. The only hope for some real improvement in their relationship seemed—to them both—the distant possibility of an idyllic old age.

Blok's leave, indeed, proved disappointing in every respect. He succeeded in finally offending and alienating Leonid Andreyev by a rather tactless refusal to contribute to his patriotic newspaper *Russkaya Volya*, and the staging of *The Rose and the Cross* (it was to help with this that he had been granted leave in the first place) had again lost impetus, so that he was not, as expected, called to Moscow, but spent the time in his empty flat in Petrograd. Even so, this brief sojourn in the capital served to remind him that he was a private person and a man of literature and was unsettling.

During the summer, he had rather enjoyed sharing a crowded peasant's *izba* near the construction site with a few congenial young officers. For the winter, however, he returned to the headquarters of the *druzhina* at the house of Prince Drutskoy-Lyubetskiy, and this meant a stiffer atmosphere, more complicated social relationships, and much time wasted in eating, drinking, and playing chess:

The Princess gives our company enormous suppers that are enough to kill you; a good chef, turkey, different kinds of stuffing; I could hardly breathe yesterday. The Princess is very talkative and hectoring, but I like her because her first husband committed suicide, the second is jealous and beats her, she used to be a trainer of boa constrictors in the circus—and has other similar merits.[28]

[ii] Blok had expressly wished Dobuzhinsky to design the sets for his play, and had demanded historical accuracy and realistic detail. Neither the artist nor Blok himself was altogether happy with the result.[25]

As the winter wore on, the atmosphere at headquarters became increasingly claustrophobic and relations correspondingly strained—though Blok himself seems to have suffered from this only indirectly. Still, it was a relief to escape out of doors into a wide landscape of peat bog and black alder, with a sky enlivened by 'very pretty' puffs of bursting shell.

Not that Blok complained. He was the moving spirit of a New Year party (which he himself actually enjoyed!). After the New Year, Count Aleksey Tolstoy, on the staff of a general making a tour of inspection of work behind the lines, visited Porokhonsk:

In January 1917 one frosty morning ... I got out of the train at a little station all buried in forests and snow and went on foot to a settlement of plywood huts which was the headquarters of the *druzhina*. My job was to make enquiries about some Bashkirs who were working for them.

I was led into a light, warmly heated hut where there were some clerks at work who ran off to call the man in charge. He appeared a few minutes later, a lean, tall, good-looking man, his face flushed from the frost and his eyelashes all rimed with it. The last thing I could have expected was that the man in charge would turn out to be—Aleksandr Blok.

He bade me welcome merrily and immediately opened up his books. When we had dispatched the required information to the General, Blok and I went for a stroll. He told me that it was a fine life here, how he had been promoted from *desyatnik* to works manager, how much time he spent in the saddle; we spoke of the war, of the beauty of the winter. When I asked if he were writing anything just now he answered with indifference: 'No, I'm doing nothing.' In the twilight we went to supper in the old, dark country mansion where Blok was quartered. In the long corridor we met the mistress of the house, a faded woman; she looked at Blok with gloomy, deep eyes and gave us a haughty nod as she passed.

Lighting the lamp in his room, Blok said to me: 'If you ask me, there'll be a crime in this house....'[29]

The gloom in the house notwithstanding, there were moments to which Blok knew it would always be stimulating to look back:

In spite of the fact that these marshes have been forgotten not only by the Germans but by God as well, there is wonderful air here, constant changes of wind, deep snow, and at night—lights in village windows; all that, as always, is real. Last night, for instance, we heard the firing at the front suddenly hotting up, saw the searchlights and flares come into play and the horizon all lit up with blazing shells; we mounted our horses and rode into the little hills which look towards the front; while we were on our way, of course, it all petered out, but the ride itself was very pleasant and interesting. A dark night, a path through the snow, trees and bushes looming up like sleighs as though they were actually coming to meet us, the ruins of a windmill with broken sails and a strong wind. At last I've got them to send me the mare I rode in the First Division, I love her very much, she has an English head. . . .³⁰

There was, however, one thing that worried him both at the time and after he had left the *druzhina*: a nagging feeling of guilt towards the workmen under his command. Naturally, the *druzhina* got only men who were unfit for battle: the old, the sick in mind or body, the halt and the lame, '. . . and there's nothing you can do about it. You can't cure them all. You can't even get them properly shod . . .' (VIII. 475).

This feeling of guilt Blok brought home with him. It shaped his attitude to 'the people'—one of unbounded tolerance—and his attitude to the bourgeoisie and all people of privilege, himself and his family included: an exigent, uncompromising attitude. It also gave a sense of emotional, humane urgency to his ever-mounting opposition to the war.

CHAPTER VIII

The Revolution

(March 1917 – November 1917)

'Are you writing or not?—He's writing. He's not writing.
He can't write.'
Leave me alone. What do you call 'writing'? To mess
up paper with ink?—That's something within the scope of
every chief clerk in the 13th *druzhina*. How do you know
whether I am writing or not? I don't always know myself.
(*Z.K.* 318, entry for 22 April 1917)

'Is this the beginning of life?' Blok wondered as he resumed his notebooks on his return from six months' quasi-military service in the
Pinsk marshes.

I have 'run wild': physically (deceptively) in good form, morally off
balance (neurasthenia—Doctor Kannabikh). I need to get down to my *own
work*, to be inwardly free, to have the time and means to be an artist....
    I have no clear opinion of what is going on, and this when, by the will
of fate, I have been set to be witness to a great epoch. By the will of fate
(and not by my own *feeble strength*) I am an artist, that is a witness.
(*Z.K.* 316, entry for 14 April 1917)

For the beginning of life, as he suspected, it was too late, but after
the February revolution Blok did feel an imperative need to make
some kind of a new beginning. The Pinsk marshes had been all right
while nothing much was going on—and for Blok the 1914–18 War
was just that: nothing much, 'every superfluous day' of which was
'sweeping away culture'. Now, however, that things were happening, as he wrote to his mother, 'in the spirit of my forebodings' (VIII.
484), he was irresistibly drawn back to Petrograd, to the centre of
events.
    Without the least qualm of conscience, he 'deserted' from his *druz-
hina* and took steps to get himself usefully employed in the capital

in such a capacity as would protect him from recall, conscription to the ranks, and military tribunals.

1

When the news of rioting in Petrograd, the enforced abdication of the Tsar, and the establishment of a Provisional Government reached the front in February 1917, Blok determined to take some overdue leave; but he did not hurry. In Petrograd, no one was expecting him. His mother, whose nerves and general condition had deteriorated badly without his sustaining presence that winter, was in a sanatorium at Kryukovo near Moscow. Lyuba had not yet returned from her acting in Orenburg. Maria Beketova was holding the fort in their flat, and it was she and her faithful Annushka who eventually welcomed him home on 19 March 1917. The journey had thrilled him, as did the free, festive atmosphere of 'the bloodless revolution', though there were things about the new democracy which he admitted would take some getting used to, which were just a little 'shocking'.

It would be some time, he realized, before he would be in a state to perceive anything beyond how pleasant it was to be home and bathed and in civvies again: '... My mind is still rusty. I am very well, exorbitantly hardened by riding, fresh air, and continence, so that I cannot yet see anything clearly through my own involuntary fitness ...' (VIII. 479). Waiting for Lyuba to rejoin him in Petrograd, which she did a few days after his arrival, he wandered about the city enchanted by the 'simple miracle' of freedom. A visit to the Merezhkovskys brought him much inside information about recent events, and with them he again felt himself 'a person and not the pariah I had become accustomed to feel myself at the front' (VIII. 480–1).

Before he put the front temporarily out of his mind, however, he spent some hours in the second-hand bookshops buying in a small library for his workers, which he then dispatched to Poro-khonsk. After Lyuba's arrival Blok decided to go to Moscow to visit his mother and to look in on Nemirovich-Danchenko and *The Rose and the Cross*. That this would mean overstaying his leave he was aware, and was not yet certain how he would deal with the situation, but the heady atmosphere of general permissiveness made him optimistic:

Quite extraordinary is the feeling that nothing is forbidden, menacing, breath-taking and terribly exciting. Almost anything might happen and the moment—for the country, for the state, for 'property' of all sorts—is a perilous one, but all is overcome by the awareness that a miracle has taken place and, therefore, we may expect more miracles.... You might think that there was everything to fear but there is nothing frightening about it, freedom has an extraordinary majesty, the armoured cars with red flags, soldiers' trenchcoats with red armbands, the Winter Palace with a red flag on the roof. The Lithuanian Castle and the Court Rooms have been gutted by fire and the eye is riveted by the beauty of their façades, licked clean by the flames. All the foulness that made them so hideous within has burnt out.

(VIII. 480, letter to his mother of 23 March 1917)

On Easter night, as usual, he walked down to the square before St. Isaac's Cathedral:

Mama, this year Easter has passed less painfully than I ever remember. Only now does one see how the brute force of autocracy penetrated everywhere, even into things one would have thought immune. Last night I was at St. Isaac's Cathedral. There were far fewer people than usual and very good order. They allowed everyone there was room for into the church and the rest milled about quite freely in the square, there were no mounted police to create panic, nor the crowds of cars with high-society occupants which used to make it impossible to walk around. There were almost no illuminations, only the usual salute and from all parts of the town a fusillade of guns and revolvers—fired into the air in honour of the feast day.... 'The dregs of society' are keeping a low profile everywhere, which delights me rather more than it should, really—to the point of malice.[a]

Easter week, even in this first year of the revolution and third year of the war, meant people: Blok lunched with the artists Dobuzhinsky, Benois, and Igor Grabar and saw or gathered news of Aleksandra Chebotarevskaya, Zorgenfrey, Remizov, Meyerhold—now full of plans to secure *The Rose and the Cross* for the cinema, and Poliksena Sergeyevna Solov'eva:

...Everyone you see and talk to is worried, each in his or her own way, about the way things are going and only I, thrown out of life by the war, am serene in my attitude. When I've had time to get my eye in I shall probably have to rethink a great deal. One thing is certain and that is that a great deal more is going to happen, almost everybody feels this.

(VIII. 481–2, letter to his mother of 2 April 1917)

[a] The Russian word is *zloradstvo*—the exact equivalent of the German *Schadenfreude*. By 'the dregs of society', Blok meant the élite—his point of departure being Tolstoy's definition of the working people as '*le vrai grand monde*'.

The trip to Moscow convinced him that the Art Theatre was in a state of revolutionary turmoil and that it was unlikely his play would be staged that year. Rehearsals, however, were still going forward and Blok was able to watch the whole of Act One and Scene 2 of the second act. Gzovskaya was changing theatres and Blok left with the opinion that

...In essence the *only really great artist* is Stanislavsky, who says a lot of very stupid things; but he really does love art because he himself *is* art. *The Rose and the Cross*, though, is quite alien and incomprehensible to him; I think he is insincere (is fooling himself) when he praises the play. He would only tire himself out on it.

In the same letter of 17 April 1917, he admitted his unfitness to judge the work of the theatre on his play, because 'I have lost acuteness of perception and impressions; as an instrument, I am out of order' (VIII. 485).

Blok returned from Moscow depressed and disoriented. A visit to his mother at her sanatorium had done nothing to cheer him up. Neither had his reunion with Lyuba, who had seemed rather sad and intended to go on with her acting in the summer season, this time in Pskov. She had broken with Kuzmin-Karavayev and seemed uncertain of her future as an actress.[b] Nevertheless, she did not choose to keep Blok company while he decided what to do about the future and had already left Petrograd when he got back from Moscow, so that he was again alone with his aunt.

For a few days, he could hardly bring himself to speak to anyone. He saw Del'mas once, then avoided her in spite of her efforts to re-establish their relationship. He wanted to be alone to think and to define his own attitude to what was going on.

Once again, it was the 'yellow peril' that was gnawing at his mind. In many Russians, including Blok's erstwhile allies against the war, the Merezhkovskys, the February revolution had brought out a latent patriotism. In liberal circles it was widely accepted that, now that it was Russia and not the autocracy they were defending, the war must be carried to a victorious conclusion. Blok could not share this opinion. '... Let Europe go on fighting if she wants to,' he wrote to his mother, 'let her, old exhausted *cocotte* that she is: all the wisdom of the world will run out through her fingers, soiled by war and

---

[b] In a long and friendly letter of 14 January 1917, Lyubov' had informed her mother-in-law of this break and assured her that she did not intend to continue indefinitely her nomad life of acting in the provinces.[1]

politics, and others will come and lead her "whither she would not". The yellow peoples, perhaps?"[2]

The war still seemed to him a gigantic act of self-deception: *'We're fed up with it,'* he wrote to his mother on 2 May,

and this Europe cannot understand, for it is *simple*, but in her muddled mind—all is dark. Yet, while despising us more than ever before, she is at the same time mortally afraid of us—or so I think because, if the worst came to the worst, there would be nothing easier for us than to give a free passage to the yellow peoples and allow them to flood not only the *cathédrale de Reims* but all their other sacred shopping centres into the bargain. We, after all, are a dam, in the dam there are sluice-gates, and from now on there is nothing to stop anybody from opening those gates 'in full awareness of their revolutionary power'....

(VIII. 487)

To some extent, Blok was projecting his own mood on to Russia (the capricious: 'we're fed up with it...'). On the other hand, his mood reflected that of an ever-growing number of other people: above all of the huge silent majority of 'soldiers, workers, and peasants'.

The euphoria of the 'simple miracle' of freedom wore off very quickly. So long as the war continued, he realized, nothing would or could radically change. For one thing, though this would certainly not have influenced his thinking had he seen any reason for it, he was not free himself: his position as a deserter was clearly untenable.

Having stalled off his commanding officer, who had sent a telegram demanding his return, he wrote to Tereshchenko, whom he had seen briefly in Moscow, where he had been at the same time as Blok in his new capacity as Minister of Finance to the Provisional Government, and who had now received the portfolio for Foreign Affairs, explaining his dilemma and asking his help.[f] Tereshchenko,

---

[f] A draft of this letter is preserved in Blok's notebook for 30 April 1917 (*Z.K.* 319–20) and reads:

Mikhail Ivanovich,
My service in the 13th Construction Engineering Division is repellent to me because of its indefiniteness and uselessness. The period of my leave is up and I am being recalled and threatened with dismissal. To be a private soldier is beyond my capacity; to enter an officers' training corps it is, presumably, too late, and I doubt I should be a really useful officer. (Help me to find a way out of this situation. If I am of any use, then most probably it would be possible to find some way of applying my powers now, until the war is over: not *my* powers, exactly, but those of the second-class soldier of 1902 Blok). [Bracketed words struck out in manuscript.]
  To pursue my own calling in this situation is impossible, as I am subject to call-up and do not wish to evade it. If it is possible for you, I would ask you to help me by act or advice to find a way out of my present predicament.

for all that he had told Blok in Moscow how his poetry, a small
volume of which he carried with him everywhere, had served him
as a kind of touchstone throughout this chaotic spring, procrasti-
nated. Blok made every allowance for his friend's failure to respond
(he was indeed extremely busy for it was precisely at this time that
he was transferred from one ministry to another), but admitted that
there was an element of 'not wanting to'. To Lyuba he wrote that
to have involved Tereshchenko was, perhaps, 'going too high' for
his small personal problem, but that he had had recourse to him
because he genuinely liked him: he was 'a true artist' and had always
been 'cruelly honest' with him.

While Tereshchenko hesitated, the poet found his own channel
of escape through N. I. Idel'son, Pyast's mathematician friend who
had served with Blok in Porokhonsk and who had connections with
the legal world.[d] Idel'son, thanks to his friendship with N. K. Murav'ev, chairman of the Extraordinary Investigatory Commission
appointed by the Provisional Government to enquire into unlawful
acts committed by Tsarist officials and court dignitaries, had been
recalled especially to work on the Commission, and was able to
recommend Blok for the post of verbatim reporter. On 8 May, the
poet was taken on by the Commission and, in spite of the protests
of his superior officer, officially seconded from the *druzhina*.[e] He was
still 'on military service', had to wear uniform and had less time than
ever for his 'own work'. On the other hand, as 'a witness', he cannot
but have felt that Providence, in the unexpected guise of Idel'son
whom he rather disliked, had presented him with a seat in the front
row.

2

At first, Blok could make nothing of the situation. His carefully cultivated artistic sensibilities did not help him but, on the contrary, left

[d] Idel'son is described in *S.S.* as a lawyer (*prisyazhnyy poverennyy*).

[e] The correspondence went on for a long time. Blok, who considered his work in the
druzhina of little value and who set up to be nobody's judge, was so tickled by the final
formula of release that he quoted it to his mother in a most uncharacteristic nest of exclamation marks: 'The *druzhina* expressed "profound regret at the loss of a comrade of such
rare qualities" and considered that if the Investigatory Commission were to conscript such
people "Revolutionary Democracy can be at ease and certain that the traitors and despots
of our Fatherland will not escape the just sentence of the People's Justice". (!!! There's
what all that correspondence with Lodyzhensky [the superior officer in question] has led
to!!!)' (VIII. 502, letter of 15 June 1917).

him a prey to every fleeting impression, every cross-current of emotion:

As before, 'I can't choose'. For choice an effort of will is required. Strength for that I can find only in heaven, but heaven now is empty for me (all my life from that *point of view* and how it came about). That is, having established myself as an *artist* I paid for it by legalizing, by granting recognition to the 'centre' of life—which (naturally) is empty, because too full of transient content. . . .

(VII. 280)

Throughout the summer of 1917 Blok's work kept him standing at 'the centre of life', trying, fact by fact, to make a pattern of the snarled tangle of 'transient content'. His first attempt was set down in painstaking detail near the beginning of the new diary begun after his return from the front:

The old Russian regime ... required people of faith (faith in the divine right), of courage (undivided in themselves), and honesty (the axioms of morality). Given the enormously swift development of Russia in depth and in breadth, it also required—with mounting insistence—genius.

For a long time those invested with power in Russia had lacked all these qualities. The upper strata declined, demoralizing the lower. All this went on for many years. During the last years, as those invested with power themselves admit, they were already absolutely lost. Nevertheless, the balance was not upset. The lack of power from above was balanced by indifference from below. The Russian regime found support in the inborn characteristics of the people. Denial answered denial. Since the support was purely negative, all that was needed to upset the *status quo* was a push. The push, because of the enormous size of Russia, had to be a very hard one. It was provided by the war of 1914–17. . . . 'The revolutionary people' is a rather doubtful concept. It is not possible that a people for the majority of whom the collapse of the regime was an unexpected 'miracle' would suddenly become revolutionary; indeed, the most striking thing was the utter unexpectedness of it, like a train crash in the night, like a bridge crumbling beneath your feet, like a house falling down.

Revolution presupposes will; has there been any effort of will? There has been, on the part of a small body of people. I do not know even whether or not there really has been a revolution?

It is all in a minor key.

(VII. 254–5, entry for 25 May 1917)

Throughout the summer of 1917, Blok's work on the Investigatory Commission led him into close contact with those who, but a few short months ago, had still been 'invested with power': not the gangster-type reign of terror to which the twentieth century has become all too accustomed, but an organic power hallowed by time and tradition, a net of loyalties and sentiments as complicated and as closely interrelated as the veins and arteries of the human body: 'I am now seeing and hearing something that almost no one hears or sees, that only the very few have the opportunity to observe once in a hundred years' (VIII. 491), he wrote to Lyuba soon after embarking on his work for the Commission. This was true. He heard the whole story of the abdication from first-hand witnesses—all those, indeed, who had themselves played a part in the tragedy, with the exception of the principal figure.ᶠ Contrary to scandalous rumour and suspicion, the Commission established that neither the Empress nor the Tsar had had pro-German sympathies, or was at all fond of 'Cousin Willi'. The Empress, moreover, had never been Rasputin's mistress (as was freely rumoured), nor had Vyrubova (as was almost universally believed). On the other hand, Blok learnt that the sheer incompetence of yesterday's rulers of Russia was greater than could have been imagined, and so was their distrust of one another. Stolypin had had even his own relations watched. Ex-officers of the police explained at length about the use of *agents provocateurs* and the censorship of letters. Blok also learnt that he had been right to sign a protest against the conduct of the Beylis case and another paper expressing relief at the man's acquittal (of the rightness of which he had never, in fact, been 100 per cent certain). He was initiated into the 'dense pornography' befogging the extraordinarily dominant figure of Grigoriy Rasputin.

Blok was, however, forced to admit that Adam Feliksovich, several of whose cronies were being held and interrogated by the Investigatory Commission, had not exaggerated when, on the point of beating a strategic retreat to his country estate, he had informed his nephew that, legally, 'his' Commission had not a leg to stand on. With one or two exceptions, the Commission's 'clients', as they came to call them, could not be held juridically—or even politically—responsible for the misconduct of the war.

When we see that the majority show no vestiges of conviction as to the rightness of the ideas they were professing and the actions they were undertaking only three months ago—we should not forget that this is a *Russian* government; if it was not actually supported by the people, then at least it supported itself on them, nourished itself from them; characteristics exhibited by these people were and still are very much alive in the populace

ᶠ After some hesitation, the Commission decided not to interrogate 'Nikolay Romanov' or his consort, though they did examine their correspondence ('mutually loving', Blok commented).

Blok and his brother officers in the Pinsk marshes, winter 1916–17.
Blok is seated, at left.

Frants Feliksovich Kublitsky-Piottukh,
about 1916.

Lyubov' Dmitriyevna in nurse's
uniform, 1915.

Sketch of Blok by M.P.
Miklachevsky, dated 21 July 1917.

Blok (second from right) with S. F. Ol'denburg (centre) and other members of the
Investigatory Commission. (From the collection of N. P. Il'in)

at large; many strata of the nation have a similar psychology; these characteristics penetrate far more deeply into the body of the people than it might
seem to the abstract eye. Loving Russia, it is still possible to react in various
ways to these characteristics; in indignation, one may love; in contempt,
one may forgive....

(VI. 443)

To his mother he wrote on 18 May 1917:

This absorbing novel with a thousand characters and the most fantastic
combinations, mainly in the spirit of Dostoyevsky (whom Merezhkovsky,
with such unexpected insight, called 'the prophet of the Russian revolution'), is entitled *The History of Russian Autocracy in the Twentieth Century*.

(VIII. 493)

Blok looked at the characters of this 'novel' with the dispassionate
eye of the artist, observing and noting for himself peculiarities of
speech, gesture, facial expression, the way they held their hands. His
diary is like a sketchbook with here a carefully executed portrait,
there the line of a nose, the tilt of an eyebrow, the rough outline
of a figure. A rumpled Vyrubova, half-reclining on her bed, a crutch
pushing up one shoulder; old Goremykin's eyes—'looking into
death'; Protopopov—'moving his ears and all the skin of his face';
General N. I. Ivanov—'A good, kindly, efficient man ... wrinkles
his nose like—now I remember!—General Grek used to do';
'Dzhunkovsky has a talented palm'; Frederiks—'lean, firmly
modelled face, a cane, has kept his dignity ... drums with his fingers
on the table ... most elegant hands, extremely well-bred voice and
manners. Charming—of the olden days. One of the *best* and most
characteristic figures. Elegance'. Markov—from the Union of
the Russian People—'angry, fit and tanned', sitting opposite his
interrogator, the tense, sick, overworked Murav'ev, 'plucking at
his beard and stroking his moustaches, baring his white teeth. Speaks
in a tone verging on insolence ... a terrifying Russian Stenka ...'.
Sobeshchansky, whose function it had been to be present at
executions and whom Blok had often seen in the low haunts he himself frequented: 'Free, he was more terrible than in prison, where he is
just a pathetic, criminal bird: there's a gauze patch of some sort on
his long neck, and where there ought to be a forehead is sorrow
and anxiety....'

Even as he watched the prisoners, so he watched the weary, simple
faces of the soldiers who guarded them: Blok noted when they began
to nod off, when they pricked up their ears to listen. He noted the
wretched latrine smell in the cells of the Peter-Paul Fortress. He and
Idel'son even tried to taste the prisoners' food as they used to taste

their workers' in the *druzhina*, but never got time, trotting from cell to cell after the ever-hastening figure of Murav'ev. He observed how Murav'ev conducted his interrogations, where he gave free rein to his emotion, where he controlled them, to what extent the effect was calculated. He tried to understand the garrison's attitude to the prisoners, which vividly reflected the dichotomy of power between the Provisional Government, represented by the Commission, and the Soviets, represented by the garrison:[g]

... They do not trust the Commission. They don't give milk and eggs to the prisoners who should be on special diet. It is always the same company of Streltsy who are on duty. There is talk of appealing to the Soviet of Soldiers' and Workers' Deputies. Manukhin and the commandant have gone to see Lunacharsky to ask him to use his influence.

In this outwardly absurd situation there is a *deep* Russian idea of justice. The Russian (or a part of his soul) does not judge a man for what he has done but for how he has conducted himself. Hence this: 'Just try the same food as we soldiers get for a while.' Rasputin would have understood that. All these are the abysses of the Russian spirit (so is Bolshevism without any politics whatsoever, in the guise of so-called 'anarchy', insubordination, and Rasputin)—its fathomless abysses. Apart from such abysses, there are hundreds of versts of level fields, empty steppes. But the mountains, the heights?

(*Z.K.* 359)

At the prisoners themselves he tried to look dispassionately:

One should never judge. In misery and humiliation people become like children.... The heart is drenched with tears for the pity of it all; and, remember, one should never judge. Remember again, what Klimovich said in his cell and how he said it; how old Kafafov wept; how Beletsky wept at the interrogation, that he was *ashamed* of his children.

Remember more—more, more, weep more, it may cleanse the soul....
(*Z.K.* 340, entry for 21 May, Trinity Sunday, 1917)

'One should never judge': it was not so much pity as empathy which

[g] The revolution in Petrograd had begun with 'hunger riots': the Provisional Government came into being in February as an improvised attempt on the part of the establishment to control the populace and to introduce reforms which would make it possible for the country to go on being governed at all. The workers and soldiers, however, had their own authority in Petrograd, a Soviet or Council of Deputies. From the beginning, the Soviet had great influence in the capital, where (except for the Bolshevik faction after the arrival of Lenin on 18 April) it was prepared to work under the umbrella of legitimacy provided by co-operation with the Provisional Government—which in its turn, thanks to the recommendation of Nicholas II himself, commanded the loyalty of the High Command of the armed forces.

produced this exclamation.[h] The very next evening, having worked all day on the depositions of Sazonov and Voeykov, he wrote:

I'm tired.... It's as if my nerves had lost their edge from all I've seen and heard. The moment I let myself go—that Rasputin who sits within me raises his head. Of course, it would be like that on All Souls'. All, all of them—the living and the dead children of my age—are within me. How many, many of them there are!

(Z.K. 342)

The 'children of his age'—such as Protopopov,[i] for instance, the last and most disastrous Minister of the Interior—were the products of the same cultural climate as Aleksandr Blok the poet and, indeed, as the other members of the Investigatory Commission were:

Protopopov (even) is a personality of tremendous interest from the psychological, historical, etc. point of view, but of no interest whatsoever *politically*. One might say not so much that *he was* as that he was *brought into being* [*ego bylo*] and the same could be said of any of them.

(VII. 288, entry for 25 July 1917)

When S. V. Ivanov, temporarily replacing Murav'ev in the chair of the Commission, exclaimed: 'What are all these people? We ourselves are guilty for having lost control over them, and I more than others. We are more guilty than they are', Blok considered that he had 'lit up the whole situation as though by a searchlight' (VII. 289).

Nevertheless, he did his best to beware of pity:

The situation is that tomorrow I shall again be looking at all these people. I see them in grief and humiliation, I did not see them in all their 'inaccessibility' and the 'glory of power'. It is necessary to observe fixedly, with intense concentration, in full awareness of a *terrible* responsibility....

(Z.K. 347, entry for 26 May 1917)

---

[h] Cf. also Blok's letter to his mother of 26 May 1917 in which he says: ' "I am crucified together with all of them", as A. Bely says somewhere. It really is very, very sad. Yesterday the commandant of Tsarskoye Selo came and gave us a detailed account of what the royal family are doing. That is sad too. In fact, everyone is right—the Kadets are right, and Gorky with his "two souls" is right, and in Bolshevism there is a terrible rightness. I do not see ahead at all. "The old" and "the new" are in us ourselves; in me at least. And I am suspended in mid-air; there is neither earth just now, nor heaven. And with all that Petersburg is extraordinarily beautiful again just at the moment ...' (VIII. 495–6).

[i] Protopopov, almost breaking under the strain, began to beat his head on the walls of his cell, call himself a villain, and finally threw his teapot at one of the guards. He said he 'heard other voices' and was called up for interrogation 'to take his mind off it'. Blok was sympathetic but sceptical: 'I don't know really whether that's possible: to take someone's mind off "other voices"?' he noted, reserving judgement.

3

This awareness of responsibility he called 'a special feeling—revolutionary'.

Blok, of course, was not called upon to sit in judgement but to produce records: to edit the typewritten versions of the stenographic accounts of the prisoners' depositions and, finally, to make a summary of all the evidence concerning the events leading up to the Tsar's abdication which was to be presented to the Constituent Assembly and eventually received the title: *The Last Days of the Imperial Regime.*[j] Correcting the typescripts, together with attendance at the interrogations at the Fortress and at the editorial conferences in the Winter Palace, kept him busy for eight to ten hours a day, sometimes more, throughout that summer.

The form the Commission's report should take occupied his thoughts a good deal. At first it seemed to him that this 'account to the people' should be full of 'revolutionary pathos' and the 'majestic romanticism of our days'—something in the style of Carlyle's *History of the French Revolution* (cf. *Z.K.* 365, entry for 20 June 1917). Soon, however, he began to take a more sober, 'classical' view of the task. Some of his best thoughts on the subject were scribbled down for his own benefit after a bath on 8 July:

What do you think of first and foremost when you think of a report from a high institution appointed by the state (the Investigatory Commission, whose duty it is to pass sentence on a 300-year-old regime) to a still higher institution: the Constituent Assembly of the new regime?

You think of a Russian that is clear, laconic, calm, dignified, and convincing. . . . Such a language will be comprehensible to the people (it is a mistake to think that the people will not understand anything that is genuine and accurate). It is, on the contrary, popularization which might lead to misunderstandings.

Any popularization, any attempt to be original, any attempt to go halfway to meet something as yet unknown, will deprive thought of its creative conviction, water it down, make it wobbly, like brawn: *Caveant Academia, ne quid ratio detrimenti capiat.*[k] . . . No people should be insulted by adaptation [to their supposed level]—popularization. Vulgarization is not democratization. In time the people will appreciate everything and pronounce their

---

[j] Murav'ev suggested in addition to this that Blok should write pen portraits of the prisoners, but the only two he attempted, Protopopov and Vyrubova (VI. 446–7), are more self-conscious and literary than the jottings in his diary and notebooks, and of correspondingly less interest.

[k] 'Be on your guard, Academy, lest reason suffer any harm': Blok is playing on the tag: '*Videant consules, ne quid res publica detrimenti capiat*'.

own judgement, a cold and cruel judgement, on all those who thought
them ... inferior to themselves.

(VII. 276–7)

On 25 July there was a special meeting devoted to the report: to
whether it should take the form of individual 'papers' or of a single
compilation. Blok said at this session that he saw it either as an
exhaustive work of research, written from an impartial, *historical*
viewpoint, or as a *political* report, compressed, giving few details
and not dwelling on personalities (who, he repeated yet again, were
almost all politically negligible). Obviously, the second was what was
required of the Commission at this time:

... a two-hour address, every sentence of which would be clothed in invisible armour ... offering few details, but inwardly ardent, brimming with
the fire of life that pulsates in all the documentary material at the disposal
of the Commission. As a result, every phrase of such a speech would be
capable of being thrown out into the midst of the people, bandied about
in all directions. It should stand up to being played with, to being tossed
back—it won't break, because it has a firm foundation, it is a firm generalization built on irrefutable facts.
    Concurrently with such a speech there might be a report devoted entirely
to criminal actions. And, most important of all, there will be the materials
themselves, all the great mass of which should always be at the disposal
of the Constituent Assembly.

(VII. 288)

The document which Blok eventually compiled[1] was not an
address; neither was it 'political' in the sense he obviously intended
when he spoke at the meeting. It does not contain the kind of sentences that can be taken out of context and tossed back and forth
by the crowd. It is quiet and totally self-effacing. The story itself
draws one in and the exact words of documents and depositions
quoted suggest the gentle but inevitable collapse of a house of cards.
    One of the most remarkable things about this eminently fair,
rather pedestrian, report is the note on which Blok chose to end it.
Perhaps recalling the Black Knight on the roof of the Winter Palace,
ready 'to lay down his life for an ancient legend', he gave the

[1] The whole question of a report to the Constituent Assembly naturally lapsed together
with the Assembly itself. Blok's *Last Days of the Imperial Regime* was eventually published
by Shchëgolev, who, as a historian, was also a member of the Commission, in his journal
Byloye, no. 15, 1919 (which actually came out in 1921), and as a separate book. The stenographic reports were published in full, in seven volumes, edited by Shchëgolev, after Blok's
death: *Padeniye tsarskogo rezhima* (1925–7). This was the first, 'academic' variant, a publication of the materials in full, which Blok had foreseen as a valid alternative to the report
conceived in terms of a two-hour speech.

last words to the old Russia, to the 'primitive and loyal-hearted Cavalry':[m]

Tsarskoye Selo, to his Imperial Majesty the Emperor Nikolay Aleksandro-vich.

    With a feeling of satisfaction we have heard that it has pleased your Majesty to change the form of government of our country and to give Russia a responsible ministry, by which you have put off from yourself a heavy burden of work, too much for one man alone to bear.... But, your Majesty, forgive us if we have recourse to ardent pleas to our God-given Tsar, do not desert us, your Majesty, do not deprive us of the legal heir to the Russian throne. Only with you at our head is the unity of the Russian people, of which your Majesty was so good as to write in your manifesto, at all possible. Only with our God-given Tsar can Russia be great, strong, and firm and achieve peace, prosperity, and happiness.

On 8 March, concludes the impassive chronicler, 'The ex-Emperor left the Stavka and was confined to the Palace at Tsarskoye Selo' (VI. 270).

4

The actual writing of this report occupied Blok from August 1917 to the beginning of April 1918. The concentrated lyrical attention the poet accorded the contemporary world was counterpointed throughout the year he worked with the Investigatory Commission by the sustained, clerkly, and artistic attention he gave to the recent past. Yet, even amongst Blok's contemporaries, the legend persisted that the poet knew nothing of politics and did not understand what was going on. In fact, few literati at that time were better informed— certainly as to the immediate past—and never was there a year in history when the present so quickly slipped back into the past, for the Commission which had begun in May by interrogating Prince Golytsin and Protopopov, was, by August, hearing the evidence of two deposed ministers from the original Provisional Government: Milyukov and Guchkov.

    This intense study of 'a past now vanished without trace' cannot but have affected the poet's attitude to the 'transient content' of the ever-shifting present that still, it seemed to him, offered no firm basis for choice, no foundation on which to base an act of will.

    Perhaps, as Blok had suspected on his return from the *druzhina*,

[m] As Winston Churchill called them in his *History of the Great War*.

the collapse of autocracy had not been a revolution and, for the moment, he saw the task of the Provisional Government as being

... to keep the swing from going over the top yet not allow the trajectory to decrease. That is, it must lead the country, which has taken to a nomad existence, on to a place where it can settle and put down roots again, guiding it always along the edge of a precipice, not letting it fall or lose itself, nor yet retreat on to a less dangerous and precipitous road where it might fail in the way and the Spirit of Revolution take flight from it.

(*Z.K.* 378, entry for 13 July 1917)

To begin with, it seemed as though this miraculous equilibrium had been achieved. Blok was deeply struck by the order in the streets, the fact that public services still functioned and that riot and brawling were the exception rather than the rule. This order, maintained not by the police but by 'the whole revolutionary people', was, he knew, a matter of hair's-breadth balance: but all the more precious for that. The Spirit of Revolution, which Blok felt had 'not so much as spent the night' (VII. 268) in his own Commission, was very much present at the All-Russian Congress of Soviets of Soldiers' and Workers' Deputies," which he attended on 16 June 1917 to hear Murav'ev's report to the Congress on the progress of the Investigatory Commission. At this Congress, Chkheidze, an old Menshevik, told a delegation from the American Labour Conference that the only way to help the people of Russia was to hasten the end of the war, a statement which met with a roar of applause. After this, Murav'ev's report, delivered with due legal dryness but with incisive vigour towards the end, was met with approval, and there was enthusiastic support for the statement that the Commission had no wish 'to inflict on the prisoners the kind of treatment which "they" used to inflict upon us'.

Afterwards, Blok made for the buffet and listened with real interest to a young soldier's impressions of war and memories of peasant life (VII. 262–4). This was a new experience: a far cry from the awkward conversations with Kluyev or the master/servant relationships at Shakhmatovo or at Porokhonsk. Blok's glimpse of the Congress of Soviets left him in no doubt that a revolution was indeed in progress. Its 'swelling music' was all around him. It seemed to Blok that the

" In the provinces, Soviets on the Petrograd model had very soon begun to take power everywhere, the Provisional Government's attempt to rule through the Zemstvos proving ineffectual. The All-Union Congress, convened by the Central Executive Committee of the Petrograd Soviet, thus represented an extremely influential body of opinion throughout the country. There were 285 Social Revolutionary deputies, 248 Mensheviks, and 105 Bolsheviks. The Bolsheviks called for an immediate take-over of power by the Soviets but were overruled by the majority, who wished to avoid civil war.

'will', missing in February, had now been found; in the elections to the city Duma at the end of May he had voted for the Left S. R. (Social Revolutionary) and Menshevik bloc. 'Many auguries', he had written to Aleksandra Andreyevna on 30 May 1917, 'which, as usual, I am inclined to believe, tell me that so far it is necessary to be with the Socialists' (VIII. 497).

The concierge of his block of flats, who served him throughout that summer as a kind of barometer to public opinion, approved his choice. Yet he began to feel increasingly isolated because, amongst the intelligentsia and particularly amongst the Kadets 'to whom I belong by blood' and who were 'in many ways, in general culture and morality, especially in morality, my superiors' (VII. 284),° he found a kind of cramped hanging on to the outward shell of established values, cultural and material, which expressed itself in irony and withdrawal at the very moment when Russia required a tremendous, united effort on the part of all her people: of 'the brain of the country' as well as its muscle.[3] There were moments when he felt he hated the 'intelligentsia' (VII. 265, entry for 19 June 1917), that they deserved anything that might come to them:

... I should not be in the least surprised if (even if not very soon) the people, clever, calm, and with an understanding of things the intelligentsia is incapable of understanding (that is, with a *socialist* psychology which is something completely, diametrically the opposite), begin with equal calm and majesty to hang and rob the intelligentsia (to re-establish order, to clean the rubbish from the mind of the country).

I am writing fresh from impressions of the Winter Palace, where (in contrast to the Fortress),[p] I hate to go. It is a realm of disorder, rumours, intrigues, and inefficiency.

(VIII. 503)

This 'irritable' letter, as Blok himself called it, was written the day after the reluctant and divided Soviets had given Kerensky their support for the reopening of an offensive at the front, a day filled with

° Between Blok and the Kadets there was a kind of failure of communication. In a letter of 7 June 1917 (VIII. 499–500), he told his mother how he had been too tired to accept 'Madame Kokoshkina's' invitation to attend a meeting of writers on preparatory work for the Constituent Assembly. He had tried to explain over the telephone that he was, in any case, out of sympathy with Kadet attitudes and 'inclined to the Social Democrats', even sympathetic 'to the Bolsheviks'. Politely but inexorably the Kadet lady brushed all this aside as not expressing his true opinions, a kind of poetic licence, and Blok, never good at explaining himself, gave up the attempt.

[p] At the Peter-Paul Fortress the Extraordinary Investigatory Commission pursued its enquiries, examining prisoners and witnesses, while a subsection known as the Editorial Commission, on which Blok also served, discussed how best to present its findings to the public. The subsection's headquarters were at the Winter Palace.

rumours of Russian advances all along the line and of major demon-
strations being organized against the Provisional Government by the
rebel Bolshevik faction and its supporters in Petrograd.[q]

That confrontation was inevitable Blok knew full well, had
known since 1908 when he had 'found his theme' of 'the people and
the intelligentsia'; when he had written *On the Field of Kulikovo*. He
was exceptional in that he recognized the line of confrontation: not
between the 'old regime' and the democratic parliamentarians, not
between one political party and another, but between the people of
Russia and the Europeanized professional classes. The practical grasp
of the hard realities of power that was a part of his heritage gave
him the certainty that, in view of the head-on clash of opinion now
clearly preparing, only a miracle could avert further violence. His
feeling for events was still running parallel to that of Zinaida Hippius,
who had noted to herself right at the beginning, on 28 February
1917:

In the manifestos of the Soviets of Workers' Deputies there is the will to
action and to power; and this is set over against the tender lack of authority
of the Duma deputies.... They are foreigners, but these others, the left-
wingers—are masters in their own home. ... There will be more fighting—
Lord! Save Russia! Help, help, help.[4]

The only 'miracle' that Blok could foresee would be the end of
the war and whole-hearted, energetic co-operation on the part of
educated Russia with 'the people', who alone had 'the will to action
and to power'. 'The people have wings', he wrote, 'but in skills and
knowledge they need our help. Gradually I am coming to understand
this. But surely it cannot be that many who could help will not go
over to them?' He was not blind to the obverse side of social revolution, but the superior attitude adopted by men and women he had
formerly thought enlightened exasperated him: 'What do you
expect of life? That having destroyed what was dropping to pieces
with age people will immediately start to build up something new
strictly according to plan?' (*Z.K.* 347, entry for 26 May 1917), he
apostrophized them.

His diaries and notebooks are full of such inconclusive debates with
some more hidebound and cautious *alter ego*. The details of everyday
life would set his mind ticking over furiously along the same lines:

---

[q] The motif of 'if I were they I'd hang the lot of us' first crops up in Blok's notebooks
much earlier, on 18 April/1 May 1917, 'the first day of the International' (*Z.K.* 317), and
is reiterated from time to time in various contexts, usually concerned directly or indirectly
with the question of the war.

A tree has died under my window. The bourgeois, especially the snotty-faced aesthete, will look and say: those workers playing the hooligan again. But one ought to make sure first: maybe something heavy was dumped there, perhaps they couldn't help scraping the tree, perhaps it was just some very clumsy person at work. . . .

(VII. 265)

He explained the erratic postal system to his mother, whose letters from the country were taking anything up to ten days to reach him:

It's no good being surprised if letters take a long time or even get lost. In all departments, including Tseretelli's,[1] the same thing is going on: they've thrown out many 'experienced' civil servants who exacted fines, were strict, etc. I'm not inclined to be irritated by that or by many similar things, because that *is* Revolution. If the proletariat is going to take power, then, we'll have a long wait for 'order', and maybe it won't come in our lifetime; but I think power should go to the proletariat, because only children can make anything new and interesting out of that old toy.

(VIII. 505)

But 'Alas', he added in a sceptical footnote, 'what will actually happen will be as always a compromise, with the grown-ups, as they always do, taking away some of the children's toys and calling them to order.' Blok's attitude was paternalistic rather than patronizing. Fatherhood does not necessarily entail smugness. After his first real contact with 'the proletariat', for instance, he had written to Lyuba:

There's nothing new to tell you about myself and if there were it would be impossible to work up any excitement over it because the whole content of life has become the World Revolution, at the head of which stands Russia. We are so young that in a few months we could recover completely from a 300-year-old sickness. . . . I was at the Congress of the Soviets of Soldiers' and Workers' Deputies and, in general, I see my future, although I am still up to my neck in work on a past that has gone without trace.

All this is nothing but a generalization, a summary of anxious thoughts and impressions which are daily rubbing and polishing themselves against others' thoughts and impressions, alas, often the opposite of mine, which keep me in a constant state of suppressed anger and nerves and sometimes of simple hatred for the 'intelligentsia'. If 'the brain of the country' is going to go on nourishing itself on the same old ironies, the slavish fears, the slavish experience of weary nations, then it will stop being the brain and will be ripped out quickly, cruelly, and authoritatively, as everything is done which really does get done nowadays. What right have we to fear

---

[1] Minister of Posts and Telegraphs and Minister of the Interior to the Provisional Government.

our great, clever, and good people? And our experience, bought with the blood of children, could be shared with these children....

(VIII. 504)

5

As the clash over the issue of the renewed offensive gathered momentum, Blok retreated into the role of a spectator, minding his own business: 'I have no voice,' he wrote, 'but I have eyes.'[5] Yet there were moments when the strain was so intense he even thought he might be going mad (VII. 268–9). Possibly the absorbing, regular work on the Commission (there were days when he did not return from meetings until after midnight) saved him from complete nervous breakdown, though he was beginning to long again for his 'own Russian language', and, occasionally, to look wistfully out of the window:

The moon is on the wane beyond the window over the roofs to the east— a terrible, sharp sickle. And beneath the window a couple is embracing, embracing long and sweetly. The woman is bent back against the man's shoulder in such a long and languorous curve and does not withdraw her lips. How beautiful! And I sit here between two candles....

(VII. 270–1)

Before May was out, he had begun to see Del'mas more often again, although there was a muted quality about their meetings. Her visits, he noted, ended rather than crowned his days, and once, when he came across the box in which he had 'buried Del'mas', it moved him to write the only 'poem' of that summer, an elegy in prose, scribbled in his notebook and not published—in deference to the singer's feelings—until almost half a century later:[5]

O God, what madness it is that everything passes, nothing is eternal. How much happiness I had (yes, 'happiness') with that woman. There are hardly any words left from her. What is left is this heap of petals, all kinds of dried flowers, roses, pussy-willow, ears of barley, reseda, one or two big, single petals and leaves. All that rustles beneath your fingers. I burnt some notes I didn't like when I got them; but how many are left. And what captivating words and phrases there are amongst heaps of nonsense. Hairpins, ribbons, flowers, words. And everything in the world passes. How she wept the other night and how, for one minute, I felt drawn to her with the old impulse, a cruel impulse, seeing a spark of that former youthfulness in her face, grown younger from the white night and from passion. And that cruel

[5] First published without Del'mas's name in Z.K. (Moscow, 1965), the passage has since been quoted in full in an article written after her death.[6]

(because momentary) impulse of mine brought nothing but her tears. . . .' ¹
Poor thing, she was happy with me. Different-coloured ribbons, red, pink,
pale blue, yellow; roses, ears of barley, coppery, wiry, supple strands of
hair, ribbons, barley, hairpins, pussy-willow, roses.

(Z.K. 339–40)

Indeed, it was not the time for romance. Provisions in the city
were running very low and on 30 June Blok wrote to his mother:
'. . . for the moment this is doing me a power of good, sometimes
I eat only once a day, and feel more and more winged . . .' (VIII. 505).

On 3 July opposition to the offensive erupted in violence, and the
Editorial Commission devoted a long session to spelling reform!
Naturally, the resignations of the Kadet ministers provided a more
exciting topic, and formal discussion kept breaking down into talk
of what was going on: 'In fact—chaos, in which the only question
that we really discuss the whole time is: how to overcome chaos?
To overcome ourselves' (VII. 271).

Tired, Blok went home and forced himself to work. It was quiet
in his dark green study with the heavy, simple furniture and the view
of factory chimneys and distant masts, but the streets below were
in hubbub: lorries, shouting, little boys rushing hither and thither.
. . . Del'mas came, she left after midnight and phoned from her flat
to say that people in the streets were shouting 'Down with the Provisional Government' and 'praising Lenin'; that the 'islands' were
up, as in 1905, and workers bearing placards 'Down with the Provisional Government', together with several regiments which had
gone over to them, were advancing on the centre of the city.

The following day, Petrograd was in uproar. Blok had to walk
to the Winter Palace for there were no trams. One of the members
of the Commission had his car confiscated in the streets. When he
showed his permit, signed by Kerensky, he was told: 'Kerensky was
arrested long ago! You might as well show us a permit from Nicholas
II' (VII. 273). The garrison of the Peter-Paul Fortress, it was
rumoured, had gone over to the insurgents, and the Commission
feared for the safety of its 'clients', but could do nothing about them.

Blok, now informed that the rising was definitely the work of the
Bolsheviks, turned over in his mind the persistent rumours that Lenin
had 'German money' and had been specially sent to disrupt morale
at the rear, rumours which his Commission was promptly called
upon to investigate. That evening he wrote Aleksandra Andreyevna:

Mama, these days there is a revolution in the town and a committee meeting
in the Winter Palace. You will probably read about the revolution in the

¹ Blok's ellipse.

papers; in fact, though, as always, everything is much simpler. There is
some beauty (not much as yet), some idiotic things, some rather sad. There
is little danger so far as I can see; the thought of that German money
is in my head, taking form from various impressions. But I see little, because
I am very tired, now at the Palace, now at home, and since yesterday there
are no trams, so you can't even get a ride....[7]

Two days later, a sub-committee of the Editorial Commission at
the Winter Palace was brought to its feet and across the lustreless
parquet to the mighty windows by the racket of a company of armed
cyclists from the front, tearing along the embankment to 'liberate'
Ksheshinskaya's Palace from the Bolsheviks. The insurrection was
over. 'It is very difficult for me to go on sitting on the fence politically
...,' Blok wrote his mother,

but all that is going on either fails to come up to the level of politics or
exceeds it. All these new rumours of treason, spying, etc. are, of course,
only partially justified, but behind all this there is the truth of legend.

In general, Russian Bolshevism is so permeated, saturated to overflowing
by elements that are quite foreign to its own essence, that it is almost impossible to speak of it as a political party.

Thanks to this sitting on the fence I am deprived of all political activity;
what's to be done? One must simply assume that this is something not given
to me....[8]

Indeed, the Bolsheviks still seemed to him no more than 'a small
group active on the surface' (Z.K. 346, entry for 25 May 1917).
Beletsky, one of the Commission's most informative 'clients', the
penitent ex-Chief of Police, had compared the life of Bolshevik revolutionaries to that of 'the early Christians', and the comparison had
settled deep into Blok's mind. At the same time, the setbacks at the
front were blamed on organized Bolshevik treachery. Opinion in
the Commission was as divided as Blok's own heart. Some
clamoured for more stringent measures against Lenin (now fled to
Finland under threat of arrest) and against the Bolsheviks generally;
others, notably Murav'ev (coldly) and Miklashevsky (in tears), disapproved of any such 'counter-revolutionary' notions. Rodichev,
also in tears, advocated a strong line against the 'traitors'. Shchëgolev
arrived with news that the Russian army was attacking all along
the line in the north, but that the remnants of the 11th Army had
broken and deserters had been shot by their own comrades in
arms.

Blok was torn between disgust at the mounting war fever" and an upsurge of patriotism which took him unawares:

The 'devolution' of Finland and the 'Ukraine' suddenly scared me today. I began to be afraid for 'Great Russia'. Yesterday I had to formulate to Ol'denburg" how, basically, nationalism, even Kadetism, is in my blood, and that I am ashamed to love 'my own', and that a 'bourgeois' is anyone who has hoarded up any treasures whatsoever, even spiritual treasures. (That is the psychology of the '*lanterne*' and of all extreme, 'senseless' insurrections; Kiprianovich backed me up, but added that all this has an economic basis, whereas I think that it comes out like that of itself and that brains, morality, and particularly art—are objects of hatred in themselves. This is one of the most terrible tongues of the revolutionary flame, but it *is* so, and it is peculiarly typical of Russians, more so than of anyone else.)
(VII. 279, entry for 12 July 1917. Cf. also *Z.K.* 377, entry for 13 July 1917)

One question which exercised Blok's mind at this moment was whether the explosive power of the revolution would prove sufficient to produce a chain reaction of decentralization and dissolution all over the world, or whether Russia alone would 'blow up' and thus enter upon a period of servitude to stronger 'state organisms' (VII. 280). The Commission was in possession of documents showing a connection between devolutionist and Bolshevik forces and enemy espionage. Yet when, on 12 July, the Provisional Government reintroduced the death penalty at the front at the request of General Kornilov and of the political commissars instituted by Kerensky, Blok noted bitterly:"

'The state cannot do without capital punishment' (Kerensky). The state cannot do without secret agents, i.e. *agents provocateurs*. The state cannot do without counter-espionage, which means among other things capturing enemy soldiers 'for information'....
People are cursing Kerensky for having begun this offensive when some

---

" 'Officers and their tarts in Luna Park' and a rumour that officer cadets were drinking the health of the Tsar were among the 'facts' he noted over these days. Newspapers, too, were taking a militant tone.
" S. F. Ol'denburg (1863–1934), Academician and Orientalist. He was one of the members of the Commission most respected by Blok and was to make a profound impression on the poet by determining to go and serve in the ranks at the front—a few days after the conversation recorded here—at a time when all the newspapers were predicting he would be the new Minister of Education. Kerensky, however, persuaded him that he would be more useful in the government. He was, Blok noted, a Kadet and came from a military background (*Z.K.* 377).
" For Blok's reaction to the reintroduction of the death penalty see also his letters to his mother over this period—rather fuller and more redolent of his general bewilderment in *Pis'ma k rodnym* II than in *S.S.* VIII, particularly the letter of 12 July 1917.

were for it, but others—not. Without the offensive and with fraternization the war would have been over....

(VII. 282)

On 18 July, a new offensive was launched which began well for the Russian troops, but rapidly turned into a rout and a shambles. Exasperated by the emotional reactions of his family at Shakhmatovo, behind which he suspected the influence of Adam Feliksovich, then staying near by at his own Safonovo, Blok, on 28 July, dispatched one of his more bracing scolds to his mother:

At the beginning of the 'offensive' on 18 July, you and Auntie were crying 'hurrah' and that is why you are now convinced that everything is going flying into the abyss (Auntie more so than you). Be glad it is not you who are in power; at least, don't 'be glad' exactly, but try not to take this agony of the state so emotionally to heart. We are—'passengers' just now; people a great deal more prescient than we are bewildered.[9]

In his diary he wrote:

I shall never take power into my hands, I shall never join any party, I shall never make a choice, I have nothing to be proud of, I understand nothing.

I can only whisper, and sometimes—cry out loud: leave me in peace, it is no business of mine how reaction sets in after revolution, how people who don't know how to live, who have lost the taste for life, begin by making concessions, then take fright, then begin to terrorize people who have not yet lost the taste, who have not yet 'lived' in 'a civilized way', who desperately want to live a little, like rich people....

(VII. 281, entry for 13/26 July 1917)

6

Exhausted by indecision, poor food, and his struggle against vulgarization, which had earned him the reputation in the Editorial Commission of an unrepentant aristocrat,[x] Blok began to retreat somewhat into private life. He spent as much time as he could in the park at Shuvalovo, where there was a lake the yellow waters of which were said to contain salubrious iron. Here he bathed and thought longingly of Shakhmatovo: 'How I'd love to live (even for a little while) in the country, and with Lyuba' (VII. 283, entry for 14 July 1917). He relaxed mentally, and began to read a Kadet newspaper, Russkaya Svoboda: 'But not for long, I hope ... I love the

---

[x] Cf. the backlash in his diary for 13 July 1917 (VII. 283): 'You reproach me with "aristocratism". But the aristocrat is closer to democracy than the average "bourgeois".'

Kadets in my blood . . . but I would be *ashamed* to support them' (VII. 284).

Gradually, his private life emerges once more in his notes and letters: 'The swing of the pendulum in me has slowed down and does not these days reach as far as the element of Bolshevism (or if it does it is only seldom and fortuitously); and I am "resting" a little, working and getting out and about' (VIII. 508, letter to his mother of 16 July 1917).

The sun came out and, he wrote, 'warmed me, poor animal that I am'. He went to have supper with Zhenya Ivanov and his new god-daughter; took some thought for his own family's plans and discouraged his mother and aunt from returning prematurely from the country on the grounds that the winter in Petrograd would be very hard and they must build up their strength. Also, Auntie liked to live alone, and this was now a major problem. The city was over-crowded. Manya, the maid who had been in Pskov with Lyuba, arrived with her mistress's clothes and a loving letter, which Blok read with mixed feelings, in which his wife promised to return to him at the beginning of August.

Just before Lyuba did return, Murav'ev and Ol'denburg officially requested Blok to take part in writing up the Commission's final report: thinking that Ol'denburg, whom he respected, would be editor-in-chief, he agreed, but it was that very night that Kerensky persuaded Ol'denburg to take on the Ministry of Education. Blok found himself bogged down once more in time-consuming bickering with his fellow editors. Tired and frustrated, he wrote to his mother: 'I am again thinking of "serious work", which is how I inwardly think of art, and, connected therewith and sacrificed thereto, my neglected "private life", all overgrown with weeds.'[10]

Although Lyuba's insistence on remaining in Pskov from May to August had thrown him back into the company of Del'mas, Blok's relationship with his wife had taken on a new depth over the summer months. They wrote constantly, exchanging impressions. 'How strangely you write,' he replied to one of her first anxious letters from Pskov. 'You have still not woken up. . . . Can it be that you don't understand that it is not the Leninists who are frightening, that everything is going in quite a new way, that the only frightening thing is the old philistinism [*poshlost'*], which still nests in many bastions?' (VIII. 488, letter of 3 May 1917).

Humbly, she replied that it was only just that events should have 'turned their grandiose aspect' towards him, whereas she was beset by their petty reflections in everyday life: the wholesale lowering of standards, work-dodging, bad manners and the scramble 'for places about the pie'. She knew he would not agree with her, but wrote: 'You explain where my mistakes lie; I just wanted to tell you my own reaction to the present time....'[11]

Manya had brought Blok this letter on 25 May, on a day when he was suffering from a particularly severe attack of depression—'an excellent letter', he noted, 'clever, sad (about life in Russia just now), but not loving enough ...' (Z.K. 346), and answered:

I am not really inclined to quarrel with what you write. All I can say is this: if it is indeed true (and there is a great deal of truth in it, but there are other truths to be taken into account as well) it only intensifies the tragedy of Russia. There is a terrible truth of its own in what now goes by the name of 'Bolshevism'. If you could see and know what I know, your attitude would be different, in spite of everything; your point of view is rather limited, it is essential to rise above it....

(VIII. 406, letter of 28 May 1917)

After Aunt Maria's departure for Shakhmatovo on 7 May it had been very lonely in the empty flat, to which he would return, often late at night, a prey to an obsessive fear of being caught unawares by something he could not quite define: 'it', 'something chaotic and senseless', 'probably relating to the war' (VIII. 289).

'As far as material things are concerned', he had written to Lyuba on 14 May, '(in the sense of looking after myself, etc.) I could manage quite all right without you.... But the time is such, the situation is such that there is no knowing what will happen tomorrow, everything is charged with electricity, I am myself, and sometimes there is such a need to have at one's side someone one trusts and loves' (VIII. 49).

So long as he concentrated on editing the sheets of ill-typed stenographic reports he brought home from the Fortress, he was protected from doubt and fear; but the moment he looked up from his work he was overwhelmed by the need for some other human presence, 'very unsettled; terribly lonely, you can't really talk to anyone and there's no one to advise' (VIII. 496). 'All that you write is fine,' he had answered Lyuba, not wishing to call her back from the provincial stillness and comparative plenty of Pskov, '...that in the mornings you walk to the Pskov Detinets[y] and that you think of me. Sometimes I miss you so much, I can't tell you; now, for instance: I have a quiet hour, how I'd like to be sitting with you' (VIII. 406).

In early June she had paid him a flying visit: 'so wonderful, I shall

[y] The inner part of a kremlin or fortress.

remember even the smallest details'. It meant so much to have her there, even asleep on the sofa as he worked.

How I need Lyuba in these days, how long it is since she was with me. Just to live with her for a while; no one will ever appreciate her as I do, in spite of everything—all the greatness of her purity, her mind, her appearance, her simplicity. And those little worthless traits (inherited from her mother)—never mind them. She will always be a shining light [*Ona vsegda budet siyat'*].

(Z.K. 339)

In her memoirs, Lyubov' Dmitriyevna says that she accepted the revolution together with Blok and under his influence. For them both it was a tragic acceptance, involving the final sacrifice of the way of life and habits of mind of their youth, of much that was dear in tradition and ceremony, of the good will of friends and relations: 'I knew what a burden I was taking upon myself, but I did not know that the burden which fell upon Blok would prove to be beyond his strength—he was quite young, strong, and even full of a kind of youthful dash....'[12]

In a sense, they were able to do it because they had little to lose, because all their life together had been one long internal revolution, a protracted series of preparatory 'manoeuvres' in which they had tried, almost consciously, to train themselves to do without all security, material or spiritual:

Hardly had my fiancée become my wife when the lilac worlds of the first revolution seized us, and cast us into the whirlpool. I first, as one who had long secretly wished for perdition, was drawn into the grey purple, the silver stars, mother-of-pearl and amethyst of the blizzard. After me followed my wife, for whom this transition (from the difficult to the easy, from the impermissible to the permissible) was a torment, more difficult than for me. Behind the storm that had passed there opened up the iron emptiness of the day which, however, continued to threaten a new storm, to secrete a threat. Such were the years between the revolutions, exhausting and wearing for both soul and body. Now—another squall is upon us (the colour and scent of which I cannot yet define).... When, whither, and how will we emerge from it, will Lyuba and I emerge at all?

(VII. 300–1)

So Blok reviewed the situation on 15 August 1917, a fortnight after Lyuba's return from Pskov, where, aware of his continuing involvement with Del'mas, she had been thinking of a 'collective suicide'. 'All is full of Lyuba,' he wrote after discussing—and rejecting—this plan, which had occurred to them both. 'The weight and responsibility for her hard life' weighed heavily upon him—and he was sorry, too, for Del'mas, who haunted the street where they both lived and the lake at Shuvalovo where she knew he went to bathe. He avoided her.

Physically, Lyuba's warmth and energy made life considerably easier and more homely. She got up at six o'clock and went to the railway station for milk; procured fuel for the winter for her mother-in-law and found a room for Maria Beketova in the flat next door to their own, a real coup which would keep Auntie under their eye but preserve the illusion of independence so important to elderly relatives. Not only this, but Lyuba actually took over some of Blok's work, editing the stenographic report on Vissarionov and checking the voluminous file on Kryzhanovsky. When the time came, it was she who obtained the necessary permits for Aleksandra Andreyevna and Maria Andreyevna to return to the capital.

Blok himself was now so overwhelmed with work for the Commission that he had to farm some of it out to other friends and acquaintances: Zhenya Ivanov proved totally inefficient; V. A. Pyast offered to help but then changed his mind; M. V. Babenchikov,ᶻ a recent acquaintance, proved more satisfactory; for Knyazhnin, a reliable, scholarly person, Blok managed to obtain regular employment and eventually passed on to him many of his own responsibilities.

7

12 August saw the opening in Moscow of the conference between representatives of the three centres of power: the Provisional Government, the High Command of the Army, and the Central Executive Committee of the Petrograd Soviet. Murav'ev left Petrograd to attend the conference and Blok took the opportunity to play truant from work and go for a long bathe at Shuvalovo.

The night after this unaccustomed outing was inexplicably ominous:

... strange explosions in the sky right in front of my window, far off. Thunder? Summer lightning? But the air is cold. Rockets, perhaps. Or a searchlight.

ᶻ An ex-admirer of Lyuba's at Terioki, Babenchikov later wrote one of the first books about Blok.[13] His later reminiscences,[14] published in 1968, though interesting, should be approached with caution. The conversations, much less fully reported in the book written shortly after Blok's death, appear to have been expanded with near-quotes from Blok's diaries and even from his poetry.

The night (Saturday/Sunday) seems like a working night, the noises in the city have not calmed down, sirens blow, the lights are on at the factories. And the shimmering explosions, sometimes yellow, sometimes pale, sometimes covering a great stretch of sky, go on and on, and it begins to seem as though behind the roar of the city, I can hear another roar. . . .

(VII. 299)

The next day: 'Of course, it *was* thunder . . .' (VII. 300).

Nevertheless, he was haunted by dark premonitions and, since the days were full of work, they came upon him at night, often in sleep. A heavy smell of smouldering turf lay over Shuvalovo, over Petrograd, and ate its way into his very dreams:

Between two dreams:—'Help, help!'—'Help what?' Russia, the Motherland, the Fatherland, I don't know what to call her; that there may be no grief nor bitterness nor shame before the poor, the embittered, the ignorant, the oppressed! Only help us! The yellowish-brown billows of smoke are already menacing the villages, bushes and grass are flaming in wide strips, and God sends no rain and the crops have failed and what there is will burn . . . other such yellowish-brown billows, behind which everything is fermenting and smouldering . . . are surging over millions of souls; the flames of enmity, barbarity, Tatarshchina,[aa] anger, humiliation, oppression, revenge—flare up, now here, now there: Russian bolshevism is on the loose, and there is no rain and God sends none. . . .

(VII. 296–7)

By Russian bolshevism, Blok did not here mean the political party. They were not yet 'on the loose' but, on the contrary, on the run. Three of their leaders, as he well knew, were in the cells of the Peter-Paul Fortress. He was speaking rather of some mixed quality of fanaticism and vitality, one aspect of which he had perceived long ago in the Sectarians and amongst the Old Believers.[16]

With a chain they beat the honeyed clover, the fat clover that has overgrown all the fields of Great Russia. . . . Bolshevism (the element) leans towards 'eternal rest' (like a crooked cross). It is only to begin with that there is blood, violence, bestiality, but then—clover, the pink clover. Sensuality (Rasputin) goes by the same road. This storminess springs from eternal rest and culminates in the same. My 'The People and the Intelligentsia', 'The Element and Culture'.

While binding it with iron, it must be possible to find some way of preserving this precious storminess, this non-tiredness.

[aa] Babenchikov, who saw a lot of Blok at this time, stresses the poet's awareness that popular passion could be whipped up by the right as easily as by the left: 'Amongst those dark elemental forces which might lead Russia to Tatarshchina Blok included Kornilovshchina.'[15]

Yes, things aren't as bad as that. 'The heavy hammer breaketh glass but forgeth steel.'[bb]

(VII. 292)

Waking from his dream of burning, he struggled, throughout the varied impressions of the 'iron day',[cc] to work out how—and whether—he could serve the people, how the 'intelligentsia' might serve 'the element':

But that is the *task of Russian culture*—to direct this flame on to what must be burnt, to set such limits to the destruction as will not weaken the force of the fire but will organize that force; to organize ungovernable freedom, to direct the slothful fermentation which also secretes the possibility of violence into the Rasputin-dominated corners of the soul and there to blow it up into a sky-high conflagration so that our cunning, slothful, servile sensuality may burn....

(VII. 297)

Just before Lyuba's return, Blok had refused an invitation from P. B. Struve to speak at the inauguration of the League of Russian Culture, because of pressure of work and 'the division in my soul'.[dd] He did, however, attend a meeting of the League and one of his reasons for not joining it, even then, was his 'inclination towards the mists of bolshevism and anarchism (the element, "perdition", to hasten "the faces of the roses above the dark earth"'.[ee] Yet, at the same time, he felt he *ought* to join, for Struve's League offered an opportunity to 'work for enlightenment ... the link with *life*, participation in life, which is still necessary to me ("the iron day"; one cannot hasten "the evening")' (VII. 292).

But there was no need now to 'hasten' anything and precious little time to 'work for enlightenment'. The front was crumbling and Petrograd was directly threatened by the Germans. On 21 August Riga fell. Voices in the trams said: 'What's the odds. We'll all die of hunger, anyway' (VII. 303). Savinkov, now Minister of War, was sent by Kerensky to negotiate with Kornilov to form a semi-military

[bb] The quotation is from Pushkin.

[cc] This particular day involved the interrogation of P. N. Milyukov, the ex-Foreign Minister to the Provisional Government; trouble with the stenographers; work at home with Babenchikov on the Voeykov file in the evening.

[dd] In a letter to P. B. Struve of 30 July 1917 (VIII. 509–10), Blok also makes it clear that, though honoured by the invitation which he would have liked to accept, he did not feel happy about joining a League which did not have Gorky's name among its founders and did have—Rodzyanko's. 'In the history of Russian culture the name of the author of *Confession* and *Childhood* is of more significance than that of the President of the Duma. ...' Cf. also VII. 291–2.

[ee] A favourite quotation from Vladimir Solov'ev.

coalition capable of carrying on the war and controlling the Soviets. At the last moment, however, Kerensky, fearing reaction, made common cause with the Soviets, legalizing the Bolsheviks and demanding Kornilov's resignation.

Observing all this in conjunction with the reactions of his own relatives (the patent approval of Kornilov, for instance, by the more worldly elements as represented by Lyuba's mother) and of the literary world (he heartily endorsed the Provisional Government's decision to close down his old *bête noire*, the newspaper *Novoye Vremya*), Blok concluded that Kornilov would inevitably become a symbol of reaction: 'On his banner is written: "food, private property, a constitution not without a hope of monarchy, strict disciplinary measures [*Yezhovye rukavitsy*]"' (VII. 306).

Before the end of August, Blok's aunt and mother arrived in Petrograd with flowers and food from the estate and, almost immediately, began to talk of moving back to Shakhmatovo in order to be nearer Moscow if Blok and Lyuba were evacuated there with the Commission.

Petrograd was hungry, and on the eve of Blok's name day, 29 August, his pride received a severe jolt when his mistress sent his wife flour to make a pie. 'My personal life has become one long *humiliation* and that is noticeable the moment there is a lull in work' (VII. 307), he wrote distressfully. Nevertheless, on the 30th, the customs were observed. Lyuba, 'all dressed up', he noted affectionately, presented him with a bouquet of shaggy pink asters ('children's flowers') and entertained his mother, aunt, Zhenya Ivanov, Babenchikov, and Chulkov. It was that day he began an endless Socratic discussion with Babenchikov about Kerensky, Kornilov, and the Decembrists,[f] which was obviously important to him. As so often in conversations of this sort, however, Blok 'spoke in short, broken phrases. He liked to draw out other people's opinions by putting unexpected telegraphic questions. One had the impression that he was thinking hard all the time and, not certain of his conclusions, was sounding the opinion of the person he was talking to. Such probing conversations probably tired him and as for me, even now, after many years, I remember them with a feeling of exhaustion. Nevertheless, I was always drawn back to "play catch at thoughts" with Blok....'[17] All Babenchikov retained of this particular discussion was the harshness with which the poet finally dismissed the past (including the Decembrists as 'romantics' and 'gentlemen') and his intense desire

---

[f] During the months immediately preceding and following the February revolution, many young officers—naturally enough—saw themselves as followers of the Decembrists.

that the 'New' should be 'something quite different—neither Romanov, nor Pestel', nor Pugachëv....'

On 1 September Kornilov was arrested. Savinkov resigned from the Provisional Government to found a newspaper and fight the Bolsheviks, now unprecedentedly strong, in print. Yet still the agony dragged on and life continued as before. On 7 September Blok was informed that he had been elected a member of a theatrical-literary commission: the first of a series of onerous advisory jobs. After the first session on 9 September he was given four plays to review for the Commission and 'a mass of tickets for the Aleksandriynsky and Mikhaylovsky Theatres' (VII. 309).

As always when all the family were together, he began to quarrel with Lyuba; his mother had one of her epileptoid seizures. Hunger was already at the door and behind it the terrible threat of winter cold. The war ground on disastrously.

The summer lull over, people had begun inviting Blok to participate in various literary and theatrical projects and his work with the Investigatory Commission irked him more and more. Andrey Bely turned up in Petrograd and came to dinner. The phone rang constantly: Remizov, Ivanov-Razumnik, Pyast, Tereshchenko.

Z. N. Hippius, now as ardent an advocate of war as she had been of peace, was helping Savinkov to rally the anti-Bolshevik intelligentsia about his newspaper *Chas* (The Hour). Having scarcely seen Blok all summer, she rang him up on 15 October and asked him to contribute:

If I was a little late in inviting Blok it was because it had never entered my head to doubt him.... I invited him to the first meeting. A pause. Then: 'No. I won't be coming.'—'Why? Are you busy?'—'No. I can't take part in a paper like that.'... 'But you ... you don't want to be with us ... I suppose you're not with the Bolsheviks by any chance, are you?'— Even as I put it, the question still seemed absurd. And here's what Blok answered (he was very straightforward, never told lies): 'Yes, if you put it that way, I am more with the Bolsheviks.'[18]

Perhaps Hippius helped him to make up his mind. Only three days later, the news of the threatened armed uprising by the Bolsheviks was in the newspapers. Blok noted that Trotsky and the others wanted it 'out of despair' whereas Lenin alone believed that the seizure of power by the Soviets would end the war 'and put everything in the country to rights' (VII. 312). On the same page, he had noted his agreement with his mother over 'the necessity of putting an end to the war: the crassness of the word "shame". We have the riches, the West—the experience' (VII. 311). During these days when, to borrow a simile from Babenchikov, everything was breaking up like ice on the river in spring, Blok appeared quite undismayed. 'It was as if he were striding with stubborn determination on and out over a thin film of ice which was already cracking and splitting beneath his feet. But he strode on, ignoring the danger, his eyes fixed on some point far ahead, avidly breathing in the cold wind off the sea.'[19]

8

At the second All-Russia Congress of Soviets, the Bolsheviks went over to the offensive and declared that all power had passed from the Provisional Government to the Soviets. On the night of 26 October, the new government, with Lenin at its head, adopted a Decree of Peace, calling upon the belligerent countries to conclude an immediate armistice for a period of not less than three months to permit negotiations for peace, and upon 'the workers of the three most advanced nations of mankind and the largest states participating in the present war—namely Great Britain, France, and Germany', to help 'bring to a successful conclusion the cause of peace...'.

Blok's decision to abandon his position of nonalignment and to come out on the side of the Soviets must be seen in the light of this decree and of his loathing of reaction. Some kind of dictatorship, given the tremendous pressures of the war, must have seemed inevitable. Blok opted for those he thought of as the obscure, the ignorant, the threatened—'children in an iron age' (VII. 330). In faith and hope, he committed himself to the 'mists of Bolshevism', to the destructive element. More we cannot know, for his diary breaks off on 19 October and is taken up again, like the notebooks, only in the following year.

Two facts, sharply contrasted as so often in Blok's life and poetry, stand out for November 1917.

At the beginning of the month, Blok was present at a meeting of 'representatives of the literary and artistic intelligentsia' called on the initiative of the All-Russian Central Executive Committee at the Bolshevik headquarters at the Smolny Institute. Many were bidden: actors, artists, writers. Few came. Amongst these few were the artists Konstantin Petrov-Vodkin and Nathan Al'tman; the theatrical producer and actor Vsevolod Meyerhold; the poets Vladimir Mayakovsky and Aleksandr Blok.[20] A motion was carried declaring the readiness of those at the meeting to co-operate with the new Soviet government.

A week or so later, Aleksandra Andreyevna received a letter from Shakhmatovo:

Your Excellency Gracious Lady Aleksandra Andreyevna,
They registered the estate, took the keys away from me, took away the grain leaving me just a little flour, 15 or 18 poods.[gg] In the house they have executed devastation. Aleksandr Aleksandrovich's writing table they broke open with an axe and rooted through everything. Such outrage and hooliganism there's no describing. The door of the library is broken in. These people are not free citizens but barbarians, human beasts. From today, in my own feelings, I go over to the non-party ranks....[hh] My curse on the lot of them, all 13 numbers[ii] of struggling fools.

I sold the horse for 230 roubles. I shall probably soon go away from here, if you come please let me know in advance, because I am required to report on your arrival, but it is not my wish to inform on you and I am afraid of the wrath of the people. There are people who are sorry for you and there are people who hate you. I will not accept anything from them now.

With all respect

...[jj]

1917 November

Answer as soon as you can.
They played on the piano, smoked, spat, tried on the *barin*'s caps, took the binoculars, the dagger, knives, money, medals, and what more I don't know, I felt sick and went away.[22]

This letter is glued into Blok's diary after the last entry for 19 October 1917: 'The peasants, sure that everyone in the towns has enough to eat, are giving no bread to the cities' (VII. 312).

Someone had found Lyuba's 'little end of string', and the very first tug brought Blok's own house tumbling about his ears—as he had always known it would.

[gg] One pood = 16.38 kg., or 36 lbs. avoirdupois.
[hh] In Russian, 'Otnyniya moim chuvstvom perekhozhu v nepartiynye ryady'—a sentence worthy of a character from Andrey Platonov.
[ii] Each political party had an electoral number for which people voted. The Kadets, for instance, were No. 9. The writer is presumably referring to canvassing for the Constituent Assembly, which to him seems part and parcel of the general 'outrage and hooliganism'.
[jj] Tactfully, the publisher of this letter which was first printed in 1928 did not give the writer's name. He was Nikolay Lapin, the general factotum and odd-job man whom Blok and Lyuba had engaged in 1910 and always thought well of. Lapin had received his call-up the same summer as Blok, in 1916, but had been exempted on medical grounds.[21]

CHAPTER IX

The Great Tarantella:
The Twelve and *The Scythians*

(November 1917 – April 1918)

> ... In January 1918 for the last time I surrendered myself
> to the element no less blindly than in January 1907 or in
> March 1914. I do not disavow what I wrote then, because
> it was written in harmony with the element: for instance,
> during and for several days after writing *The Twelve* I was
> physically, through my actual sense of hearing, aware of a
> great noise all around—a noise compounded of many sounds
> (probably the noise of the fall of the old world).
>
> (VII. 474–5, 1 April 1920)

Blok met the onslaught of social revolution as the wise virgins met
the Bridegroom. He had kept his lamp trimmed and his oil to hand
through the long night watches, and now he went out gladly to welcome the future. 'He walked about young and merry and wide-
awake,' Maria Beketova remembered, 'with shining eyes.'[1] The
thundering collapse of the old order was all about him, and from
the dust and rubble—so he willed it, so it had been in other ages
of the world—a new age would arise. He did not expect to see it.
He belonged to the age that was passing and would not long outlive
it. But it was his function to stand at the threshold, to bid the new
era welcome, to speed it on its way with blessings. This was his hour.

1

There was hunger in Petrograd that winter: virtually nothing to buy
and—for Blok and Lyuba, Maria Andreyevna and Aleksandra

Andreyevna—very little money to buy it with. The Extraordinary Investigatory Commission had collapsed together with the Provisional Government, so Blok—still liable to call-up, still in his well-worn but always clean and pressed Zemstvo uniform—was out of work. This, however, merely added to his exhilaration. Hungry he was, and often cold, but strong and fresh still from the sober life of the past eighteen months. Shakhmatovo was wrecked, but what was that in the general holocaust? Babenchikov was tactless enough to write a letter of condolence which remained in Blok's archive with the scathing comment: 'This piece of philistinism was received 23 November.'[a2] Later there would be 'a time for such a grief'. Not now.

Now there was the keen joy of feeling himself a free artist again, of sharing with Lyubov' the tremendous excitement of these heady days when, even to some more sober hearts, it seemed that '... Custom was no more, or rather the tempest had become customary. Soon Germany would fall—England—and the plough would cut across the needless boundaries. And heaven would unroll like a sheet of parchment. ...'[3]

Blok's only official activity during these months was to attend meetings (again at the Winter Palace) of a Commission for the Publication of the Classics[b] chaired by P. Polyansky. Also present were Larissa Reysner, a beautiful Jewess who was later to join the Red Army as a female commissar, a handful of artists including Shterenberg, Al'tman, and Benois, and A. Z. Shteynberg, for some reason known to Blok as 'the Marburg philosopher'. Also present, when he could spare the time, was the Commissar for Education, Anatoliy Lunacharsky, an old acquaintance who could not deny himself the small gratification of coming up to Blok (always rather forbidding in public) with a hearty: 'Allow me to shake your hand, *Comrade* Blok.'

In the person of Polyansky, Blok met his first hard-core, professional, 'illegal' Bolshevik. Polyansky's reminiscences of the occasion are a study in honest bewilderment. Lenin had issued a directive stating that the co-operation of the intelligentsia was essential to the success of the revolution, and Blok, an excellent catch, was potentially even better bait. There were no fish in the sea more beautiful, but a great many more useful; and Polyansky naturally

[a] In Russian, '*Eta poshlost' poluchena 23 noyabrya.*'
[b] On 17 January, 26 January, 14/1 February 1918. Blok began to give old- and new-style dates in his diary commencing from 14 (n.s.)/1(o.s.) February 1918, when the Western Gregorian calendar was officially adopted by the new Soviet state.

set out to determine, in proper conspiratorial fashion, who amongst Blok's wide acquaintance might be accounted like-minded confederates:

I watched Blok attentively.

He stood motionless. Erect, firmly poised, with head very slightly inclined to one side, with one hand at the lapel of his closely-buttoned jacket. The man he was talking to was arguing, gesticulating, seizing his head in his hands, but he stood unruffled as a piece of sculpture, his eyes attentive, majestically calm, all you could see were his lips moving.

Then he turned sharply away and came straight over to us.

'Comrade Lebedev-Polyansky, isn't it? An interesting undertaking. We'll see how we get on. We are different sorts of people and our evaluation of what is happening is different. Anyway, we'll try to do what we can. Are you from the Smolny? Is the news bad?'

'Yes. There are difficulties at the front.—What *is* your opinion of what is happening?' I asked him.

Reluctantly, drawing out the words as though squeezing them out of himself, he began.

'I ...[d] I think that the future will be all right. But have we—you, we, the whole people—sufficient strength for so great a task?'

I began to develop the thought of the progress of the revolution and the forces at its disposal.

'I'm talking about moral, spiritual strength', he interrupted me. 'We lack culture. We are inefficient about so many things....'

Polyansky was disappointed. From Blok's early photographs he had pictured him as the epitome of the *exalté* poet, and now here he was—crop-haired and khaki-clad—talking like a professor. Gradually, however, Blok warmed to his theme:

... looking me fixedly in the eyes, he said impulsively:

'What matters to you is politics, the interests of the party; I, we poets, are looking for the soul of the Revolution. It is beautiful. And there we are all on your side.'

I very much wanted to clear up the question of who he meant by 'we', but at that moment Lunacharsky made a noisy entrance. . . .[4]

Blok was aware that his words, though attentively listened to, had quite failed to convey either what he wanted to say or what his interlocutor wanted to hear:

In Polyansky there is much of the Marxist-émigré-intellectual-Lunacharsky-like-cunning-good-natured type. Very civil. He is aware of all this

---

[c] i.e., the publication of the classics. Evidently the invitation to attend this preliminary meeting had been issued in Polyansky's name.

[d] Polyansky's ellipse.

in himself (fifteen years' illegality).... The tragic aspect of the situation (there are so few of us). A kind of sadness—perhaps from clumsiness, from the stigma of belonging to the intelligentsia, from the different languages. Something encouraging, too (good will).

The work is great and responsible. The leaders of Messieurs the Intelligentsia don't wish to get involved in work....

(VII. 321)

This was in mid-January. Throughout November and December, except for his attachment to the still semi-existent theatrical-literary commission, Blok was entirely free. He haunted his beloved flea-pit cinemas, walked the streets of the town with and without Lyuba, became an enthusiastic patron of the street 'Theatre of Miniatures', where there were 'two talented impromptu versifiers: Savoyarov and Ariadna Gor'kaya'.ᵉ They were the Russian 1917–18 equivalent of calypso singers or of the present-day *chansonniers*—and Blok loved both them and their public.

Of course, Petrograd was in turmoil. Everyone was armed. Patrols of Red Guards, supposedly keeping order, were quite likely to turn round and raid a shop or a wine cellar—or to shoot up anyone who did not take their fancy. Peaceful citizens protected themselves as best they could. Blok's house was closed after dark to all but residents with a pass and protected every night by a rota of armed occupants.ᶠ

In conversation with his old friends, Blok—arguing, persuading, quite unlike his usual self—defended the Soviets. He even gesticulated and raised his voice. 'I see angels' wings behind the shoulders of every Red Guard soldier,' he is reported to have said.

Zorgenfrey recalls him in a quieter moment, at home:

I remember the first months after the October revolution, Offitserskaya Street dark in the evenings, the sound of shots under A. A.'s windows and his desultory explanations that it was like that every day, that somewhere near by men were raiding the wine cellars. I remember the cold winter morning when, coming to his flat, I heard that he 'had now got the total feel' of what was going on and that it was necessary to 'accept' everything.⁵

During these two and half months of which we know so little, free at last 'of all obligations but the merely human', Blok was hard at work, re-tuning the supersensitive instrument that had become

ᵉ Viktor Shklovsky in his *Sentimental Journey* says that *The Twelve* was written 'not even in the style of the factory workers' *chastushki* but in the underworld (*blatnoy*) genre of Savoyarov's couplets'. Maria Beketova tells us that Blok took Lyuba to hear Savoyarov to give her an idea how *The Twelve* should be recited.

ᶠ Blok loathed this 'guarding the bourgeois's sleep' and bought himself off by paying out-of-work officers resident in the house to take his turn.

all rusted and jangled during the months of service in the Pinsk marshes and in the Peter-Paul Fortress. It was Korney Chukovsky who best described, in terms of physical appearance, 'from the outside', as it were, the workings of this instrument:

I have often heard and read that Blok's face was immobile. To many it seemed petrified, like a mask, but I, watching it thoughtfully from day to day, could not help noticing that, on the contrary, it was perpetually in strong, though scarcely-detectable motion. There was invariably a quivering and trembling in the corners of the mouth and beneath the eyes, and all the pores of his face seemed to be absorbing impressions. He only appeared to be calm. To anyone who looked for long and lovingly into that face it was quite clear that this was the face of a man excessively, uniquely sensitive, experiencing every slightest impression as pain or delight.... Sometimes, when he spoke of Russia, it seemed to me as though he felt Russia, too, with his whole body, like physical pain.[6]

2

In November, Blok had declared his willingness to co-operate with the Soviets, not 'to work under their direction'. This he made very clear when an overenthusiastic *Izvestiya* announced a meeting at which he, Ivanov-Razumnik, and Petrov-Vodkin would publicly exhort the intelligentsia to accept the party's tutelage. The meeting, which was to have been held in the Hall of the Army and Navy under the auspices of Lunacharsky and Aleksandra Kollontay, fell through. 'Ivanov-Razumnik—won't be there; Petrov-Vodkin— won't be there; I—won't be there,' Blok wrote firmly on 2 January (*Z.K.* 381 and notes).

His concept of art was too austere to admit the possibility of an artist being 'used' for limited political ends. The artist, he believed, could only give what he has to give by remaining absolutely true to himself (a difficult thing to do at any time or in any historical climate). At this moment in history, however, Blok's private experience coincided absolutely with what was happening in his country. 'I was living through contemporaneity,' he later said,[7] and stuck to it that what he wrote in this period had a peculiar value for this very reason.

All that he had written about the people and the intelligentsia in 1907–8 and 1908–9 seemed suddenly, devastatingly apt. He collected and revised these articles at the request of Ivanov-Razumnik ('I have quite a special relationship with him ... —comfortable and full of care and excitement at the same time' [VIII. 512], he wrote to Andrey Bely in April 1918). They were published one by one in the Left S. R. newspaper *Znamya Truda* (The Banner of Labour), of which Ivanov-Razumnik was literary editor, and later reprinted as a book under the title *Russia and the Intelligentsia*.[89]

To begin with it seemed to Blok that it could only be a matter of time before everyone saw things as he did. The Russian intelligentsia had always worked for the revolution—but why should they expect to direct it? Why, having preached social revolution, should they be shocked at the inevitable excesses? Blok, in spite of Shakhmatovo, in spite of the raided cellars, in spite of the summary trials and executions and even atrocities such as the lynching of the Metropolitan of Kiev, considered that, on the whole, such excesses had been 'very few'. Later, he spoke out against blood-letting: now, he saw it as a ritual act of purification and even if it had not been the Metropolitan but 'Another'—he told Zorgenfrey—all would have been as it should be. He, who had never preached revolution but only warned against the holocaust to come, now unhesitatingly laid all he had to offer upon the altar: his home, his material means of subsistence, the future security of his family, even.[h] Yet those who had sown the wind, now that the time had come to reap the whirlwind, were crying halt, were ready to bring in troops against the Soviets, even to welcome a German occupation of Petrograd. To Blok, this seemed contemptible.

The situation in Russia was still fluid: intellectually, materially. The Bolsheviks' hold on the country was not secure. Criticism of the regime could still be voiced openly in print: newspapers were not infrequently confiscated, but the only one so far to have been closed down was *Novoye Vremya*, under the Provisional Government. Criticism, moreover, was led not so much by reactionaries and conservatives as by old revolutionaries and democrats such as Korolenko and Maksim Gorky, humane men of liberal, rational sentiments and common sense, who were horrified to see what the unleashed fury of the people was doing to Russia's war effort, her

[g] Blok wrote in the copy of this book which he presented to Maksim Gorky in August 1919: 'To Aleksey Maksimovich Peshkov— this little book, fortuitously broken off in January 1918, though the end is not yet in sight. With profound respect and affection [*predannost'*]. A. BLOK.'[8]

[h] Cf. Blok's answer to the questionnaire on the law of literary inheritance (by which the relatives of dead artists continued for some time after their death to receive royalties from their work): 'I can find nothing to say against the revoking of this law ... all my wish is that hands may be found that are competent to pass on, in the best possible way, the proceeds of my labour to those who have a use for them after I am dead ... (VI. 7, 1 January 1918). His wife helped him to compose this answer.

economy, her cultural heritage, not to mention some of her best and noblest citizens. Apart from this, the Germans—should they take Petrograd, which at that juncture seemed highly probable—would undoubtedly begin by liquidating the Soviets.

Meanwhile, general elections to the Constituent Assembly had been proceeding all over the country; in the minds of many, the Soviets were still only a caretaker government until such time as the country should have its own elected Parliament. It was rumoured that the Constituent Assembly, with the help of the Semyënov Regiment and anyone else prepared to support them, would turn the tables on the Soviets and force them, if force were needed, to submit to its authority.

Blok was inclined to share the opinion of his mother's anonymous Shakhmatovo correspondent as to the '13 numbers of struggling fools'. He was too well aware of the realities of power to believe in a democratic[i] takeover by a newly elected Assembly claiming to represent the vast diapason of interests of the one-time Empire of 'all the Russias'. It was rather like trying to call a Parliament elected on the basis of universal suffrage to decide the fate of the entire British Empire in 1917. Sooner or later, there would be a putsch and it would be organized by a few effective people with military backing: Blok accepted the fact that the putsch came sooner—on the very day the Constituent Assembly first forgathered—and from the left.

Perhaps it was easy for him. As an artist, he had never really thought very deeply about representative government, or worked to establish it. 'The *Uchredil'ka*': Blok pondered the contemptuous diminutive bestowed on the Assembly by the people. Why did they call it that? Why did they not want and respect it when supposedly it was to represent *them* after free elections? It was because, he decided,

... we ourselves have brought civil servants to trial for abuses during election campaigns; because even the civilized countries (America, France) are to this day still choking on their own electoral dishonesty, electoral bribes.

Then (I'm being simplistic on purpose), I want to 'control' everything myself, I don't want to be 'represented'. ...

Then there was the question of the difference in languages. The language of politics was as incomprehensible to the mass of the people as was the language of law. Dostoyevsky and Tolstoy had both described the plain man's reaction to the learned pomposity of the law courts: the same would apply to the lawmakers. And lastly, it was

---

[i] In the English sense of government by majority rule through elected representatives. Blok himself used the word in a different sense to mean government by the common people, and applied it to the Soviets.

'... because God alone knows who was elected and how and to what end by the illiterate Russia of this present day; Russia who cannot even get it into her head that the Constituent Assembly is not the Tsar ...' (VI. 15).

For these sentiments, Blok found considerable support with Ivanov-Razumnik and the Left S. R.s gathered about *Znamya Truda* and later about Razumnik's journal *Nash Put'* (Our Way). Andrey Bely had responded to the October take-over with a fiery paean of verse, 'Christ is Risen', in which he drew a parallel between the immolation of the Old Russia and the Crucifixion. Esenin, too, had written a number of revolutionary poems, on a note of bravado and blasphemy reminiscent of Dostoyevsky's village youth who shot the Body of Christ in the form of the consecrated Host. He came to read one of these poems to Blok on 4 January and this time the two poets found plenty to talk about. As so often, Blok listened more than he talked, drawing Esenin out about his Old Believer background, his life as a boy in Ryazan, and noting the peasant poet's optimistic remark that the intelligentsia was 'like a bird in a cage, fluttering desperately to avoid a horny, gentle hand that wanted only to take it out and to let it fly free'.

As the date of the convening of the Assembly approached and news of the peace talks at Brest-Litovsk grew grimmer, Blok felt it incumbent upon him to make a statement in print. 'Towards evening—a hurricane (the invariable accompaniment of putsches)...,' he noted on 3 January. As this 'hurricane' grew to a 'cyclone', as the Assembly met and was disbanded, as shots rattled beneath his windows and an enemy plane droned overhead, dropping leaflets announcing the imminent advent of the German armies, he sat writing 'The Intelligentsia and the Revolution':

'Russia is perishing', 'There is no Russia', 'Eternal memory to Russia'—so I hear all about me.

Yet before me I see—Russia: that same Russia which our great writers saw in terrifying and prophetic dreams; that Petersburg which Dostoyevsky saw, that Russia which Gogol called a run-away troika.

Russia is storm. Democracy comes 'girded with storm', says Carlyle.

Russia is doomed to live through torments, humiliations, divisions, but she will emerge from these humiliations renewed and—in a new way—great.

He thought back to the theme to which in 1908 he had 'consciously dedicated' his whole life: the theme of Russia and the intelligentsia:

In that flood of thoughts and premonitions which swept me off my feet ten years ago, there was a mixed apprehension of Russia: longing, horror, penitence, hope.... Now, when all the air of Europe has been changed by the Russian revolution, beginning with the 'bloodless idyll' of February and growing unceasingly and menacingly, it sometimes seems as though those years,[j] so recent and yet so ancient-seeming now and distant, had never been: but listen! The stream which had gone underground, flowing silently in the depths and the darkness, has broken out again in a roaring torrent. And in this roaring there is a new music....

(VI. 11)

Music. It was a feeling for 'music', for the underlying harmony of things for which he had listened ever since he began to write serious poetry, that Blok now demanded of 'the intelligentsia', of educated Russia. On 14 January, somebody rang him up to ask for a newspaper statement on the theme: 'Can the intelligentsia co-operate with the Bolsheviks?' 'It can and should,' Blok replied in his statement:

... The music of the intelligentsia is the same as the music of the Bolsheviks.

The intelligentsia has always been revolutionary.... The intelligentsia's bitterness against the Bolsheviks is all on the surface. It seems to be passing already. People's thought is not always truly in accord with what they say. Reconciliation will come, a musical reconciliation....

(VI. 8)

He did not see it as the calling of an artist to look at the *details* of 'what has been purposed' or of *how* that purpose is to be accomplished. It was enough, as he maintained in 'The Intelligentsia and the Revolution', to realize that the ultimate purpose was '*to remake* everything. To organize things so that everything should be new; so that our false, filthy, boring hideous life should become a just, pure, merry, and beautiful life' (VI. 12–13).

Almost like a man addressing frightened children, he went on:

Don't be afraid. Surely you don't think that so much as one grain of what is truly valuable can be lost? We have loved but little if we are so afraid for that which we love. 'Perfect love driveth out fear.'[k] Do not fear the destruction of fortresses, palaces, pictures, books. They should be preserved for the people; but, having lost these, the people have not lost everything. A palace destroyed is no palace. A fortress wiped off the face of the earth is no fortress. A Tsar who tumbles off his throne of his own volition is no Tsar. Fortresses are in our hearts, Tsars in our heads. Eternal forms which have been revealed to us, are taken from us only with our hearts and with our heads.

(VI. 16)

---

[j] i.e., the years between 1908 and 1917.   [k] I John 4:18.

'He walks on the steps of eternity,' stormed Zinaida Hippius, 'and in eternity we are all of us Bolsheviks. But there in that eternity there's not so much as a whiff of Trotsky, oh no....'[10]

But Blok continued, soberly, sternly: 'What did you think? That revolution is an idyll? That creation destroys nothing that gets in its way? That the people—are good little children?' Then, with mounting passion:

Love works miracles, music tames wild beasts. And you (all of us) have lived without music and without love. It is better to be silent now if there is no music, if you can't hear the music. For everything other than music will only rouse and anger the beast.[1] The only way to get through to the human being is through music.

(VI. 16)

Yet all about him the intelligentsia were proclaiming their 'disappointment' in the Russian people, seeing *only* the brute ('when the human being is here, right beside you', VI. 16). Those who but a few months before had been defeatists, internationalists, atheists, were now bewailing the collapse of their country's armed might and mourning Holy Russia. Blok made it clear that his article was not addressed to the politicians, whose disapproval of the Soviets was based on reasoned arguments about matters of short-term policy, nor yet to the bourgeoisie, who had indeed something to lose, whose whole life centred round family, property, stability: 'God on His icon, the Tsar on his throne'. He was addressing the intelligentsia, who had no stake in property or government and who had energetically devoted themselves for the past sixty years to opposing and undermining all established values, that same intelligentsia to which he was so proud to belong, but to which he had brought his own aristocratic, military sense of a class trained to power and to facing up to the consequences of its own actions:

What it amounts to is that we have been lopping off the branch we were sitting on. A sorry situation! Positively revelling in malice, we piled up knotted roots that had long lain damp under the snow and the rain, dry twigs, shavings, chips; and when the flame suddenly flared up and unfurled, blowing skywards like a banner—we run round and squeal 'Oh! Oh! We're burning!'

(VI. 18)

[1] Cf. *Lightnings of Art* (v. 386, Autumn 1909–April 1918). These ideas of the uprooted, mechanized urban proletariat as a beast which is angered by culture but may be turned back into a human being by love and music are based at least partially on Blok's reading of the European classics: notably Ruskin and Flaubert.

The people, he went on urgently, would take their tone from the intelligentsia. Behind the few criminal types who tended to take the lead at such moments of anarchy were millions of people, ignorant and unhappy at the present moment, great and creative in potential.

'But it is not you who will bring them enlightenment ...,' he wrote bitterly, dropping the proprietary preacher's 'we'. In this emergency, he concluded, the spirit, not the emotions, must condition the approach of responsible people: 'For the spirit is music. The Demon once ordered Socrates to hearken to the spirit of music. With all your body, with all your heart, with all your mind—hearken to the revolution' (VI. 20).

This article, written over the first nine days of the New Year and published on 19 January in *Znamya Truda*, was pronounced 'sincere—but unforgivable' by many of the poet's erstwhile friends: Hippius, Aleksandra Chebotarevskaya, Sologub, and Ariadna Tyrkova-Williams amongst others.

Nevertheless, it was the context in which the article appeared, more than the article itself, which gave a new bitterness to what was, in fact, an old argument. Blok said little in 'The Intelligentsia and the Revolution' that he had not said before, in very different political circumstances, in 1908 and 1909. There was, perhaps, a greater underlying anger,[m] but the essential message was the same as in 1908: the abyss between the 'two camps' is widening; much has been given to you, much is asked; jump, leap, fly across the gap before it is too late. The only way to do this is on the wings of the spirit, the spirit of music.

3

'The Intelligentsia and the Revolution', although it shocked some of Blok's friends and colleagues, was generally considered rather naïve and did not put him beyond the pale. The liberal intelligentsia could read it tolerantly, as the statement of an irresponsible enthusiast who had not shared the heat and burden of the day in preparing social reform, in planning and advocating representative government. They could repeat what they had said in 1908, 1909: that Blok was, of course, a very talented poet, but a stranger to politics and sociology; that he should confine himself to things he understood.

[m] This anger can be seen in the rough notes, all bearing on this article, which Blok made in his diary for 5 January 1918, notes which reach a climax with: 'It is essential to take a better, purer attitude to *everything*. Oh, the scum, my own, native scum!' (VII. 314–15).

It was not until he spoke out with his own voice, as a poet, that he brought the swarm about his ears, provoking boycott, ostracism, and a controversy that has lasted for over fifty years and will last, most probably, as long as the Russian language. The Bolsheviks themselves were chary of having *The Twelve* read aloud at public gatherings—though read it was." It is on the Vatican index. Representatives of Russian Orthodox thought are still disputing as to whether or not it should be classed as a demoniac vision.[11] It has been anathematized as a coarse work of no artistic merit, yet one great Russian scholar went so far as to say (in the English periodical press) that if he had to choose between *The Twelve* and all the rest of Russian literature, he would hesitate.[12]

The Twelve is, indeed, a quintessential work, not only for Blok but for the whole Petersburg period, but at the time it grew naturally and immediately out of events.

On 6 January 1918, it became known that the Constituent Assembly had in fact foregathered on the previous day, had had time to elect a Right S. R., Victor Chernov, as speaker, and had been dissolved. That morning, Blok noted, the Bolsheviks had confiscated most of the newspapers from the fat woman who sold them on the corner of his street. For the 7 January—curiously, amongst all this chaos—the only entry in the poet's notebook is: '*Vie de Jésus*'. He was reading Renan. The next day, on a whirlwind of rumour, came the certain news of the murder, in hospital, of Shingarev and Kokoshkin, two deeply respected Russian democrats who had devoted their lives to political reform. Again the newspapers were confiscated. Amongst those reported killed was Mikhail Tereshchenko.[o]

That evening, Remizov rang Blok: 'And Blok told me that, above all that was happening, above all the "horror", he heard music and was trying to write. It was *The Twelve* he was writing.'[13]

Blok himself noted: 'All day—*The Twelve* ... I am trembling inside' (*Z.K.* 382, 383, entry for 8 January 1918). The poem began to grow from the couplet in section 8 about the slashing knife:

> *Uzh ya nozhichkom*
> *Polosnu, polosnu.*

The repetition of the sinister sibilants[p] seemed to express something of the violence which, over these dreadful days, had reached so shocking a climax.

" Cf. *Z.K.* 394, entry for 9 March 1918.

[o] This rumour proved false. Tereshchenko emigrated.

[p] The first *zh* is pronounced *sh*, the second as *je* in French.

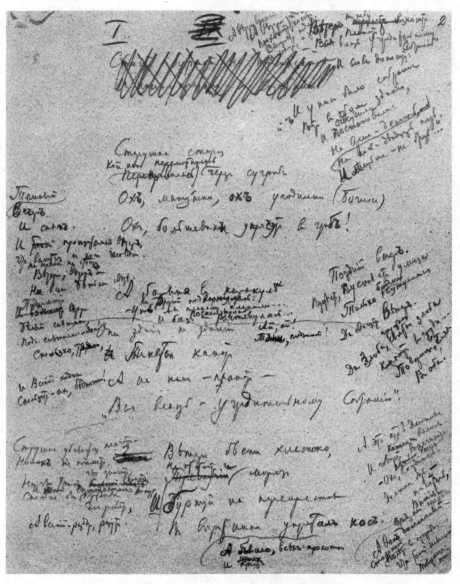

Blok's rough draft of the opening section of *The Twelve*.

But Blok was hurrying to finish 'The Intelligentsia and the Revolution', and the next day he returned to prose, leaving the poem to lie fallow.

'The other day I lay in bed with open eyes and listening to something roaring, roaring: I thought it was the beginning of an earthquake' (Z.K. 383, entry for 9 January 1918).

Blok's mother, horrified by the murders, asked him not to come to see her for a few days. It was cold and there was not enough to eat. Snow fell heavily and no one cleared it away. A raw wind blew off the sea. Yet throughout these perilous and comfortless days, the music was all about him: 'A different music. Could it be—yellow?' he wrote on 11 January when the negotiations at Brest-Litovsk finally broke down and the Germans renewed their advance on Petrograd. He read Gogol's *Correspondence with Friends*, that *bête noire* of the progressive intelligentsia, which he now found supremely apt. He read the Gospel, sent by his mother, and Renan, and thought of writing a play about Christ—not a divine, sinless Christ but a kind of emanation of the spirit of the people and the herald of a new age. The Sermon on the Mount was to be represented as a meeting and St. Peter was to talk (like Scryëzha Esenin) about different ways of catching fish. 'Thoughts, thoughts and plans—so many that they prevent me concentrating on any one thing' (Z.K. 386, entry for 25 January 1918).

Then, on 27 January, he returned to the poem. Now that the moment had come, he wrote with consummate ease. He had once—in that other life before the revolution—copied out a passage from Ruskin (Z.K. 157) in which the English critic said that all truly great works of art come easily. It was a matter of not losing concentration, of biding one's time. Gradually, the work would take shape of itself. A few words, expressions, would glow ever brighter like stars in the gathering dusk and then there would come the moment to fling over them a fragile net of words and rhythms. After days, months, years of patient waiting—the unswerving practised throw and then gently, easily, you would pull in your catch and present your fellow men with these marvellous alien bodies, recovered at the cost of a lifetime of concentration from some quite other sphere of being.

Two days later *The Twelve* was finished and he had already begun to write *The Scythians*. That evening he wrote: 'A terrible noise, growing within me and all around. This was the noise Gogol heard (and to silence it exhorted men to return to Orthodoxy and an orderly family life). Steiner: "regulates" it? *Today—I am a genius*' (Z.K. 387, entry for 29 January 1918).

The Twelve was the triumphant justification of the poet's search for form, of his long, slow struggle to introduce 'the personal and particular organically into the objective and the general'. Superficially, the form was one he had often used, more suited to his gift than the sustained narrative poem in a single metre which he had attempted in *Retribution*. As in 'Invocation by Fire and Darkness', for instance, as in *On the Field of Kulikovo*, 'Autumn Freedom', 'Florence', 'The Dance of Death', or 'Black Blood', Blok wrote, in *The Twelve*, a cycle of poems which tell a story or evoke a state of heart and spirit, a kind of symphony in which each movement has its own characteristic rhythm.

Like a musician, Blok wove borrowed melodies[q] into his symphony, making them his own. The sounds of the street: staccato shouts, murmured imprecations, snatches of talk, marching feet. Popular rhythms: the Russian dance, the cruel romance, the *chastushka*,[r] the folk-song. Words: snatches of slang; revolutionary jargon with its indigestible foreign words; popular mispronunciations; phrases from the Liturgy. Then a growing cacophony: hoarse, angry curses; the rattle of rifle-fire; the long laugh of the wind in the alleyways and, at the last, a total change of key: a soft, compelling music that bursts upon the reader with majestic serenity, as inevitable yet totally unexpected as the choral finale of Beethoven's Ninth Symphony or the swelling prayer at the end of Schoenberg's *Survivor of the Warsaw Ghetto*.

The poem opens with a cosmic vision of roaring black night and driving snow.[s] Gradually, the reader becomes aware of the locale in time and space: the city of Petrograd as it was on the eve of the

---

[q] A brilliant analysis of the elements of folk culture and carnival woven into this poem, conceived during the twelve days of Christmas and containing ancient processional elements as well as more modern ingredients from the peepshow and other fairground amusements, is given by B. M. Gasparov and Yu. M. Lotman in the 1975 collection of articles published by Tartu University in honour of D. E. Maksimov.[14]

[r] An improvised quatrain, popular amongst factory workers and semi-industrialized peasantry.

[s] There have been at least a dozen more or less unsuccessful attempts to translate *The Twelve* into English.[15] I have no reason to think any effort of mine would improve upon the better of these: Maurice Bowra's, Alex Miller's; the 'beat' version by Anselm Hollo; the very English but curiously beautiful rendering of Jon Stallworthy and Peter France. The German language being rather closer in structure to the Russian, those who read German may prefer to try a German translation: Gröger's, Guenther's, Walter's, Paul Celan's are all very tolerable, and the first is often considered the best. The poem goes no more happily into French than it does into English. It has been translated into many other languages, including ancient Hebrew. Nevertheless, it is worth learning Russian to read it in the original. Always laconic, Blok here invested every word with such a resilience of meaning, sound, associative significance, that one cannot hope to reproduce more than a fraction of the effect in translation.

Constituent Assembly, deep in drifted snow. People appear in the streets: all figures we have met before in Blok's earlier poetry, his prose or his notebooks: the helpless old woman (like the old peasant woman in the 1906 poem, 'The Red Cock', who sets fire to her own wooden house and dies in the flames); the bourgeois with his nose in his collar, and the lady walking up the Nevsky Prospect in her ill-gotten Persian lamb; the priest, his majestic stomach reminding us of that other priest in the cycle *Iambs* who—so the poet had foretold when the 1905 revolution had just begun to recede into history—would not have time so much as to read the last rites over the agony of the Old World (III. 87); the writer, murmuring words from Georgiy Chulkov's latest feuilleton; a huddled group of prostitutes; a lonely passer-by.

With section 2, a new rhythm is introduced: the advancing patrol of Red Guards, marching in step, their looted Austrian rifles slung across their backs on black straps, ruffianly as a gang of convicts. In the hearts of these twelve men an incoherent struggle is being waged which permeates the poetry as a dialogue of rhythms: the steady beat of the march and the wild Russian song-and-dance, the *chastushka* and the *plyasovaya*, which express, on the one hand, the revolutionary will to power and, on the other, the destructive and self-destructive revolutionary temperament.

The action of the poem seems simple enough. A renegade comrade of the twelve, Van'ka, goes flying by in a horse-drawn sleigh with Kat'ka, a prostitute but also the special girl of one of the patrol, Petya. The twelve surround the sleigh and start shooting. Vanka and the driver gallop off unharmed, but Kat'ka tumbles out into the snow—shot through the head.

The twelve march on, leaving her to lie. Columbine is dead at last, and with her the very last hope of rosy warmth, of human happiness.

Only Petya mourns and calls on the Saviour for forgiveness, but soon he is caught up again in the inexorable rhythms of the moment: the lust for wine, the lust for pleasure, the sullen anger of a dark, frustrated life and the imperative need to keep watch, to defend the revolution.

> *Uzh ya nozhichkom*
> *Polosnu, polosnu!*
>
> (Now with my knife
> I will slash, I will slash!)

This section 8 where the poem began lies at its very heart. Here

Petya, the transgressor, goes berserk, lashing himself into an ugly fury, a tarantella, a bacchanalia of destruction to drown out the voice of conscience and the sheer misery of having murdered the only thing he loves. Yet the misery remains, at the end as at the beginning, and, sounding through the wild cacophony like the tolling of a passing bell through an impassioned *dies irae*, one line of prayer:

Upokoy, Gospodi, dushu raby tvoyeya.

(Receive into Thy rest, O Lord, the soul of this thine handmaiden.)

Quite unexpectedly, as this cyclone of wrath and sorrow fades back into the savage boredom from which it sprang, come the sweet strains of a sentimental ballad, a wistful popular song about silence over the city and the main thoroughfare of the Nevsky Prospect. To this incongruous music 'the bourgeois' again materializes on the corner of the street, a silent question mark, monumental, threatened yet menacing, and at his heels cringes a starving, lousy dog: the Old World.

The blizzard grows more fierce and obliterates the figures, the street itself: again a new rhythm, exclamatory, troubled. The twelve are on the scene once more: Petya, frightened, calling on the Lord for help; the others exhorting him not to weaken, reminding him that he has gone too far in crime to seek help of the old certainties, steeling his will with rough talk of worse to come. Then again the refrain, a reprise, here repeated for the third time since the twelve's first appearance and their first attempt to pull themselves together after Katya's murder:

> Keep in step with the revolution!
> Sleepless, the enemy is very near!

followed, for the first time, by the rousing chorus from the old Polish revolutionary song, the *Varshavyanka:*

> *Vperëd, vperëd, vperëd,*
> *Rabochiy narod.*

> (Forward, forward, forward
> The working people).'

'Without the Cross', 'without one holy name', the twelve march on into the distance, sticking at nothing, regretting nothing, ready to destroy anything and everything in their path.... Through empty streets where their boots stick in the drifts, where the blizzard

' Slightly misquoted, if quotation it be, but near enough to evoke all the associations.

blows like dust in their eyes, they march into an infinity of blowing snow, day and night, a red flag flapping before their blinded eyes, on and on, night and day

$$—'—'$$
$$—'—$$
$$—'—'$$
$$—'—$$

Vperëd, vperëd,
Rabochiy narod.

'With sovereign tread', as the rhythm changes once more at the beginning of section 12, the patrol steps out after the red flag that so mysteriously precedes them through the blinding storm. As frightened as they are dangerous, they challenge the flag, but only the wind replies with a long laugh echoing among the snows. Behind them limps the starving dog, the Old World—they threaten it with their bayonets, but then turn their attention back to the flag, challenging, warning, shooting into the night, only to send the echoes ricocheting from house to house through the white darkness.

Still they march on 'with sovereign tread'. Behind them, the hungry dog. Before them, bearing the flag, invisible, invulnerable, walking lightly above the storm, haloed in a pearly scattering of snow, wreathed in white roses—Jesus Christ.

Blok never explained the image. In the margin of his rough copy is scribbled, with the same winged haste as the whole poem: 'And He was with the thief'....[u]

Later, the constant questioning of an astonished public made the poet think and analyse. Now, he merely hurried on to the next poem.

4

The Scythians[v] had been boiling up in him since the breakdown of the peace talks at Brest-Litovsk. He who had doubted throughout

[u] Another inexact quotation recalling Isaiah, 'And He was numbered with the transgressors...', the Gospel account of the crucifixion between two thieves, and the Orthodox Maundy Thursday canonic hymn of the good thief, the first to be 'with Christ' in Paradise. The quotation is qualified by a second marginal note from a Nekrasov ballad: 'There lived twelve robbers', the word *razboynik* in Russian being the same in both contexts and emphasizing the allusion in the title of the poem to the number of Christ's disciples, and the parallel between the Red Guard and the whole tradition of outlawry.

[v] Blok took the name at hand—suggested by Ivanov-Razumnik's almanac, two numbers of which had been published during his absence with the *druzhina* and while he was too

the long summer had no doubts now. When Esenin rang him up to tell him that, at a meeting in the Tenishev Hall, there had been cries of 'traitors' at the mention of Blok, Bely, and himself, and that people had refused to shake hands, Blok wrote firmly in his note-book, 'Gentlemen, you never knew Russia and never loved her.' Then, taking up the red crayon from his ever-tidy desk, in larger let-ters: 'The truth leaps to the eye' (Z.K. 385, entry for 22 January 1918). As great as his rising indignation against the intelligentsia ('cowards, rabble-rousers, hangers-on of the bourgeoisie', VII. 318), was his disgust at the blindness of the Europeans (Germans, French, and English alike), at their stubborn pursuit of war and death, their heedless, irreverent disregard of the new life that had come into the world in Russia, of the green shoots already breaking through the burnt and blackened stubble. The thoughts of 'opening the sluice-gates' that had visited him the previous spring now came flooding back:

If you do not wash away the shame of your wartime patriotism with at least a 'democratic peace', if you destroy our revolution, then you are no longer Aryans. And we shall open wide the gates to the East.

We looked at you with Aryan eyes, so long as you still had a face. But your animal muzzle we will run over with our squint-eyed, cunning, glanc-ing look; like changelings we will turn into Asiatics, and the East will flood over you.

Your skins will go for Chinese tambourines. He who has brought down such shame on his own head, who is so sunk in lies—is no longer Aryan. We're barbarians? All right then. We'll show you what barbarians really are. And our cruel reply, our terrible reply, will be the only answer worthy of man.

(VII. 317)[16]

So Blok had written on 11 January. Now, on 29 January, hearing the extraordinary unilateral declaration of peace ('The war is ended, the peace treaty has not been signed'), by which the Soviets announced that, while not willing to agree to the very stiff German

---

busy working on the Investigatory Commission to contribute. For technical reasons, the third *Scythians* almanac, which was to have contained both *The Twelve* and *The Scythians*, remained unpublished and much of the material went into the first number of *Nash Put'*.

Of course, Blok did not mean to refer to any specific ethnic group, though he noted with annoyance that he had made a mistake in confusing Mongols and Scythians. He had meant what Vladimir Solov'ev meant by pan-Mongolism, Bryusov by 'The Coming Huns', Cavafy by 'The Barbarians': aliens without reverence for Aryan civilization. The fascination of the term 'Scythians' (originally a tribe inhabiting the southern plains of Russia beyond the Greek colonies along the coast of the Black Sea) was that Russians, as 'Eurasians', could identify with them, seeing themselves either as pagan barbarians *or* as the front line of Christendom and European civilization.

peace terms, they no longer considered themselves at war, Blok wrote: 'Asia and Europe. I have understood Faust's: *Knurre nicht, Pudel . . .*' (*Z.K.* 38).

That evening and the following day he wrote *The Scythians*. Printed within the week,[w] supremely topical, written for and from that particular moment of history, the poem has retained its relevance. Yet even when time has worn away all political significance, *The Scythians* will still stand as a splendid monument of rhetorical verse.[x] It does not bear comparison with *The Twelve,* for it lacks the lyrical and what one contemporary critic called the 'supra-spatial' dimension,[19] but, in its own genre, it is unsurpassed. In the trough of her humiliation, Russia welcomed this defiant affirmation of the national spirit:

> O, ancient world! While yet life lingers on
> > While yet your sun in sweet pain sinks,
> Halt, wise as Oedipus, and seek to solve
> > The riddle of the Sphinx.
>
> The Sphinx is Russia. Now, exulting through her tears,
> > As black blood from a thousand gashes flows
> It is at you, at you, at you she stares
> > With hatred—and with love.
>
> Aye, so to love as our hot blood can love
> > Not one of you has loved these many years!
> You have forgotten that there is a love
> > That burns, and wrecks, and sears!

[w] Ivanov-Razumnik, in his speech at the 1921 session of the Free Philosophical Association in memory of Blok, implies that the Left S. R.s, who were so quick to publish *The Scythians,* accepted it as an expression of their own point of view on the war: i.e. that it must be fought to the bitter end. He even gave his listeners to understand that Blok's 'disappointment with the revolution' dated from the final signing of the peace of Brest-Litovsk.[17] This was a misunderstanding. It is clear from Blok's notebooks that, while he found the Left S. R. attitude 'touching', he thought that the Bolsheviks, by settling for peace at any cost, were doing the only possible thing. His poem was not written in opposition to those in his own country who wanted to make peace, but as a warning and an appeal to 'the Old World'. It advocates internationalism. Ivanov-Razumnik was bound, by his own personal philosophy which made an ultimate value of the individual at any given moment of being, to misunderstand a poet who regarded the present as non-existent, no more than an imaginary point of contact between past and future, and a man's true friends as those who see him as he might become rather than as he is.

[x] One of the best translations of the poem is by Alex Miller, a free version which preserves the rhetorical poetic tone though it makes no attempt to follow the metre. A better idea of the latter is given by Robin Kemball who, in the first line, brings off an almost exact reproduction of Blok's sound pattern.[18]

> For the last time, Old World, think well, think deep.
> A feast of peace and toil is spread before you.
> For the last time, as brothers, join our feast.
> Hear well! The savage lyre calls you.

5

The Scythians was published on 20/7 February, the very day that the Soviet of People's Commissars (theSovnarkom, as the government of the country was now called) declared its readiness to accept the humiliating German terms for a separate peace, and the Left S. R.s seceded in protest.

Rumours were rife that the Commissars would evacuate to Moscow. 'Monstrous days are upon us,' Blok noted, and began to hurry Ivanov-Razumnik to print *The Twelve* before Petrograd was occupied and the revolution temporarily crushed. At the same time, he noted Lyuba's sudden bout of weeping for the old world:

She says: 'I go out to meet the new world, perhaps I shall come to love it.' But she has not yet broken with the old world and suddenly she saw in her mind's eye all the glories of the last nineteen centuries.
Yes.

(VII. 325)

To drown out such regrets, he launched into a diatribe more violent than any he had permitted himself in print:

Patriotism is filth....
Religion is filth (priests and so forth). The terrible thought of these days: it is not that the Red Guard are 'not worthy' of Jesus, Who is with them now; it is precisely that it is still He Who is with them, whereas it should be Another.[y]
Romanticism is filth. All that has been buried in dogma, in delicate dust, in the aura of *fairy tale* has become filth. All that is left is ÉLAN.
Only—flight and impulse; fly and break away, otherwise perdition waits on every road.
It may be that all the (European) world will take fright and settle back more firmly than ever into the old lies. *That will not be for long*. It is hard to fight against the 'Russian infection', because *Russia has already infected mankind with health*. The foundations of all dogmas are shaken, they cannot last for ever. Movement is infectious.

[y] Cf. also *Z.K.* 388, entry for 18 February 1918: 'That Christ is going before them is beyond a doubt. The question is not "whether they are worthy of Him", but it is terrible that again it is He Who is with them and as yet there is no other; but there should be Another—? I feel exhausted somehow. Either I am giving birth, or simply tired.'

Only he who has loved as I have loved has the right to hate. And it is my lot to become a catacomb.

A catacomb is a star, flying through the empty deep-blue ether, giving light.

(VII. 326)

The Germans continued to advance on Petrograd. On 21 February Lenin issued his proclamation: 'The Socialist Fatherland is in danger.' Volunteers from among the workers of Petrograd—soon to become the hard core of the Red Army—marched out to defend the capital. Sergey Esenin, Blok heard, was among them.[z]

Rumours: counter-rumours: plans. Without rest or pause, Blok embarked on an introduction to Wagner's *Art and Revolution*, which seemed to him an apt expression of the time, but other impressions— from the past—kept rising up to obscure that vision of the New Age he was striving to keep before him. Doubles, fragments of his own guilt, appeared to him in the shape of real people he met, and demanded to be exorcised.

There were the young people: Zhenya Knipovich, a girl with eyes like 'great dull agates', who had run away from home and soon became almost a part of Blok's family. *Five* of her friends, admirers of modernist literature, had committed suicide. Then there was the nightmare conversation with Stenich, a young poet who claimed Blok and his generation were responsible for what he and his generation had become, reared on ambrosia when they might have thrived better on porridge, unfit for survival, bisexual, suicidal, drug-takers, living for poetry alone. Irony—even more than for Blok's own generation—was the air they breathed. The October revolution, said Stenich cynically, was an improvement on the February revolution because there was 'a flavour of the autocracy about it'. The most fashionable poet, because the most self-mocking, was Ilya Ehrenburg (VII. 323–4). This conversation revolved in Blok's head until he described it in an essay entitled 'Russian Dandies' (VI. 53–7). Byron, Pushkin's Onegin, Poe, Baudelaire, Wilde—how he had loved them! But they must not poison the roots of the new Russia as they had poisoned this strange boy and his milieu, as they had destroyed Zhenya Knipovich's five dead friends. . . .

Then, in the next-door flat and on guard duty downstairs, more revenants, more doubles. Blok's own distant relative, an officer called von Schulman, was courting the daughter of his next-door

---

[z] According to Gordon McVay, Blok's diary is the only evidence for this action of Esenin's. Like the story of Tereshchenko's murder, it may have been one of the countless rumours of the revolutionary period.[20]

neighbour, an inoffensive society miss whose tinkling on the piano together with Aunt Maria's rustlings beyond the other wall combined to transform Blok's study 'into a torture chamber'. This 'last echo of the hey-day of the bourgeoisie', the serene singing while the Germans were advancing beyond Pskov and people were saying that all that stood between them and Petrograd was fear of taking responsibility for feeding its three million inhabitants (cf. *Z.K.* 390, entry for 25 February 1918), irritated Blok to an almost pathological degree. On the day that the Red Guard re-took Pskov and the Germans, at the first sign of serious resistance, agreed to sign the peace treaty which ceded them vast territories and promised total disarmament, Blok sat down to exorcise his furious resentment against these former patriots:

I live in a flat and behind the thin partition wall is another flat inhabited by a bourgeois and his family (there's no need to write down his name or occupation). He has a crew-cut, he is good at getting things done, having served all his life as an important official, has bags under the eyes, under his paunch, too, smells of clean male underwear, his daughter plays the piano, his voice, a reedy tenor, sounds behind the wall, on the stairs, by the latrines in the courtyard where he is in charge (of hygiene), etc. Wherever you go, there he is.

Lord God! Give me strength to shake off this hatred for him which makes it almost impossible for me to go on living in my flat, strangles me with resentment, interrupts my thoughts. He's the same kind of carnivorous two-legged animal as I am. Personally, he has done me no harm. But I am choking with hatred, which mounts to a pathological, hysterical revulsion, poisons my life.

Be gone from me, Satan, be gone from me, bourgeois, somewhere where I need not touch you, or see you, or hear; whether I am better than he or worse I do not know, but I am revolted, sickened, be gone from me, Satan.

(VII. 327–8, entry for 26 February 1918)

This violent revulsion, too, had to be reduced to its proper proportions and, little more than a month later, Blok managed a humorous feuilleton, 'Fellow Citizens' (VI. 49–52), whose cool malice suggests nothing of the white-hot fury of these dreadful days of February 1918.

It was not until 5 March, the day on which *The Twelve* appeared in *Znamya Truda*,[aa] that the Germans finally did sign the peace treaty.

[aa] It was also to have appeared in a separate edition with a cover by Petrov-Vodkin, but this project came to nothing. (Petrov-Vodkin was one of the first to object to Christ's wreath of white roses, which, for an artist of his calibre, one of the few at that time to have a real knowledge of the Russian icon, must have seemed incongruous indeed.) In

Nobody, however, seemed to think that it would really mean peace. Noting again the fateful 'trembling inside', Blok looked out at the melting icicles on the roofs and gutters and called again on the spirit of music: 'Something is going on. Be ready. The only salvation is music.' Europe, old Russia, had transgressed against this spirit and now, 'so that music *should consent to make peace with the world*', there had to be a complete about-face, a 'betrayal' of the old values: of patriotism, particularly.

Yet he hated the idea of betrayal, compromise. Was it not just another sign of the decline of Europe, an injection of 'yellow blood'? Russia, maybe, was young enough to recover from such an injection. Yet even Russia—what could she do when, by agreeing to the German peace terms, she had ceased so dramatically to be a great power?

Nine-tenths of Russia ... really has ceased to exist. It was sick, had long been rotting; now it is dead; but it is not yet buried; it stinks. Paunchy shopkeepers spitefully reverence the dear memory of the corpse (without intending it I am writing in trochees, that means, perhaps, that I shall perish)....

(VII. 328)

Later, he was to weave this lapse into the metre of death into something approaching a funeral chant:

> Something there is that has passed with her passing
> Irretrievably
> But we may not mourn it
> And we may not reverence it
> Because that here and there
> Dully huddling together
> Paunchy shopkeepers
> Spitefully reverence
> The dear memory of the corpse—
> Here and there
> Here and there ...

(VII. 334)

But there he broke off. It was too soon for tears, and when they came they would be too bitter for poetry.

Now he was suddenly excited again by the newness of everything. It was a strange feeling to be such a little country, 'a waifish wooden

April 1918, both *The Twelve* and *The Scythians* were republished in the periodical *Nash Put'*, in company with poetry by Andrey Bely and Sergey Esenin and an article by Ivanov-Razumnik. *The Twelve* was also published as a separate pamphlet before the famous Alkonost edition with almost definitive illustrations by Yuriy Annenkov.

church in the midst of a drunken and debauched market-place', Blok
said of Red Russia in the spring of 1918, momentarily enchanted
by the sudden cosy sense of 'smallness', the idea of a breathing space.
In this, he differed radically from Ivanov-Razumnik: 'A repulsive
socialist-petty-bourgeois-Bolshevik Paradise', he called what remained of his country, over the telephone to Blok.

6

Though the fruits and warmth of Paradise were notably lacking
throughout that cold and hungry spring, the more orderly atmosphere did indeed make itself felt almost at once and life began to
separate from poetry. Symptomatic was the fact that O. D.
Kameneva, Commissar of the Theatrical Department, told Lyuba
that it would be better not to read *The Twelve* aloud at public gatherings:

Aleksandr Aleksandrovich's poem (*The Twelve*) is a very talented depiction
of what is happening—almost a work of genius. Anatoliy Vasilievich
(Lunacharsky) is going to write about it, but it should not be read (aloud),
because it glorifies something that we old socialists fear more than anything
else.

Blok recorded this remark on 9 March, and added: 'The Marxists
are clever—they may even be right. But where—again—is the artist
and his homeless calling? (*Z.K.* 394).

Next day, musing over the criticisms of his poem now pouring
in from all sides, he defined art for himself as extracting from life
and the everyday that alien essence which comes from some other
source: to loot the looted? he queried, his all-too-absorbent ear suggesting—and at once half-rejecting—a now familiar catch-phrase:

The Marxists are the cleverest critics and the Bolsheviks are right to be
afraid of *The Twelve*. But ... 'the tragedy' of the artist is still a tragedy.
Apart from this:

   If in Russia there was a true priesthood and not just a class of morally
dull people of ecclesiastical calling, they would long since have 'taken into
account' the fact that 'Christ is with the Red Guards'. It is hardly possible
to dispute this truth, self-evident for people who have read the Gospels
and thought about them. But here instead of that, they are 'excommunicated from the Church' and this storm in a tea-cup still further confuses
the already confused (monstrously confused) minds of the upper and lower
middle classes and of the intelligentsia.

   'The Red Guard' will keep the wheels of the Christian Church turning (as did the Sectarians etc. who were so zealously persecuted),[bb] (as wealthy Jewry did for the autocracy, something not one 'monarch' ever realized in time).

Did I really 'glorify' (Kameneva)? I merely set down a fact; if you look into the pillars raised by the blizzard along *that* road, you will see 'Jesus Christ'. But sometimes I myself deeply hate this feminine apparition.

(VII. 329–30, entry for 10 March 1918)

It was only two days after this, when the Bolshevik government, still apparently far from certain that the German army would refrain from occupying Petrograd, was in fact—after all the rumours—preparing to evacuate to Moscow (with Ivanov-Razumnik and the editorial board of *Znamya Truda* in its wake) that Blok finished his introduction to Wagner's *Art and Revolution*. Wagner, and the '*sociological tragedy of The Ring*', had always been an integral part of his adult experience, but here, in writing of the composer, Blok gave expression to his own duality. 'How is it possible', he asks, apropos of Wagner's attitude to Christ, to love and to hate at the same time? And continues:

If this attitude is extended to something 'abstract' like Christ,[c] then, perhaps, it is possible; but if this becomes the general attitude, if this is the way people are going to react to everything in the world? To their country; their parents; their 'wives' and so on? It will be unbearable, because there will be no peace. . . . The new age is unsettled, not peaceful. He who understands that the meaning of life lies in anxiety and concern has already ceased to be a parasite. . . .

(VI. 25)

'Anxiety and concern' for the most various things show in all Blok's articles of that, for him, extraordinarily fecund spring. 'One

[bb] Sergey Hackel, in his book *The Poet and the Revolution*, contends that Blok's Christ was essentially an Old Believers' or Sectarians' Christ, and cites this passage among others in support of his thesis, but it does not seem to this writer that Blok deliberately *set out* to write of an 'Old Believer Christ' or, indeed, as has often been suggested by other scholars,[21] of a compilative, 'Russian', 'People's' Christ. He set out, as always, to write of perdition and salvation, broken in the prism of experience. 'Christ' is the 'hidden Yes', the path of light leading up into the sky, the resurrection and regeneration that Blok had always longed to attain by his own strength, 'under the sign of courage and will', but of which he had never been able to conceive other than in terms of religion.[22] As in the dream of 1910, the angel must come to roll away the stone that the poet would rather have moved by his own 'demonic' strength; as in the 1904 conversations with Zhenya Ivanov, Christ alone can join the Demon in his rebellious tarantella, to raise him up at the last. The final interpretation of 'the apparition' (whether it were a spiritual and psychological defeat, as the poet himself tended to see it at that time, or a demoniac vision, or a great grace granted) must depend on whether or not you believe in 'the objective existence of other worlds'. Blok did.

[c] A few lines above Blok wrote that Christ has, as it were, been always 'outside the brackets' of modern civilization.

of the blessings' of revolution, he wrote, 'is that it brings the whole man to life; if he goes out to meet it, it harnesses all his forces and opens gaping abysses of the kind which have long been closed ...' (VI. 38–9). So it was, incongruous as it may seem, in this April that he returned to 'The Diary of a Woman whom Nobody Loved', looking back once more from the watershed of history at a pathetic chance acquaintance in whose story, six years before, he had perceived 'a kind of surfeit of despair, the last cry of a long sorrow' (VI. 37). Even here, he thought, there might be some 'unknown ore' which could be quarried and polished and 'set into the crown of the new culture'. He thought of the article as one of a series 'on human unhappiness'. If the new world was to be brought into being indeed, then Blok demanded of it—ultimately—not one whit less than Ivan Karamazov demanded of heaven: justification of all things, down to the last tear of the last frightened child, the last unloved woman.

So it was in that imperilled, exhausted April that the poet, acutely conscious of the Lenten season, looked back to his school days to write the 'Confession of a Pagan', and, in the introduction, made one more attempt to delineate his love-hate relationship with the Russian Church:

I do not know for how long, but the Russian Church is no more. I and many like me are deprived of the right to mourn for this because, although the Church is no more, the churches are not locked and not boarded up; on the contrary, they are crammed with people trading and selling Christ, as they have not been crammed for a long time. The Church is dead, and the church has become an extension of the street. The doors are open, in the midst lies the dead Christ.[dd] All around Him crowd and whisper pious old women in male and female garments....

But I am Russian, and all Russians always think about the Church; there are few who are altogether indifferent to Her; some hate her very much, others love Her; both, with pain.[ee]

[dd] From Good Friday to just before midnight on Holy Saturday a representation of the dead Christ lies in the centre of the church and people file past to kiss it before the ritual re-enactment of the burial.

[ee] Blok's attitude to the Church was not unique. Very similar was that of a man who, although he contributed at this time to the same newspapers, was never a close friend: E. Lundberg. In his *Diary of a Writer* Lundberg had written, *before* reading *The Twelve*, that the real Christ had always been followed by 'those who had nothing to lose' rather than by respectable citizens or people of intellectual distinction, and although a convinced Christian had, like Blok, perceived in the Easter processions of 1918, nothing but 'shop-keepers demonstrating, petit-bourgeois, policemen-in-hiding, hysterical women, people who have been paid by somebody, dark *pogromshchiki*, left-overs of the clergy who have lost their political power—greed, stupidity, resentment'.[23] Others reacted otherwise. The ex-Marxist philosopher Sergey Bulgakov, for instance, whose opinions are said to have

I, too, used to go to church. True, I chose times when the church was empty, because it is vexatious and humiliating to assist at the animal howling of unshaven people who happen to earn their living that way. But, in an empty church, I have sometimes found something for which I have sought in vain in the world.

Now, there is no longer even an empty church.

It is a very long time since I made a confession, and I need to confess. . . .

(VI. 38–9)

What follows is not a confession at all, though the fact Blok called it one confirms, perhaps, that his school days were the origin of his duality. Briefly, he tells the story of his youth: of his first day at school, his first friendship, the white horse at home and his first meeting with the rosy girl amongst the apple blossom.

These articles were part of the backwash of the tidal wave that had culminated in *The Twelve* and *The Scythians*. Blok was still living in a state of creative tension and everything he touched—whether personal or historical, artistic or political—demanded to be taken up, considered, made sense of, harmonized with the music of the revolution. Hence this plethora of apparently disconnected articles. He had been 'looking into the rainbow' and now he was catching single drops of the spray as they fell back into the ocean of life, for he felt sure that never again would they reflect such intensity of colour. But he was very tired.

The Twelve, which he never fully understood himself, inspired a bewildering battery of reactions, varying from unqualified enthusiasm (Meyerhold), unexpected gratitude (Chebotarevskaya), to opprobrium, and insult (Prishvin, Hippius, and many others). Not infrequently, it even called forth diametrically opposed reactions in one and the same person. Sologub, for instance, who had called 'The Intelligentsia and the Revolution' an 'anti-religious article', rang up to ask Blok to join the Academy of Art, yet later refused to make a public appearance with him. A newspaper, the *Petrogradskoye Ekho*, asked him to contribute one day and (literally) the next compared his latest poetry to 'soldiers' songs from provincial garrisons' and even 'old potato peelings'. Minich, the young girl poet of whom Blok had written with such affection before leaving for the war, first sent him an abusive letter, then flowers and an apology. Remizov, the author of the tragic *Lament for the Destruction of the Russian Land*, admired *The Twelve* unreservedly for the marvellous evocation of the revolutionary city. Sergey Bulgakov, on 13 May, wrote

---

impressed Blok profoundly during his last years, chose 1918 as the year in which to take Holy Orders.

that Blok had confused Christ with the Antichrist; yet a month later in the Vvedensky church a priest called Yegorov took the poem as his text for a sermon.

Lyuba, in spite of Kameneva's initial disapproval, gave public readings of *The Twelve*, and when Blok accompanied her and recited other poems in the same programme they never knew what to expect. At an evening arranged by Arzamas, for instance, Akhmatova, Pyast, and Sologub all declined to recite their poems in a programme that included *The Twelve*. Blok was still sufficiently exhilarated to attend the evening in a spirit of defiance. The auditorium was split. In the interval, Blok entered the foyer on a buzz of conversation about his poem, which dwindled to a hostile silence. In that silence, a voice behind him hissed audibly: 'See—even his back view looks guilty.' Blok turned round at once, seeking the speaker with cold eyes, his face a study in exhaustion 'as though covered by a cobweb of contemptuous indifference'. There was a body of younger people in the room for whom *The Twelve* was little short of a revelation, and one of those, Vsevolod Rozhdestvensky, unable to bear the poet's isolation—for several hands had been demonstratively thrust into pockets or behind backs at his entrance—rushed up and began to pour out incoherent thanks. '... Blok listened in silence. Then suddenly he smiled. His eyes grew warm and I recognized something of the freshness of his youthful portraits.'[24] Yet only a few days later he and Lyuba were given an ovation by Left S. R. workmen in the building of the Pazheskiy Korpus. 'Lyuba read wonderfully,' Blok noted.

At this time when people Blok loved and respected were condemning him out of hand, Andrey Bely wrote from Moscow:

Dear, beloved, close Sasha,—What a strange fate. Again we have echoed one another's thoughts. I am reading you with a feeling of awe. *The Scythians* (the poem) is great and epoch-making, like *On the Field of Kulikovo*. Everything that you write touches off the old notes of foreboding in my soul again: with these notes I lived in Dornach: THIS I KNOW. For me, what you write about Russia is equally applicable to Europe....

In my opinion, you strike some notes overboldly. Remember—you will not 'be forgiven' 'ever'.... There are things in your articles with which I am not in sympathy, but I am amazed at your valiance and courage.

Remember: you will always be needed by us in our STILL MORE DIFFICULT future.... Be wise: combine valiance with discretion. I embrace you and love you more than ever before.

Your brother 'whether he will or no'.

                                        (B. BUGAYEV)[25]

To this letter, Blok replied gratefully on 6 April 1918:

Dear Borya,

Your letter was a great support and I much appreciated the warning. There was such a state of tension (in January and February) that I began to hear a great noise within me and around me and to experience frequent fits of physical trembling. For myself I called it the *Erdgeist*. Then, at about the time I received your letter, there was a reaction and only now am I feeling better. Otherwise—it was very hard: a kind of lost feeling of total exposure....

I should like to think that you yourself (and all of you) should not take fright at *The Twelve*—not because there is nothing 'to seduce you' (perhaps there is), but because we have known each other too long for that, and it seems to me you 'took fright' as you did eleven years ago at *The Snow Mask* (also, January and snow)....

I kiss you firmly

Your AL. BLOK
(VIII. 512)

All these reactions, these conflicts with many he had looked up to and admired, these uneasy alliances on a knife-edge of enthusiasm and intuition, caused Blok to make one last effort to draw up some sound historical, or perhaps rather historico-philosophical, basis to his thought.

Towards the end of April, fired by an almost forgotten early play of Ibsen's about the Roman revolutionary Catilina, he went back to the Latin sources and became absorbed in the uncannily familiar, tragic world of ancient Rome.

From this study he was distracted on 13 May to make one last statement of his own position with regard to contemporary events; a statement intended for publication in Fyëdor Sologub's one-day newspaper *Puti vozrozhdeniya Rossii* (Ways to the Renaissance of Russia).[f] In answer to the question 'What is to be done now?' Blok wrote:

... since 'a writer's words are his deeds', I consider it my duty to answer a question that does not so much touch me as burns me up: what is the artist to do at this present time?
(1) It is the duty of an artist to know that the Russia which was is no more and never will be. The Europe which was is no more and never will be.

[f] Edited by S. Kondrushkin, the 'newspaper' never saw the light of day and Blok's uncompromising 'Answer to a Questionnaire', written for his friends the artistic intelligentsia at that particular juncture of history, was first published as an academic curiosity almost twenty years later in *Literaturnoye Nasledstvo* (Moscow), v, 1937, 27–8.

Both may, perhaps, reappear in ten times more horrific form, so that it will become unbearable to live. But the particular type of horror that has been will not be any more. The world has entered upon a new era. *That* civilization, *that* concept of the nation-state, *that* religion—are dead. They may return again and exist, but they have *lost their being*, and we, present at their hideous death agonies, are now condemned to be present while they disintegrate and rot; to be present for as long as each one of us can find the strength. Do not forget that the Roman Empire continued to exist for almost five hundred years after the birth of Christ. But it only *existed*, it swelled and rotted, disintegrated—already dead.

(2) It is the artist's duty to flame with wrath against anything that attempts to galvanize the corpse. In order that this wrath should not deteriorate into sullen anger[gg] (and this is a great temptation), it is his duty to preserve the fire of awareness of the greatness of the age, which is far above any such sullen anger. One of the best ways to do this is not to forget *social inequality*, not lowering the great content of these two little words with 'humanism', or sentiments, or political economy, or journalistic sensationalism [*publisistika*]. The knowledge of social inequality is a high knowledge, cold and wrathful.

(3) It is the duty of the artist to prepare to meet still greater events which may come about, and, having met them, to be able to bow before them.

13 May 1918
(VI. 58–9)

It was in the spirit of his answer to this questionnaire that Blok had become involved with Catilina. In this amoral, patrician revolutionary he saw the forerunner of a new age.

The article 'Catilina' was the last upsurge of the creative energy of that spring. It was written with intense empathy, as though the events described had been in the newspaper only yesterday. Yet the language is measured and classical. Blok, in this new context, defends his old idea that all the facts add up, that the individual and intimate is the surest key to the general and historical, that each epoch has its own poetic rhythm. The 'rhythm' of Catilina he finds not in the measured accounts supplied by Cicero, Plutarch, and Sallust, but rather in the frenzied cadences of the lyric poet Caius Valerius Catullus, singing of the rebellion of Atys, the Phrygian shepherd who, in an ecstasy of defiance against the goddess Cybele, destroyed his own manhood.

Yet Atys, after the fury of rebellion, became tame to the goddess's hand, her priest and servant. There is an undertone of weariness in Blok's account of Catilina. Catilina rebelled, perished, and the world

---

[gg] The Russian words Blok uses are *gnev* ('wrath'), and *zloba*, which implies anger with resentment and bitterness: an impotent, unloving anger.

changed: so what?[hh] And now the world was changing again. And so? Blok quoted Ibsen that the most interesting thing about the struggle for freedom is the struggle. Once the object is achieved, freedom becomes licence. It must be worked upon and reconquered constantly from within.

Nevertheless, Blok ends on a note of hope, the same note as that sounded in the finale of *The Twelve*, 'outside the brackets' of our civilization. Here, it is garnered not from the Latin sources but from the 'naive' epilogue to Ibsen's drama. Ibsen's Catilina, believing he will be condemned to Hell after his death, is nevertheless allowed to pass 'to the right', into the fields of Elysium, at the intercession of the quiet wife whom he himself had slain:

I have neither the time, nor the space, nor the *right* to develop that theme *now*. All I will say is that here the crux of the matter is not democracy or aristocracy, but something totally different: it follows from this that the critics should not particularly rejoice that Catilina goes 'to the right'. . . .

What the critics *should* take into account is rather the fact that . . . *he who is found worthy of Elysium and accepted in love is none other than the rebel, the murderer of the most sacred thing in his own life:—Catilina.*

(VI. 91)

[hh] Cf. Blok's note in his diary for 25 April 1918: 'Catilina. What a close, FAMILIAR, sad world!—And immediately—the *bitterness of the fall*. How boring, all known in advance. Christ will come, and so what? Catilina wanted something not boring, not solemn, not beautiful, unattainable. And that, too, is boring' (Z.K. 492).

CHAPTER X

The Iron Day

(May 1918 – May 1920)

A weary soul sits down on the threshold of a tomb. Again it is spring, and again the almond trees are in blossom on the steep slopes. Magdalena passes with her jar of ointment (Peter with his key; Salome with the head). 'Where is your body?'—'My body is still wandering about the earth and trying not to lose its soul, though it was lost long ago. It is trying to persuade itself that it wasn't.'

The chief devil, thoroughly out of patience: 'Do you know what I'm going to do with you? I'm going to send you to live in Russia.'

The soul humbly agrees—even to this.

The junior devils applaud their chief's monstrous ingenuity.

The soul passes through many trials in twentieth-century Russia.

'Fragments from autumn dream at Shakhmatovo.' 13.xi.09.

(VI. 489–90)

1

Blok finished writing 'Catilina' on 19 May 1918, at about the time he would, in that other life, have been wondering whether to recuperate from the tensions of the 'season' at Shakhmatovo, or to go abroad, or to stay on in a sleepy, empty Petersburg, walking in the white nights, writing in the sustained quiet which sometimes came to him during the city summer.

This year, there was to be no rest, no change, no period of healing seclusion. Aleksandr Blok the poet had given all he had to offer and now, if the man and his family were to survive even for the next few months, he would have to begin bringing in money. It was almost two months since he had noted: '... and while cruel *Realpolitik* continues its irresistible incarnation in various parts of the world, "simple" and "not-so-simple" people grow weak, tired, and begin to die...' (*Z.K.* 395).

A few days after that, Maria Timofeyevna had telephoned to tell him that Angelina, who had been working as a nurse in Novgorod, had succumbed to a typhus epidemic.[a] Blok did not attend the *panikhida* in his sister's memory, at which, he suspected, 'it was planned to demonstrate something' (*Z.K.* 399). When on 24 March he heard of her death, he simply entered it under the actual date—the 4th— and went on to the next day.

At this time he was hurrying to finish his report on the findings of the Investigatory Commission, *The Last Days of the Imperial Regime*, which he completed in rough on 29 March, and was still absorbed in the compulsive flow of articles he had been writing throughout the spring. He could not yet shake off this absorption and work 'to order'. In response to a request for a lecture on Apollon Grigor'ev, he said only a few words about Grigor'ev's defence of Gogol's *Correspondence with Friends* against Belinsky (VI. 26–8). It was not, he considered, the time to 'stir up bookish dust' or to recollect anything that had no direct bearing on the given moment. In addition, he lacked the physical stamina. When they rang to remind him that he was due to speak he noted, 'No, no, no, I can't, don't torture me, I'm hungry' (*Z.K.* 398). But he spoke.

His first attempt to earn money was made on 4 April 1918 when he resumed work for the theatre, attending the opening session of the re-formed Committee for Theatrical Repertory. He was more interested than he had expected, but felt he had little to contribute: 'After the exultant moods of January I am all wretchedly sclerotic indifference and dullness' (VII. 332). Then, on 11 April: 'I am destroyed. There has been no me these three days. To die?' (*Z.K.* 399).

For the moment, however, it seemed more likely that his mother might be the next one to die. She was weakening fast, though she still had things to sell which somehow kept body and soul together. On 16 April, the arrival—back from the front—of Frants Feliksovich

---

[a] Though his letters to her were unfortunately later destroyed, along with many other Belayev family papers, Blok had not lost touch with Angelina. They had corresponded on philosophical and religious subjects and, from Novgorod, she had sent him an icon of Hagia Sophia. Angelina had been a beloved spiritual daughter of the Bishop of Novgorod, Sergiy, a prominent figure at the original pre-1905 Religious-Philosophical Meetings and eventually the second Patriarch of the Orthodox Church under the Soviets. The Bishop had himself administered the last rites and had buried Angelina, Maria Timofeyevna informed Blok, 'like a saint'.

(bringing bread and flour, old, bent, but just the same, 'as though nothing had happened') temporarily relieved Blok and Lyuba of the necessity of taking Aleksandra Andreyevna into their flat.

While still full of plans for his writing, the poet fought off the constant demands to sit on committees and to lecture: 'I am old, it's difficult enough for me to earn my bread: I cannot sit any longer and listen to speeches by the clever and the stupid, the young and the old: I'll die of hunger. I'll just go on getting quieter and quieter' (*Z.K.* 401).

He tried disconnecting the telephone, but still people got at him through Lyuba, who was busily arranging a 'Workers' Theatre' in Luna Park.[b] She was 'absent-minded and powdered', and kept passing on messages from Chukovsky, Meyerhold, Lunacharsky, Aleksandr Hippius, Georgiy Ivanov ... unending demands on her husband's time and energy. He snapped her head off and was immediately sorry: Ivan Mendeleyev, Lyuba's brother, was in prison; Boblovo was threatened; her theatrical career was beset by difficulties; and she was no better fed or more rested than he.

Then Auntie began to behave strangely and Blok 'hurt her feelings', too. On 26 April there was a family explosion, after which he wrote to his mother who had evidently said some unpleasant things to him:

It is true that I am 'wrapped in cotton wool' but it is no less hard for me to live than for you, physically and emotionally and materially, apart from which I am writing from morning till night, concentrating on one subject that is very difficult and painful for me.[c] Lyuba also has great difficulties and she is out of sorts. That is why the atmosphere in our flat is so gloomy. So don't let's quarrel.

SASHA
(VIII. 513)

A few days later, Blok was standing at the window when he caught sight of the painfully thin figure of Maria Andreyevna tottering home along the street below. He noted this at the time and then, on 1 May: 'Auntie came in to me and Lyuba with a queer, happy expression, poor little thing. Auntie, Auntie, dear little Auntie, what a strange day you have had today, no one will understand it ...' (*Z.K.* 404). Maria Andreyevna had temporarily gone quietly out of her mind. Overcome by the hardship and distress of the winter, she was

[b] A great disappointment, as Aunt Maria remarks with her usual imperturbable benevolence, because the workers did not come: just the same old intellectual, St. Petersburg public!
[c] The article 'Catilina'.

unable to comprehend that it was not safe to go back to Shakhmato-vo,[d] and for a few weeks she had to be put into a sanatorium. Here she threatened suicide and turned against her nearest and dearest, blaming her sister and Frants Feliksovich for all her troubles. Soon, however, she was sufficiently recovered for Frants Feliksovich to escort her to Safonovo, where her sister Sofia and family were firmly in residence, holding out against riots and levied contributions.

On 7 May it was still snowing in Petrograd. It was clear that, if they were not all to lie down and die, Blok *must* begin to earn regular money, and he agreed to so many lectures and so much committee work over the summer that the mere thought of it filled him with panic: and with good reason. Blok was incapable of taking advantage of a sinecure, of living on the capital of reputation and accumulated knowledge. All through the next three years every lecture was care-fully prepared, every manuscript on which he was asked to give an opinion painstakingly read, every sack of frozen cabbage he received from the State honestly earned.

Yet in spite of all the commitments he had undertaken, he still could not see how he was to make ends meet. 'Where am I to get money from? Petersburg is emptying, and we need between 1,000 and 1,500 roubles a month' (*Z.K.* 408). He even thought of writing a scenario for a film ('Lyuba advises it, for money', *Z.K.* 408).[e]

A bout of 'flu in the middle of May made everything look still more hopeless. No sooner was he out and about again than huge posters appeared all along Offitserskaya Street bearing his name, Lyuba's, and—Chaliapin's. It seemed that he was to become a concert performer. This particular occasion Blok dreaded so much he almost balked at the last moment, but overcame panic and exhaustion to recite 'after Chaliapin'. 'It went off all right,' he noted with relief on 4 June (*Z.K.* 410).

2

It was not easy to live under the intense pressure of disapproval to which Blok was subjected by the majority of his acquaintance

---

[d] The house at this stage was still standing, and she and Aleksandra Andreyevna were in correspondence with Nikolay Lapin, who reported that there was a movement on to install one Fyedot in the 'good' kitchen and that the countryside was plagued by bands of 'anarchists' who were 'arresting' people and then holding them to ransom.

[e] This plan came to nothing; Blok was too conscious of the necessity of working out a completely new technique. Cf. letter to A. A. Sanin of 10 September 1918, VIII. 515–16.

throughout that spring and summer. On 31 May Zinaida Hippius
sent him her anti-Bolshevik *Last Poems*: in the first half of 1918, it
was still possible to publish such things. Blok sat down to write her
a letter:

I am answering you in prose because I want to say more to you than you
have said to me; something more than the purely lyrical.

I address myself to your humanity, to your brain, to your generosity,
to your sensitivity, because I have not the least desire to hurt your feelings
and get under your skin, as you seem to want to do to me; for that reason
I do not address myself to that 'mortal innocence',[f] of which there is quite
as much in you as in me.

There is a 'fateful emptiness'[g] in both you and me. Either this is something
very great, in which case we should not reproach one another with it; it
is not for us to judge; or it is very small, our own, private, 'decadent', in
which case it is not worth speaking of in the face of the events that are
about to happen.... Nothing has changed in me (that is my tragedy, as
it is yours)....

I do not know (or rather I do know) why you did not see the greatness
of October behind its grimaces, which were VERY FEW—there might have
been many times more.

Can it be that you do not know that 'there will be no Russia' just as
there was no Rome—not in the fifth century after the Nativity of Christ
but in the first year of the first century? In the same way—there will be
no England, no Germany, no France. That the world has already changed?
That the 'old world' is already at melting-point?

(VII. 335–6)

Perhaps unfortunately, Blok did not send this letter, but chose instead to send a reply in verse which merely deepened the misunderstanding:

> It is my joy, my fear, my fate, my calling,
> To fling myself into the foam-flecked wave
> While you, a green-eyed naiad, are disporting
> Yourself and singing by the Irish caves....
>
> And high above us both, above the billows
> Like the dawn above black, jutting cliff-heads
> The International its banner waves.

(III. 372)

[f] In a poem dedicated to Blok, Hippius had written:

> I'll not forgive; your soul is innocent.
> But I shall not forgive you. Never more.

[g] This expression is from the poem about 'the children of Russia's dreadful years' (III.
278) which Blok had dedicated to Hippius in 1915.

Hippius says in her memoirs that Blok dedicated to her some 'extra-ordinarily bad verse' in which she was supposed to be 'splashing about beside the Irish cliffs(!)' while he—'I don't remember what, and then sang the *Internationale*!'[1]

This, however, was not the end of the story. Blok knew that the Merezhkovskys' rejection of the revolution was as disinterested as his acceptance. He missed them very much.[h] Zinaida Hippius, as kind and faithful to her friends at heart and in practice as she was malicious in words, left a poignant account of their last meeting, in a tram, on 3 October 1918:

The tram begins to fill up and by the time we reach the Sennaya there are passengers standing.

The first person to get in took up his stance just by my seat, and said suddenly: 'How do you do?'

There was no mistaking that voice. I raised my eyes—Blok. His face under some sort of cap (it was a cap, not a hat) was long, parched, yellow, dark.

'Will you give me your hand?' Slow words, spoken with the same old effort, the same old heaviness.

I put out my hand. 'Personally—yes. Only personally. Not socially.'

He kissed my hand. And, after a moment's silence, 'Thank you.' And after another moment: 'They say you are leaving?'

'What else is there to do...? You either die or you leave. Unless, of course, one is placed as you are....'

He said nothing for a long time, then, speaking particularly grimly and distinctly: 'One can always die, however one is—placed.' Then added suddenly: 'I love you very much, you see...'

'You know perfectly well that I love you, too.'... I stand up, it is time to get off.

'Good-bye,' Blok says. 'Thank you for giving me your hand.'

'Socially all the bridges between us are blown. You know ... Never ... But personally. As we always were.'

Again I put out my hand to him, standing in front of him. Again he bent his yellow, sick face, slowly kissed the hand. 'Thank you.'... And I am out on the dusty pavement with the tram car swimming by me and on the step I see Blok, who had escorted me to the door. I can just make out something dark he is wearing, yes, a dark blue shirt....

And that was all. That was the end. That was our last meeting on earth.[3]

[h] K. Chukovsky writes that, while there was no foundation in the persistent rumours that Blok 'repented' of having written *The Twelve*, he did regret publishing this poem to Z. N. Hippius. 'There was a word there that I don't like now,' he told Chukovsky in March 1921. Chukovsky also quotes from a letter Blok wrote to him on 18 December 1919: 'If it comes up, tell Zinaida Hippius that I don't think she has drawn the right conclusion from my verses; that I love and respect her as much as before and sometimes more than before.'[2] The Merezhkovskys left Petrograd for Poland on the 24th of that month.

3

Particularly hard to bear, right from the first, was the conviction
of Blok's fellow writers that, in his position as an honoured collaborator with the Soviets, he must enjoy material privileges denied
to them. True, he was not out of work. He was even in demand
in the Theatrical Department of Narkompros (the People's Commis-
sariat for Education), where he had begun work that spring, and was
elected chairman of the Repertory Section and on 4 August (in his
absence) editor of the section's almanac; on 8 August he had been
elected to the presidium of the Commission for the Reorganization
of Theatres and Spectacles and, on 22 September, invited to take part
in the work of the publishing house Vsemirnaya Literatura (World
Literature) under Maksim Gorky. This led to a commission to edit
a volume in a Russian edition of the Collected Works of Heinrich
Heine.

Blok, however, had no notion of how to exploit this situation to
his own advantage. 'How tired I get from the pointlessness of all
these meetings' (Z.K. 409), he confided to his notebook as early as
1 June 1918. Yet that month he attended at least seven such meetings
and went as many times to the theatre, preparing reviews of productions he saw and plays he read, producing two essays on what he
considered a desirable repertory for the revolutionary theatre, and
drafting an appeal to the intelligentsia to provide new plays and
translations.[4]

... he wrote, he wrote a great deal, only not verses but protocols, official
papers, articles to order.

They told him: 'Make a list of the hundred best writers.' And he meekly
compiled not one but several lists and set out with his funereal gait God
knows how far to some meeting where these lists would be discussed, turned
down, thrown away.

They told him: 'Write a play about life in ancient Egypt.'[i]

And he meekly took Maspéro and sat down to fulfil the commission.

They told him: 'Edit the works of Heine.' And for whole months he
would immerse himself in the minute and exacting work of comparing
texts, reading a mass of quite untalented translations and, choosing the
least untalented, rewriting them and rearranging them and writing the
translators long letters, that such-and-such a line required revision or that
such-and-such a line was lacking one syllable.

He was told: 'Give us your opinion on these manuscripts which are scheduled for publication as soon as possible.' And with the conscientiousness

---

[i] This was *Rameses*, Blok's contribution to the series 'Scenes from History'; see below,
p. 338.

of genius he would write one report after another on anything they put before him.

So wrote Korney Chukovsky, who had managed to earn his living from literature all his life-long and knew with the instinct of the professional just where to exert himself and where to take things easy. Exasperated at Blok's helplessness, exaggerating both the uselessness of his last years and the ease with which he used to write poetry (he says in this same article that Blok's life 'was one unending, indivisible poem ... which poured forth without a break day after day for twenty years from 1898 to 1918'), but generous in his disinterested indignation, he wrote:

This was how the poet's contribution to the revolution was understood: take your portfolio, go to the meeting. And if you don't want to, die. We won't even give you that wet cabbage that you carry back home over your shoulder....[5]

In 1918, however, Blok still had no suspicion that such was to be his 'contribution to the revolution' or that *The Twelve* and *The Scythians* were to be his last great poems. Always, through the times when he had been prevented from writing poetry either by outside events or by periods of inward stress and dryness, he had done whatever other work was nearest to hand and held himself in readiness until such time as his vocation should reassert itself. During this last and longest three-year wait, he continued to love, to care, to laugh, and to grow angry, to try to understand what had happened to him, what would happen to Russia. Over this period he wrote some of his best prose and put his mind and integrity at the service of all who asked him, not, as Chukovsky seems to imply, like an automaton doing what it is told, but often with keen interest, though at other times he was indeed deadly bored and forcing himself against the grain of his nature.

Zorgenfrey said that Blok was explicitly critical of many aspects of the new order (or, as it so often must have appeared, disorder) and he was certainly critical, as he had ever been, of incompetence and 'yellow' absence of aspiration and care, yet when he spoke out against such things it was 'never in order to condemn but rather trying always to understand and to hallow'.[6] There is sarcasm, misanthropy, and despair in his post-1917 as in his pre-1917 notebooks, but their subject is the human condition rather than specific political circumstances. In the summer of 1918, moreover, the fires of Blok's enthusiasm, though no longer blazing high, were still burning fairly steadily.

Whenever he could do so, he escaped from the town to bathe and walk around his usual out-of-town haunts: Olgino, Lakhtina, Shuvalovo. Living on the edge of chaos, with rumours of 'occupation within the fortnight' still rife, cholera gaining ground in the city and on its outskirts, and the certainty of the approaching winter being still hungrier and bleaker than that of 1918,[j] his physical vitality was waning somewhat; but he was borne up by the heroic newness of this living from day to day amongst the ruins of a crumbling world, and by a genuine desire to salvage and to be of service.

To begin with it seemed that in the Theatrical Department of Narkompros he had found a niche where his experience of the theatre would make him really useful. The committee meetings were dull, but it suited him to visit the theatres, both the old, classical state theatres (the Mikhaylovsky, the Mariynsky, and the Bolshoy Dramaticheskiy) and the various popular theatres which provided entertainment for a more democratic public 'embittered by an indescribably hard life ... and on the lookout for rest and distraction' (VI. 276). His first two reports on the theatre, composed over this summer, must be among the most personal and most poetic documents in the history of bureaucracy.[7]

Blok took a lofty tone. Now was the moment to set the theatre's course for many years to come, and his advice to the state was, on the one hand, to hold fast to the 'mighty tears and mighty laughter' (VI. 282) of the classics and, on the other, to what pleased the people, not to scare away life which might so easily 'flutter off never to return, leaving us sitting about a broken trough' (VI. 280). To force the pace or to impose any ready-made criteria would inevitably entail mistakes: 'For the waves are running high and neither we nor the comrades rowing at our side can yet make out the shore' (VI. 293).

Having said his say and duly been appointed chairman of the Repertory Section, Blok found himself up against formidable practical difficulties. There was a grandiose plan for publishing the world's best plays with competent introductions and simple directions for staging. Blok appealed to the intelligentsia at large for help with this project, the sheer 'revolutionary' scale of which delighted him, but the technical snags proved insuperable. It was difficult even to obtain the texts of many plays, and Blok personally hunted through second-hand bookshops and publishers' storerooms in search of the odd copy of Aeschylus, Racine, Schiller. As to the State Printing Works, they

---

[j] Blok records in his notebook that the peasants were already starving in the districts about Petrograd, having eaten the grain they should have sowed the previous spring.

had a waiting list and the Repertory Section had to take its turn. There was an acute paper shortage and what there was available was in demand for newspapers, proclamations, political pamphlets.

During the summer, however, Blok had made a new friend whose services—true to his belief that every man of talent should at this juncture contribute his all to help 'the people'—he proceeded to enlist for Narkompros

4

Samuil Mironovich Alyansky had entered Blok's life with the modest intention of buying up any spare author's copies the poet might have retained from previous editions of his works. He and his friend Vasil'ev, both in their early twenties, ran a small, very hand-to-mouth second-hand bookshop. Blok's poetry was in constant demand, and unobtainable either in Petrograd or in Moscow. By now Moscow, owing to the extreme difficulty of travel in the summer of 1918, had become almost a foreign city, but Alyansky, travelling for nothing on troop trains thanks to his soldier's uniform, acted as a courier, making frequent excursions to replenish his larder of modern poetry for the novelty-starved bibliophiles of Petrograd. Nowhere, however, had he been able to find Blok's poems. With much trepidation, he and Vasil'ev had at last decided to ring the poet up. They tossed for it and the lot fell to Alyansky who, having screwed up his courage to tackle Blok in person, was put completely off his stride by the 'deep woman's voice' that answered the telephone. Its owner listened to a description of the friends' antiquarian enterprise and, to their mutual astonishment—for Vasil'ev had been pulling at Alyansky's sleeve to stem the disastrous flow of nervous confidences—civilly made an appointment for one of them to come and see Aleksandr Aleksandrovich that very evening.

'You got us into this,' Vasil'ev commented unfeelingly. 'You get us out of it!' So it was a very chastened young man—still in his private's uniform—who rang Blok's doorbell that evening:

The door was opened by a tall, fair woman. She looked at me curiously with clever, smiling, slightly crinkled eyes. . . . She led me into the room off the entrance hall, Aleksandr Aleksandrovich's study. . . . It was a light Petersburg evening. The spacious room was rather bare. Over by the window was a writing table, not very big, and some way away from it, a settee. . . . I hadn't had time to take a really good look round when from the right, from another door, with light steps there entered a slender, handsome man with the head of an Apollo, slightly thrown back.

He was taller than average, well made. The wavy hair was ashen-fair and cropped short. I remember too that the corners of the mouth drooped slightly. He was dressed in an ordinary grey suit.

The man I saw before me was not very like the famous photograph of the poet. I did not at once recognize him. But he came up to me, smiled, put out his hand and, in a rather hollow voice, introduced himself.

Seeing that I was at a loss, Blok himself introduced the topic on which I had come to see him.

'You need copies of my books? ... Sit down, please, and tell me more about yourself... about yourself,' he repeated with a warm, friendly smile.[8]

Before he knew quite what was happening, Alyansky discovered that he had once, for a few years, attended Blok's old school, and the two were soon reminiscing and laughing like old friends. Carried away by the relaxed atmosphere, the young man was soon improvising a wonderful day-dream of founding a publishing house and a regular periodical to 'reunite the Symbolists'. No one but a great lover of poetry and a complete innocent in the complicated cross-currents of the literary world would have made such a suggestion at such a time. Blok, fascinated, asked him to come again....

Even the cautious Vasil'ev was impressed by the fifteen volumes of Blok's poetry (five sets of the three-volume Musaget edition) Alyansky acquired at this first encounter, though he poured cold water over his friend's newly conceived publishing projects. To Alyansky's horror, however, he found that Blok had taken him at his own evaluation: the second time he came to Offitserskaya Strcct, although the poet expressed doubt as to the possibility, or even the desirability of uniting the Symbolists, he was obviously keenly interested in the idea. He told Alyansky of the breach *The Twelve* had created between him and the majority of his erstwhile literary allies and, through the dry words, the younger man sensed his 'vulnerability and his bitterness'. In the past, however, the foundation of a new Symbolist journal or publishing house had always proved a rallying point; people tended to forget personal differences when there was real work to be done. Blok had decided to back this enthusiastic boy who admired their work and knew little or nothing of their deep-rooted disagreements.

To Alyansky's utter confusion, the poet presented him with the text of a long poem which had only been printed in a newspaper and had passed almost unnoticed because of the war: *The Nightingale Garden*.

Blok was suggesting I undertake a perfectly concrete task: these few sheets of paper had to be turned into a book. What should I do? How should I react? I had to say something, but what—I had no idea. Perhaps I should say thank you, or ask something about the honorarium or the proofreading, or something.... How was I expected to know what one said or did in such cases?

My confusion and anguish must have shown on my face, for again Blok read my thoughts and came to my rescue:

'You needn't give me any answer now, read the poem at home, take your time and think about it, have a word with that friend of yours, Vasil'ev, and decide if it's worth printing as a separate publication. Unfortunately, I have nothing else free at the moment to support you with. I believe in you.'[9]

Vasil'ev sent Alyansky to talk to a friend of his who worked at a printing house on the Nevsky Prospect. Miraculously, the friend was so enthusiastic about the poem, which was new to them all, that he offered to get on with the printing of it on credit while Alyansky arranged for distribution.

Vasil'ev and Alyansky thought up a name for the new publishing house: 'Alkonost', after a mythical bird with the gift of prophecy. They ordered a colophon from the 'only artist' they knew, Alyansky's school friend, Yuriy Annenkov. Alkonost was spelt wrong in the design, with a soft sign after the 'l', but nobody, not even Blok, noticed this in the general excitement.

And so, only a few days after Blok had entrusted Alyansky with the poem, his new 'publisher' brought him the first proofs. Blok's old passion for making books reasserted itself and he entered with enthusiasm into all the practical details. A fortnight later Alyansky had 3,000 copies of The Nightingale Garden in print, which he peddled from shop to shop along the Liteynyy Prospect, transporting them by bicycle in a rucksack. The following week he was in a position to pay his bill with the printers and persuaded Blok to accept half of the small total profit.

Delighted with his success, he determined to follow it up by publishing Andrey Bely and Vyacheslav Ivanov, whom he judged to be the closest in spirit to Blok of all living writers. Blok was doubtful of the success of his plans, 'but I felt that in secret he would have been pleased to hear that they had come off because this would have meant a reunion with old friends.'[10]

So, armed with inscribed copies of The Nightingale Garden ('I don't know what kind of a reception you'll get from Vyacheslav Ivanov,' Blok had said. 'I don't know if he will accept the gift'),[k] Alyansky set out for Moscow determined to return with new manuscripts.

Almost unbelievably, he did. Vyacheslav Ivanov, moved by Blok's proffered reconciliation, made no attempt to repudiate his copy of the book. He put Alyansky right as to the spelling of 'Alkonost' and, having satisfied himself that this strange young man really did want to reunite the Symbolists and not to 'colour them red', he presented him with the manuscript of his own narrative poem *Infancy*. From Bely Alyansky received the manuscript of a book of poetry: *The Queen and the Knights*. Bely made him very welcome, and talked him almost into the ground. 'His long hair waved up from his head like tongues of fire. It seemed as though at any moment he would burst into flame—and all the crises and world catastrophes would immediately break about us and their rubble would bury us both for ever.'[11]

On Alyansky's return to Petrograd, Blok kept him talking on the telephone for a full hour and then invited him round to continue his 'report' over tea that evening:

Blok invited Lyubov' Dmitriyevna to hear how I had fared.

My account of my visit to Bely was frequently interrupted by bursts of laughter. Blok explained that listening to me they had a vivid mental picture of Bely whom they hadn't seen for a long time. My account of my meeting with Vyacheslav Ivanov interested them still more. Blok made me remember absolutely every word Vyacheslav Ivanov had said.[12]

After this Alkonost went from strength to strength.[l] In November 1918 Alyansky published *The Twelve*, with illustrations by the same school friend, Yuriy Annenkov, who had designed the colophon, and the following year, 1919, saw the miraculous birth of the last Symbolist journal: *Zapiski Mechtateley* (Dreamers' Notes), with its supremely romantic cover thought up, in a last firework of symbolist 'collective creation', by Golovin and Meyerhold, Meyerhold posing for the lonely figure who stands on the cliff-edge, perceiving the City of the Future through the smoke and steam of a contemporary industrial town.

[k] Vyacheslav Ivanov had broken off relations with Blok after the publication of *The Twelve*.

[l] Alkonost went on to publish works by Zinov'eva-Annibal, Anna Akhmatova, Aleksey Remizov, Khodasevich, Zamyatin, and other luminaries of Russia's Silver Age. The first version of Andrey Bely's memoirs of Blok appeared in *Zapiski Mechtateley* and it was Alkonost that published Maria Beketova's biography of the poet. After the collapse of the Menshevik Imnayshvili's publishing house Zemlya, to which he was under contract when he first met Alyansky, Blok published exclusively with Alkonost and with Grzhebin, who had undertaken to bring out his Collected Works.

The first number of the Symbolist journal *Zapiski Mechtateley*, 1919.

Annenkov's illustrations to *The Twelve* were unexpectedly felicitous and are a lasting monument to the blizzard-swept Petrograd
of 1918 as well as to the poem itself. The first sketches elicited a letter
from poet to artist which, together with a note on Christ added
separately (and somewhat reluctantly) on the insistence of Alyansky,
bear witness to Blok's extreme, impressionistic laconism. From the
letter to Annenkov, it is clear that Blok had a detailed visual picture
of all his characters, of which he left only one or two telling details
in the actual work:[m]

12 August 1918

I was terribly afraid of the drawings for *The Twelve* and even afraid to
speak to you about them. Now, having looked at them at leisure, I want
to tell you that certain angles, details, artistic thoughts—are inexpressibly
close and dear to me, and the whole is more than acceptable.... For me,
personally, most unquestionable are Kat'ka dead (the big drawing) and the
dog separately (a smallish drawing). These two taken as a whole give me
great artistic pleasure.... The reason I have to write is because: the more
acceptable the work is to me as a whole the more decisively must I object
to two things and these are: (1) Katya alone (with the cigarette); (2) Christ.

(1) 'Kat'ka' is a splendid drawing as a drawing, but less original than
the others and, I suspect, less 'yours'. It is not Kat'ka at all: Kat'ka is a healthy,
plump-cheeked, passionate, snub-nosed Russian lass; fresh, simple, kind—
swears like a trooper, weeps over novels, kisses as if her life depended on
it; none of this is in contradiction to the *elegance* of all the middle of your
big drawing (the two bent fingers and what surrounds them). And it's right,
too, that the little cross has fallen out (also—in the big picture). The mouth
should be fresh, 'a mass of teeth', sensual (in the little drawing it is old).
The *esprit* could be less refined and a bit sillier (perhaps without the bow
at the neck). The 'plump cheeks' are very important (healthy and clean,
to the point of childishness).[n] The cigarette would be better out (perhaps
she doesn't smoke)....

(2) About Christ: He's not like that at all: small, crouching like the dog
behind, carrying the flag as though on parade and *walking away*. 'Christ
with the flag'—it is—well, 'it's like that and then again it's not'. Do you

---

[m] This ability to select characteristic detail was a quality Blok admired in Merezhkovsky
who, he noted, left only the dimple in the chin of his Alexander I. Gzovskaya tells in her
recollections of Blok how impatient the poet became when she failed to grasp the topo-
graphy of the castle in *The Rose and the Cross*, every detail of which was quite clear in
his imagination.

[n] Significantly, all we see of Blok's Kat'ka in the poem are the plump cheeks and gleaming
teeth. We also know she has a knife-scar under her breast and a birthmark on her shoulder,
but this we learn from Petya, her jilted lover. Annenkov subsequently spent many hours
searching for a model for Kat'ka. The final version, Chukovsky tells us, pleased Blok immensely. 'About the other illustrations he said different things at different times, but with
this one he was always content.'[13]

Yuriy Annenkov's illustration of the death of Kat'ka, for the Alkonost edition
of *The Twelve* (1918).

know (what I've felt all my life), that when a flag flaps in the wind (through rain or through snow and *most important* through the dark of the night), then *underneath* it I imagine someone enormous, related to it in some way (not holding it, not carrying it, but how—I can't put into words). In general it is the most difficult thing, you can only find it, but I can't say it, just as perhaps I said it worst of all in *The Twelve* (in essence, though, I do not repudiate it, in spite of all the critics).

If from the upper left-hand corner of the 'murder of Kat'ka' there was a flurry of thick snow and through it—Christ;—that would be a *definitive cover.* . . .

(VIII. 514)

When Alyansky insisted he try to be more specific about the figure of Christ, Blok checked through the younger man's notes on what he himself had told him and this account, 'heard from the lips of A. A. Blok on 12 August 1918 on the day I showed him the sketches of drawings for the poem',[14] was also shown to the artist. The account emphasizes the way in which—on a wild night of snow when everything loses its shape and it is hard to keep one's feet— a 'light or luminous patch', 'a great flapping flag or a placard torn by the wind', can seem to materialize through the blizzard, beckon and draw one on, then take on 'the outline of someone walking or floating through the air'. 'It was on such a winter's night', Blok concluded, 'that I saw this patch of light;[0] it grew, becoming immense. It moved me and drew me. Behind this immensity the thought came to me of *The Twelve* and of Christ. . . .'[16]

5

The unexpected recrudescence of Symbolist publishing represented by Alkonost and the renewed contact—albeit at second hand—with old friends like Bely and Vyacheslav Ivanov, injected a new youthfulness into Blok's working life. Day-to-day existence, however, became predictably more difficult as the summer drew to a close. From the last day of August 1918, when Frants Feliksovich was arrested at four o'clock in the morning in connection with the attempt on Lenin's life and the assassination of Yuritsky, Blok seemed to be constantly involved in trying to get people out of prison or helping those who had been reduced to total penury. His stepfather, obviously old, infirm, and innocent, was released the same day, but

---

[0] Corroboration comes from Nadezhda Pavlovich (see p. 355), who tells how, when walking with Blok one snowy evening of the winter 1920-1, he pointed out a swirl of snow about a dimly-glowing street lamp and told her that that was how he had 'seen Christ'.[15]

Blok also had to intervene, successfully, for a friend of Zorgenfrey's, seized as a hostage on the same occasion. He worried about Baron Drizen, an ex-censor who had once objected to the title *The Rose and the Cross*, and about Burenin, the much-disliked feuilletonist of *Novoye Vremya*, who had once declared (and proved by printing it that way), that Blok's 'Steps of the Commendatore' read just as effectively backwards as forwards.[17] It was only a year since the poet had rejoiced at the closing down of *Novoye Vremya* and (to himself in his diary) advocated Draconian measures against the newspaper and its proprietors, but it was different when you heard that a real old man who had once made you laugh was quietly dying of hunger.

Blok's own family still weighed heavily on him. Aleksandra Andreyevna and Frants Feliksovich did not have enough to live on. Lyuba suggested that she and Blok should contribute 500 roubles a month to their upkeep; Aleksandra Andreyevna consented to accept 300. Auntie, much recovered after her summer at Safonovo, returned to Petrograd at the beginning of September and Blok managed to find her some work with Gorky's Vsemirnaya Literatura, but this was little more than a sop to her pride.

The Beketovs were, indeed, a proud and independent lot, and Blok, in his turn, was embarrassed by gifts of food from female admirers, particularly Mme N. A. Nolle-Kogan and Del'mas, though the latter was so tactful and so warmly attentive to his mother and aunt that here he was less humiliated. Nevertheless, sitting at home in the September slush, unable to go out because neither boots nor galoshes were proof against the wet, absorbed in an attempt to write a prose commentary to the *Verses about the Most Beautiful Lady* (as Dante once pieced together his memories of Beatrice),[18] he noted: 'the telephone kept on ringing and Mama succeeded in forcing me to answer it, which is a good thing. (I am afraid of calls from L. A. Del'mas and, particularly, Mme Kogan)' (*Z.K.* 426, entry for 11 September 1918).

His gums were troublesome again, and he had begun to dream of Shakhmatovo: 'a-a-a ...' (*Z.K.* 428, 22 September 1918), and, on 12 December; 'Why was it my face was all drenched with tears for Shakhmatovo in my dreams tonight?' (*Z.K.* 439).

His mother's depression, complicated by a growing nervous revulsion for her husband, tormented him. On 8 October the Kublitskys moved into a flat and Aunt Maria into a new room in his own building. Throughout that autumn, in amongst pages of business notes about committee work, he gave vent to rebellious exclamations, such as: 'Despair, headache: I am not a civil servant but a writer' (*Z.K.* 430, entry for 2 October 1918).

On 18 October, Boblovo went the way of Shakhmatovo.

Yet there were still good moments. On 30 September, Lyubov's name day, Ivanov-Razumnik had come to call and continued a conversation begun a few days previously on the telephone by another 'Scythian', the poet K. A. Syunnenberg, about the possibility of turning their publishing projects (the newspaper *Znamya Truda* and the journal *Nash Put'*), both now defunct owing to practical and political causes, into a new centre of oral culture to be known as the Volnaya Filosofskaya Akademiya (Free Philosophical Academy), Volfil for short. This promised to be, and was, a much more lively undertaking than any of the editorial boards, commissions, and committees on which Blok was then sitting.

Then, on 7 November, came the first anniversary of the October revolution. Petrograd—in defiance of cold and hunger, to the embarrassment of the Bolsheviks and the horror of the philistines—had been decorated with tremendous verve and talent by a bevy of the most brilliant artists of the twentieth century. Blok was enchanted by the whole occasion:

7 November. The celebration of the October anniversary. In the evening Lyuba and I went to Mayakovsky's *Mystery-Bouffe* at the Musical Drama.... An historic day—for Lyuba and me—complete. In the afternoon we walked about the town together: the decorations, the processions, rain at the graves.[p] In the evening—a hoarse and sorrowful speech by Lunacharsky, Mayakovsky,[q] much besides. I hope I never forget today.

(*Z.K.* 434–5, entry for 7 November 1918)

And the next day, touchingly: 'I am writing an appeal for the Theatrical Department. Marvellous illuminations in the evening. But Lyuba and I have grown old again' (*Z.K.* 435). Then, on 8 December: 'All day I read Lyuba Heine in German and felt younger' (*Z.K.* 439).

Such happy moments, however, were few and far between. The new society seemed to have little need of Aleksandr Blok, the poet; a magazine called *Rabochiy Mir* (Workers' World) turned down his verses as 'unsuitable' for its readers (*Z.K.* 434, entry for 4 November 1918), and, in the Repertory Section, Blok's attempt to speed up the publication of plays by involving Alyansky only led to trouble.

---

[p] The graves of the fallen Bolsheviks at Marsovo Polye.

[q] Lunacharsky made a speech before the opening of Mayakovsky's play in which Mayakovsky himself acted 'the man' and two other parts.

His Heath Robinson methods and gift for accomplishing the impossible had led Blok to picture the young editor of Alkonost as a kind
of Robin Hood of Bolshevik publishing:

Everything will have to be achieved in revolutionary fashion. It may be
you'll have to take a detachment of Red Guards, explain the purpose of
the operation and its importance to the country, lead them to some paper
factory—confiscate all the paper and transport it to Piter [Petrograd] at full
speed under escort of those same Red Guards.[19]

So Blok had urged the physically unimpressive young man, and he
and Meyerhold gave their unconditional backing to Alyansky's
active 'Americanism', and had actually succeeded in pushing through
the publication of quite a number of plays, even without the help
of 'detachments of Red Guards', before some more self-effacing civil
servants thought it incumbent on them to complain to Kameneva,
now head of the Theatrical Department of Narkompros and working with the rest of the government from Moscow, that their protégé
was exceeding his brief. Alyansky offered to resign, but Blok—
almost gleefully—undertook to stand by him and penned an energetic defence of his methods (29 January 1919, VI. 297–301), and of
his own and Meyerhold's theoretical position which, he declared,
'can be summed up by saying that our task is to capture the market
... by an avalanche of truly nourishing books' (VI. 300).

Blok carried the day and though, shortly afterwards, he himself
resigned from the Repertory Section, Alyansky worked on with the
publishing bureau until the liquidation of the Petrograd branch. It
is understandable, however, that Blok's romantic approach, particularly his sweeping demands for 'avalanches of books' and 'trainloads
of paper' for the starving ex-capital, must have seemed childish to
those in positions of greater responsibility and that Kameneva, his
immediate superior, reacted with an irritation which she expressed
with all the tact of an authoritarian schoolmarm.

Conditions were indeed appalling. There was a general feeling that
Petrograd was returning to the Stone Age. Zamyatin compared the
desolate houses to cliffs honeycombed with caves,[20] and Viktor
Shklovsky wrote:

At the beginning of 1919 I happened to be in Piter. The time was fearful
and primitive.... At first we fed the stoves with furniture of the kind we
were wont to consider necessary, then we simply stopped lighting them.
We moved into the kitchens. Things were divided into two categories:
the combustible and the non-combustible. ... We slept in our coats, covering ourselves with the carpets.... Particularly many died in houses with

central heating. . . . It was not yet known that in order to survive one has
to eat fats. We ate only potatoes and bread, bread with avidity. Without
fats wounds do not heal, you scratch your hand and the hand festers and
the rag you have bandaged it with festers too. . . . The ration of bread was
one pound per day, salt herring, a few grammes of rye, a piece of sugar,
you'd come home and it would be frightening to look at such minute portions. As though they were making fun of us. Once there was cow
udders. . . . Occasionally you could get frozen potatoes and sometimes fruit
purée in the co-operative of Narkompros. . . .[21]

Blok put a brave face on all this, but day-to-day life was becoming
more and more exhausting. At the beginning of the winter the Bloks'
maid had left them, and Lyuba wept over the salt herring and what
it was doing to her smooth actress's hands.

Towards the end of December 1918 the old people began to die.
One of the first was Nanny Sonya's husband. Somehow, the family
scraped together 200 roubles for the funeral and immediate expenses
and managed to place Sonya herself in an old people's home. Blok
noted the death of the mother of the vice-chairman of his Theatrical
Department; the mother of the pianist of the Prival Kommediantov,
where Lyuba was reading *The Twelve* every night, died too, but,
Blok noted wonderingly, he turned up to play just the same:

19 December. I am so exhausted I shout at Lyuba.

20 December. The horror of the frost. I eat like a horse [*zhru*]—money melts
away. Life is becoming horrifying, monstrous, senseless. Robbery everywhere. The Mendeleyevs' flat with their collection of Ambulants' will be
the next to go (the tenant is vacating it and it's sure to be broken into). . . .
Mama called in—hungry.

21 December. What extraordinary dreams—terrible, barbarous, vivid.
There's no telling them in words.

24 December. . . . I have been 'called up' to the 'home guard' [*tylevoye opol-
cheniye*]. . . . Horrors with Mama. Horrors with Lyuba.[s]

                                                              (Z.K. 441)

And, for the last day of the old year:

Bu's part for the Prival (Lenore) is not ready and she won't recite today.
With difficulty I make myself go on working at the proofs of 'Catilina'.

' A society of artists, so called because they arranged travelling exhibitions and famous
in their day for their defiance of the Academy and the social criticism suggested by their
realistic genre pictures.
   s The word *uzhas* ('horror') used in a similar context recurs all through Blok's notebooks.
It can denote quarrels, awkwardnesses, any situation that is not as it should be.

There is a rumour (from our shop) that all shops are to be closed. The most basic essentials are unobtainable. What is obtainable is a crazy price. Frost. People in the street carrying odd-looking sacks. Almost total darkness. There's an old man crying out, dying of hunger. Shining in the sky—one large, clear star.[1]

(Z.K. 443)

6

Throughout the rest of the winter, death and disaster formed a grey, turgid undertone to all everyday life:

1 January. An unheard-of absence of food and unprecedented prices.

3rd. Darkness and silence.

11 January. Bu's birthday (thirty-seven years old). I and everyone else forgot—and she only remembered in the evening.

15 January. There's a typhus epidemic.

(Z.K. 444–5)

Zorgenfrey went down with raging typhus at this time and recalled with gratitude that, on hearing of his illness, Blok wrote to his wife, hurried the payment of his honorariums, counted the lines in his manuscript for him and brought the money for it to his home himself: 'a genuine act of self-sacrifice in a man habitually careful and, with regard to illnesses, even over-cautious.'[23]

A rare celebration at Vsemirnaya Literatura on 21 January elicited Blok's heartfelt but self-reproachful comment: 'Cigars, cigarettes, food—all these are a source of incommunicable delight when they are expensive and rare, and of virtually none when available. Damned sensuality!'

[1] This clear Christmas star (under the old calendar it was still only 17 December, the last week in Advent) was destined to awake a response across the years, at the end of another, no less terrible war. In 1946, Pasternak, for whom Blok was the embodiment of 'that freedom which is wider than political or moral freedom ... that freedom in dealing with life and the things of this world without which there is no great art', thought of writing a study of his verse. Instead, because he saw in Blok's poetry 'a revelation of the Nativity in all spheres of Russian life', he decided that 'there was no need to write an article' and undertook instead 'a Russian Epiphany, in the style of the Dutch, with the frost and wolves and a green forest of fir trees'.[22] So it was that, in the hunger and cold of 1946, Dr. Zhivago's 'Star of the Nativity' shone out from the sky of Russian poetry as if in answer to Blok's 'one large, clear star' of that no less terrible winter of 1919....

The circumstances of Blok's mother and aunt continued to be a source of constant worry:

24 January. Evening with Mama, poor Mama.

31 January. Auntie called in (quite mad). All plans come to nothing....

5 February. Mama's got Auntie away to Luga." Auntie's completely lost her wits.

13 February. Mama came, Mamochka....

19 February. Auntie came to see me this evening. She's better but every tenth word is mad. Complained of Mama and Annushka. Said how nice it was in Luga.

(Z.K. 446-50)

February and March brought another rush of deaths, beginning with Vasiliy Rozanov, dead in the arms of Father Pavel Florensky in the Monastery of St. Sergius at Zagorsk, and culminating, for Blok, with the death of Aunt Sofia, his mother's elder sister, on 6 March. Blok's relationship with the other Kublitsky-Piottukhs had been cool since after the first revolution, but he had the happiest childhood and boyhood memories of his aunt, and the previous summer at Safonovo she had nursed Maria Andreyevna through the worst of her nervous breakdown.

Then, on 7 March, Zhenya Ivanov rang to say that he was at the end of his tether—could Blok help? As soon as he could get away, Blok made his way out to Tsarskoye Selo and found Zhenya 'all swollen, with sores on his legs'. 'I must find him some sort of sinecure in the Department—930 roubles,' he noted distractedly. Not surprisingly, Blok was by this time beginning to feel at the end of his own tether:

20 March. Dreams, dreams again. Shakhmatovo—in a peculiar way.

8 April. In the evening I have a recitation.... Pointless—no audience, no success.

14 April. Lyuba took the proofs to Alyansky this morning. She's been at a rehearsal since early morning, having quarrelled with me; this acting of hers will be the death of me.

15 April. I am to recite at an evening in the '*Expeditsiya* for the Preparation of State Papers'.—I am tired and no longer have any success. Time to put me on the shelf?

" A provincial town near Petrograd.

22 April. Some day I shall go mad in my sleep. Such terrible dreams I had last night. There's no describing them. I cried out. Such horror that I am not even frightened any longer but feel my mind becoming sweetly confused.

3 May. Announcement of some kind of call-up. Because of that to Vsemirnaya Literatura. But I can't really do anything about it. What has destroyed the revolution (the spirit of music)?—The war.

4 May. Worked a little but I can no longer work properly now....

8 May. ... I have been allowed a temporary exemption as far as military service is concerned.

10 May. It's true that Meyerhold has left.[v]

18 May. Weariness to the point of despair. 'Nerves?'

23 May. I feel very rotten and there's something wrong with my eyes.

25 May. Intercede for Vl. Zlobin and Sergey Syunnenberg to Maria Fyëdorovna Andreyeva.[w] ... I still feel a total wreck.

27 May. In the morning—Zhenya. I must go and see Maria Fyëdorovna about his call-up....

(*Z.K.* 453–61)

And so on, and so forth.

Yet in spite of all this private anguish, confided only to his diary, Blok gave an outward impression of remarkable fitness. His handiness with axe and saw and his sheer physical strength gave him a long start over most of his fellow intellectuals and he managed to plough through enormous quantities of paper work. Throughout January, February, and March 1919 he was still working actively for Kameneva's Theatrical Department and putting in a great deal of time at Gorky's Vsemirnaya Literatura. There, his work on Heinrich Heine ('whose poetry is so beautiful but whose personality leaves so much to be desired', VII. 355), really interested him. Then there were still the odd good days when he felt 'full of thoughts and plans' (*Z.K.* 445). These plans, however, seldom even began to burgeon, never mind to bear fruit, not so much because of the hardships of life as because something else always cropped up to demand all his strength and attention: time-consuming incidents such as his brusque

[v] Meyerhold left for the south of Russia to recuperate from the hardships of the winter in a sanatorium at Yalta.

[w] Maria Fyëdorovna Andreyeva (Gorky's wife) was Blok's second female boss in the Theatrical Department. As personalities, he found both rival 'ladies'—Andreyeva and Kameneva—tryingly authoritarian, and exasperation was enhanced by the constant necessity of interceding for friends and obtaining papers (*spravki*).

engagement (the first of many) with I. Ionov, the dictatorial official in charge of state publishing at the Smolny Institute.

Ionov had designs on Alkonost and wanted to reissue *The Twelve* with Annenkov's illustrations. This, at a time when the state was not yet capable of satisfying the demand for books and when private publishers, in theory at least, were being encouraged, was against the party line, and Blok and Alyansky had no difficulty in enlisting Gorky's support for Alkonost (VII. 352). Nevertheless, Ionov continued in office and was later to remember the incident against Blok. After calling on the Commissar in the Smolny to plead Alyansky's cause and finding him surrounded by literary sycophants, Blok noted: 'one becomes quite unlike oneself: coarser, dry, businesslike, ageing'. In the same breath he recorded, as one who remarks on an extraneous fact somehow pertinent to one's own condition: 'E. F. Knipovich's father ... was perfectly healthy. Carried on as though nothing had happened, then suddenly a nervous seizure, and he fell dead on the spot' (VII. 355).

Oddly, Blok understood Ionov's resentment of his own independent conduct very well, just as he had understood the sacking of Shakhmatovo:

All culture, whether scientific or artistic—is demonic. And the more scientific, the more artistic it is, the more demonic it is.... But demonism is strength. And strength is power over weakness, is *to offend against the weak*.

The unfortunate Fyedot[x] has soiled and spoiled *my* spiritual treasures, for which I weep *demonically* in the night. But who is the stronger? I, who weep and suffer, or Fyedot? Even if Fyedot should actually come into full legal possession of all these things that he has no idea how to use (and he has not done so; there was nothing left for him, because everything, most probably, had been stolen, and there was little enough of value to steal at Shakhmatovo anyway), yet what for Fyedot is something worth only a few coins remains, for me, a source of priceless ecstasy, enthusiasm, tears.

So it follows that to this day I am the stronger, and this strength I owe to the fact that someone, some ancestor of mine, had leisure, money, and independence.... So even if hands a good deal dirtier than my own (of which I know nothing and, good Lord, do not take it upon myself to judge) have thrown out from the printing machine the works of even such a poet as A. Blok who is supposed to have done some 'service' to the revolution, *I have not the right to judge*. It is not those hands that are throwing them out, not they alone, but those distant, unknown millions of poor hands; and all this is watched by millions of other eyes.... And the eyes will laugh

---

[x] Fyedot had taken over what was left of the house at Shakhmatovo, but Blok later appended a footnote to this entry recording that, shortly after writing it, he had learnt that Fyedot was already dead.

a little: how's this, they'll say, the *barin* went prancing by, the *barin* had a good time, and now the *barin* is on our side? Oy, but *is* the *barin* on our side?

The *barin* is a demon.

The *barin* will get out of this present dilemma. And a *barin* he will remain. But as to us—we have only this present hour [*Khot' chas, da nash*].

That's how it is.

(VII. 352–4, entry for 6 January 1919)

Blok noted that Ionov and Kameneva, Mayakovsky, he himself, and Meyerhold all understood this 'sociological instinct', whereas Gorky[y] and his wife Maria Fyëdorovna Andreyeva did not. Lunacharsky, 'not in the least a Bolshevik by temperament', tried to reconcile the two factions.

7

In general, although a retrospective glance through his plays on Christmas Day (7 January 1919) had convinced Blok that his way between the two revolutions had been 'the right way', his faith in the efficacy of his work under the aegis of Gorky at Vsemirnaya Literatura and of the 'two ladies' in the Theatrical Department of Narkompros was more than a little tarnished by the spring of 1919, and his hopes of serving the people were now beginning to centre round Ivanov-Razumnik's Volfil.

These hopes, however, were to prove short-lived. On 16 January the poet had found 'a certain mental relaxation' in a meeting to discuss further the foundation of the Free Philosophical Academy, in Syunnenberg's office at Narkompros. Blok was keen enough to copy out an extensive extract from the manifesto of the Academy in his diary.[25]

Couched in the grandiose language of the period, the manifesto envisaged the Academy as a free teacher-pupil association, a link between the present day and the classical tradition of the ancient

---

[y] Where Blok saw just retribution for centuries of unnatural inequality, Gorky, as a man of the people, saw the spoliation of his own heritage. In a sense, this was a refraction of the old Westerner/Slavophile controversy, with Blok, who saw himself as a natural Westerner, coming out on the side of the Slavophiles and Gorky, the great 'son of the people' and, as Blok himself called him, a man 'of the East', playing precisely the opposite role. The two men thus had very different views and, in spite of a mutual respect which was at its height in 1919, did not work easily in double harness. Gorky's verdict on Blok, however, was a generous one: 'He was uniquely beautiful, both as a man and as a character,' he is reported to have said. 'Enviably beautiful.'[24]

world.[z] On 19 January 1919, Kameneva was persuaded to grant the project official sanction. On 23 January Blok, Andrey Bely (newly come from Moscow), Alyansky, and Syunnenberg spent the evening at Meyerhold's discussing their plans and, three days later, most of the founder-members (with the notable exception of Lunarcharsky) forgathered at Ivanov-Razumnik's house in Tsarskoye Selo. There they were informed that Moscow objected to the word 'Academy' and had suggested 'Society' (and a state subsidy). It was evidently felt that this initiative from Petrograd on the part of Left S. R.s, 'Scythians', and unpredictable idealists should not be allowed to set itself up in rivalry with the official Socialist Academy in Moscow, founded the previous year.

In the circumstances, however, it was extraordinarily difficult to get any project off the ground, even with official permission and a subsidy. The first 'casualty' was Andrey Bely, who had looked ill at Ivanov-Razumnik's, and subsequently felt so weak he thought it better to return home to Moscow, though not before he had bestowed the influenza from which he was suffering on his host.

Then, the discovery in Moscow of a new 'Left S. R. plot' led to widespread arrests among the party membership both there and in Petrograd. In this connection, on 14 February, came news of the arrest of Ivanov-Razumnik, taken from his home with a high temperature. Blok, more concerned for his friend's health than for his actual arrest, which he must have assumed would soon be proved a mistake, spent the day in the Theatrical Department, organizing a collective appeal to the head of the Cheka, Skorokhodov. Next morning, Serafima Pavlovna rang to say that Remizov, who had also been present at the meeting at Ivanov-Razumnik's, had been arrested. With the disappearance of Shteynberg, Petrov-Vodkin, and Syunnenberg, it became clear that someone had monitored the gathering in Tsarskoye Selo. Blok went with Bakrylov, a friend from Narkompros, to inform Lunacharsky. Then, after a walk about the town, came home to find 'Commissar Bulatsel' and a soldier waiting to arrest him. It was late and, after undergoing the ritual search of his flat, Blok had to spend a sleepless night in a Cheka waiting room before being called for cross-examination.

The interrogator wanted to know about the poet's connections with the Left S. R. press, and Blok, trained up from school days never to present the authorities with gratuitous information, replied

---

[z] Apart from Blok, Bely, and Ivanov-Razumnik, others who had undertaken to participate in its work were Ars. Avramov, B. Kushner, Lunacharsky, E. Lundberg, Artur Lur'e,
Meyerhold, Petrov-Vodkin, A. Shteynberg, and K. Erberg (i.e. Syunnenberg).

briefly that he had contributed to *Znamya Truda* and *Nash Put'*
'because, while sympathetic to the general trends of socialism and
internationalism, I was always more inclined to populism than to
Marxism'. The protocol of the interrogation includes a statement
in Blok's hand which reads: 'I have never been a member of the
Left S. R. Party and would not join any party as I have always been
far from politics.'[26] To this, as he replied to all further questions, he
had nothing to add.

So, instead of being allowed to go home after this routine interrogation, as the majority of his fellow writers and artists had been,
the suspiciously unforthcoming Blok was packed off to a large communal cell until his case could be further investigated. One other
founder-member of Volfil, A. Shteynberg, had also been detained.[aa]
After prisoners scheduled for removal to a more permanent place
of confinement had been called out from the communal detention
cell in Gorokhovaya Street, Shteynberg had made haste to secure
a bunk:

No sooner had I spread my fur coat on the hay mattress and put my travelling grip as a pillow than I was struck by the sight of the tall, stately figure
of Blok just entering the cell.

It was strangely incongruous. Blok's whole being stood out so sharply,
somehow, against this macabre scene of human misery....

Blok came in just as he always came into a place where there were many
chance-met, unknown people. I had seen him mount a crowded tram just
like that: his head just a little thrown back, his lips compressed, his eyes
looking calmly around for some object on which they might rest. He came
in as though he were going to walk right through us or as if, having had
a word with someone, he would just turn round and go back again with
that same light, springy step with which he had entered. And it was strange
to see how this man, free even in captivity, must inevitably bump into the
blank wall and would have to stop or even spring back. I felt somehow
shy to go up and greet him although, after a bad night, this was the first
ray of comfort.

But his eye had already met mine and we involuntarily smiled at one
another and shook hands....

Shteynberg invited Blok to share his bed, as all the others were
by now filled up again, and the poet lay down to catch up on his
sleep. Shteynberg had struck up a cell friendship with a group of

---

[aa] Afterwards, at the session of the Association devoted to Blok's memory held on 28
August 1921, Shteynberg was able to give a vivid account of the whole incident.

Left S. R. sailors, one of whom knew all about *The Twelve* and Aleksandr Blok's support for the Soviets:

'It can't be! It can't be!' kept repeating the sailor [Sh——], who had spent
years in Tsarist prisons and had already succeeded in making the acquaintance of revolutionary ones—'At least, *anything* can be, I suppose,' he interrupted himself. 'Only, you know, this little fact is not just biographical, it's
historical!'

The sailor was well read, and had even published something on
the history of the revolutionary movement in the fleet, but some
of his companions were still more bewildered:

'But, comrade,' one of them addressed me. 'It was comrade Blok who made
up *The Twelve*, wasn't it?'
　'Yes, of course.'
　'And what would you say it was: revolutionary or counter-revolu-
tionary?'
　'I should say it was—revolutionary.'
　'Well then, how can the revolutionary regime put comrade Blok in pri-
son on the Gorokhovaya?'

Meanwhile the object of all this bewilderment slept peacefully,
while various other prisoners, hearing that 'the famous writer'
Blok was sharing their misfortunes, tiptoed up for a closer look—
even those who had never heard of him becoming infected by the
general curiosity. Contrary to Blok's own conviction that, as an educated man and a *barin*, he should be the object of a certain malice
on the part of the people, he was surrounded by good will. His
appearance, as Shteynberg observed with wry understanding,
accorded so very well with how everyone imagined a 'famous
writer' ought to look....
　At the dinner hour it was the sailors who made him feel at home
over the common bowl of horse-meat soup, a large wooden vessel
designed to feed five:

... Blok, who had just heard about this dinner-time custom, was torn
between his habitual fastidiousness and a sharp appetite.
　'Are you going to dine?' he asked me.
　'Yes, I think so, like everybody else!'
　... We joined the queue and Sh—— began to explain to Blok in detail
why he was glad to see him here:
　'Writers should see everything with their own eyes. Who can say they've
lived through the Russian revolution if they've never once been in the
hands of the Cheka? Now you've seen it from that angle too.'
　'But I never wanted to see it from this angle,' Blok objected.

'You mean you're only interested in the façade!'

'No, not the façade,' Blok objected again; 'but the real truth, surely that is not here?'

... However, as it transpired, this was not the moment for philosophizing. The soup had already been poured into our bowl, each of us had received a piece of bread and a wooden spoon and we returned to our table. Each had some sort of eatables with him which we pooled on the table. Then we began the rite of the meal: each in turn dipped his wooden spoon into the bowl at the bottom of which swam the pieces of horse meat and, having swallowed his mouthful of soup, waited until it was his turn to dip again. Evidently we were all equally 'considerate' and, when the bowl was empty, all the horse meat was left on the bottom.

'Very polite you all are!' exclaimed the worker P—— and immediately took a piece of newspaper, tore it into five pieces, got out his penknife and began to dole out the meat in equal portions.

Blok was all flushed from the hot soup: the whole ceremony had obviously put him in good spirits and, chewing painfully on the tough meat, he began to joke....

Blok spent the rest of the day in conversation with various other prisoners. Shteynberg left him for a time to go and play chess and came back to find him talking to a very young sailor, arrested by chance but found to have a Left S. R. proclamation in his pocket. As Shteynberg came up the sailor rose and held out his hand. 'I'm for a long voyage!'

'How nice he is,' said A. A. 'How nice they all are!'

'You haven't been bored?'

'No, there's a great deal here that interests me very much, you know.'

One prisoner, however, awoke Blok's active distaste, reminding him strongly of some of his former 'clients' in the Peter-Paul Fortress. It seemed to him, moreover, as though this personage—who looked, he said, like a general of the Tsarist police—was 'fulfilling the function of one of his ex-subordinates' (i.e. listening in to the other prisoners' conversations).

When Blok was called out 'to the interrogator' at four o'clock in the morning[bb] (he was sleeping soundly again and proved hard to wake), this man moved across to talk to Shteynberg and asked for a light. He *was* a general, but now in command of Red Artillery on the Eastern Front, and was waiting for Trotsky to intervene and secure his release. Noting Blok, a 'distinguished revolutionary', in the same predicament, he had made a kind of bet with himself that either both of them, or neither, would emerge from prison. Shteyn-

[bb] According to Shteynberg. Blok, probably the more accurate, has it at 2 a.m.

berg objected that Blok was no distinguished revolutionary but a
poet. The general's reply proved that the 'poet's' sensitive antennae
had warned him all too well: '... nonsense, those are the most
dangerous people of all. I have always thought so. If we hadn't had
all those Count Tolstoys, etc., all this would never have come about,
I'm convinced of it.'

When Blok returned, Shteynberg told him about the general.
'"We evidently recognized one another at first glance." He smiled.
"Well, I suppose we'd better try to go back to sleep."' Soon after
they awoke, Blok was summoned: 'Pack your things; for release.'
The general received an identical summons at the same time.

Blok sought out his table-fellows of the previous day, shook hands,
asked Shteynberg to give his best wishes to another prisoner, an
ardent admirer of his poetry, gave him a piece of bread he had kept
from the previous day and embraced him: '"You and I spent the
night just like Shatov and Kirillov," he said.'[27]

His own diary reads: 'Home and a bath. Telephones. It appears
it was M. F. Andreyeva and Lunacharsky who intervened for me'
(Z.K. 450, entry for 17 February 1919). The next day he was back
at work.

8

On 27 February 1919, an invitation to work in an advisory capacity
for the Soyuz Deyateley Khudozhestvennoy Literatury (Union of
Practitioners of Literature as an Art) gave Blok the opportunity to
resign his increasingly irksome chairmanship of the Repertory Section, which he did on the following day.[a]

On 1 March there was a moment of light relief. Alyansky decided
to celebrate the ninth birthday (in terms of months) of Alkonost,
and invited Blok, Ivanov-Razumnik, now safely back from a series
of interrogations in Moscow, Syunnenberg, Kupreyanov, Meyerhold, and others to what Blok describes as 'pancakes' and Alyansky
himself as a '*pâté*' of dried fish and frozen potatoes, salt herring, *vobla*
(dried fish again!), and 'some sort of buns'. 'To this *hors d'œuvre* I
had managed to add three bottles of pure spirits.'

Blok arrived first, full of plans to discuss Alkonost's journal *Zapiski
Mechtateley*, the first number of which had just been published. He

---

[a] In fact, this new appointment proved short-lived, as Blok, together with Gorky and
Gumilev, felt it incumbent upon them to resign within two months because of financial
corruption within the Union.

was the first to write in the album Alyansky had prepared for the occasion:

Dear Samuil Mironovich,
Today I have been thinking about 'Alkonost' all day. You did not know yourself what a name you gave your publishing house. 'Alkonost' it will be (in all the fullness of the word), and it will continue to be as a part of history, because everything begun in 1918 will be a part of history. And it is very important that it was begun in June (and not before), because every month, if not every day, of this year is equal to a year or to ten years.
  Long live Alkonost!

ALEKSANDR BLOK
1 March 1919

A 'joy unhoped-for' on this occasion was the arrival of Olga Glebova-Sudeykina, the exquisite dancer and wife of the artist Sudeykin, friend of Akhmatova and heroine of her *Poem without a Hero*.[dd] It was 'a good evening', Blok noted, and afterwards they all went on to a masquerade where they continued the celebration until seven o'clock in the morning.[ee]

On 8 March Blok was elected to the editorial board of a section of Gorky's Vsemirnaya Literatura which was attempting to organize a series of dramatizations of historical events by leading writers. 'Another tower of Babel: to show the whole of world history through a cycle of historical plays, no more and no less,' commented Evgeniy Zamyatin, an ex-Bolshevik engineer lately returned from building icebreakers in Newcastle and one of the most original prose-writers of the twentieth century, whose play *Attila* was, in fact, the only memorable result of this initiative. Blok warned from the start that he did not think 'Art could carry science' and eventually, having toyed with the idea of Tristan and Isolde, of the battle of Kulikovo,

---

[dd] In the *Poem without a Hero* Blok figures as the successful rival of a young poet who, in 1913, shot himself for love of Sudeykina. If there was a romance between poet and dancer, no trace of it remains in Blok's diaries nor surviving letters. Akhmatova was most probably weaving a poetic fiction, justified by Blok's Don Juan image.

[ee] In his memoirs, Alyansky merges this incident with another recorded by Blok as 'At Alyansky's all night after getting drunk', on 3 June 1919. It must have been on this occasion that Alyansky provided 'too much spirits', and 'not enough food'. The city being under curfew, the guests had to stay the night, a circumstance of which Alyansky had neglected to inform the 'House Committee of the Poor' (in its shortened form this sounded like the House Committee of Misfortunes—*Domkombed*), who informed on him. He was awakened by the patrol, a commissar in the classic revolutionary leather jacket and two sailors festooned with belts of machine-gun ammunition. Alyansky confessed to harbouring unexpected guests and pointed out Blok, dozing uncomfortably upright on a chair. The commissar accepted his explanation and was already on his way when, seeing Alyansky hovering at the door, he came back and demanded angrily: 'Do you mean to say you can't find somewhere for Aleksandr Blok to lie *down* to sleep?'[28]

and of Isabella Malatesta, he settled for ancient Egypt and produced the unreadable *Rameses* (IV. 247–63, written in March and April 1920), which he himself was glad to see shelved. 'Better not try to stage them', was Blok's own final verdict on those 'Scenes from History'.[29]

9

In spite of almost daily committee meetings, the long hours of preparatory work, and his constant and time-consuming involvement with less fortunately placed friends, Blok was writing again that spring, and with genuine inspiration: the article 'The Collapse of Humanism' (VI. 93–115).

This article was the immediate result of a workaday committee meeting in the Translators' Section of Vsemirnaya Literatura at which Blok had read a report on the progress of his work on the edition of Heinrich Heine. Entitled 'Heine in Russia' (VI. 116–28), the report touched on the question of the Romantic challenge to the settled humanism of eighteenth- and pre-eighteenth-century Europe.[30] Blok's opinions had infuriated 'the professors', some of whom had hotly defended the values of nineteenth-century humanism, as interpreted by Turgenev and Herzen in literature, by rationalists and liberals in politics. But Maksim Gorky—a Nietzschean and a romantic at heart—had found Blok's paper 'prophetic'[ff] and suggested that the committee devote an entire session to the questions he had raised (VII. 355–7). Yet Blok, in spite of his Wagnerian fire and dislike of humility, was no ally of Gorky's against the specifically Christian humanism of Myshkin and Alyosha Karamazov, those 'just persons' always ready, as Gorky himself had complained so vigorously in his 1918 anti-Bolshevik series of articles 'Ill-timed Thoughts', to take upon themselves 'all the revolting little sins' of the Russian people. For Blok, 'humanism' (and thus also 'anti-humanism') was a cultural, not a religious, concept, for in his view humanism stood for classical individual morality, not Christian coinherence,[32] and for precisely that *rationalistic* idea of progress to which Gorky, for all his temperamental romanticism, so desperately clung.

The alliance was thus based on misunderstanding, but Gorky's

[ff] 'Humanism', Gorky wrote to Fedin five years after Blok's death, 'in that form in which we have absorbed it from the Gospels and the "Holy Writ" of our artists about the Russian people and about life, that humanism is a bad thing, and A. A. Blok is, I think, the only one who had some slight inkling of this.'[31]

encouragement did serve to set Blok writing again 'in his own Russian language', did set him free to hearken for the last time to the dread roaring of a world in flux. The day after the committee meeting saw Blok already totally absorbed in his theme:

27 March. A day of tense thoughts, flooding over me—to the point of exhaustion.

28 March. All the evening I wrote of the collapse of civilization. A depressing day.

29 March. The depression of yesterday has grown even stronger. Have been writing the lecture all day. Everything is very difficult.

(Z.K. 454)

The next day Blok interrupted his writing to speak at a reception in honour of Gorky, emphasizing the responsibility of the great popular writer's position as 'intermediary between the people and the intelligentsia'. Coming after a plethora of rather sycophantic tributes, Blok's quiet words about the artist's responsibility to the Spirit of Music which alone, he said, 'is capable of putting an end to this blood-letting which becomes nothing but a wearisome banality once it has ceased to be a sacred madness' (VI. 92), rang very soberly.

The war in Europe being at an end, civil war was in full spate. Internal resistance to the Bolsheviks, supported by the erstwhile allies of the Provisional Government, had by now got firmly under way; Kolchak was advancing from the east and other White forces were closing in on Petrograd. In Soviet-occupied territories, terror had become an acknowledged instrument of government, and it is against this background—and the Stone Age conditions of that winter—that Blok was writing.

During the last days of March and the first week of April 1919, while he was working on the article, Blok went almost every night to the opera to hear Chaliapin, or to the ballet: *Ruslan and Lyudmila*; *The Barber of Seville*; Rubinstein's *The Demon*, to which his father had once invited his mother and which now seemed to him 'a mixture of infinite profundity and infinite vulgarity—both in the music and in the production' (Z.K. 454-5); *Don Quixote*; *Giselle*; *Prince Igor*; *The Queen of Spades*; *Esmeralda*. He would join the starving citizens in their greatcoats shuffling into the magnificent white-and-gold Mariynsky Opera House to hear the marvellous bass voice of the legendary singer or to watch the frail gleam and colour of the classical ballet, while outside the mighty eighteenth-century capital was crumbling into ruin as the snows melted to show the scars of war, and people left the theatre not knowing what the night would bring, as insecure now in their own homes as in the desolate streets. No wonder it seemed to Blok that only 'the artist' was capable of surviving the bitter years until a new civilization would arise from the ashes of the old; that only 'music' could remind people that life was more than a dull, dangerous, and miserable struggle for survival.

On 9 April Blok read his lecture 'on anti-humanism' to the Translators' Section of Vsemirnaya Literatura. He postulated four key concepts: culture, civilization, 'the element', and the 'Spirit of Music'. Culture he saw as the real qualitative achievement of mankind throughout the ages: quantitively small, very vulnerable, and easily destroyed. Civilization was culture moribund, a cracking outer shell, no longer bound and quickened by the Spirit of Music. Humanism, for instance, had been culture, but was *now* civilization. Like every true culture, it had emerged from 'the element', the untutored people (or, as Blok called them, harking back once more to the fall of Rome, the barbarian masses), generators and guardians of that Spirit of Music which, in a finely sustained metaphor, the poet compared to a distillation of life-giving water; now playing in a rainbow of spray about the head of the 'last humanist', Schiller; then falling back into the ground with the rains and mists of Verlaine and the European decadents; accumulating in the depths of the earth; and, at the last, breaking out in a deluge whose intolerable roar could no longer be recognized as harmony. This flood, he said, was still rising, threatening to engulf all civilization, and the flotsam of true culture was 'being whirled along on the very crest of the tidal wave of revolution'. The only protection for it was the frail ark of perfect form.

Neither civilization nor the civilized individual ('the social animal, the moral animal') would, it seemed to him, survive: only culture itself would survive, and the individual artist who would prove capable of adapting himself to 'the age of whirlwind and storm that is opening up before us, into whose vortex the whole of humanity is being irresistibly drawn' (VI. 114–15).[gg]

Showing signs of weariness and haste, the paper contained some very dangerous statements, open, if quoted out of context, to terrible misinterpretation. Perhaps the best comment on it was provided by Blok himself. Walking back from Vsemirnaya Literatura with a

[gg] Blok's thoughts which provide the basis for and to some extent modify this article, clearly tracing its origin back to the polemics about the Heine report in Vsemirnaya Literatura, are recorded in his diary (VII. 358–63 for 28 March 1919, and under 1 April and 7 April 1919, 363–5).

young poet who afterwards tried to reproduce his exact words, Blok
said something like this:

... You know, I think a lot about the revolution just now. For me it is
not just a fundamental change in all our outward life but something much
more. First of all, it is the birth of a new kind of man such as has never
been seen on earth before. And what I was saying just now about chaos
in the mind was about myself exclusively. You don't have to listen to me,
but you asked me whether I was writing poetry and I have to give you
an answer. It is true that my inward ear is full of roaring and sound just
now, and perhaps that is my only consolation, although a painful one, I
must admit. But you see I still have not lost faith that the chaos will form
itself into sounds. If not for me, then for others. Cosmos is born of chaos—
that was what the Greeks used to say. It is a sadness to me that I haven't
the words to say this as clearly as they did, so many centuries ago. But
they had a naïve, childish soul. Whereas we, expecially people of my generation, are trammelled with doubts and anxieties. So much strength has been
wasted....[33]

10

'Trammelled' as he was, Blok had certainly failed to convince Gorky,
who was later to recall:

The article seemed unclear to me, but full of tragic forebodings. Blok as
he read reminded me of a child in a fairy tale, lost in the forest: he feels
the approach of monsters out of the darkness and mutters some kind of
incantation to make them go away. When he turned the pages of the manuscript, his fingers trembled.

Certain phrases, such as Blok's statement that 'to civilize the masses
is both impossible and unnecessary' or his declaration that 'discoveries' were being superseded by 'inventions', struck Gorky as
pessimistic to the point of obscurantism.

Shortly after the reading, strolling with Blok along the ruinous
streets through the pale spring sunshine, he attempted to draw him
into a real conversation of a kind that was hardly possible in committee. The poet bypassed Gorky's strictures on his paper, welcoming rather the new departure he perceived in the older man's recent
books, from 'deciding the problems of society' to the 'childish questions' of life and death and human happiness. Gorky, who did not
feel he had made any such departure, refrained from contradicting:
'Let him think so if it pleases him, if he needs to do so....' This was
a line of thought Blok was constitutionally incapable of following.

All his dialogues with himself, or with others, were attempts to overcome the terrible isolation suggested by Tyutchev's dictum, 'The word once spoken is a lie.' That someone he admired should, in an important conversation, a genuine attempt to communicate, deliberately *disguise* his thought was something new to him: and totally alien.

'Why don't you write about those questions?' he asked insistently.

I said that questions of the meaning of being, of death, of love—were strictly personal, intimate questions for myself alone. I do not like to air them in public, and if, from time to time, I do so involuntarily, then the result is always clumsy, awkward. 'To speak of yourself is a subtle art, I do not possess it.'

And so Gorky retreated behind that charming, bear-like persona which, for so many years now, had served him to disguise an aspiring and vulnerable heart. Blok, however, was not to be put off. The two men turned into the Summer Garden, which they happened to be passing, and sat down on a sunlit bench.

'"You are hiding yourself. You hide your thoughts about the spirit, the truth. Why?" And before I had had time to answer, he began to talk about the Russian intelligentsia. . . .' The two argued: Gorky, as usual, defending the intelligentsia. Utterly absorbed in his theme, Blok contradicted him:

'When you have conjured up the spirit of destruction out of the darkness, it is not honest to say: that was not our work, but that of those people over there. Bolshevism is the inevitable conclusion of all the work of the intelligentsia in professorial chairs, in editorial offices, in the political underground. . . .'

A pretty woman who was passing greeted him sweetly, he replied drily, almost contemptuously, and she went her way, smiling but crestfallen. Looking after her, at the small, uncertain feet, Blok asked: 'What do you think about immortality, of the possibility of immortality?'

He asked insistently, his eyes held mine stubbornly. I said that maybe Lamennais was right; . . . that it was possible that in a few million years' time, some frowning evening in a Petersburg spring, Blok and Gorky would again be speaking of eternity, sitting on a bench in the Summer Garden.

He asked: 'Do you mean that—seriously?'

His insistence surprised and rather irritated me, although I felt that he was not asking out of simple curiosity but as if from the desire to quench or to suppress some heavy anxiety.

Gorky changed his tack and launched, in considerable pseudo-scientific detail, into the explanation of another theory involving the 'transformation of so-called "dead matter" into psychic energy'. But Blok shook his head with mounting impatience. 'What a gloomy dream,' he exclaimed. 'Luckily the law of the conservation of matter is against it!' And finally, in a burst of impatience:

'All that is a bore....

'It's simpler; the thing is that we have become too clever to believe in God and not strong enough to believe only in ourselves. As a foundation for life and faith there can only be God—and "I". Humanity? But—how is it possible to believe in the reasonableness of humanity after this war and on the eve of other, inevitable, still more cruel wars? No, that fantasy of yours ... it's creepy! But I don't think you were speaking seriously.'

He sighed: 'If only we could stop thinking completely for ten years. Simply switch off this deceitful will-o'-the-wisp that is leading us deeper and deeper into the night of the world and listen in our hearts to the harmony of the universe. The brain, the brain....[hh] It is not a reliable organ, it is monstrously large, monstrously developed. A swelling like a goitre.'

He fell silent, his lips tightly compressed, then said quietly: 'If only movement would cease, time would stop ...'

'It would stop if we could give all types of movements the same speed.'

Blok shot a sideways look at me, raising his brows, and launched into rapid, confused speech.... I ceased to follow him. It was a strange impression. As though he were stripping off worn-out, ragged garments....

Unexpectedly he rose, shook hands, and set off for the tram. His walk at first sight appears firm but when you look closely you can see that he is almost staggering, as though not sure of his direction....[34]

So Blok appeared to Gorky. To Blok, who had so long admired and consistently championed Gorky the author, the fundamental disingenuousness of the man, now already virtually inextricable from the public figure, was a puzzle and a real disappointment.

Blok's last appointment that season was to the chairmanship of the directorate of the Bolshoy Dramaticheskiy Theatre, an honour of which Maria Fyëdorovna Andreyeva informed him on 24 April 1919. After the first meeting of the directorate on 26 April, Blok sat down to write a long letter explaining why he had been wrong to accept: he had taken on too much already, he wrote; the basic questions of the theatre's repertory (classical tragedy and comedy and high romantic drama) had already been decided. He was no good at theatrical 'politics', finance, or administration.

What remains? To sit on committees again, which is something I should so much like to avoid. When I left the Theatrical Department I was really

[hh] Gorky's ellipse.

deliberately trying to escape from the specifically theatrical, from 'theatri-cality', into literature, which is more my native element and where, it seems to me, I can be of more use.   (VIII. 520–4)

On the very day he wrote this letter, however, he received one from Andreyeva, who had after all done a great deal to help him: 'Impos-sible to refuse.'

And so, weak and exhausted after the murderous winter, Blok reluctantly shouldered yet another burden, exposing himself to back-stage intrigue, tying himself to more committee meetings, more speeches, more long winter walks through the icy streets. As it turned out, however, the Bolshoy Dramaticheskiy Theatre was perhaps the most rewarding, certainly the most agreeable, of all his post-revolu-tionary obligations. The actors loved him and called him their 'con-science'. He did not know it, but already he was above and beyond intrigue: it quailed before those tired, clear eyes, before the hesitant speech that never uttered dogmatic truisms or sought to shield the speaker behind the ready-made phrases of official propaganda.[ii] As with all his other duties, Blok took infinite pains: never kept any-body waiting, never left anybody without an answer.

11

The summer of 1919, was, if anything, worse than the winter. Blok was again obliged to 'guard the sleep of the bourgeois' at the gates of his own house, a duty which annoyed him out of all proportion to the inconvenience caused. The only light relief came when a com-plete stranger, recognizing him hovering at the doorway, looked at him sympathetically and murmured, on a note of ironic interrogation: '*I kazhdiy vecher, v chas naznachennyy?*' (a quotation from 'The Stranger': 'And every evening, at the hour appointed . . .').

This sentry duty however, was a mere pinprick. Towards the end of May, the White general Yudenich advanced almost into the suburbs of Petrograd. A state of siege was declared. To be out after curfew a special pass was necessary, which had to be renewed monthly. Blok's summer expeditions out of town to bathe and to walk, so necessary to his mental and bodily health, were curtailed. Lyuba, with great trouble, obtained a special paper enabling him to go out to Strel'na to swim. As every summer, he was soon tanned

---

[ii] His speeches for the Theatre, which take up almost 100 printed pages in his Collected Works (VI. 347–421) and are dated from May 1919 to 22 January 1921, are works of litera-ture, each in its own right.

View from the balcony window of
Blok's last flat, in Offitserskaya
Street, 1920–1

The house where Blok lived after 1912,
with the icebound river in the
foreground.

One of Blok's favourite walks, downriver from his house.

Aleksandr Blok in 1920.

Aleksandra Andreyevna on
the balcony of Blok's flat,
1919.

and appeared fit, but in his notebooks he complained of weakness.
In the parks the decay of nature affected him in a way that the ruinous
condition of the city did not. Where man had built, he would build
again, but the neglected, depopulated, vandalized outskirts of Petersburg reduced him almost to tears.

11 July. Olgino and Lakhta.
    One thing one must accord the Bolsheviks and that is their quite unique
ability to stamp out custom and to liquidate the individual. I don't know
whether that is particularly bad or not. It is a fact.
    Last year I was struck by this in Shuvalovo. But what one can see this
year in Lakhta is incomparably more striking.
    There are virtually no residents left, and no holiday-makers [*dachniki*].
Depressed-looking women drag themselves along every morning to the
local Soviet, to which they are obliged to deliver milk. There, so they say,
it is distributed....
    'The castle' has some very complicated name such as 'an excursion point
and museum of nature' (at least that's what's written on the gate). They're
supposed to give tea to schoolchildren there.[jj]
    Today what looked like a number of schools arrived, but they got no
tea because there was no hot water: 'they hadn't had notice in advance'.
The teacher had to lead the children off to the tea-room where they were
provided—very unwillingly—with tea for a vast sum of money.
    It's empty in the tea-room. There are almost no tables, and the gramo-
phone has disappeared. Round the pretty waitress with slippers on her feet
are hovering four or five insolent youths in boots that were the height of
fashion in 1918. And the girls they've picked up.
    No one wants to do anything. Before millions were forced to work for
the benefit of thousands. That's the reason. But why should the millions
wish to work? And why should they understand communism otherwise
than as robbery and card-playing?

                                                        (VII. 365–7)

    Throughout that summer, Blok was involved in prolonging his
exemption from call-up, then in fighting a decision to billet sailors
in his flat. 'Try to look at it impersonally,' he had advised Zorgenfrey
in 1918, and now his friend ironically referred him to his own
advice. The combined pressures of call-up and billeting reduced him
to thoughts of suicide (*Z.K.* 468, entry for 23 July 1919), but Lyuba,
as so often before, saved the situation by energetic wire-pulling and
tramping from one committee to another.
    Then there were the rumours: culminating in the remarkable

---

[jj] Blok had just been pained to discover that the castle was administered by Narkompros,
for which he himself had been working in various capacities ever since the October revolution.

notion that Blok, Remizov, Merezhkovsky, and Sologub were to be taken to Moscow as 'hostages'. Naturally, it was Blok who had to find out whether this was true, and 'Maria Fyëdorovna rang up Zinov'ev who begged to say that this rumour emanated from fools and idiots . . . ' (*Z.K.* 463).

The searches, however, were real enough. Blok's mother was again disturbed by a night search. The telephone no longer worked.

Real, too, were the difficulties in getting things published: Alyansky had to appeal to Moscow for Alkonost through Gorky, over the head of the Petrograd censorship.[35] There was a rumour that Blok's book of old but previously unpublished poems, *Za gran'yu proshlykh dney*, had been forbidden by the censor, but this turned out to be unfounded. Amazingly, books did continue to come out. On 30 July Blok received Rozanov's last work, published posthumously, *The Apocalypse of Our Time*, sent by the author's daughter from Zagorsk; on 7 August, his own collection *Iambs*, which he had dedicated to the memory of Angelina, was published by Alkonost, and earlier that summer *The Song of Fate*, with a very satisfactory cover by Golovin. Also brought out by Alkonost was the collection of articles on *Russia and the Intelligentsia* for which Blok had written a new introduction, explaining the terminology and historical context.

Amongst the few pleasures of the summer was the fact that Lyuba was freer than she had been the previous winter and could give him more of her time. Together they worked on Heine, went to the cinema, to the theatre, out to Strel'na where she watched him bathe in the cold sea. Nevertheless, writing to her sister on 10 August 1919, his mother said: 'What should I write of Dushen'ka? He's in a bad mood, tired from the disorder, the tyranny, the terror and everything else. . . . He is an extremely sensitive accumulator. . . .'[36]

As August came to an end and the committee meetings started up again, the problem of winter fuel began to loom large in Blok's life and diary. Pyast, who had been one of the first to break with Blok after *The Twelve*, called to return a manuscript and a book Blok had given him, still pointedly refusing to shake hands. He had recently suffered a second nervous breakdown and Blok was terribly sorry for him (*Z.K.* 473).

Almost unbelievably, the material situation was still getting worse. It had begun to look as though the Bolsheviks would lose the civil war. Blok still had to renew his exemption from call-up every month and the threat of requisitioning became acute. A document from M. F. Andreyeva stating that his personal library was the property of the theatre saved his books, but he had to beg letters from the detest-able Ionov and from Zinov'ev himself requesting the housing com-mittee to leave him his flat. On hearing of the proposal to place a sailor in the Bloks' spare room, Hippius remarked spitefully that it would have done him good to have a round dozen billeted on him, but Merezhkovsky rang up to offer a useful contact. 'Seems strange', Blok noted bemusedly in his diary. On 10 September a sailor and his wife actually came to 'look over' the flat but temporarily waived their claim on being shown *The Twelve*!

The first of the winter's deaths to affect Blok directly was the sui-cide of Leonid Andreyev. He wrote an article 'In Memoriam' (VI. 129–35, 29 October 1919). It was a sad account of two souls that had 'called to one another through chaos' but had never quite found each other:

One thing I know about him for certain: the really important Leonid Andreyev, who lived in the famous writer Leonid Nikolayevich, was infi-nitely lonely, unrecognized, and always facing out into the empty blackness of the window that looks over the islands to Finland, into the damp night, into that heavy autumn rain that he and I loved with the same love. . . .

(VI. 135)

September went by in concentrated work. Blok wrote the article 'On Romanticism' for the actors of the Bolshoy Dramaticheskiy—an article in which he developed his concept of romanticism as the essential, elemental spirit of culture, including Shakespeare and Plato among the great romantics and conceding only fifth-century Greece and seventeenth-century France altogether to classicism (VI. 359–71). He was still busy with work on Heine.

On 11 October he and Lyuba 'said good-bye to the sea at Strel'na' and Blok noted 'the first night of hoar-frost' (*Z.K.* 477). Winter came with sudden cold, still worse news from the front, more searches in the night ('in our flat, too'), the almost total cessation of all services (telephones, shops, and theatres, failing, closing, being shut down), and hunger more terrible than ever before.

Blok went on working. A typical entry in his diary this autumn reads: '*25 October*. Second act of *Othello*. Interesting argument with Monakhov and Yur'ev.—I saw up some furniture. In the night—change the position of the furniture.'

When Syunnenberg invited him to address the Free Philosophical Association he noted wearily: 'Is this the time?' but nevertheless read his piece on 'The Collapse of Humanism' at the opening evening. This time his hands did not shake. So apt were his words that to

Konstantin Fedin, a young disciple of Zamyatin's sitting huddled in the audience,

> ... it seemed that, filled with panic, we should have fled from the cell-like little room out into the slush of terror on the street, to flee, to cling to passing trams, to drag our sacks through the mud. But no one left while he was reading. Lofty he was, and fear did not envelop him but wreathed in swirling eddies about the soles of his feet and beneath them. And it was good that he had not taken off his greatcoat, and that his fingers evenly sorted through the pages of his manuscript, and that he was, as ever, unhurried and upright: for he stood high above all those whose only passion was how, in those dreadful days, to save their own skins.[37]

Indeed, the public appearance of so beloved a member of the old literary establishment at a time when the majority of his fellow Symbolists were living retired in their own corners—many, now that Europe was at peace again, desirous only to escape abroad—meant a great deal to the literary youth of his city. Blok, though he felt for individual cases, could not envisage leaving Russia. With great sympathy, he would quote Akhmatova's poem about the temptation to abandon Russia and to forget the shame and sorrow of the time, which ends:

> But I, indifferent and tranquil,
> Raised hands to ears to block it out,
> That no such unbecoming counsel
> My sorrowing spirit should pollute.[38]

Yet Anna Akhmatova, too, had refused to appear in public with Blok after *The Twelve*, and took no part in the life he now led. They met occasionally, as acquaintances.

The only person he could talk to as a fellow poet at his work with Vsemirnaya Literatura was Akhmatova's divorced husband Gumilev, whose poetry he did not admire and whose views he found intensely alien.[39] The hostility was mutual, but so was an element of respect. Rozhdestvensky loved to watch the two poets in conversation:

> ... They clearly did not like one another, but never allowed this any outward expression. Rather the opposite: their every conversation took on the character of a subtle duel of courtesy and irreproachable affability. Blok's interlocutor would shower him with elegantly ironic compliments. Blok listened unsmilingly and, with a particular cold clarity, rather more often than was strictly necessary, would pronounce the name and patronymic of his opponent, enunciating every letter, which in itself sounded almost like an insult.

Eventually, it would be Gumilev who gave up the argument, though patently irritated and unconvinced. He maintained that Blok was stubborn and ignorant of the most elementary laws of versification, but when Rozhdestvensky asked him why he continued to address the older poet so respectfully he replied: 'Well, what else could I do? Imagine yourself arguing with a live Lermontov!'[40]

Isolated, harassed, doubtful of the efficacy of his work, Blok was gradually losing even that sense of 'creative chaos' which had upheld him for the last two years. 'Why do they pay us for not doing what we ought to be doing?' he asked, staring over Gumilev's shoulder into the ruddy cold of the windswept sky beyond the window of their committee room. 'He did everything as if it were "real work". But at the same time he felt—never for one minute did he cease to feel—that it was not what he should be doing, not the real thing.'[41]

He still had the energy, though, to exchange verses with Chukovsky who had accused him, with high-toned comic pathos, of betraying the 'embraces of The Stranger' to ensure his fuel ration from Sovnarkhoz. To this, Blok replied with a vigorous jingle, 'On Bare Essentials':

> No, I swear, enough has Roza
> Preyed upon our scanty gains[kk]
> Believe, oh madman, it's not 'proza'
> That rations from on high yet rain
> Without which, in our place, von Posa
> Would surely have blown out his brains!
> But wilted prose is now the rose,
> The nightingales' enchantment wanes.
> No food in on our railway flows
> Because there are not any trains
> And even—since the heavy snows?—
> The electric current's failed again
> And no tram through the dark street goes ...
> In vain supply-lines we'd maintain ...
> Eastward and southward—nothing shows,
> Our city's going down the drain:
> So where, then, should the Sovnarkhoz
> The *blaue Blume* now obtain?

[kk] Roza Vasilievna ran a stall at Vsemirnaya Literatura where she sold food, soap, etc. to the writers at speculative prices. Blok, the least astute and suspicious of men, she cheated mercilessly, but since she was for long their only source of supply they continued to pay her, pillory her in verse, and observe with a feeling bordering on affection how she invariably occupied one of the best seats at all their functions, sleeping soundly in her best satin blouse through philosophy and philology, unable to resist a complimentary ticket to the most obscure lecture, the most recondite debate.

In this world, now sad and savage,
If you can find it—go and see,
And, having found it, call it cabbage,
Put it daily in your *shchi*
Ne vzyshi, chto shchi ne gusti—
Budut zhizhe vperedi . . .

6 December 1919
(III, 426–7)

Blok's 'romantic Pegasus' jogged along very smartly harnessed to the springless cart of comic verse. But after a second effort 'in the style of Bryusov' (VI. 427–8), even this spark faded.

12

Irony, and the remains of a genuine enthusiasm, a real desire to serve, saw Blok through the grind of his public life and the appalling physical hardships of that second revolutionary winter, but his home was gloomy. On the day after he read his paper on 'The Collapse of Humanism' at Volfil the electricity was cut off and he noted wearily: '*17 November*. How far can despair go? The little cupboard is broken up for firewood—my childhood, and Mama's' (*Z.K.* 480).

All that year, Blok had borne a part of his mother's anguish. Aleksandra Andreyevna's feeling of loathing for her husband grew: Frants Feliksovich was prematurely senile, and she could feel neither warmth nor compassion for him and reproached herself bitterly. She wrote to her sister:

> . . . you will never understand our[II] 'causeless sufferings'. In this we are alike, but each in his own way. You get up in the morning and love the world, whereas I get up and almost always, with rare exceptions, my first thoughts are of a noose, a rope, or some other means of putting an end to my existence. . . . I get up from my bed and move about out of habit and a sense of duty. Hatred of my husband—that is the only live feeling. I am cut through and through with it, as with a knife. I am repelled by his walk, figure, hands, gestures, temperament, all his *noises*.[42]

In a typical passage, which Blok himself might have written, she tells her sister,

> As to your not being needed in the world, your standpoint is not valid: I am no more needed than you. I am a burden on many people. Yet I go on living. Presumably it is the will of God. And apart from that people

[II] i.e., her own, Blok's, and Lyuba's.

live for *themselves*. You write of your sins. You *have* no sins. Therein is your sin, if you like.[43]

When Frants Feliksovich was ill it was Lyuba who nursed him, and towards the end of the year it was on her shoulder he wept as his last strength began to fail. Blok knew all this.[mm]

On 28 December, Maria Andreyevna, still living out of town in Luga, paid them a visit and Blok noted: 'Auntie came back from Mama—depressed, quite another person from the one who arrived yesterday and spent the night with us. I don't know how to help Mama, either' (*Z.K.* 484). At the end of the year he wrote: '... Frants, Mama—no way out. A symbolic act: on the day of the Soviet New Year I broke up Mendeleyev's desk' (*Z.K.* 484, entry for 31 December 1919),[nn] and on 13 January 1920: '... New Year—Lyuba and I alone together' (*Z.K.* 485).

January 1920 brought a slight material improvement. The blockade was lifted from the Baltic, peace made with Estonia, and there was an amnesty on death sentences. Blok's private life, however, went from bad to worse. On 23 January, Frants Feliksovich died, '... from a cold and my rotten nursing',[44] Aleksandra Andreyevna wrote to her sister. After the funeral, Blok took his mother to live with him and, on 23 February, having sold a good deal of furniture and many books, he and Lyuba moved into her smaller flat (no. 23 in the same building), abandoning their own at last to the patient sailor.

The funeral, the move, all these practical arrangements, were major undertakings:

They do everything for me, feed me, my room is beautifully arranged ... and Dushen'ka is attentive in his own way and takes care of me. Apart from which I see that I don't bother him, that he's even glad that I am here ready to hand, in better conditions. But Lyuba ... I can see that my presence is a burden to her, I can't do a thing right and either she does not answer me when I speak or answers resentfully. In a word, she can't bear me. And how well I understand that. I couldn't bear Frants. And it's the same thing. For the moment I'm still weak,[oo] haven't quite recovered and can't help her....

Perhaps I shall succeed in winning her over when she is calmer and the chaos in the flat subsides. Only I haven't much hope. If *I do not*, I shall

[mm] *Z.K.* for 3, 17, and 20 December 1919.

[nn] It is some measure of a new feeling of distance from the 'new era' he had so wholeheartedly welcomed that Blok had reverted unquestioningly to the old system of dates in his private life.

[oo] Shortly after the funeral, Aleksandra Andreyevna had had a bout of 'flu with a very high temperature.

have to think how to get away, where to. But for the moment we will
live as we are....[45]

Of course, they were civilized people and tried to make the best of
one another, but the atmosphere was thundery and as before it soon
led to Lyuba spending as much time out of the house as she possibly
could. For the moment, however, the main object was simply to
keep alive:

If you could see how crowded we are, how dirty everything is, how Sasha
and Lyuba have changed. Lyuba is pale, and her irritability can be explained
to a large extent by the general upheaval. And my Dushen'ka has grown
so thin and he has boils from nerves and lack of fats. His hand, leg, and
neck are bandaged.

... Dushen'ka had to go to the Commune, to the surgeon to get his dressings
changed yesterday. He has grown thinner, weaker.... Again he carried the
fuel up to the fourth floor ... then me, then the furniture and the books.
And overstrained himself, because he's not getting the right food, meat is
a rarity, fat of any kind—a rarity. And Lyuba has gone all quiet, and
pale....[46]

On 17 March 1920 Blok was subjected to his first really painful
blow in the course of his post-1917 literary duties. He had been writing an introduction to the works of Lermontov—of all poets the
closest to him in spirit—for Grzhebin, and it was turned down. Presumably he destroyed the manuscript, for it has not reached us; all
we know is that he wrote of the poet's prophetic dreams, of his search
for God—and that his article was judged unsuitable for the kind of
edition Grzhebin had undertaken to publish. Blok turned out
another which might have been written by any competent peda-
gogue but from then on 'his alienation from those with whom he
was obliged to sit in committee grew from month to month'. As
Chukovsky, who was present, remembered, Blok said nothing in
defence of his article, but his face simply 'grew sadder, more arrogant, more closed'. For the first time, he began to feel superfluous.

He was a poet and a creative artist and was not qualified to act as a com-
mercial traveller for ready-made ideas. But, as poets and creative artists,
writers were at that time of no use to anyone—they were valued as propa-
gandists of generally useful and easily comprehended knowledge.
    When he had understood that this was so, that as Blok he was of no
use to anybody, he withdrew from active participation in our work and
continued to sit through the committee meetings in silence.[47]

He began work on a companion volume to Lermontov—on Tyutchev—but soon abandoned it. In the intervals he continued his

endless, courteous argument with Gumilev, defending Symbolism,
attacking Gumilev's formalistic attitude to poetry as 'non-Russian'.
During the meetings he would joke quietly with Chukovsky, scrib-
bling parodies in verse and prose into his album 'Chukokkalo'.[48]

Between agony at home and increasing alienation at work, the
time passed heavily. For most of April 1920, Blok was ill and confined to the house. It was almost a relief: '*1 April*. Have at last given
in Lermontov to Grzhebin. A few thoughts of my own thanks to
the illness.' But now there was no rest at home, either: 'In the evening—horrors (I, Mama, Lyuba)' (*Z.K.* 490).

He returned to his revision of his first book of poetry and to work
on *Lightnings of Art* (the articles written in rough after his return from
Italy), for publication by Alyansky, who had also organized several
public readings for him in Moscow. He made arrangements to stay
there with N. A. Nolle-Kogan and her husband, the literary critic
P. A. Kogan, who were ready to help him in every way, even to
act as his agents in selling books.

13

On 7 May 1920, Blok and his young editor-entrepreneur left for
Moscow. Alyansky was in an agony of nervousness. He had seen the
sort of crowd who gathered to hear Mayakovsky in the Polytechnic
Museum where Blok was to give his first reading on 9 May, not
at all like the polite assemblies of refined Peterbourgeois to which
Blok was accustomed. The Moscow crowd was drawn from every
conceivable walk of life: they hooted and booed, cheered and bar-
racked the speakers, yelled out requests and questions. At the end
of the first half, a snowstorm of notes had descended on the stage
and in the second half Mayakovsky had answered questions contained in these screws of paper . . . 'which, as it appeared, had nothing
to do with the poems he had been reading but were on the most
general subject of politics, literature, and art. There were awkward,
even anti-Soviet questions, and a number dictated by vulgar curiosity. It was like a game of questions and answers, one in which
Mayakovsky had great expertise and which he presumably enjoyed.
He answered quickly, with a ready wit.'[49]

Alyansky took care to ascertain in advance that the Futurists, 'from
whom anything might have been expected', did not intend to create
any disturbance at Blok's reading. Nevertheless, there was every
reason to be anxious. Blok had not Mayakovsky's temperament, and

Chukovsky records how, on one occasion in Petrograd, having taken an unreasoning dislike to an individual in a large fur hat near the front of the auditorium, he had flatly refused to continue:

I begged him to get back on the rostrum, I said that there was only one man like that in the hat and it was no reason to penalize all the others, but looking at Blok's face I shut up. The whole face was trembling, the eyes colourless, the lines suddenly deeper.

'He's not the only one,' said Blok. 'Every single one of them out there's got exactly the same sort of hat!'

Still, we persuaded him to go on again. He came out frowning and instead of his own poetry, read out to the great confusion of those present the Latin verses of Politian:

> Conditus hic ego sum picture fama Philippus
> Nulli ignota mee gratia mira manus
> Artificis potui digitis animare colores
> Sperataque animos fallere voce Diu ...[50 pp]

The Petrograd audience had been indignant but orderly. In hot-headed, warm-hearted Moscow such a reaction might well have led to a near-lynching.

Approaching the Polytechnic, Blok and Alyansky became separated in the crowd round the door. To the younger man's intense relief, the poet's farewell glance over his shoulder as he was borne irresistibly forward in the scrum had been merry and encouraging. They came together again in the foyer—no less chaotic than the street:

In the room to which the manager led us Aleksandr Aleksandrovich was immediately surrounded by his Moscow friends who had come to shake him by the hand. And it is a moot point which moved and excited Blok the more—the recital he was about to give or this meeting with old friends.

I suddenly felt I wanted to hear Blok from the auditorium.

I forced my way back to the doors. When I at length managed to find a firm stance against the wall my anxiety for him came back in full measure. ... I looked into the faces of the people who had come to hear Blok and they looked to me exactly the same as the people I had seen at Mayakovsky's performance.... And now, ... the Muscovites were going to be shown

----

[pp] The Latin poem was inscribed on the tomb of Fra Filippo Lippi and Blok had translated it for the end of his *Italian Verses*. The lines quoted here from Chukovsky's account read, in Blok's translation:

> Here I lie, Filippo, a painter immortal for ever,
> The wondrous charm of my brush is on everyone's lips.
> By the skill of my fingers I could imbue colours with a soul
> And I could touch the hearts of the pious with the voice of God.

shy, quiet, modest Blok, reciting in front of a vast audience, to an unpredictable assembly of people.

When Blok came out on the rostrum he was met by applause that lasted so long he looked quite lost, turning back to the table behind him where the organizers of the evening were sitting: but they just smiled and clapped too.

Only when their palms were sore did the applause die down. The poet began his recital.

He read standing in the centre of the stage, both hands resting on the back of a chair. . . . Aleksandr Aleksandrovich read in his usual rather hollow voice, simply and quite quietly, almost monotonously as it seemed, without intonation. He recited as he did at home for his own friends and family. There were no external or internal techniques of recitation. And it was impossible to understand by what secret the poet riveted people's attention. . . . It was so quiet in the room you could hear the crowd breathing. . . .[51]

After the interval all Blok's friends who had gone backstage came out on to the platform behind him so that there was only a tiny space left for him to stand during the second half. From the auditorium the public surged up to the edge of the stage. The poet was surrounded by a living wall of people on all sides. A few notes fluttered on to the stage. One of the bystanders picked them up and quietly pocketed them.

Blok began to recite again. A young woman poet, Nadezhda Pavlovich, was sitting in the audience with Blok's old friend Knyazhnin. Deeply religious, the daughter of a judge, she was yet an ardent supporter of the Soviets and worked as secretary to Lenin's wife, Krupskaya. She remembered the occasion:

. . . the impassive, hollow, bitter voice was incorruptible. It was impossible to listen to it and experience only aesthetic pleasure. He brought each listener face to face with truth itself. . . . He had an all-too-acute sense of the forces that played in him himself and in us. The intonations of one who is older and in some way an initiate sounded more and more clearly in his verse. It seemed he had every right to say:

Oh, children, if you only knew . . .

. . . I was shaken by Aleksandr Aleksandrovich's poetry, by his whole personality, and by the suffering which was evident behind those wonderful verses.

Knyazhnin offered to take me backstage. I refused.

However, Pavlovich did ask Knyazhnin to show Blok some of her own poetry and the next time he read, at the Polytechnic Museum, she plucked up courage to be introduced.

In the entr'acte I went behind the scenes with Knyazhnin. The table and
the sofa were littered with flowers and notes. In the corner there was a
group of people arguing furiously. I caught single words, shouts: 'Russia',
'Bolsheviks', 'art on a new basis', 'the ninth wave'.

Blok stood at the window, pale, with a cold alienated face. He was clearly
not with us; people asked his opinion, came up to speak to him, he scarcely
answered. Seeing Knyazhnin he smiled and came towards us. At once he
said to me: 'I've read your verses. What do you want to hear from me?'
I didn't know what to answer. He said, 'I liked them, I recognize something
of myself in them, echoes of something I feel at home with.'

At that I got my courage back. 'That is a great joy to me, but it would
mean more to me if you could tell me what I do wrong. What ought I
to do? I'm only a beginner, you see, and I may never see you again.'

Then his face grew warmer....

Praising one line of verse he had found particularly evocative, he
invited her to come and see him in Petrograd: ' "I don't remember
the bad bits now. And I should like to talk to you, too. Will you
come to Petersburg?" '[52]

So, even in the midst of a personal triumph such as he had never
known before, Blok found time for the young, the obscure. The
Moscow trip put him on his feet again after that terrible winter. The
sun shone; the stalls in the street were laden with lily of the valley
and early lilac. Vyacheslav Ivanov came to listen to him and asked
him to read 'The Stranger'—an echo from that summer of 1906
when he had captured the heart of literary St. Petersburg with his
recital of the poem on the roof of the 'tower'. Now he seldom read
from the *Second Volume:* only 'A young girl stood in the church
choir singing', with which he often concluded his recitals.[qq] But
it was an unexpected bonus to think of nothing but art and poetry
for a few days, to meet all this good will, all those old friends: Bal-
trushaytis, Chulkov and his wife, S. A. Polyakov, Vyacheslav
Ivanov.

Aleksandra Andreyevna, who for all her difficult character had a
great capacity for rejoicing for others, wrote a glowing account of
the visit to her sister, obviously based on Blok's own:

...today Dushen'ka returned from Moscow. I feel myself a happy mother.
He was eleven days in Moscow, gave three readings. A landslide of enthusiasm. At the end, on the square outside the Polytechnic, he received an ovation. The table before which he stood to recite was invariably loaded with

---

[qq] He had mistrusted, since 1910, the undisciplined mysticism of the 'Stranger' period,
but towards the end of his life he came actively to dislike 'people who preferred the *Second
Volume*'.[53]

flowers, lily of the valley, lilac. And there in the room itself people sent him notes, poems dedicated to him. And not just young girls—there were men who came up with tears in their eyes to shake him by the hand.... Amongst others a shock-headed man came up to him, just out of prison, and said that he had recited Blok's verses to three men condemned to be shot and that afterwards they had gone calmly to their deaths....

Detochka was living all the time as a guest of Nadezhda Aleksandrovna Kogan. They fed him very well, he even looks a bit fuller in the face. He travelled there and back with Alyansky, who took upon himself literally all the intolerable part, and they had a carriage to themselves in an international train there and back. He had dinner with Stanislavsky who still firmly hopes to stage *The Rose and the Cross* in the autumn, although half his troupe is in the Caucasus." They gave him money in advance and at the readings he also earned quite a lot. He visited the Kublitskys and actually spent the evening with them. He says that there are no people so alien, i.e. that for him they are the most alien people imaginable ... they have adapted themselves wonderfully, and are getting on very well. Bread and butter they get from Safonovo. They seem to have enough of everything. A fine flat, terribly satiated and infinitely distant. They received him *with all courtesy*. Dushen'ka came home in a very mellow frame of mind. More than anything, I am struck by the modesty with which he tells about his own successes.

Then, always strictly fair, she adds: 'Lyuba was not unkind to me once in Sasha's absence....'[54]

" In White-occupied territory with no immediate possibility of returning to Moscow.

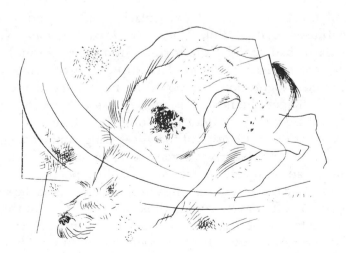

CHAPTER XI

Coda

(May 1920 – August 1921)

A writer is a man marked of fate; he is put into the world
to lay bare his own soul before the spiritually hungry . . .
Perhaps it is the writer's duty to give them his whole soul,
and this is particularly true of the Russian writer. Perhaps
why Russian writers die so young, perish or simply come
to the end of all they have to give is that nowhere is
literature so vital as it is in Russia, that nowhere else does
the word pass into life and become bread or stone as it does
in our country. That is why Russian writers have less right
than anybody else to complain of their fate; for good or for
ill, they are listened to, and whether or not they are understood at least half depends on them.

(v. 246–7, 1908)

1

Petrograd must have seemed particularly cold, poverty-stricken,
and unenthusiastic after Blok's success in Moscow, mellowed and
tempered as it had been by the sorrows and losses through which
he and his friends had all come. The impression of being needed,
of an immediate emotional response to his poetry from a wide
audience of all ages, did not last long. Alyansky organized readings
for Blok and Bely that summer for Volfil, but these were orderly,
highbrow occasions with none of that life-giving contact with a new
public that Moscow (older yet always warmer and less formal than
Petersburg) had been able to accord the failing poet.

The summer passed much like the summer before, and the summer
before that. As often as he could, Blok would get away for whole
days to the edge of the sea, or to wander again through the ruined
parks. Sometimes Knipovich, the young girl with eyes like 'great
dull agates' who had first entered his life in 1918 and had since

become a devoted friend to Aleksandra Andreyevna, would accompany him. 'He loved to sit on the back platform of the tram dangling his feet,' she remembered. 'Like all good men, he had a lot of the little boy in him. It would give him real enjoyment to see a squirrel run across his path, to feel the sun.'[a]

Knipovich, like Alyansky, was a blessing to the Blok household, for she brought with her something of the unimpaired, self-effacing energy of generous youth; she loved them all and she was one of the few people to 'get on' with both Lyubov' Dmitriyevna and Blok's mother.

Another devoted female friend, of a very different sort, was Nadezhda Aleksandrovna Pavlovich, the young Moscow poet, who appeared at Blok's flat on 22 June with—to Blok's delight and her own lasting confusion—two large green caterpillars on her broad-brimmed hat. Having tenderly removed the caterpillars, he discovered that she had come not only to talk about poetry, but to discuss the founding of a Petrograd branch of the Poets' Union.

The Poets' Union, dominated in Moscow by Valeriy Bryusov and having on its presidium such names as Vyacheslav Ivanov and Boris Pasternak, had been founded, in the first place, 'simply to ensure the physical continuation of such live poets as were left, not to let them die, and gradually to find means of giving them some material security and obtaining for them at least the most elementary conditions of work (fuel, clothes, paper, food).' Beyond this the organization also had ideological aims but these, at the time, were entirely secondary.

Pavlovich had come, in part at least—for she was deeply and unconcealedly in love with Blok and had been even before she met him— as an emissary of Bryusov. Of the foundation of a Petrograd branch of the Poets' Union, Blok said:

'I don't know if anything will come of that. All of us here are very different and it may be we won't find a common language. But a lot of people are in need of material help, we need regular rations [payki]. We need a writers' bookshop. A Union should be able to organize all that. And then, perhaps, there will be new people, as Bryusov hopes.... If we begin with some material care for our poets, something more may come of it.'

To judge from Pavlovich's recollections of the Bloks' flat, the chaos of the move was a thing of the past:

At that hour it was light and sunny in the white room with two windows opening on to the Pryazhka. Everything was somehow extraordinarily

[a] From an interview with the author, Moscow, 1961.

tidy. Behind a screen was Blok's bed, between the windows stood a small writing table and against the wall a cupboard on the top of which were stacked various editions of the poet's works. It was a passage room with a door on to the hall and into Lyubov' Dmitriyevna's room and it was also used as a dining room. In summer the dining table was moved nearer to the window, in winter to the white-tiled Dutch stove.

Blok also had a separate study, '. . . a narrow room with one window. Darkish wallpaper. An old writing desk at which he had written most of his works. On the wall, a black tray with yellow roses from Shakhmatovo and faded Shakhmatovo photographs. . . .'

Pavlovich did not like Lyubov' Dmitriyevna, whom she found at once prosaic and unpredictable, nor could she perceive any traces of beauty in the raddled actress's face, the rather clumsy, heavy movements. The first evening she came, Lyubov' was patently bored and sat with absent eyes, giving little heed to the talk going on around her, not trying.[b] Blok's mother, on the other hand, became very dear to the young Moscow poet: she was prepared to talk for hours on end about her 'Detochka', and Nadezhda Aleksandrovna asked nothing better than to listen. Also, Aleksandra Andreyevna was a loyal and wise friend, and she drew young people like a magnet.

She knew her son through and through, in all his weaknesses and passions, but also in all his loftiness of soul. Smiling, she would say: 'There is only one anxiety he has not caused me—he never flew in an aeroplane. But otherwise—I've always been afraid for him, either he'd drown like Sapunov, or he'd go walking along a railway line and start gazing at something, a girl perhaps . . . and a train would come and run him over, or something else of that nature.'[1]

Even his day-long absences at the seaside were a torment to Aleksandra Andreyevna and it was with a sort of submissive wonder that she wrote to her sister that both he and Lyuba considered these expeditions essential to his health.

Indeed, the first few days of July 1920, when a fierce heat wave came to Petrograd ('There's a rumour that the heat has gone up to 40°'), brought Blok a greater well-being than he had known for a long time: 'heat and bliss'; 'intoxication'; 'drunk with nature' (Z.K. 495). With his sunburnt face, high boots, and white sweater, Blok began to look more and more like a Scandinavian skipper, and once, to his pleasure, was actually mistaken for one when standing in a queue for apples.

[b] Alyansky gives a very different picture, of someone who habitually 'set the tone' for a lively and laughing table.

On 22 June Blok told Gumilev about the Union of Poets and after some preliminary discussion the first meeting was called on 4 July on the premises of Volfil. Blok made a brief opening speech (VI. 433–4), introducing N. A. Pavlovich to explain how things were done in Moscow. The aims of this 'rather monstrously named' society, he said, were purely material:

We are making no attempt to achieve internal unity; in the first place, such a unity, if it is possible and necessary, will come of itself and every attempt to bring it about by constraint can only put it off still further; in the second place, we all have in common certain purely professional requirements— and why should we not unite so as to make these more easy to satisfy?

(VI. 433)

Blok began this work with two adoring aides-de-camp, Pavlovich and Vsevolod Rozhdestvensky, the young poet who had rushed up to shake his hand after the first reading of *The Twelve*. As ever, he could not maintain a purely formal attitude. His speeches at the evenings devoted to Sergey Gorodetsky and Larissa Reysner (4 August 1920) and to Mikhail Kuzmin (29 September 1920), were carefully thought out and delicately worded so as to give no offence to nervous poetic individualism. Without trespassing on their right to follow their own paths, without trying to sound new notes of revolutionary emotion which would have rung false in the general atmosphere of dogged exhaustion and ironic disillusion, he could yet say that 'although it is almost impossible to breathe the air of the present', it was still possible 'to breathe the air of contemporaneity, that thin air that smells of the sea and of the future' (VII. 437).

To Kuzmin, who was to outlive him by many years,[c] he said tenderly, 'We are all ... worried about how to preserve you. To lose a poet is very easy, but to acquire a poet is very difficult; and there are very few poets like you in the world today' (VI. 439). As the good steward of a great inheritance, Blok found words for Kuzmin which his colleagues quite failed to find for him:[d]

In you we would preserve not the civilization which, in essence, never really existed in Russia (and God knows whether it ever will!), but something of that Russian culture which was, is, and will be. For neither you yourself nor any of us can really imagine what a wonderful thing it is that when we are gone new people will be born for whom your 'Alexandrian

[c] Mikhail Aleksandrovich Kuzmin died on 3 March 1936 in Leningrad.
[d] After his death, Zamyatin told Gorky, in a bitter outburst: 'Blok's dead. We're all of us to blame—unforgivably.'[2]

Songs' and your 'Chimes of Love' will sound again—those same waves of music that washed round and nourished and stung with salt so many of us in the evenings and the nights on the Tavricheskaya Ulitsa, for instance, in the tower of Vyacheslav Ivanov.... We all know what a difficult thing art is. We know how capricious and whimsical is the soul of the artist and we wish from our hearts that eventually a milieu should come into being where the artist will be able to be capricious and whimsical, as he needs to be, where he will be able to remain himself, without being an official, a member of a collegium, or a scholar....

(VI. 440)

The Poets' Union was soon inundated with applicants. Again, Blok could not deal with them formally but examined each one as a human being and a poet. Rozhdestvensky preserved some of his 'recommendations', and tells how, amongst many others, there came an elderly man in a worn-out soldier's coat, smelling strongly of spirits and quite obviously not altogether in his right mind. Calling Blok his 'dear brother', he recited 'a whole fountain of verses' and left with him a fat exercise-book, scribbled over with a mass of verses in microscopic handwriting with lines going in all directions.

Aleksandr Aleksandrovich read it carefully from beginning to end and sent in the following recommendation:

'A. S. seems to me not devoid of talent. There are well-chosen words and images, ... but everything about him is very mixed up. I have some acquaintance with him personally and, apart from this, he writes to me in a letter that it would mean a lot to him to be accepted in our literary circle and particularly, into our Union, which may "help him to become more like a human being again". After such letters with a touch of "Dostoyevshchina" (and there's something of Captain Lebyadkin in the verses) I cannot pretend to be objective, and so I would very much ask my comrades to judge in this matter on the basis of the poetry alone, as we should do.'[3]

Blok's recommendations were not always so charitable, but each was personal, based on a thorough study of the individual case.

Nevertheless, he was not really at home in the Poets' Union. The majority of the members were admirers and imitators of Gumilev, convinced formalists and politically well to the right of their chairman. They began by getting rid of Blok's supporters: Maria Shkapskaya, Nikolay Otsup, Konstantin Syunnenberg, Rozhdestvensky, and Pavlovich. Blok looked on this as a happy opportunity to resign himself, but Gumilev, who—as Blok protested to various people— was as strong-willed as Gorky,[e] led a delegation to his flat and 'forced'

[e] 'However much they dislike one another,' he noted a few weeks later, 'they are alike

him to remain (*Z.K.* 504, entry for 13 October 1920). Reluctantly, Blok consented, only to be voted out of office a few months later^f by 5 votes to 4 when not all the members were present. Naturally, he was fed up and flatly refused to have anything further to do with the Union, though it is to be doubted whether he took the event as tragically as his supporters tended to do.[4] To be relieved of an obligation was, by that time, an unmitigated boon.

Blok rounded off his long polemic with Gumilev in the article 'Without Divinity or Inspiration' (VI. 174–84). In this article, not published until four years after both their deaths (as Chukovsky remarked, Russia never bothered to stop and find out which was the Symbolist, which the Acmeist), Blok deployed a kind of lazy sarcasm to demolish the Acmeists' claim to be a separate movement, advocating a larger 'synthetic' culture rather than a multiplicity of schools. The true poets were Akhmatova, whose muse he saw as 'ascetic' and 'monastic', and Mayakovsky. It was they who mattered, not their Futurism or Acmeism. As to Gumilev and his followers, he concluded:

... if only they would untie their own hands, and become, even if only for a moment, tough and rough, hideous even, and so more like their native, crippled, trouble-scorched, devastation-scoured country! But no, they won't and they can't; they want to go on being distinguished foreigners....

(VI. 183–4)

2

In this last year of his life, Blok thought back over a great deal of old ground and confirmed, for himself, that his way in art, from the *Verses about the Most Beautiful Lady* to *The Twelve*, had been consistent. He told several people that, of all his poetry, the most significant for him was still the *First Volume*.[5] In looking back to Vladimir Solov'ev, the prophet of the Eternal Feminine and the teacher of his youth, he perceived many links between the beginning of his road and its ending. On 15 August 1920, in a talk to Volfil on 'Vladimir Solov'ev in our Time', he said:

Our time is often compared to the time of the great French Revolution ... the more events unfold before us, the more I am confirmed in the

---

in that neither knows anything of tragedy, of the "two truths", ... both are (north) eastern....' (VII. 371).

^f In February 1921.

thought that such a comparison is not enough—it is overcautious, in some ways even cowardly. More and more clearly there seem to shine through our time the features not so much of a transitory epoch as of a new age, our time is reminiscent not so much of the end of the eighteenth and beginning of the nineteenth centuries as of the first centuries of our era.

Solov'ev he saw as a 'man who had found no shelter between the enemy camps' and was still not acknowledged by either side because he was a bearer of some part of that third force, of that new world which, Blok believed, was advancing through all the chaos of the present 'dark ages'.

Now, well and truly embarked upon the 'exhaustingly slow' dark ages of transition, all that remained was to set one's teeth and to go on. At the theatre, where, in spite of mounting differences with Andreyeva, the poet's work continued to afford him many reward-ing moments, they were rehearsing *King Lear* in a translation re-edited that spring by Blok and Zamyatin. On 3 August 1920, Blok introduced his actors to the play in a 'dry, bitter, adult speech' which echoes the old Tyutchev theme of courage in the face of a hopeless struggle: 'Why was all this written?' he asked in the peroration and answered his own question:

In order to open our eyes on those bottomless pits which do exist in life and which it is not within our power to avoid. But, if there are such fright-ful abysses in this life, if it really does happen that there are times when, although vice does not conquer and does not triumph, virtue does not triumph either, for she has come too late—must we not then look for another and more perfect life?

Not one word of this crosses the lips of that cruel, sad, bitter artist Shake-speare. Courageously, he ends on a full stop, on the exhortation: 'The weight of this sad time we must obey.' After all, he is an artist, not a priest, and he seems to repeat the ancient words: 'Learn through suffering.'

(VI. 409)

When, at one of the last rehearsals of *Lear*, the company decided to scrap the scene of the blinding of Gloucester, Blok objected, saying: 'Our time is very like the sixteenth century. We are quite capable of watching the most cruel scenes.'[6] He would not admit the ultimate triumph of evil and death, but neither would he conceal from himself or others their temporary victories.

His forebodings for the immediate future appear clearly in Rozh-destvensky's account of an informal reading at the Poets' Union:

... he read not more than five or six poems. Everyone was silent, enchanted by his voice. And when no one expected him to go on, Aleksandr Aleksandrovich began the last: 'A Voice from the Chorus.' His face, calm up till then, was distorted by an agonized line by the mouth, his words rang hollow, as though cracked. With his whole body he leant a little forward in his chair, the heavy lids drooped over his eyes, half-hiding them. The final words he pronounced almost in a whisper, with an anguished effort, as though forcing himself.

We were all overcome with a feeling of hopelessness. No one wanted to go on reciting. But Blok was the first to smile and said in his usual voice:

'Most unpleasant verses. I don't know why I wrote them. It would have been better for those words to have remained unsaid. But I had to say them. The difficult must be overcome. Beyond it will be clear day. You know what,' he added, seeing that no one wanted to break the silence, 'let's have something from Pushkin. Nikolay Stepanovich, it's your turn.' ...[7]

'Why was all this written?' 'I don't know why I wrote them. It would have been better for those words to have remained unsaid. But I had to say them.' For Blok, it was as if the great works of literature had some absolute pre-existence, as though the writer literally recorded truth.

When, earlier that summer, Gumilev, in a lecture on Blok's poetry, had said that the end of *The Twelve* seemed to him to be artificially stuck on and the apparition of Christ a 'purely literary effect',

Blok had listened, as always, with no change of expression, but at the end of the lecture said thoughtfully and carefully, as though listening for something:

'I don't like the end of *The Twelve* either. I would have liked it to be different. When I'd finished, I was surprised myself: Why Christ? Could it really be Christ? But the more I looked, the more clearly I saw Christ. And that's when I made a note of it for myself: unfortunately, *Christ*. Unfortunately, Christ and no one else.'[8]

Now, in the autumn of his last year, it came almost as a surprise to hear that real poetry was still being written. Mandelstam, returning at the end of October from the South and a brief sojourn in White captivity, recited wonderful verses 'arising from dreams—very unusual, altogether confined to the sphere of art ... his way from the irrational to the rational (the opposite of mine)' (VII. 371). But Blok had no dreams now. To Chukovsky he said: 'All the sounds have gone silent. Can't you hear that there aren't any sounds any more?'[9] and to Pavlovich he compared himself to the hero of Kipling's *The*

---

[8] The last words, often omitted when this passage is quoted, are in Russian 'K sozhaleniyu, imenno Khristos'.

Light That Failed, 'Only he went blind, whereas I have gone deaf—for ever.'[10] 'It would be blasphemous and false to try by any rational process to recall sounds in soundless space,' he explained in a letter.[11] It was a state which overcame him gradually in the course of that last year, but he did not yet give up all hope of a return to poetry. Zorgenfrey, an old and dear friend, tried more than once to talk to him about it:

... but his explanations were broken and far from clear. 'The air has become very thin ... so many responsible, absorbing projects ...' 'It would not be quite honest to blame everything on these hard times,' he said at the end of 1920. 'It's partly a very exacting attitude to myself that prevents me from writing.' At the very beginning of 1921 he felt, in his own words, 'as though something were beginning to stir in him, parts of the run-down mechanism were beginning to tick over again'; in early spring he began to speak with conviction of the approach of other conditions which might make creative work possible—but it was then he was taken mortally ill.[12]

3

Indeed, after a difficult autumn and a miserable New Year which Lyuba met with her fellow actors, the cast of *The Merry Wives of Windsor* (there were whispers that she was enamoured of one of the clowns), Blok rallied once again, made a courageous effort to resume his poetry, and produced his greatest statement about art: 'On the Calling of the Poet'.

A growing tendency to use strong-arm methods in the world of art had been edging the poet into a more and more nonconformist attitude throughout that winter. Defending Yur'ev, an undisciplined actor of whom he heartily disapproved but whose colleagues wished to have him 'called to order by the police', he 'found the strength' to put across his own point of view 'that art is incompatible with any forcible measures whatsoever on the part of the powers that be' (VII. 385).

The next long entry in his diary after this incident confirms what he had always thought but had now come to understand in a new way:

... Conscience encourages man to seek what is best and helps him at times to reject the old, comfortable, and dear but *dying and disintegrating* for the sake of the new which at first is uncomfortable and not dear, but which promises fresh life.

On the contrary: beneath the yoke of oppression man's conscience falls silent; then it is that people lock themselves up in the old; the more open the oppression, the more firmly do people lock themselves up in the old. That's what happened to Europe under the yoke of war, to Russia—now.

(VII. 388, entry for 24 December 1920)

At Vsemirnaya Literatura too, Blok's silent irritation against authority reached new peaks. He recorded how, returning from one of their sessions,

I was angry, I committed a sin: a little boy was sliding along towards me on the frozen pavement as they always do (it's a long way from Mokhovaya Ulitsa and there was a frost and a strong wind); I pushed him aside so hard that he fell over. I am ashamed, forgive me, Lord.

(VII. 390)

After the New Year, he had had to call in Dr. Pekelis. His heart was giving him trouble and the long walks from his home to Vsemirnaya Literatura and to the theatre were becoming a torment because of a pain in one leg—which he ascribed to 'gout'.

Now, however—fighting down a growing malaise of mind and body—he was seeking to concentrate on Pushkin, about whom he had been asked to speak on the 84th anniversary of the poet's death. Pushkin, Blok felt, would help him on two fronts: to confound the Acmeist conviction that poetry was a matter of formal calculation and, at the same time, to establish that it cannot be subjugated to outside authority. 'What the poet is trying to do', he said, 'cannot be defined in advance, either by himself or by anyone else. . . . Even a cab driver hired from his stand for an hour wants to hold the reins himself and resents a back-seat driver' (VII. 399, entry for 21 January 1921).

On 11 February, he wrote into the album of the Pushkin House his last complete poem, his last tribute to Petersburg, and his last statement of hope: in the fiery distances that poets of his generation had once perceived from the banks of the Neva, it was not the 'brief illusion' of these present, 'oppressive days' that they had conjured from the 'blue-pink mists', but 'centuries to come'. Apostrophizing Pushkin, Blok wrote of that 'secret, inner freedom' of which Russian poetry as a whole had always sung, and called on him to reach out a hand to his successors 'in the ill weather' of the present time. For the joyful sweetness of Pushkin's verse was the inspiration of all their youthful visions: 'And that is why, in the evening hour,/About to walk away into the dark of the night/From the white square of the Senate/I quietly make my bow to him.'

Afterwards, these lines took on the solemnity of 'last words'. It is doubtful whether they were intended as such. In January, Blok had fallen into a veritable trough of depression ('Evidently, I am ill: I am tired, my head doesn't work properly, terribly depressed ..., black dreams, and also very ominous half-dreams, half-waking' (*Z.K.* 400–1). Yet this was not yet surrender. It was the other side of the final struggle, for precisely at this time Blok made an attempt to return to *Retribution*, comparing his struggle to wrench Pegasus to his will to a fight with a real wild horse:

> And you will go where I require,
> Though bit be champed and reins in foam
> Till evening cool and welcome fire
> Fill me with thoughts of rest and home ...
> But now, tempestuous dream, obey!
> Your will to man, your master, bend....

And, for a little while, Pegasus bent his fiery head and bore the poet once again: but not out into the 'shining emptiness' of his demonic dreams nor down the complex labyrinths of past history. He cantered gently into 'a corner of paradise', bought for a song long years ago, where every blade of grass was familiar, every tree and shrub alive with memory. An old woman came out on to the porch to greet them, shielding her face from the sun:

> And there, at once, all was familiar
> As though it always had been so,
> The grey house, and the tall French windows
> The annexe, and the coloured glow
> Of stained glass, red and blue and yellow,
> As it had been from year to year.
> So with an old, stiff key they opened
> The house. The old man bore the child
> And nothing could disturb the stillness—
> The crying babe, dogs barking wild,
> All fell to silence, just the buzzing
> Of one fly bumbling at the pane,
> And then the fly itself ceased humming,
> And on the pale blue wall again
> The sun threw leafy, dancing shadows,
> And winds beyond the window rocked
> The hundred-year-old lilac bushes
> In which the old house drowned, leaf-locked.
> And then a sound, half-heard and muffled,
> As though the stillness still could sing

> Or church bells, ringing in the distance,
> Or the unceasing roar of spring ...
> And out after that distant ringing
> (That brought news of a world reborn)
> The father, mother, daughter, grandson,
> And even their good dog were drawn....

The last lines of poetry Blok wrote were neither the trumpet call of *The Scythians* nor the elegant Alexandrian farewell of the Pushkin House poem, but these stanzas about Shakhmatovo, dated January, May, July 1921, and some scattered attempts at Chapter 3 of *Retribution* (May–July 1921) which invoke death and birth, and, at the very last, the *mea culpa* of all great spirits:

> I have not done ...
> What I ought to have done ...
>
> (III. 473)

Now, however, one more public triumph awaited Blok: on 13 February 1921 he made his Pushkin anniversary speech 'On the Calling of the Poet' (VI. 160–8). In it, he appealed to the officials into whose hands power was now flowing to leave the poet that 'secret freedom', that 'peace and independence' of which Pushkin had written with such longing before he himself succumbed to the stifling atmosphere of a repressive era. But Blok ended on a high note, and a gloriously hopeful one:

We are dying, but art will remain. Its final aims we do not know, nor can we know them. It is one in essence and indivisible.
    I would like, just for fun, to pronounce three simple truths:
    Art cannot be filed away into compartments; it is wrong to call anything art except that which merits the name; in order to create a work of art, one must have the know-how.
    On those three merry maxims of common sense, against which we have so often offended, we may take our stand in the joyful name of Pushkin.

(VII. 168)

There were no hidden meanings behind Blok's words, neither were they, as is frequently implied, the fruit of alienation and withdrawal. He was still thoroughly embroiled in Soviet literary politics, endeavouring to keep Ionov and other overweening literary officials in their place, defending the views of Zamyatin and Alkonost that art cannot be regimented because it is about the future, fighting vigorously for the practical right to variety and 'caprice' in life and publishing as well as in thoughts and dreams.[13] As far as day-to-day politics went, if he involved himself at all he fought openly and from within the given situation, maintaining to the end his contempt for intellectual 'criticism from behind the fence', whether this emanated from outside Russia or from those within the country sufficiently arrogant to disclaim responsibility for what was happening. In his Pushkin speech, however, Blok rose above the conflicts of the day to make a broad statement about art rather than about the petty concerns of politics.

Many said the speech was his apotheosis, but this is not so. *The Twelve* was his apotheosis: the supreme expression of his great and simple idea of a Third Force, a sound from some other shore beyond all the warring clash and clamour of this agonizing and terrible world. Only few had ears to hear it. 'On the Calling of the Poet' was a gentle speech composed of comprehensible words, delivered in a minor key to bewildered people in the dusky twilight of a fearsome night. But the speaker, as always, spoke of the free morning, of the green garden beyond the dark corridor, and this time he was heard and understood by all.

4

March and April 1921 were very hard months. The Kronstadt rising had reduced the city again to a state of siege; then to a state of war. Blok's breathing became laboured, his knee hurt, and he had begun to walk with a stick. His heart troubled him more every day. He and Lyuba had so-called 'hot rations' (*goryachiye payki*), which meant they received a reasonable allowance of meat and fat, but they were chronically short of money, and could afford no extras.[h] Nobody thought of vitamins, but Blok did consciously miss wine, and tobacco was a luxury he could ill afford. Dr. Pekelis, consulted again, had ventured the opinion that Blok was suffering from arteriosclerosis.

The human relationships in the poet's life were hopelessly confused and painful. He had faced up to the fact that his wife and mother would never live together in harmony and had told them so, loving both. He, who had always sought refuge in his home, now referred to their flat as 'that place', 'that house'. Every now and again, the strain between the two women would explode into ugly scenes: once, literally, over a pail of slops. Always, the atmosphere was strained and gloomy.

[h] It was at this time, for instance, that Blok's mother had to sell Frants Feliksovich's briefcase to buy potatoes on the market.

Del'mas he sometimes felt he loved but their relationship was not settled. He had been seeing more of her since Lyuba's retreat into her own affairs the previous autumn. She always had something interesting to tell him, and had preserved her glamour and gaiety. Blok still found her 'seductive to the last degree' (*Z.K.* 503). And his mother wrote to her gratefully:

To understand so well how to care for the writer and poet in him, to know with such tact when to leave him alone, when to come close: such insight can only be dictated by real love. No one is able to cheer him up and to make him see things in a reasonable light as you do.[14]

But Del'mas could not take upon herself the care of a sick man, nor was there any question of her doing so.

'At the beginning of the Kronstadt days' Blok broke off relations with Pavlovich, what she herself called her 'passionate but superficial' curiosity proving unbearably intense: this was painful to both, for her understanding of his poetic destiny had been profound and brave, and she was very young, and very unhappy. Also, she had brought about a reconciliation between him and Pyast. Blok had grown accustomed to having her around and she was one of the few people he could still eat with.[i] When they met in a queue for *payki*, she looked so stricken that he could not resist going up to her and silently pressing her hand.

'My illness progressed,' he was to recall that summer; 'weariness and depression were eating me up. In our flat I never opened my mouth' (VII. 420). Walking with a friend, Blok had asked him suddenly: 'Do you want to die?' The friend, taken by surprise, stammered something incoherent. 'I want to—very much,' Blok had said simply.

Strange though it may seem, Blok had been deeply upset by the initiation of the New Economic Policy, or at least by its results. After three years of deprivation such as the citizens of Petrograd had endured under war communism, it was painful to see the recrudescence of inequities and vulgarity. Alyansky, who was as fond of Aleksandra Andreyevna as of Lyuba and Blok, tells how they had been sitting talking when Blok's mother's voice suddenly trailed off. She had tried to go on but suddenly pressed her fingers to her temples and, in a weak, scarcely audible voice, had said: 'You know, something's happened to Sasha.' Maria Beketova had told Alyansky that there was some telepathic contact between son and mother. Now he was convinced of it, for even as Aleksandra Andreyevna gazed

---

[i] Eating in front of strangers brought on a kind of nervous spasm.

fixedly at the door of her room the outer door of the flat had banged
and a few moments later 'a pale and extremely distressed Aleksandr
Aleksandrovich burst into her room'. ... Not noticing Alyansky,
Blok had spoken directly to his mother as though in answer to some
wordless question:

'... when I was coming home just now, on the streets, out of all the gate-
ways, doorways, shops, out of every cranny, everywhere—crawling noises
of the foulest vulgarity, repulsive foxtrots, pseudo-gipsy music. I thought
these noises had disappeared from our life long ago—but they're still going
on.... Mama, surely it's not all coming back....'[15]

Alyansky had never seen the poet so upset and, looking back, it
seemed possible to him that this March evening had marked the beginning of his friend's serious nervous deterioration.

5

On 7 May 1921, the first day of Easter, well supplied with *kulich*
and other Easter fare, Blok set out again for Moscow, this time with
Chukovsky and Alyansky. He was in good spirits, or so it seemed,
and Chukovsky kept him laughing all the way, though he would
occasionally stir uncomfortably in his seat and straighten out a painful leg.

For Chukovsky he had conceived something like an affection. The
great gangling man with his marvellous gift for children's poetry
was writing a book about him in collaboration with Zhenya Knipovich.[16] Moreover, at Blok's last poetry reading in Petrograd, on 25
April, Chukovsky had made a bad introductory speech, and had had
the grace to realize it. Blok had been terribly sorry for him and had
sat by him throughout the interval comforting him, 'and so we were
photographed together', Chukovsky recalled, 'I looking absolutely
crushed and he kindly and attentive, like a good doctor'.

The gaiety on the way to Moscow, however, was a momentary
reaction to the change of atmosphere. Blok afterwards said that Chukovsky, who had been in sparkling form, had 'talked away' the pain
in his leg.

The purpose of the visit was to help Blok recuperate: financially,
physically, and morally. He was met by N. A. Nolle-Kogan in one
of the Tsar's cars, commandeered by Kamenev and sporting a large
red flag: a macabre beginning that did nothing to restore the festive
atmosphere of the previous year. The poet's friends had not realized

they had to deal with a dying man. Their chief anxiety was to see he earned enough money to allow him to spend the summer at a sanatorium and to rest a little. The Moscow Art Theatre was still promising to stage *The Rose and the Cross* 'next autumn', but this time would offer only a small advance. Eventually, with the help of the Kogans, he signed a contract with another theatre, for 5,000,000 roubles of which then and there he received 1,000,000 in advance. These vertiginous sums,[j] together with a last-minute attempt by Stanislavsky to reserve the play for the Moscow Art, and offers of additional readings and of state publications which smacked of charity and which 'thank God I managed to refuse' (VII. 419), confused Blok and increased the nightmare feeling of weariness.

The readings themselves were not unmixed triumphs. At one of them, a literary critic in the audience called out that Blok was a living corpse. It was a put-up job. Pasternak and Mayakovsky had heard that a row was brewing, but arrived too late to stop it. Mayakovsky, however, was privately in agreement with the critic and afterwards wrote coldly of a man reciting the old 'gipsy' verses and other poetry which had no reality for the world of 1921, a man clearly waiting for death. Alyansky recalled that, though Blok reacted quite calmly at the time, the hostile barracking stuck in his head and he talked about it on the way back from Moscow.

From the House of the Press, where he had been told he was already dead, he went on to the Italian Society, and some of the public followed him. It was Easter, it was May, the weather was southern, there was a scent of bird-cherry, Blok walked alone recalling his *Italian Verses* which he was about to recite. No one went up to him for fear of disturbing his concentration. There was something moving in all this. Along the moonlit streets walked the solitary poet and behind him, at a considerable distance, with flowers in their hands, reverently followed these people who *loved* him, and it was as if they felt they were walking with him for the last time.

At the Italian Society Blok had perhaps his greatest success: the *Italian Verses* brought out a richness in his voice and he read them in a slow, sorrowful sing-song.

On the whole, he managed to disguise his weariness pretty well. Only Andryusha Kublitsky, the deaf and dumb cousin who had always been specially attached to him, was unusually affectionate when he called to see his relatives. Blok was moved, the more so as the Kublitskys' circumstances had taken a dramatic turn for the worse and they could no longer be numbered among the 'satiated'.

[j] By the beginning of 1921 prices were 16,800 times what they had been in 1913.

One incident, however, shocked Chukovsky:

He had been reciting his verses in the Writers' Union and afterwards we returned to the crowded flat where he was putting up. We sat down to drink tea, and he retired to his room; then, a minute later, reappeared, saying:

'How strange! How confused I'm getting. I quite forgot we had been to the Writers' Union and I was just going to sit down and write my excuses that I couldn't come.'

That frightened me. It was not yesterday he had been at the Writers' Union, not the day before, but today, ten minutes ago.[17]

At the station in Petrograd, Lyuba met him, not in an Imperial car but with a shabby borrowed horse-drawn cab: 'I wanted to cry, one of the few live feelings in all this time (for so long; a shadow of feeling)' (VII. 420).

'Sasha returned from Moscow', Lyubov' Dmitriyevna recalled in her memoirs:

There was our piercing tenderness, the joy of seeing one another again after the strain of that unhappy winter. After the first few hours his mood grew dark and oppressed again, and when on one of the days before the 17th I persuaded him to come for a walk with me through our favourite places, along the Pryazhka to the Moyka, to the crossing and back via the Franco-Russian factory (it was a sunny day, the young grass was growing, and the Neva was blue—everything that we love), he did not smile *once*, neither at me, nor at all the rest; that could not have happened before.[18]

6

From 17 May onwards, Blok was confined to bed or to the house almost the whole time. In June, he suddenly felt a great longing to see the sea again, and Lyuba went with him on the tram. They had a pleasant quiet day but when he got home he went to bed and, after that, did not go out any more.

Aleksandra Andreyevna had gone with her sister to Luga, wanting to give 'the children' a rest from her presence. That winter Lyuba had told her that she permeated the atmosphere with her anxiety, and she knew this to be at least partly true.

Lyubov' Dmitriyevna, in her turn, seeing that her husband was seriously ill, was conscience-stricken. She gave up her theatre, her clowns, and all her life outside, devoting herself to him entirely. In May he had taken leave of Zhenya Ivanov, who came on a day when he felt so ill he could scarcely speak, and of Del'mas, making the sign of the cross over her and giving her messages for his mother.

To Chukovsky, on 26 May, he wrote the famous letter quoting ironically from one of his own parodies: 'And so, "We keep fit to this day" is something I can say no longer. She's gulped me down at last, that filthy, grunting, own-mother of mine Russia, like a sow her piglet ...' (VIII. 537). After this, he wanted to see no one but Lyubov' and Alyansky, who helped him sort out his diaries and albums and brought him news of his books, proofs, new publications, and as much literary gossip as he could still enjoy. All through the second half of May and almost all through June, Blok worked at his archive, sitting for an hour or two at a time with his papers, then lying down to rest for a while on the sofa, then forcing himself to go on. When Alyansky found him destroying some of his diaries, he appealed to Lyuba to stop him. 'I had the impression that he was out of his mind.' But she replied: 'Oh no, how can you say so? He has been going through them for the last two days....'[19]

Towards the end of June Blok had to take to his bed and his doctor now insisted on his earlier advice that he be sent abroad to a sanatorium.[k] Blok, who had resisted this idea up till then, at last consented, but the permission was delayed because of some unwise things Bal'mont had had to say to the Western press about life in Soviet Russia when he had been given a similar permit; when greater pressure was applied, a visa came through for Blok but not for his wife. Gorky was still pleading their case in Moscow and Knipovich was on her way to collect Lyuba's permit on the day Blok died.

In the meantime, as he wrote to his mother (VIII. 539), Blok was taking a 'vaudeville quantity' of medicines. At times his mind was clear, at others he would have terrible attacks of apathy or anger. On one occasion he deliberately broke all the bottles of medicine (which was extremely difficult to get hold of), and on another took the poker from the stove and smashed in the head of the Apollo Belvedere that always stood on his writing desk.

Lyubov' took this 'growing habit of smashing things' as a mere exacerbation of his normal highly nervous state, and wrote that it was not accompanied by any signs of 'clinical abnormality'. It was a greater grief to her that, after he grew seriously ill, Blok could not take refuge with her in that world of childhood where 'we always felt full of light and hope':

When Sasha fell ill he could no longer find sanctuary there. It was in the

---

[k] On 28 May 1921 Lyuba had written Blok's mother that the Writers' Union in Moscow was trying to get leave for Blok to go abroad but that this was 'a secret from Sasha who still does not want to!'[20]

middle of May he drew a caricature of himself—'from there'—and that was the last. His illness took this relief from him too. Only a week before he died, opening his eyes from a kind of coma, he asked me suddenly in our language why I was all in tears—the last tenderness.[21]

On 1 August, Lyubov' warned Alyansky, who still came almost every afternoon to see what he could do to help although he had not been admitted to the sick man for some ten days, that Blok would like to see him.

Aleksandr Aleksandrovich lay on his back. Desperately thin. The features of his face had grown so sharp that I hardly recognized him. The face was surprisingly calm. The voice was weak, quite lacking in resonance....
    He asked me to sit down and as always asked me how I was doing, how my wife was, what was the news. I began to tell him some tale but soon noticed that his eyes were fixed on the ceiling and he was not listening. I broke off and asked how he was feeling and whether he needed anything.
    'No, thank you, I have no pain, only, you know, I don't hear anything at all now, as though a great wall had grown up. I hear nothing at all any more,' he repeated.... I understood that he was not speaking of any physical deafness.

And so the young 'American', as Blok had so affectionately called him, sat on, fearing to speak or move lest he break down and cry. Blok appeared to have drifted off into a doze, but, when Alyansky got up to go, he opened his eyes, gave a helpless little smile, and said quietly: 'Forgive me, dear Samuil Mironovich, I'm so tired.' 'Those were the last words I heard from him. I didn't see Blok again.'[22]

On 2 August, Lyuba wrote Aleksandra Andreyevna:

Pray again, and again and again.
    Yesterday Sasha was very bad, today he is a little easier—what is there now but all our prayers? Pekelis still insists there is hope, I too have prayed myself into a state of hope....
    There can still be no talk of your coming—precisely because the situation is critical we must not 'try' anything. But afterwards everything will be all right; how could I possibly be the same as I was before his illness? If God saves him—he will be happy with me, and you too. But now, he is never in a healthy state of mind.[1] He reacts to me in a different way, as

---

[1] The Russian is 'A on ved' teper' vsyë vremya ne v zdorovom soznanii'. Lyubov' Dmitriyevna in her memoirs expressly denies that Blok was actually out of his senses at any time. The doctor's insistence on the possibly beneficial effect of a 'shock' and 'a complete change' also suggests acute depression rather than madness. Khodasevich was told by Nadezhda Pavlovich that Blok had gone mad[23] and was under the impression that she had come straight from the poet's flat, but in fact Lyubov' Dmitriyevna admitted no one but Alyansky, Knipovich, the doctor, and, the day before he died, his mother and Del'mas.

Blok with Korney Chukovsky after the latter's unsuccessful
introduction, at the poet's last Petersburg reading, 1921.

Blok on his deathbed.

Blok's funeral, August 1921.

The grave of Aleksandr Blok.

though I were a stranger, although he gets my name right, how can he want to see anybody? Or even think of anything real?... For the moment just pray for him, pray for his salvation.[24]

Lyuba later told Aleksandra Andreyevna that, in these last days, Blok murmured constantly: 'God forgive me'. In spite of the morphia prescribed by the doctor he raved through the nights, suffering mentally and physically. The pain about his heart made it hard for him to breathe and he could get no rest.

At last, Aleksandra Andreyevna came up from Luga and was allowed to be at her son's bedside. When she entered his room he recognized her and appeared to take her presence for granted. There was a long-standing pact between them that, should one be mortally ill, the other would not conceal the fact. It was a pact of that devastating candour, that absolute integrity which had made their whole relationship at once so uncomfortable and so unique.

'Mama, am I dying?' he asked.

Courage failed her and she struggled for words of hope. Coldly, he turned his face to the wall, and she tiptoed out to spend the whole night on a stool before his closed door. He was in great pain from his heart, crying out and groaning.

In the morning, he called for her and, asking her to stand on one side of the bed and Lyuba on the other, stretched out and died.

7

Early that spring, Blok had told his mother that only the death of one of them could solve their dilemma. She had rejected the ever-present temptation of suicide, aware that this would be final defeat for them all. Now that Blok himself had provided the most drastic, most unexpected solution, Lyuba's animosity evaporated and she found strength to care for the wispy little grey-haired woman for the few years she had left to live.[m] As for Aleksandra Andreyevna, she had always said: 'It's impossible not to love Lyuba.'

[m] Aleksandra Andreyevna lived entirely in the hope and expectation of death and her thoughts were constantly with her son. Nevertheless, she found some joy still in the many young people who came to her both to hear her talk of Blok and for her own sake—and in the flowers they brought her. Lyubov' Dmitriyevna was, according to Maria Beketova,[25] a good daughter to her until her death, though later, in her memoirs, she was to refight the old battles, as she was to reassess her marriage, still struggling to assert her right to a life of her own outside Blok and his poetry. At the time, however, Lyuba wrote to her sister that the weight of sorrow was not unbearable because, quite simply, her life had come to an end together with his.

Now, together, they awaited Sasha's friends—and prepared to make the final gift of this man each had loved with so private and deep an affection. For the first time in her adult life, Lyuba formalized her relationship with God, feeling that it would be unfitting to mourn Blok alone in empty churches, as she had prayed as a young girl. It was Aleksandr Blok who must be mourned, not just her Sasha, and she achieved dignity and a generally acceptable form by insisting on strict traditional observance."

The first person to be informed was Alyansky, who took it upon himself to circulate the news and to arrange for the funeral. Zhenya Knipovich, who was at the station about to board the train for Moscow, telephoned before leaving and, on hearing what had happened, returned post haste. '... Aleksandra Andreyevna sat at his bedside and stroked his hands ... when she was called out to receive fresh arrivals, she said to me: "Go in to Sashen'ka" and those words, that I had heard so often in his life, took away the sense of death. ...'

Knipovich helped Alyansky with the funeral arrangements, herself choosing the place 'near his grandfather's grave in the Smolensk cemetery, underneath an old plane tree', where the poet was buried.'[26] She went to fetch Nadezhda Pavlovich. By the time they returned the body had been laid out in traditional fashion.

The white rainwashed light of Petersburg in the window and a long table set diagonally. Blok dead, half-covered by a white muslin sheet (they had not yet bought the grave clothes); the cold of death was not yet on him. The beautiful, stern face, the face of the Last Judgement. The hands folded and in the pale, yellowish fingers an icon of the Mother of God. Later, Lyubov' Dmitriyevna replaced this by the image of Hagia Sophia. As yet there were no wreaths or flowers or weeping crowds. Only a few roses in a tall vase on the chest of drawers by his bed and the spluttering of a newly-lit *lampadka*.

Then friends began to come.[27]

All day people came. Somebody took a photograph. Yuriy

" The question is bound to arise, how would the poet himself have reacted to this? One can only quote from his letter to N. A. Nolle-Kogan, to whose child he had been asked to stand godfather: 'Understand how I say this, I say it with pain and despair in my soul; but I cannot go to the Church yet, although she is calling me' (VIII. 532, 8 January 1921). Lyubov' Dmitriyevna, it may be fairly presumed, would not have acted deliberately against her husband's wishes.

° Regrettably, Blok's body was not permitted to lie undisturbed beneath the white wooden cross and the clover. Subsequently his remains were removed and re-interred beneath a heavy black marble tomb in the literary Volkovo cemetery. Though undoubtedly done with the best intentions to honour the memory of the poet, this was, as Pavlovich says firmly in her memoirs, 'everything Blok didn't like, everything he didn't want'.

Annenkov made a drawing. A young girl whom nobody knew brought the first flowers, four white lilies.[p]

All night, in true Orthodox tradition, the Psalter was read over the dead man. Next morning, Pavlovich records, the face was calmer and more mild.

Meanwhile, notices had been posted all over the town, and the next day more people came. Olga Forsch, among the first, also made a drawing; so did Lev Bruni and Lyuba's mother, Anna Ivanovna Mendeleyeva, but those who came on that day remember a corpse, not Blok. Akim Volynsky came, the father of Russian 'decadence'; Ivanov-Razumnik; Zamyatin; Kuzmin; Somov; Benois; and many others. There was a queue on the stairs and out into the street and the little flat was crowded; the air grew heavy with the scent of flowers and incense.

On the day of the funeral, 10 August 1921, the process of reconciliation continued. Andrey Bely, Vladimir Pyast, Vladimir Hippius, Zhenya Ivanov, Zamyatin, and Zorgenfrey bore the open coffin out into the August sunshine. 'Down the narrow, curving, rather dirty staircase ... across the courtyard. By the gateway out in the street a crowd was waiting. . . . All that remained of literary Petersburg. And only there did it become evident: how few remained.'[29]

Lyubov' Dmitriyevna walked steadily, supporting Blok's mother. Del'mas, tactful as always, walked quietly beside Pavlovich. But it was not only the women who wept. All the way across Petersburg and the Vasil'evsky Island where he had been born Blok's friends carried him, with the hearse plodding empty and unwanted behind.

> In a silver coffin we bore him
> Alexander, our pure swan,
> Our sun extinguished in torment.

So Anna Akhmatova, full of dread presentiment for her ex-husband, Gumilev, arrested with many others but a few days before Blok's death, mourned the older poet. It was only one of a deluge of memorial poems, of memorial speeches and articles. Akhmatova's poem begins with the cryptic line: 'Our Lady of Smolensk holds fête today,' and the church and graveyard were full of flowers, for the funeral happened to fall on the Feast Day of their patron. At

[p] The appearance of the girl was noted by several people. In her memoirs, Nina Berberova, then a very young poet just making her literary début in Petersburg, recalls how she saw the announcement of Blok's death in the Writers' House and, seized with 'a feeling of sudden and sharp orphanhood such as I never again experienced', went straight out to buy the flowers and on through a part of Petersburg where she had never been before to find Blok's flat.[28]

the church, the choir of the Mariynsky Theatre sang Tchaikovsky's liturgy.

... More and more flowers were brought. Girls whom nobody seemed to recognize came up to the coffin, kissed the dead man and walked away, containing their tears. From the right, from somewhere high above us, broad sunbeams slanted down upon the coffin and upon the crowd.[30]

At the end of the service they carried him out into the sunshine and, beneath a plain white cross, consigned his body to the poor, autumnal soil of his native city.

Principal Sources for Volume Two
Reference Notes
Select Bibliography
Index

PRINCIPAL SOURCES FOR VOLUME II

This list comprises the principal sources, published and unpublished, for Volume Two, with the shortened forms by which those sources cited frequently are referred to in the Reference Notes which follow. Other sources less frequently drawn on are cited in full in the notes.

The two major repositories of unpublished Blok material in the Soviet Union are the Tsentral'nyy Gosudarstvenyy Arkhiv Literatury i Iskusstva (Central State Archive of Literature and Art), Moscow (cited as TsGALI), and the Institut Russ-koy Literatury (Institute of Russian Literature) (Pushkin House), Leningrad (cited as IRLI). The late N.P. Il'in also supplied much manuscript material which will now have passed into the keeping of the State.

I BY ALEKSANDR BLOK

PUBLISHED

Cited as

Sobraniye Sochineniy v vos'mi tomakh, ed. V. N. Orlov, A. A. Surkov, K. I. Chukovsky (Moscow-Leningrad, 1960–3) — *S.S.*

Zapisnye Knizhki, ed. V. N. Orlov, A. A. Surkov, K. I. Chukovsky (Moscow, 1965) — *Z.K.*

Pis'ma Aleksandra Bloka, with introductory articles by S. M. Solov'ev, G. I. Chulkov, A. D. Skaldin and V. N. Knyazhnin (Leningrad, 1925) — *Pis'ma A. Bloka*

Aleksandr Blok. Pis'ma k zhene, introduction and notes by Vl. Orlov, *Literaturnoye Nasledstvo*, no. 89 (Moscow, 1978) — *Pis'ma k zhene*

Pis'ma Aleksandra Bloka k rodnym, ed. M. A. Beketova (Leningrad): vol. I (1927); vol. II (1932) — *Pis'ma k rodnym*

Pis'ma Al. Bloka k E. P. Ivanovu, S. prilozheniyem pisem Al. Bloka k M. P. Ivanovoy i 'Petersburgskoy poemy' Bloka, ed. Ts. Vol'pe, preparation of text and commentary A. Kosman (Moscow-Leningrad, 1936) — *Pis'ma E. P. Ivanovu*

UNPUBLISHED

Letters to his wife Lyubov' Dmitriyevna Blok *née* Mende-leyeva, 29 Nov. 1901–20 July 1917. Arkhiv A. A. Bloka, TsGALI. F.55, Op. no. I, ed. kh. nos. 97–105. Now published with a few cuts in *Pis'ma k zhene*.

7 letters to L. Ya. Gurevich, 1907–16. Arkhiv L. Ya. Gurevich, IRLI. 19.814 (XXXV b 3)

Letters to A. V. Hippius, 1900–15 (copies). Arkhiv A. A. Bloka, IRLI. F.654, Op. no. I, ed. kh. no. 419

Letters to E. P. Ivanov and M. P. Ivanova. Arkhiv E. P.   *Cited as*
Ivanova, IRLI. F. 662, nos. 71, 86
4 letters to A. M. Remizov, 1913–18. Arkhiv A. M. Remizova,
IRLI. F. 256, Op. no. 1, ed. kh. no. 33
Letters to Anna Akhmatova; Fyëdor Sologub; El'tsina Rozalia
Semënovna (copies). Arkhiv A. A. Bloka, IRLI. F. 654, Op.
no. 1, ed. kh. no. 422
Zapisnye Knizhki 1–49 (nos. 13, 15, 19, 34–8 and 40–3 missing).
Arkhiv A. A. Bloka, IRLI. F. 654, Op. no. 1, ed. kh. nos.
321–60. Mainly published.
25 drawings. Arkhiv A. A. Bloka, IRLI. F. 654, Op. no. 1, ed.
kh. nos. 167–8
Album with photographs of ancient Egyptian, Greek and
Roman art and Western art 1909–11, and an album of repro-
ductions of western European painting. Arkhiv A. A. Bloka,
IRLI. F. 654, Op. no. 1, ed. kh. nos. 401, 402
2 albums of postcards: (1) Italy, Berlin, Antwerp, Ghent
(Flemish pictures), Bruges, Heyst-sur-mer, Revel, Bad
Nauheim, and 3 postcards of Vrubel's 'Demon'; (2) Brittany,
Paris, Bad Nauheim, Shuvalovo, Ozerki; circus posters
(1912). Arkhiv A. A. Bloka, IRLI. F. 654, Op. no. 1, ed. kh.
nos. 403, 404

II   OTHER SOURCES

PUBLISHED

M. A. Beketova, *Aleksandr Blok. Biograficheskiy ocherk* (Peters-   M. A. Beke-
burg, 1922)   tova, 1922
——*Aleksandr Blok i ego mat'* (Leningrad–Moscow, 1925)   M. A. Beke-
                                                            tova, 1925

Andrey Bely, 'Vospominaniya o Bloke', *Epopeya* (Moscow–   A. Bely,
Berlin), nos. 1, 2, 3, 1922   *Epopeya*
——*Vospominaniya ob Aleksandre Aleksandroviche Bloke*, with an   A. Bely, *Vospo-*
introduction by Georgette Donchin (Letchworth: Bradda   *minaniya*
Books, 1964). Reprinted from *Zapiski Mechtateley* (Peters-
burg, 1922)
Aleksandr Blok i Andrey Bely, Perepiska, ed. V. N. Orlov   *Perepiska*
(Moscow, 1940)
L. D. Blok, *Byli i nebylitsy*, text prepared by I. Paul'mann, intro-   L. D. Blok,
duction and commentary by L. S. Fleyshman, *Studien und*   *Byli i*
Texte, no. 10 (Bremen: Verlag K-presse, 1977)   *nebylitsy*
Blokovskiy Sbornik (Tartu): I, ed. V. Adams, B. Egorov, Yu.   *B.S.*
M. Lotman (responsible editor), D. E. Maksimov (1964);
II, ed. Z. G. Mints (responsible editor), V. I. Bezzubov, Yu.
M. Lotman, D. E. Maksimov (1972)
Uchenye Zapiski Tartuskogo Gosudarstvennogo Universiteta.   *Trudy*
Trudy po russkoy i slavyanskoy filologii (Tartu): vol. IV (1961);
vol. XI (1968)
Zapiski Mechtateley (Petersburg: Alkonost), 1919–22, nos. 1–6   *Z.M.*

UNPUBLISHED   *Cited as*

M. A. Beketova, 'Shakhmatovo. Semeynaya Khronika' (unpublished reminiscences), 1930. Arkhiv M. A. Beketovoy,
IRLI. F. 462, no. 4
——'Dnevnik.' Arkhiv M. A. Beketovoy, IRLI. F. 462, no. 1
L. D. Blok, Letters and telegrams to Blok, 22 Nov. 1901–
18 July 1917. Arkhiv A. A. Bloka, TsGALI. F. 55, Op. no.
1, ed. kh. nos. 159, 163, 164, 166, 167
—— 65 letters and 1 telegram to Al Bely. Arkhiv A. Belogo,
Manuscript Room, Lenin Library (Moscow). Bel. 9.18
—— 26 letters to Blok's mother, A. A. Kublitskaya-Piottukh,
1907–10. Arkhiv A. A. Bloka, IRLI. F. 654, Op. no. 7, ed.
kh. no. 24
——'I byli i nebylitsy o Bloke i o sebe' (unpublished memoirs).   L. D. Blok,
Arkhiv A. A. Bloka, TsGALI. F. 55, Op. no. 1, ed. kh. no.   memoirs
520. (Copy in the possession of the author, mainly published,
as *Byli i nebylitsy*)
G. I. Chulkov, 7 letters to A. Bely and 1 postcard, 1905–7, 1917,
1925. Arkhiv A. Belogo, Manuscript Room, Lenin Library.
Bel. 25.12
N. Chulkova, 'Vospominaniya o Bloke'. In Chulkova's possession, Moscow, 1964, and (Moscow, 1974) in the collection
of N. P. Il'in
L. A. Del'mas, Memoir about her relations with Blok, in the   L. A. Del'mas,
collection of N. P. Il'in. Partially published as 'Moy golos   memoir
dlya tebya', *Avrora* (Leningrad), 1971, 66–72
Ellis (L. L. Kobylinsky), Letters to A. Bely, 1907–11. Arkhiv A.
Belogo, Manuscript Room, Lenin Library, Bel. 25.31
S. M. Gorodetsky, 3 letters to Blok's mother, 7 March 1906–
23 Aug. 1921. Arkhiv M. A. Beketovoy, IRLI. F. 462, no.
166
Z. N. Hippius, Letters to A. Bely, 1902–10, 1917–18 (some un-
dated), Arkhiv A. Belogo, Manuscript Room, Lenin
Library, Bel. 14.6
E. P. Ivanov, Letters to Blok, 8 Apr. 1904–17 July 1920. Arkhiv
E. P. Ivanova, IRLI. F. 662, no. 42.
—— Letter to V. N. Dyukova, written from Shakhmatovo,
summer 1910. In the collection of N. P. Il'in
—— 'Mat' i syn' (unfinished study). In the collection of N. P.
Il'in
A. V. Kartashev, Letters to A. Bely, 26 Nov. 1905–5 Feb. 1917.
Arkhiv A. Belogo, Manuscript Room, Lenin Library. Bel.
17.8
N. A. Kluyev, Letters and postcards to Blok, 19 Feb. 1908–
1916. Arkhiv A. A. Bloka, TsGALI. F. 55, Op. no. 3, ed. khr.
no. 35
A. A. Kublitskaya-Piottukh, 20 letters to A. Bely. Arkhiv A.
Belogo, Manuscript Room, Lenin Library. Bel. 18.5

A. A. Kublitskaya-Piottukh, Letters to E. P. Ivanov, June 1906   *Cited as*
et seq. Arkhiv E. P. Ivanova, IRLI. F. 662, no. 60–2

—— Letters to M. P. Ivanova, 20 Sept. 1907–1922. Arkhiv
A. A. Bloka, TsGALI. F. 55, Op. no. 1, ed. kh. nos. 534–
44

—— 68 letters to M. A. Beketova and 2 to Annushka, 1915–
1921. Arkhiv A. A. Bloka, IRLI, F. 654. Op. no. 7, nos. 16,
17, 18

D. S. Merezhkovsky, 24 letters to A. Bely, 1904–9. Arkhiv A.
Belogo, Manuscript Room, Lenin Library. Bel. 19.9

N. A. Pavlovich, Manuscript of chapter on Angelina Aleksandrovna Blok and the Belayev family. Partially published in
Prometey (Moscow), no. 11, 1977, 243–6

Pyast (V. A. Pestovsky), 3 letters to A. Bely, 13 Apr. 1908 and
2 undated. Arkhiv A. Belogo, Manuscript Room, Lenin
Library, Bel. 21.36

A. M. Remizov, Letters to A. Bely, 1905–12. Arkhiv A.
Belogo, Manuscript Room, Lenin Library. Bel. 22.5

V. V. Rozanov, Letter to Blok, 19 Feb. 1909 (copy in Blok's
hand) (published *B.S.* II). Arkhiv A. A. Bloka, TsGALI. F.
55, Op. no. 3, ed. kh. no. 55

S. M. Solov'ev, Letters to A. Bely, 1908–9, 1910. Arkhiv A.
Belogo, Manuscript Room, Lenin Library. Bel. 26.1–5, 6,
8, 9

V. P. Verigina, Unpublished reminiscences of L. D. Blok. Lent
by the author

REFERENCE NOTES

All works cited are by Blok unless otherwise attributed.

CHAPTER I

[1] Letter to his mother of 10 Apr. 1908, *Pis'ma k rodnym* I, 203.

[2] L. D. Blok, *Byli i nebylitsy*, 61–5.

[3] Letter to his mother of 18 May 1908, *Pis'ma k rodnym* I, 211.

[4] Cf., for instance, *S.S.* IV, 148–9; V, 323; VIII, 265.

[5] *On the Field of Kulikovo* was first published in the almanac *Shipovnik* (Moscow), no. 10, 1909; the commentary was added in the 1912 *Sobraniye Stikhov*, vol. III. Cf. *S.S.* III, 587.

[6] Letter to his mother of 24 July 1908, *Pis'ma k rodnym* I, 220.

[7] For an earlier reaction to Tolstoy's 'I Cannot Keep Silent', cf. Blok's letter to his mother of 18 July 1908 (*S.S.* VIII, 241).

[8] Letter to his mother of 4 Aug. 1908, *Pis'ma k rodnym* I, 222.

[9] A. A. Kublitskaya-Piottukh, unpublished letter to E. P. Ivanov of 28 Nov. 1908. Arkhiv E. P. Ivanova, IRLI.

[10] Z. N. Hippius, 'Moy lunyy drug', *Zhivye litsa* (Prague, 1925), 37.

[11] L. D. Blok, unpublished letter to Blok's mother of 12 Nov. 1908. Arkhiv A. A. Bloka, IRLI.

[12] For Mendeleyev's influence on Blok, cf. A. Ekinov, 'D. I. Mendeleyev v zhizni i tvorchestve Aleksandra Bloka', *Russkaya Literatura* (Leningrad), no. 1, 1950, 156–60.

[13] N. Kluyev, unpublished, undated (*circa* 19 Feb. 1908) letter to Blok, no. 1. Arkhiv. A. A. Bloka, TsGALI.

[14] Id., undated letter to Blok, no. 2.

[15] Id., undated letter to Blok, no. 5.

[16] Id., undated letter to Blok, no. 4.

[17] O. Deshart, Introduction to *Vyacheslav Ivanov. Sobraniye Sochinenyy* (Brussels, 1971), I, 119.

[18] VI. Pyast, *Vospominanya o Bloke* (Petersburg, 1923), 67.

[19] Letter to his mother of 30 Nov. 1908, *Pis'ma k rodnym* I, 236.

[20] Cf. also D. S. Merezhkovsky, 'Intelligentsiya i narod', *Rech'* (Petersburg), 16 Nov. 1908.

[21] Cf. G. Chulkov, 'Memento mori', *Rech'*, 22 Dec. 1908, and the same author's 'Aleksandr Blok i ego vremya' in *Pis'ma A. Bloka*, 112–15.

[22] Cf. *Rech'* and *Slovo* (Petersburg), both for 27 Nov. 1908, for reports of the discussions of Blok's paper at the closed session of the Religious-Philosophical Society on 25 Nov. Blok himself considered *Slovo* the more accurate (cf. letter to his mother of 30 Nov. 1908, *Pis'ma k rodnym* I, 236).

[23] For Blok and Vengerov see 'Iz neopublikovannykh pisem A. Bloka k S. A. Vengerovu', ed. N. T. Panchenko, *B.S.* II, 333 ff. and *S.S.* VIII (index), 644.

[24] L. D. Blok, unpublished, undated letter to Blok's mother of December 1908. Arkhiv A. A. Bloka, IRLI.

[25] K. I. Chukovsky, 'Aleksandr Blok', *Lyudi i knigi*, vtoroye dopolnennoye izdaniye (Moscow, 1960), 520–1.

[26] Z. N. Hippius, op. cit., 39–40.

[27] K. I. Chukovsky, op. cit., 522.

[28] Letter to his mother of 17 Mar. 1909, *Pis'ma k rodnym* I, 251.

CHAPTER II

[1] Lucy E. Vogel, *Aleksandr Blok, the Journey to Italy* (Ithaca, N.Y., and London: Cornell University Press, 1973), 69–73. The quotation from Blok is here given in Dr. Vogel's translation.

[2] O. Elton, *A Second Book of Russian Verse*, ed. M. Bowra (London, 1947), 70 and elsewhere; J. Stallworthy and Peter France, *The Twelve and Other Poems* (London, 1970), 93–4; R. Kemball, 'Some Metrical Problems of Russian-English Verse Translation (with special reference to Blok and Akhmatova)', Schweizerische Beiträge zum VIII. Internationalen Slavisten-kongress in Zagreb und Ljubljana, Sept. 1978 (Bern–Frankfurt am Main–Las Vegas, N.M., 1978), 128–9.

[3] Cf. for instance Lucy E. Vogel, op. cit., 98.

[4] Cf. Vl. Orlov, 'Gamayun', *Druzhba Narodov* (Moscow), no. 9, 1977, 116. This work, chapters from a new life of Blok published in nos. 9, 10, and 11 of the periodical *Druzhba Narodov*, reached the author only when making the final revisions to the last chapter of the present biography.

[5] See *Pis'ma k rodnym* I, 268–70. In all, Blok wrote his mother three letters from Bad Nauheim (25 June, 27 June, and 16 [29] June, the last already bearing the Russian as well as the European date), none of which is published in the eight-volume *S.S.* A complete collection of Blok's letters would run into many volumes, but a two-volume *description* of his correspondence is now in preparation by three Russian archives: TsGALI, IRLI, and the Manuscript Room of the Lenin Library. Cf. *Aleksandr Blok Perepiska*, Annotirovannyy Katalog, ed. V. N. Orlov, compiled by N. T. Panchenko, K. N. Suvorova, and M. V. Charushnikova. Vypusk I, *Pis'ma Aleksandra Bloka* (Moscow, 1975).

[6] A. Remizov, *Akhru—Povest' peterburgskaya* (Berlin–Petersburg–Moscow, 1922), 24.

[7] E. P. Ivanov, unpublished letter to Blok of 13 July 1909, Arkhiv E. P. Ivanova, IRLI.

[8] D. E. Maksimov, 'A. Blok. Dvoynik', published in the collection *Poeticheskiy stroy russkoy liriki* (Leningrad, 1973), 211–35, and (as 'Ob odnom stikhotvorenii "Dvoynik"') in the book *Poeziya i proza Al. Bloka* (Leningrad, 1975), 144–74.

[9] In the article 'On the Present State of Russian Symbolism' (*S.S.* v, 425–36), originally read as a lecture to the 'Society of Lovers of the Artistic Word' on 8 Apr. 1910. Very considerable extracts from this article have been translated into English by Sir Cecil Kisch in *Alexander Blok, Prophet of Revolution. A Study of his Life and Work* (London, 1960).

[10] K. S. Makovsky, 'Aleksandr Blok', in *Na Parnasse Serebryannogo Veka* (Munich, 1962), 150–1.

[11] Makovsky returned to this old wrangle in a series of articles written for the newspaper *Russkaya Mysl'* (Paris), nos. 927 (19 July), 1956; 980 (22 Sept.), 1956; 1812 (15 Mar.), 1962, and in the book *Na Parnasse Serebryannogo Veka*, where he accuses Blok of—among other things—'insufficient knowledge of the Russian language' (op. cit., 153).

[12] Cf. K. I. Chukovsky, *Nat Pinkerton i sovremennaya literatura*, 2-oye izdaniye (Moscow, 1910).

[13] Cf. V. P. Verigina, 'Vospominaniya ob Aleksandre Bloke', *Trudy* IV, 311, 310, 349.

[14] M. A. Beketova, 1925, 150–1.

[15] Cf. F. F. Fidler, *Pervye literaturnye shagy. Avtobiografii sovremennykh russkikh pisateley* (Moscow, 1911). In 1915, at the request of S. A. Vengerov, Blok made substantial additions to this first 'Autobiographical Note' for Vengerov's *Russkaya Literatura XX veka*, vol. II (Moscow, 1915). He also deleted some paragraphs (cf. *S.S.* VII, 7–16, for the Vengerov text; ibid., 433–4, for the deleted passages).

[16] Letter to his mother of 24 Oct. 1909, *Pis'ma k rodnym* I, 276–8.

[17] These pieces have been translated into English by Lucy E. Vogel, op. cit., 182–313.

[18] Letter to his mother of 17–18 Nov. 1909, *Pis'ma k rodnym* I, 284–5.

[19] Letter to his mother of 1 Dec. 1909, ibid., 291.

CHAPTER III

[1] Cf. G. P. Blok, 'Geroy *Vozmezdiya*', *Russkiy Sovremennik* (Petrograd), no. 3, 1924, 172–86.

[2] Cf. letter to his mother of 1 Dec. 1909, *Pis'ma k rodnym* I, 391.

[3] Letter to his mother of 19 Nov. 1909, ibid., 286.

[4] Letter to his mother of 3 Apr. 1909, ibid., 253.

[5] Letter to his mother of 4 Dec. 1909, ibid., 244.

[6] Cf. *Varshavskoye Utro* (Warsaw), no. 13 (3/16 Dec.), 3, and no. 17 (7/21 Dec.), 1909, 4.

[7] E. Spektorsky, *A. L. Blok—gosudarstvoved i filosof* (Warsaw, 1911).

[8] For a remarkable analysis of the strange coincidence of father's and son's thoughts about Russia see V. D. Izmail'skaya, 'Problema *Vozmezdiya*', *O Bloke* (Moscow, 1929), 9.

[9] Vl. Pyast, *Vospominaniya ob Aleksandre Bloke* (Petersburg, 1923), 30.

[10] For a detailed analysis of Blok and Brand which perhaps overemphasizes the perfectly defensible idea of a connection between the finale of *Brand* and the finale of *The Twelve*, see M. Nag, 'Ibsen og Blok og "deus Caritatis"', *Edda* (Oslo), Argag 51, Hefte 4 (1964), 324–8. N. A. Nilsson also writes of Blok and Ibsen in his book *Ibsen in Russland* (Stockholm, 1958), 207–20, and, in Russian, there is D. M. Sharypkin, 'Blok i Ibsen', *Skandinavskiy Sbornik* (Tallin), VI (1963), 159–76.

[11] Letter to his mother of 9 Dec. 1909, *Pis'ma k rodnym* I, 293.

[12] Ibid.

[13] Cf. N. A. Pavlovich, 'Vospominaniya ob Aleksandre Bloke', *Prometey* (Moscow), no. 11, 1977, 243–6, for details of the Belayev family.

[14] Letter to his mother of 18 Jan. 1910, *Pis'ma k rodnym* II, 56. The lines quoted in the text above are from another letter of the same date, ibid., 60.

[15] Another version of these lines is in the collection dedicated to Angelina's memory: *Iambs* (III. 94).

[16] A. A. Kublitskaya-Piottukh, unpublished letter to M. P. Ivanova of 9 Jan. 1910. Arkhiv A. A. Bloka, TsGALI.

[17] Id., unpublished letter to M. P. Ivanova of 15 Apr. 1910. Arkhiv A. A. Bloka, TsGALI.

[18] Letter to his mother of 11 Jan. 1910, *Pis'ma k rodnym* II, 50.

[19] E. P. Ivanov, 'Mat' i syn'. Introduction to an unpublished study of the poetry Blok dedicated to his mother, in the collection of N. P. Il'in.

[20] A. A. Kublitskaya-Piottukh, letter to M. P. Ivanova of 25 Jan. 1912. Arkhiv A. A. Bloka, TsGALI.

[21] Cf. the notes Blok made on Remizov and Gnedich in the train to Warsaw, Z.K. 161–6.

[22] Letter to his mother of 4 Apr. 1910, *Pis'ma k rodnym* II, 68.

[23] The speech was reworked as an article for the periodical *Iskusstvo i pechatnoye delo* (Kiev), nos. 8–9, 1910.

[24] Cf. letter to his mother of 5 Apr. 1910, *Pis'ma k rodnym* II, 69.

[25] The book is M. Elik, *Blok i Muzyka* (Moscow–Leningrad, 1972). John Bowlt has written on Blok's handling of time and space with relation to Vrubel and Boris-Musatov ('Aleksandr Blok: The Poem "The Unknown Lady"', *Texas Studies in Literature and Language*, Special Russian Issue, vol. XVII, 1975, 349–56) and V. Alfonsov on Blok and Vrubel in *Slova i kraski* (Moscow–Leningrad, 1966), 13–62.

[26] Cf. letter to E. L. Znosko-Borovsky of 12 Apr. 1910, *S.S.* VIII, 308.

[27] Sir Cecil Kisch, *Alexandr Blok, Prophet of Revolution* (London, 1960), 62–6.

[28] Letter to his mother of 12 Apr. 1910, *Pis'ma k rodnym* II, 71.

[29] Letter to his mother of 11 May 1910, ibid., 79.

[30] Letter to his mother of 4 May 1910, ibid., 77.

[31] Letter to his mother of 18 May 1910, ibid., 80–1.

[32] A. A. Kublitskaya-Piottukh, unpublished letter to M. P. Ivanova of 23 June 1910. Arkhiv A. A. Bloka, TsGALI.

[33] Letter to his mother of 31 May 1910, ibid., 82–3.

[34] Letter to his mother of 22 June 1910, ibid., 89.

[35] M. A. Beketova, 1922, 138–9, 137.

[36] Based on P. A. Zhurov, 'Vpervye v Shakhmatove', talk given at the conference organized by the Blok Commission of the Writers' Organization of the Communist Party of the RSFSR at the State Literary Museum in Moscow, 27–28 Nov. 1971. Zhurov, a specialist on the 'country gentleman' (*usadebnaya*) tradition in Russian poetry, visited Shakhmatovo in 1923 and interviewed a number of the local inhabitants who remembered the Beketovs and the Bloks.

[37] Letter to his mother of 25 June 1910, *Pis'ma k rodnym* II, 90.

[38] Z. G. Mints, *Lirika Aleksandra Bloka* (Tartu, 1975), chapter I, 'Pervaya Lyubov''.

[39] L. V. Zharova, 'Pis'ma A. A. Bloka k K. M. Sadovskoy', *B.S.* II, 313.

[40] J. Forsyth, 'Prophets and Supermen: German Ideological Influences on Alexander Blok's Poetry', *Forum for Modern Language Studies* (St. Andrews), vol. XIII, no. 1 (January 1977), 33–46.

[41] A. Bely, letter to Blok of end October 1910, *Perepiska*, 239.

[42] Cf. S. Solov'ev, 'Vospominaniya ob Aleksandre Bloke', *Pis'ma A. Bloka*, 37.

[43] D. S. Merezhkovsky, 'Balagan i tragediya', *Russkoye Slovo* (Moscow), 14 Sept. 1910.

[44] A. Bely, letter to Blok of end October 1910, *Perepiska*, 239–40.

[45] E. P. Ivanov, unpublished letter to A. A. Blok of 29 Sept 1910. Arkhiv E. P. Ivanova, IRLI.

[46] Letter to his mother, 29 Nov. 1910, *Pis'ma k rodnym* II, 102.

[47] Letter to his mother of 9 Jan. 1911, ibid., 110.

[48] A. A. Kublitskaya-Piottukh, unpublished letter to M. P. Ivanova of 17 Nov. 1910. Arkhiv A. A. Bloka, TsGALI.

CHAPTER IV

[1] Vl. Pyast, *Vospominaniya o Bloke* (Petersburg, 1923), 60–1.

[2] Ibid., 51.

[3] Cf. T. Pachmuss, *Zinaida Hippius. An Intellectual Profile* (Carbondale and Edwardsville, Ill., 1971), 288.

[4] Letter to A. Bely of 6 June 1911, *Perepiska*, 261.

[5] Cf. S. Solov'ev, 'Vospominaniya ob Aleksandre Bloke', *Pis'ma A. Bloka*, 34.

[6] Letter to V. N. Knyazhnin of 6 Sept. 1915, *Pis'ma A. Bloka*, 206.

[7] Letter to his mother of 3 Dec. 1910, *Pis'ma k rodnym* II, 104.

[8] A. A. Kublitskaya-Piottukh, unpublished letters to M. P. Ivanova of 15 Feb. and 19 Feb. 1911. Arkhiv A. A. Bloka, TsGALI.

[9] N. G. Chulkova, unpublished memoir in the collection of N. P. Il'in.

[10] Letter to V. N. Knyazhnin of 30 Apr. 1913, *Pis'ma A. Bloka*, 202.

[11] E. Yu. Kuzmina-Karavayeva, 'Vstrechi s Blokom (K pyatnadsatiletiyu so dnya smerti)', ed. D. E. Maksimov, *Trudy* XI, Vypusk 209, 267–9.

[12] Ibid., 268.

[13] Ibid., 270.

[14] The letters Blok wrote to both Z. N. Hippius and D. S. Merezhkovsky on 10 Jan. 1911, together with many other valuable papers from Hippius's archive (but not, apparently, the two disagreeable letters of autumn 1910), are in a private collection in Paris.

[15] This information is owed largely to N. A. Pavlovich, who in the early 1970s did some research into the origins of the Belayev family for a chapter on Angelina Aleksandrovna Blok, partially published in her 'Vospominaniya ob Aleksandre Bloke', *Prometey* (Moscow), no. 11, 1977, 243–6.

[16] Letter to A. Bely of 8 May 1911, *Perepiska*, 256.

[17] Cf. A. A. Kublitskaya-Piottukh, unpublished letter to M. P. Ivanova of 29 June 1911. Arkhiv A. A. Bloka, TsGALI.

[18] This account of L. D. Blok's 1911 letters to her husband is based on the manuscripts in the Blok archive in TsGALI. Substantial extracts from the letters have, however, been published in the notes to Blok's letters in *Pis'ma k zhene*, 258–70. Blok's letter of 17/30 June 1911, also quoted here from manuscript, is published in the same volume, 266–7.

[19] A. A. Kublitskaya-Piottukh, unpublished letter to M. P. Ivanova of 24 June 1911. Arkhiv A. A. Bloka, TsGALI.

[20] M. A. Beketova, 1925, 153.

[21] According to the unpublished reminiscences of L. D. Blok by her friend Valentina Verigina.

[22] The whole of this account of the holiday in Aber-wrach is based on Blok's letters to his mother, printed in full in *Pis'ma k rodnym* II, 183.

[23] Letter to his mother of 7 Sept. 1911, *Pis'ma k rodnym* II, 183.

[24] Ibid., 184.

[25] S. M. Gorodetsky, 'Yunost' Bloka', in the newspaper *Rech'* (Petersburg), no. 251, 1911.

[26] Vl. Pyast, op. cit., 62.

[27] Cf. Vyacheslav Ivanov, *Sobraniye Sochineniy* II (Brussels, 1971); for a full and delicate account of Ivanov's relationship with Blok from Ivanov's point of view, see the introduction by O. Deshart to vol. I of this work, 161–5.

[28] E. Yu. Kuzmina-Karavayeva, op. cit., 269–70.

[29] S. M. Gorodetsky, 'Vospominaniya ob Aleksandre Bloke', *Pechat' i Revolyutsiya* (Moscow, 1922), Kniga pervaya, 86.

[30] Cf. L. K. Dolgopolov, *Poemy Bloka i russkaya poema kontsa XIX i nachala XX vekov* (Moscow–Leningrad, 1964).

CHAPTER V

[1] Maksim Gorky, *Zametki iz dnevnika. Sochineniya* XVIII (Moscow–Leningrad, 1927), 210.

[2] For a detailed study of this problem see Avril Pyman, 'An Introduction to *The Scythians*', *Stand* (Newcastle upon Tyne), vol. VIII. no. 3, 1966/7, 23–33.

[3] A. Bely, letter to Blok of 26 Nov. 1911. *Perepiska*, 280.

[4] A. A. Kublitskaya-Piottukh, unpublished letter to M. P. Ivanova of 6 Dec. 1911. Arkhiv A. A. Bloka, TsGALI.

[5] First draft of obituary on Strindberg, ed. D. M. Sharypkin in *B.S.* I, 555.

[6] N. A. Kluyev, unpublished, undated letter to Blok (written autumn 1911), no. 21. Arkhiv A. A. Bloka, TsGALI.

[7] A. Bely, *Epopeya*, no. 4, pp. 219–39.

[8] Cf. N. A. Frumkina and L. S. Fleyshman, 'A. A. Blok mezhdu "Musagetom" i "Sirinom" (Pis'ma k F. K. Metneru)', *B.S.* II, 385–7. Cf. also *S.S.* VII, 209–10, and, for Blok's earlier relations with Musaget, P. Kuprianovsky, 'Semnadtsat' neizdannykh pisem Aleksandra Bloka', *Sovetskaya Ukraina* (Kiev), no. 8, 1961, 175–80 (Blok's letters to Kozhebatkin).

[9] A. Bely, op. cit.

[10] M. Raeff, *Russian Review* (Hanover, N.H.), vol. XI, no. 3 (July 1952).

[11] Cf. N. V. Valentinov-Volsky, 'Aleksandr Blok i *Russkoye Slovo*', *Dva goda sredi simvolistov*, ed. Gleb Struve (Stanford, Calif. 1969, 228–35, and, for Rumanov, Struve's note on p. 240. Vl. Pyast also writes in his memoirs of Blok's flirtation with *Russkoye Slovo* and his acquaintance with Rumanov who, according to K. I. Chukovsky, served as the model for the 'living corpse' in Blok's 'Dance of Death'; cf. 'Aleksandr Blok', *Lyudi i knigi* (Moscow, 1960), 514.

[12] V. N. Knyazhnin, from an unpublished speech quoted in the excellent compilation by O. Nemerovskaya and Ts. Vol'pe, *Sud'ba Bloka* (Leningrad, 1930), 184.

[13] Cf. V. Zhirmunsky, *Drama Aleksandra Bloka 'Roza i Krest'. Literaturnye istochniki* (Leningrad, 1964).

[14] Letter to his mother of 25 July 1912, *Pis'ma k rodnym* II, 221–2.

[15] Letter to his mother of 29 July 1912, ibid., 223.

[16] A. A. Kublitskaya-Piottukh, unpublished letter to M. P. Ivanova of 14 Sept. 1912. Arkhiv A. A. Bloka, TsGALI.

[17] Id., unpublished letter to M. P. Ivanova of 26 Sept. 1912. Arkhiv A. A. Bloka, TsGALI.

[18] V. P. Verigina, 'Vospominaniya ob Aleksandre Bloke', *Trudy* IV Vypusk 104, 357.

[19] Ibid., 359.

[20] M. A. Beketova, 'Vesëlost' i yumor Bloka', *O Bloke* (Moscow, 1929), 13.

[21] Cf. D. S. Likhachev, 'Iz kommentariy k stikhotvoreniyu A. Bloka "Noch', ulitsa, fonar', apteka"', *Russkaya Literatura* (Leningrad), no. 1, 1978, 186–8.

[22] Robin Kemball, 'Dreams', *Russian Review*, October 1959, 309–10.

[23] Cf. V. Zhirmunsky, *Poeziya Aleksandra Bloka* (1922), ch. 2, pp. 26 et seq.; P. Florensky, 'O Bloke', *Vestnik russkogo khristianskogo dvizheniya* (Paris-New York), vol. IV (1974), no. 114, 169–92. These notes for a lecture delivered privately after an evening in memory of Aleksandr Blok were originally published in a slightly different form as Petrogradskiy Svyashchennik, 'O Bloke', *Put'* (Paris), no. 26 (February 1931), 214–25. The same number of this journal contained N. Berdayev's 'V zashchitu A. Bloka', 109–13. Cf. also Archbishop Ioann Shakhovskoy, 'O Bloke', *Novoye Russkoye Slovo* (New York), 10 Dec. 1961; Naum Korzhavin, 'Igra s d'yavolom (po povodu stikhotvoreniya Aleksandra Bloka "K Muze")', *Grani* (Munich), 1972, 76 107.; A. Pyman, [survey] in *Slavonic and East European Review* (London), vol. LIV, no. 4. (October 1976), 602–7.

[24] Cf. A. Tyrkova, 'Beglye vstrechi (iz vospominaniy o Bloke)', *Rul'* (Berlin), no. 256 (20 Sept. 1921), and 'Teni minuvshego vokrug bashni', *Vozrozhdeniye* (Paris), vol. XLI (1955), 78–91. Also Harold Williams's obituary in the *Slavonic Review* (London), vol. I (1922), no. 1, 218–20, and in the book *Russia of the Russians* (London, 1914), 212–13.

[25] R. D. B. Thompson, 'The Non-literary Sources of *The Rose and the Cross*', *Slavonic and East European Review*, vol. XLV, no. 105 (July 1967).

[26] L. D. Blok, unpublished letters to Blok of 17 Feb., 20 Mar., and 27 Mar. 1913. Arkhiv A. A. Bloka, TsGALI. Most of these extracts are quoted in the notes to *Pis'ma k zhene*, 290, 292, 297, 302.

[27] A. A. Kublitskaya-Piottukh, unpublished letter to M. P. Ivanova of 4 Feb. 1913. Arkhiv A. A. Bloka, TsGALI.

[28] Id., unpublished letter to M. P. Ivanova of 6 Apr. 1913. Arkhiv A. A. Bloka, TsGALI. Quoted in full in notes to *Pis'ma k zhene*, 304.

CHAPTER VI

[1] Letter to his mother of 5 Aug. (23 July o.s.) 1913, *Pis'ma k rodnym* II, 248.

[2] Letter to his mother of 9 Aug (27 July o.s.) 1913, op. cit., 249.

[3] Ibid., 248–9.

[4] For Maria Andreyevna's account of this summer see M. A. Beketova, 1925, 83–7.

[5] L. D. Blok, unpublished letter to Blok of 12 Aug. 1913. Arkhiv A. A. Bloka, TsGALI. Quoted extensively in *Pis'ma k zhene*, 320, n. 6.

[6] A. Akhmatova, 'Vospominaniya o Bloke', *Sochineniya* II (Munich, 1968) 191–2.

[7] First published with an epigraph 'To Aleksandr Blok', in the almanac *Lyubov' k trëm apelsinam* (Petersburg), no. 1, 1914; see also *Sochineniya* I, 115.

[8] A. A. Kublitskaya-Piottukh, unpublished letter to M. P. Ivanova of 29 Mar. 1914. Arkhiv A. A. Bloka, TsGALI.

[9] A. Akhmatova, 'Vospominaniya o Bloke', op. cit., 193.

[10] Cf. Vl. Orlov, 'Neosushchestvlënnyy zamysel Aleksandra Bloka—drama "Nelepyy Chelovek" ', *Uchenye Zapiski Leningradskogo Gosudarstvennogo Pedagogicheskogo Instituta Im. A. V. Gertsena*, T. 67 (Leningrad, 1948), 234–41.

[11] V. P. Verigina, 'Vospominaniya', *Trudy* IV, Vypusk 104, 364.

[12] Cf. A. Gorelov, *Groza nad solov'inym sadom* (Leningrad, 1970), 351, n. 1.

[13] L. D. Blok, *Byli i nebylitsy*, 50.

[14] Part of the note in Blok's hand sent to L. A. Del'mas by A. A. Kublitskaya-Piottukh after the poet's death. Copy in the collection of N. P. Il'in.

[15] Letter to L. A. Del'mas of 14 June 1914 (no. 16), *Zvezda* (Leningrad), no. 11, 1970.

[16] Letter to L. A. Del'mas of 2 Apr. 1914 (no. 9), ibid.

[17] L. A. Del'mas, memoir.

[18] Letter to L. A. Del'mas of 12 Mar. 1914 (no. 2), *Zvezda*, no. 11, 1970.

[19] L. A. Del'mas, memoir.

[20] Letter to L. A. Del'mas of 26 Mar. 1914 (no. 3), *Zvezda*, no. 11, 1970.

[21] L. A. Del'mas, memoir.

[22] A. A. Kublitskaya-Piottukh, unpublished letter to M. P. Ivanova of 29 Mar. 1914. Arkhiv A. A. Bloka, TsGALI.

[23] Letter to L. A. Del'mas of 31 Mar.–1 Apr. 1914 (no. 8), *Zvezda*, no. 11, 1970.

[24] Cf. *Lyubov' k trëm apelsinam* (Petersburg), no. 4/5, 1914. The cycle was printed here without the verses 'Na more prazelen', i mesyatsa oskolok' (III. 229) and 'Est' demon utra' (III. 230).

[25] Letter to L. A. Del'mas of 29 Mar. 1914 (no. 7), *Zvezda*, no. 11, 1970.

[26] L. A. Del'mas, memoir.

[27] Letter to L. A. Del'mas of 2 Apr. 1914 (no. 9), *Zvezda*, no. 11, 1970.

[28] Letter to L. A. Del'mas dated 'Easter' (6 Apr. 1914) (no. 10), ibid.

[29] Letter to L. A. Del'mas of 6 May 1914 (no. 13), ibid.

[30] Letter to L. A. Del'mas of 25 June 1914 (no. 15), ibid.

[31] Letter to L. A. Del'mas of 14 July 1914 (no. 16), ibid.

[32] Letter to L. A. Del'mas of 17 Aug. 1914 (no. 18), ibid.

CHAPTER VII

[1] L. B. [L. D. Blok], 'Iz pisem sestry miloserdiya', *Otechestvo* (Petrograd), no. 4, 1914, 78–9.

[2] Z. N. Hippius, 'Moy lunyy drug', *Zhivye Litsa* (Prague, 1925), 48.

[3] For Esenin's own account of his first meeting with Blok see Vsevolod Rozh-destvensky, *Stranitsy zhizni* (Moscow–Leningrad, 1962), 277–80, where he retells the story as far as possible in Esenin's own words. Blok noted only the appearance of 'a young fellow from Ryazan with verses' on 9 March. The letter to the peasant author M. P. Murashov, written that day, remains as evidence (VIII. 441), as does Esenin's introductory note, whether or not sent in by the cook. See Gordon McVay, *Esenin: A Life* (London and Ann Arbor, Mich., 1976), 51–3.

[4] L. D. Blok, unpublished letter to Blok of 27 Jan. 1915. Arkhiv A. A. Bloka, TsGALI. Quoted in *Pis'ma k zhene*, 351, n. 1.

[5] Id., unpublished letter to Blok of 14 Feb. 1915. Arkhiv A. A. Bloka, TsGALI.

[6] Id., unpublished letter to Blok of 3 Mar. 1915. Arkhiv A. A. Bloka, TsGALI.

[7] G. Ivanov, 'Stikhi o Rossii Aleksandra Bloka', *Apollon* (Petrograd), nos. 8–9, 1915, 99.

[8] Olga Forsch, *Sumashedshiy Korabl'* (Leningrad, 1931), 99.

[9] Cf. D. E. Maksimov, 'Pis'ma i darstvennye nadpisi Bloka Aleksandre Chebo-tarevskoy', *B.S.* I, 550.

[10] P. A. Zhurov, 'Vpervye v Shakhmatove', a lecture at a conference arranged by the Blok Commission of the Writers' Organization of the Communist Party of the RSFSR, held in the State Literary Museum, Moscow, 1971.

[11] Letter to L. A. Del'mas of 12 Aug. 1915 (no. 21), *Zvezda* (Leningrad), no. 11, 1970.

[12] A. A. Kublitskaya-Piottukh, unpublished letter to M. P. Ivanova of 6 Aug. 1915. Arkhiv A. A. Bloka, TsGALI.

[13] L. A. Del'mas, memoir.

[14] Vl. Pyast, *Vospominaniya o Bloke* (Petersburg, 1923), 69.

[15] Z. N. Hippius, *Sinaya Kniga 1914–18* (Belgrade, 1926), 51, 64.

[16] E. Yu. Kuzmina-Karavayeva, 'Vstrechi s Blokom', *Trudy* XI, Vypusk 209, 274.

[17] Ibid., 275.

[18] Cf. T. Rodina, chapters '*Roza i Krest*' and 'Blok, Stanislavsky, Meyerhold' in *Aleksandr Blok i russkiy teatr nachala XX veka* (Moscow, 1972), 193–294. Also O. V. Gzovskaya, 'A. A. Blok v Moskovskom Khudozhestvennom Teatre', *Russkaya Literatura* (Leningrad), no. 3, 1961, 197–205; Yu. Gerasimov, 'Stan-islavsky i Blok', *Neva* (Leningrad), no. 2, 1963, 166–9.

[19] There is an excellent analysis of this poem in relation to 'The Mask Motif in A. Blok's Poetry' by I. Masing-Delic, *Russian Literature* (The Hague–Paris), no. 5, 1973, 79–101.

[20] These notes of Blok's were written in the margins of the book he bought that summer which he subsequently, in 1920, presented to N. A. Pavlovich. They have been quoted in print before in A. Pyman, *Aleksandr Blok, Selected Poems* (Oxford, 1972), 198–9, and S. Hackel, *The Poet and the Revolution. Aleksandr Blok's 'The Twelve'* (Oxford, 1975), 94, 96.

[21] Cf. A. Bely, letter to Blok of approx. 23 June 1916 from Dornach, *Perepiska*, 329–31.

[22] Kupreyanov's manuscript copy of *The Rose and the Cross* was in the possession of the late N. P. Il'in. Seven letters from Kupreyanov to Blok (dated before 6

Mar. 1915 to 23 May 1921) have been published in the book *N. N. Kupreyanov, Literaturno-khudoszhestvennoye naslediye* (Moscow, 1973), 91–4.

²³ V. A. Zorgenfrey, 'Aleksandr Aleksandrovich Blok', *Z.M.*, no. 6, 1922, 140.

²⁴ Cf. *Pis'ma k rodnym* II, 481, n. 577.

²⁵ Cf. M. Dobuzhinsky, *Vospominaniya*, vol. I (New York, 1976), 387–8.

²⁶ L. D. Blok, unpublished letter to Blok of 1 Sept. 1916. Arkhiv A. A. Bloka, TsGALI.

²⁷ L. D. Blok, unpublished letter to Blok of 9 Aug. 1916. Arkhiv A. A. Bloka, TsGALI. Quoted in notes to *Pis'ma k zhene*, 365.

²⁸ Letter to his mother of 21 Nov. 1916, *Pis'ma k rodnym* II, 318.

²⁹ Aleksey Tolstoy, 'Padshiy Angel', *Posledniye Novosti* (Paris), no. 413, 1921. Cf. also letter to A. A. Kublitskaya-Piottukh of 17 Jan. 1917, *Pis'ma k rodnym* II, 328.

³⁰ Letter to his mother of 1 Mar. 1917, *Pis'ma k rodnym* II, 336–7. Cf. also the nostalgic note in Blok's diary for 4 Sept. 1917 (VII. 308–9).

CHAPTER VIII

¹ L. D. Blok, unpublished letter to A. A. Kublitskaya-Piottukh of 14 Jan. 1917. Arkhiv A. A. Bloka, IRLI.

² Letter to his mother of 17 Apr. (evening) 1917, *Pis'ma k rodnym* II, 348.

³ Cf. letters to his mother of 19 June 1917, *S.S.* VIII, 502–3, and of 7 June 1917, *S.S.* VIII, 499–500.

⁴ Z. N. Hippius, *Sinaya Kniga 1914–18* (Belgrade, 1926), 85.

⁵ Cf. letter to his mother of 4 July 1917, *Pis'ma k rodnym* II, 383.

⁶ L. A. Shilov, 'Po stranitsam Blokovskikh dnevnikov i pisem', *Yunost'* (Moscow), no. 10, 1969, 2–9. But see the review by V. Enisherlov, 'Na druzheskoy noge . . . s Blokom', *Literaturnaya Gazeta* (Moscow), no. 12 (18 Mar.), 1970, 6, for inaccuracies.

⁷ Letter to his mother of 4 July 1917, *Pis'ma k rodnym* II, 382–3.

⁸ Letter to his mother of 8 July 1917, ibid., 385–6.

⁹ Letter to his mother of 28 July 1917, ibid., 394–5.

¹⁰ Ibid., 394.

¹¹ L. D. Blok, unpublished letter to Blok received 25 May 1917. Arkhiv A. A. Bloka, TsGALI.

¹² L. D. Blok, *Byly i nebylitsy*, 77.

¹³ M. V. Babenchikov, *Al. Blok i Rossiya* (Moscow–Petrograd, 1923).

¹⁴ Id., 'Otvazhnaya krasota', *Zvezda* (Leningrad), no. 3, 1968, 186–200.

¹⁵ Id., *Al. Blok i Rossiya*, 51.

¹⁶ The connection between revolution and the Old Believers is treated very fully in Sergey Hackel's *The Poet and the Revolution. Aleksandr Blok's 'The Twelve'* (Oxford, 1975).

¹⁷ M. V. Babenchikov, 'Otvazhnaya krasota', op. cit., 195.

¹⁸ Z. N. Hippius, 'Moy lunyy drug', *Zhivye Litsa* (Prague, 1925), 59–61.

¹⁹ M. V. Babenchikov, 'Otvazhnaya krasota', op. cit., 195.

²⁰ Cf. Vl. Orlov, *Poema Aleksandra Bloka 'Dvenadtstat''* (Moscow, 1962), 28–9.

[21] For Nikolay Lapin cf. *Pis'ma k rodnym* II, 4 May 1910, 77; 7 July 1916, 301; and the note on p. 475.

[22] This letter was published by P. N. Medvedev amongst the notes to his edition of Blok's diaries, *Dnevnik Al. Bloka, 1917–1921* (Leningrad, 1928), 260–1.

CHAPTER IX

[1] M. A. Beketova, 1922, 256.

[2] M. V. Babenchikov, 'Otvazhnaya krasota', *Zvezda*, no. 3, 1968, 200; see particularly notes by Vl. Orlov.

[3] Viktor Shklovsky, *Sentimental'noye Puteshestviye* (Moscow, 1939), 284–5.

[4] V. Polyansky, 'Iz vstrech s A. Blokom', *Zhizn'* (Petrograd), no. 1, 1922—as quoted in *Sud'ba Bloka* (Leningrad, 1930), 228–9.

[5] V. A. Zorgenfrey, 'Aleksandr Aleksandrovich Blok', *Z.M.*, no. 6, 1922, 141.

[6] K. I. Chukovsky, 'Posledniye gody Bloka', *Z.M.*, no. 6, 1922, 161–3.

[7] G. P. Blok, 'Geroy Vozmezdiya', *Russkiy Sovremennik* (Petrograd), no. 3, 1924, 172–86.

[8] Cf. Vl. Orlov, 'Novoye ob Aleksandre Bloke', *Novyy Mir* (Moscow), no. 11, 1955, 156.

[9] For an excellent English translation of most of these articles see I. Freiman and Elizabeth Hill, *The Spirit of Music* (London, 1946).

[10] Z. N. Hippius, *Sinaya Kniga, 1914–18* (Belgrade, 1926), 51.

[11] P. Florensky formulated his thesis for a lecture delivered in the Soviet Union but first published anonymously as Petrogradskiy Svyashchennik, 'O Bloke', *Put'* (Paris), no. 26 (February), 1931, 214–25. This article, which touches also on Blok's poem 'To the Muse' (as further proof of the demonic source of his inspiration), gave rise to the polemics mentioned in note 23 to ch. V of the present volume.

[12] D. S. Mirsky, 'Russian Literature since 1917', *The Contemporary Review* (London), August 1922, 209.

[13] A. Remizov, *Akhru—Povest' Peterburgskaya* (Berlin–Petersburg–Moscow, 1922), 24.

[14] B. M. Gasparov, Yu. M. Lotman, 'Igrovye momenty v poeme "Dvenadtsat'"', *Tezisy I vsesoyuznoy (III) konferentsii 'Tvorchestvo A. A. Bloka i russkaya kul'tura XX veka'* (Tartu, 1975), 53–63.

[15] Translations into English include: C. Bechofer, *The Twelve* (London, 1920); B. Deutsch and A. Yarmolinsky, *The Twelve* (New York, 1920); W. A. Coxwell in *Poems from the Russian* (London, 1929); G. Reavey and M. Slonim (extracts) in *Soviet Literature* (London, 1933); G. Shelley, *Modern Poems from Russian* (London, 1942); C. M. Bowra in *A Second Book of Russian Verse* (London, 1943); A. Miller in *Stand* (Newcastle upon Tyne), Winter 1955–6; C. Kisch in *Alexander Blok, Prophet of Revolution* (London, 1960); Anselm Hollo in *Evergreen Review* (New York), vol. v, no. 19 (July–August), 1961; R. Fulton, *The Twelve* (Preston, 1968); E. Ritchie in *Ann Arbor Review* (Mich.), no. 4 (Summer), 1968; Jon Stallworthy and Peter France in *The Twelve and other Poems* (London, 1970); Arthur Clifford in *The Silver Age of Russian Culture*, an anthology ed. Carl and Ellendea Proffer (Ann Arbor, Mich., 1971); Natasha Templeton, ibid.; Sergey Hackel in *The Poet and the Revolution. Aleksandr Blok's 'The Twelve'* (Oxford, 1975).

[16] For a fuller interpretation of this passage and of the poem *The Scythians*, see A. Pyman, 'An Introduction to *The Scythians*', *Stand*, vol. VIII, no. 3, 1966/7, 23-33.

[17] Ivanov-Razumnik, speech delivered at an open session of the Free Philosophical Association, 28 Aug. 1921, *Pamyati Aleksandra Bloka* (Petersburg, 1922; repr. Letchworth, Herts: Prideaux Press, 1971), 54-63. For Ivanov-Razumnik on *The Twelve* and *The Scythians* see also 'Ispytaniye v groze i bure', *Aleksandr Blok Andrey Bely* (Petersburg, 1919), 119-63, originally published in the same number of *Nash Put'* (no. 1, April 1918) as Blok's poems, and repr. by Bradda Books Ltd. (Letchworth, Herts, 1971) in the series Rarity Reprints (no. 15), with an introduction by M. H. Shotton.

[18] Miller's translation is published in *Stand*, vol. VIII, no. 3, 1966/7, Kemball's in the *Russian Review*, April 1975, 117. Other translations are by B. Deutsch and A. Yarmolinsky in *Russian Poetry, an Anthology* (London, 1927); Jack Lindsay in *Russian Poetry (1917-1955)* (London, 1957); B. G. Guerney in *An Anthology of Russian Literature in the Soviet Period from Gorky to Pasternak* (London and New York, 1960); C. Kisch in *Alexander Blok, Prophet of Revolution* (London, 1960); Jon Stallworthy and Peter France in *The Twelve and Other Poems* (London, 1970).

[19] E. Lundberg, *Zapiski Pisatelya 1917-1920* (Leningrad, 1930), 131.

[20] Gordon McVay, *Esenin: A Life* (London and Ann Arbor, Mich., 1976), 99-100.

[21] Cf. for example Sophie Lafitte (Bonneau), *L'Univers poétique d'Alexandre Blok*, in the series *Bibliothèque russe de l'Institut d'Études Slaves*, vol. XX (Paris, 1946).

[22] Since this chapter was written some of the views here expressed have been confirmed by reading F. Flamant's percipient analysis of the Christ-image throughout Blok's poetry: 'Le Christ du poète Blok', *Cahiers de linguistique, d'orientalisme et de slavistique* (Paris), Août-Décembre 1974, 55-70.

[23] E. Lundberg, op. cit., 18, 101.

[24] Vs. Rozhdestvensky, *Stranitsy zhizni* (Moscow-Leningrad, 1962), 222.

[25] A. Bely, letter to Blok of 17 Mar. 1918; dated by Blok's note in his diary 'Received 5 (18)/III/1918, the beginning of Lent', *Perepiska*, 335-6.

CHAPTER X

[1] Z. N. Hippius, 'Moy lunyy drug', *Zhivye Litsa* (Prague, 1925), 66.

[2] K. I. Chukovsky, 'Poslednye gody Bloka', *Z.M.*, no. 6, 1922, 169.

[3] Z. N. Hippius, op. cit., 66-8.

[4] 'On the Repertory of Communal and State Theatres', 5 June 1918, *S.S.* VI, 267-83; 'Thoughts on the Inadequacy of our Repertoire', 2 June-29 Aug. 1918, *S.S.* VI, 284-91; 'An Appeal from the Repertory Section', November 1918, *S.S.* VI, 292-6.

[5] K. I. Chukovsky, op. cit., 156-7.

[6] V. A. Zorgenfrey, 'Aleksandr Aleksandrovich Blok (po pamyati za pyatnadtsati let, 1906-1921)', *Z.M*, no. 6, 1922, 143.

[7] Cf. note 4.

[8] S. M. Alyansky, *Vstrechi s Aleksandrom Blokom* (Moscow, 1969), 29.

[9] Ibid., 43.

[10] Ibid., 48.

[11] Ibid., 52.

[12] Ibid., 59.

[13] K. I. Chukovsky, op. cit., 182–3.

[14] A full translation is given by F. D. Reeve in his *Aleksandr Blok. Between Image and Idea* (New York and London, 1962), 248.

[15] N. A. Pavlovich, 'Vospominaniya ob Aleksandre Bloke', ed. Z. G. Mints and I. Chernov, *B.S.* I, 487.

[16] S. M. Alyansky, op. cit., 84–6.

[17] For Burenin's parodies of Blok see F. D. Reeve, op. cit., 241–2.

[18] Cf. diary for 30(17) Aug. and 11 Sept. (29 Aug.) 1918, *S.S.* VII, 338, 350.

[19] S. M. Alyansky, op. cit., 62.

[20] E. Zamyatin, 'Peshchera', first published *Z.M.*, no. 5, 1922, 82–9.

[21] V. Shklovsky, *Sentimental'noye Puteshestviye* (Moscow, 1939), 209, 215.

[22] E. V. Pasternak, 'Pasternak o Bloke', *B.S.* II, 448–9.

[23] V. A. Zorgenfrey, op. cit., 150.

[24] Quoted by D. E. Maksimov, 'Iz arkhivnykh materialov ob A. Bloke. K voprosu ob A. Bloke i M. Gor'kom', *Uchenye zapiski Leningradskogo gosudarstvennogo pedagogicheskogo Instituta*. Fakul'tet Yazyka i Literatury (Leningrad), Vypusk 5, 1956, 245.

[25] Blok's particular extract is not reproduced in his published diaries (see *S.S.* VII, note 4, 511–12). The manifesto, preserved in IRLI (F. 79, Op. 5, no. 1), was, however, published in full in the reminiscences of N. I. Gagen-Torn, 'Vospominaniya ob Aleksandre Bloke', *B.S.* II, 444–5.

[26] Quoted by Vl. Orlov, 'Gamayun', *Druzhba Narodov* (Moscow), no. 11, 1977, 160.

[27] A. Z. Shteynberg, *Volnaya Filosofskaya Assotsiatsiya. Pamyati Aleksandra Bloka* (Petersburg, 1922), repr. by Prideaux Press (Letchworth, Herts., 1971), 39, 40, 41–2, 45, 53.

[28] S. M. Alyansky, op. cit., 94–7.

[29] Cf. E. Zamyatin, 'Aleksandr Blok', *Litsa* (New York, 1967), 20–1.

[30] For Blok, Heine, and humanism see particularly Nikolay Otsup, 'Litso Bloka', *Literaturnye Ocherki* (Paris, 1961), 59 et seq. There are a number of studies of Blok's translations and work as editor of the German poet; among the most informative in English is James Bailey, 'Blok and Heine: an episode from the history of Russian *dol'niki*', *Slavic and East European Journal* (Madison, Wisc.), vol. XIII, no. 1, 1969, 1–22.

[31] M. Gorky, *Sobraniye sochineniy v XXX tomakh*, vol. XXIX (Moscow, 1955), 457.

[32] Most interesting in this connection is L. K. Dolgopolov, *Aleksandr Blok, lichnost' i tvorchestvo* (Leningrad, 1978).

[33] Vs. Rozhdestvensky, *Stranitsy zhizni* (Moscow–Leningrad, 1962), 232–3.

[34] M. Gorky, 'Zametki iz dnevnika', *Sochineniya*, vol. XVIII (Moscow–Leningrad, 1927), 205–9.

[35] Cf. the publication by I. A. Chernov, 'Blok i knigoizdatel'stvo Alkonost', *B.S.* I, 530–8.

[36] A. A. Kublitskaya-Piottukh, unpublished letter to M. A. Beketova of 10 Aug. 1919. Arkhiv A. A. Bloka, IRLI.

[37] K. Fedin, 'Al. Blok', *Kniga i Revolyutsiya* (Petrograd), 1921, no. 1.

[38] Cf. K. I. Chukovsky, op. cit., 16. Akhmatova's poem 'Kogda v toske samou-biystva ...' (cf. *Sochineniya* 1 [Munich, 1967], 185) was written in 1917.

[39] Cf. the article 'Bez bozhestva, bez vzdokhnoveniya', *S.S.* vi, 174–84. Also Vl. Khodasevich, 'Gumilev i Blok', *Nekropol'* (Paris, 1976), 118–40.

[40] Vs. Rozhdestvensky, op. cit., 225.

[41] E. Zamyatin, op. cit., 17.

[42] A. A. Kublitskaya-Piottukh, unpublished letter to M. A. Beketova of 17 May 1919. Arkhiv A. A. Bloka, IRLI.

[43] Ibid., letter of 3 May 1919.

[44] Ibid., letter of 2 Feb. 1920.

[45] Ibid., letter of 28 Feb. 1920.

[46] Ibid., letter of 5 Mar. 1920.

[47] K. I. Chukovsky, op. cit., 173.

[48] Id., 'A. Blok v Chukokkale', *B.S.* ii, 424–9—a publication of Blok's ironic accounts of the opening and closing of the 'House of Arts' and other matters.

[49] S. M. Alyansky, op. cit., 105–6.

[50] K. I. Chukovsky, 'Poslednye gody Bloka', op. cit., 162.

[51] S. M. Alyansky, op. cit., 109, 110.

[52] N. A. Pavlovich, op. cit., 451–5.

[53] Vl. Pyast, 'O "pervom tome" Bloka', *Ob Aleksandre Bloke* (Petersburg, 1921), 213–14.

[54] A. A. Kublitskaya-Piottukh, unpublished letter to M. A. Beketova of 6/19 May 1920. Arkhiv A. A. Bloka, IRLI.

CHAPTER XI

[1] N. A. Pavlovich, 'Vospominaniya ob Aleksandre Bloke', *B.S.* I, 455, 458, 461.

[2] E. Zamyatin, 'Aleksandr Blok', *Litsa* (New York, 1967), 27.

[3] Vs. Rozhdestvensky, *Stranitsy zhizni* (Moscow–Leningrad, 1962), 236–7. For other recommendations see the collection *Pamyati Bloka*, 2nd edn. (Petrograd, 1923), 63–72.

[4] Cf. particularly N. A. Pavlovich's account, op. cit., 476–7, 481, and the sections 'Klub poetov' and 'Bez bozhestva, bez vzdokhnoveniya' of her 'Poema o Bloke' in the book *Dumy i vospominaniya*, 2nd edn. (Moscow, 1966), 17–22.

[5] Cf. for example, N. A. Pavlovich, 'Vospominaniya ob Aleksandre Bloke', op. cit., 485; Vl. Pyast, 'O "pervom tome" Bloke', *Ob Aleksandre Bloke* (Petersburg, 1921), 213.

[6] E. Zamyatin, op. cit., 24.

[7] Vs. Rozhdestvensky, op. cit., 238.

[8] K. I. Chukovsky, 'Poslednye gody Bloka', *Z.M.*, no. 6, 1922, 160.

[9] Ibid., 158.

[10] N. A. Pavlovich, *Dumy i vospominaniya*, 32–3.

[11] K. I. Chukovsky, op. cit., 158.

[12] V. A. Zorgenfrey, 'Aleksandr Aleksandrovich Blok (po pamyati pyatnadtsati let, 1906–1921)', *Z. M.*, no. 6, 1922, 144. Cf. also E. Zamyatin, op. cit., 22.

[13] Cf. I. Chernov, 'A. Blok i knigoizdatel'stvo "Alkonost"', *B.S.* 1, 535, for the details of this last altercation with Ionov.

[14] A. A. Kublitskaya-Piottukh, unpublished, undated letter to L. A. Del'mas. Copy in the collection of N. P. Il'in.

[15] S. M. Alyansky, op. cit., 150.

[16] K. I. Chukovsky, *Kniga ob Aleksandre Bloke* (Petersburg, 1922).

[17] Id., 'Poslednye gody Bloka', op. cit., 171–2.

[18] L. D. Blok, memoirs. Passage missing from *Byli i nebylitsy*, probably indicated by [...] p. 83.

[19] S. M. Alyansky, op. cit., 150.

[20] Cf. *Pis'ma k rodnym* II, 503, notes to letter 634.

[21] L. D. Blok, *Byli i nebylitsy*, 86.

[22] S. M. Alyansky, op. cit., 153–4.

[23] Vl. Khodasevich, 'Gumilev i Blok', *Nekropol'* (Paris, 1976), 139.

[24] L. D. Blok, unpublished letter to A. A. Kublitskaya-Piottukh of 2 Aug. 1921. Arkhiv A. A. Bloka, IRLI.

[25] For Aleksandra Andreyevna's last years see M. A. Beketova, 1925.

[26] E. Knipovich, a letter to K. I. Chukovsky published in his *Lyudi i knigi* (Moscow, 1960), 552, and, originally, in *Z. M.*, no. 6, 1922, 180.

[27] N. A. Pavlovich, 'Vospominaniya ob Aleksandre Bloke', op. cit., 496, 487.

[28] N. Berberova, *The Italics are Mine* (London and Harlow, 1969), 125–8.

[29] E. Zamyatin, op. cit., 28.

[30] E. Gollerbach, 'Obraz Bloka', in the almanac *Vozrozhdeniye* (Moscow, 1923).

SELECT BIBLIOGRAPHY

The Writings of Aleksandr Blok

Books published during Blok's lifetime, and the most important posthumous publications, with a selection of bibliographies of his work.

SEPARATE PUBLICATIONS, PREPARED BY BLOK

Stikhi o Prekrasnoy Dame (Verses about the Most Beautiful Lady) (Moscow: Grif, 1905)

Nechayannaya Radost' (Joy Unhoped-for) (Moscow: Skorpion, 1907)

Snezhnaya Maska (The Snow Mask) (St. Petersburg: Ory, 1907)

Liricheskiye dramy (Lyrical Dramas) (St Petersburg: Shipovnik, 1908)
Comprising *The Puppet Booth*, *The Stranger*, and *The King in the Square*, with M. Kuzmin's music for *The Puppet Booth*.

Zemlya v snegu. Tretiy sbornik stikhov (The Earth in Snow. A third collection of poems) (Moscow: Zolotoye runo, 1908)

Nochnye chasy. Chetvertyy sbornik stikhov, 1908–1910 (The Night Watches. A fourth collection of poems) (Moscow: Musaget, 1911)

Sobraniye stikhotvoreniy v 3 knigakh (Collected Poems in 3 volumes) (Moscow: Musaget, 1911–12)
Volume I. A second augmented and revised edition of *Verses about the Most Beautiful Lady (1898–1904)*. Each year provides a separate section of the book, and there is an author's preface specially written for this edition. (1911)
Volume II. *Joy Unhoped-for (1904–1908)*. A second, augmented edition, divided into sections: Spring; Childhood; Magic; Poisons; The Ring of Suffering; 1905; Submission; Joy Unhoped-for; The Night Violet. (1912)
Volume III. *Snezhaya Noch' (1907–1909)* (The Snowy Night). Under this new title are included some published collections such as *The Snow Mask*, and other poems or cycles formerly published in *The Night Watches* or in newspapers and periodicals: Volnye Mysli (Free Thoughts); Zaklya-tiye ognem i mrakem (Invocation by Fire and Darkness); Pesnya Sud'by (The Song of Fate; Strashnyy mir (The Terrible World); Vos-mezdiye (Retribution) [the set of verses, not the long poem]; Italyans-kiye Stikhi (Italian Verses); Arfy i Skripki (Harps and Violins); Rodina (The Motherland). (1912)

Skazki. Stikhi dlya detey (Fairy Tales. Poems for Children) (Moscow: I. Sytin, 1913)

Kruglyy god. Stikhotvoreniya dlya detey (All the Year Round. Poems for Children) (Moscow: I. Sytin, 1913)

Stikhii o Rossii (Poems about Russia) (Petrograd: Otechestvo, 1915)

Sobraniye stikhotvoreniy i teatr v 4 knigakh (Collected Poems and Plays in 4 volumes) (Moscow: Musaget, 1916)

Volume I (1898–1904). A third, revised edition of their first collection *Verses about the Most Beautiful Lady*, now divided into sections: Ante Lucem; Verses about the Most Beautiful Lady; The Crossroads.

Volume II (1904–1907). A third, revised edition now divided into sections: Introduction; The Bubbles of the Earth; The Night Violet; Various Verses; The City; The Snow Mask; Faina; Free Thoughts.

Volume III (1905–1914). Second, revised and extended edition divided into sections: The Terrible World; Opyat' na rodine (Again in my Native Land); Italian Verses; Various Verses; Harps and Violins; Carmen; The Motherland; O chem poyët veter (Of what the Wind Sings).

Volume IV. Plays. *The Puppet Booth*; *The King in the Square*; *The Stranger*; *The Acts of Théophile*; *The Rose and the Cross*.

Sobraniye stikhotvoreniy i teatra (Collected Poems and Plays) (Petrograd: Zemlya, 1918)

Volume I (1898–1904). A reprint of the 1916 Musaget volume.

Volume II (1904–1908). A fourth, extended edition of the 1916 volume.

Volume III remained unpublished owing to the collapse of the publishing house Zemlya.

Volume IV. Plays. As in the 1916 edition but without *The Acts of Théophile*.

Solov'inyy sad (The Nightingale Garden) (Petersburg: Alkonost, 1918)

Dvenadtsat'. Skify (The Twelve. The Scythians) (Petrograd: Revolyutsionnyy Sotsializm, 1918)

Dvenadtsat' (The Twelve), second and third editions (Petersburg [*sic*]: Alkonost, 1918)

Rossiya i Intelligentsiya (1907–1918) (Russia and the Intelligentsia) (Moscow: Revolyutionnyy Sotsializm, 1918)

Rossiya i Intelligentsia 1907–1918 (Petersburg: Alkonost, 1919). A second edition, comprising articles: 'Religioznye iskaniya i narod' (Religious Quests and the People); 'Narod i intelligentsiya' (The People and the Intelligentsia); 'Stikhiya i kul'tura' (The Element and Culture); 'Ironiya' (Irony); 'Ditya Gogolya' (The Child of Gogol); 'Plamen'' (Flame); 'Intelligentsiya i revolyutsiya' (The Intelligentsia and the Revolution).

Katilina (Catilina) (Petersburg: Alkonost, 1919)

Yamby. Sovremennye Stikhi (1907–1914) (Iambs. Contemporary Poems) (Petersburg: Alkonost, 1919)

Pesnya Sud'by. Dramaticheskaya poema (The Song of Fate. A dramatic poem) (Petersburg: Alkonost, 1919)

Za gran'yu proshlykh dney. Stikhotvoreniya (Beyond the Bounds of Days Gone By. Poems) (Petrograd: Z. I. Grzhebin, 1920)

Comprising poems written between 1898 and 1903 but not included in any previous edition of Blok's *First Volume*.

Sedoye utro. Stikhotvoreniya (The Grey Morning. Poems) (Petersburg: Alkonost, 1920)

Comprising poems written between 1907 and 1916 but not included in any previous editions of the *Second* or *Third Volumes*.

Stikhotvoreniya. Kniga tret'ya (1907–1916) (Poems. Third Volume) (Petersburg: Alkonost, 1921)
> A third, extended edition which should have been published as Volume III in the 1918 Zemlya collected edition.

Poslednye dni imperatorskoy vlasti. Po neizdannym dokumentam sostavil Aleksandr Blok (The Last Days of the Imperial Regime. Compiled by Aleksandr Blok from unpublished documents) (Petersburg: Alkonost, 1921)

PRINCIPAL POSTHUMOUS PUBLICATIONS

Otrocheskiye Stikhi. Avtobiografiya (Adolescent Poems. Autobiography) (Moscow: Pervina, [1922]1923)

COLLECTED WORKS

Sobraniye Sochineniy Aleksandra Bloka (Collected Works of Aleksandr Blok) (Petersburg–Berlin: Alkonost, 1922–3)
> Planned by Blok to comprise nine volumes, this edition, although incomplete (vols. VI and VIII were not published), has served as a model for later publications, particularly the first four volumes—the three volumes of poetry and the plays—which Blok himself prepared for publication.

Aleksandr Blok. Sobraniye Sochineniy I–XII, ed. K. Fedin (Leningrad, 1932–6)

Aleksandr Blok. Sobraniye Sochineniy I–VIII, with *Zapisnye Knizhki* (Notebooks), ed. V. N. Orlov, A. A. Surkov, K. I. Chukovsky (Moscow–Leningrad, 1960–5)

Aleksandr Blok. Sobraniye Sochineniy v 6 tomakh (Collected Works in 6 volumes), ed. S. A. Nebol'sin, introduction by B. I. Solov'ev (Moscow, 1971)

DIARIES AND NOTEBOOKS

Dnevnik Al. Bloka 1911–1913 (Blok's Diary), ed. P. N. Medvedev (Leningrad, 1928)

Dnevnik Al. Bloka 1917–1921, ed. P. N. Medvedev (Leningrad, 1928)

Zapisnye Knizhki Al. Bloka (Blok's Notebooks), ed. P. N. Medvedev (Leningrad, 1930)

'Yunosheskiy Dnevnik Al. Bloka' (Blok's Adolescent Diary), ed. Vl. Orlov, *Literaturnoye Nasledstvo* (Moscow), nos. 27–8, 1937
> The *Diaries 1911–1913* and *1917–1921,* with the 'Adolescent Diary', are republished, on the whole more fully but with some cuts, as vol. VII in the eight-volume Collected Works of 1960–5. The *Notebooks* which Blok kept throughout his lifetime are republished, again on the whole more fully but with some cuts, as a pendant to the eight-volume edition.

LETTERS

(Separate publications only; for letters published in periodicals see various bibliographies.)

Pis'ma Aleksandra Bloka (Letters of Blok), with introductory articles by M. S. and S. M. Solov'ev, G. I. Chulkov, A. D. Skaldin, and V. I. Knyazhnin (Leningrad, 1925)

Pis'ma Aleksandra Bloka k rodnym (Letters of Blok to Relatives), ed. M. A. Beketova, 2 vols. (Leningrad, 1927, 1932)

Pis'ma Al. Bloka k E. P. Ivanovu (Letters of Blok to E. P. Ivanov), ed. and introduced by Ts. Vol'pe (Moscow–Leningrad, 1936)

Aleksandr Blok i Andrey Bely. Perepiska (Correspondence), ed. and introduced by Vl. Orlov, in the series *Letopisi*, no. 7 (Moscow, 1940)

Aleksandr Blok. Pis'ma k zhene (Letters to his Wife), ed. and introduced by Vl. Orlov, *Literaturnoye Nasledstvo* (Moscow), no. 87, 1978
> A volume of letters to various addressees is included as vol. VIII in the eight-volume Collected Works of 1960–5.

BIBLIOGRAPHIES OF BLOK
(Russian and English)

E. F. Knipovich, in the book by K. I. Chukovsky, *Kniga ob Aleksandre Bloke* (Petersburg [sic], 1922)
> Music set to Blok's words, books, a chronology of the poems.

N. Ashukin, *Aleksandr Blok, sinkhronisticheskiye tablitsy zhizni i tvorchestva 1880–1921. Bibliografiya 1903–1921* (Moscow, 1923)
> Publications by and about Blok, 1904–1923.

E. Blyum and V. Gol'tsev, 'Literatura o Bloke za gody revolyutsii (bibliografiya)', in *O Bloke*, ed. E. F. Nikitina (Moscow, 1929)
> Publications about Blok from 1918 to 1928.

E. Kolpakova, P. Kupriyanovsky and D. Maksimov, 'Bibliografiya A. Bloka', *Vil'nyusskiy gosudarstvennyy pedagogicheskiy Institut. Ucheniye Zapiski* (Vilnius), vol. VI, 1959
> Covers publications by and about Blok 1928–57.

A. Pyman, 'Materialy k bibliografii zarubezhnoy literatury ob A. A. Bloke', *Blokovskiy Sbornik* (Tartu), vol. I, 1964
> Works about Blok, publications and translations in English, French, German, Italian, up to 1962, and (with addenda covering principal books on Blok 1921–66, émigré literature about Blok up to 1962, and the other language sections 1963–8) in A. Pyman, *Alexander Blok. Selected Poems* (Oxford, 1972).

P. E. Pomirchiy, 'Materialy k bibliografii A. Bloka za 1958–1970 gody', *Blokovskiy Sbornik*, vol. II, 1972

M. Sendich, 'Blok's *The Twelve*: Critical Interpretations of the Christ-figure and Bibliography', *Russian Literary Triquarterly* (Ann Arbor, Mich.), no. 2 (Fall), 1972.

INDEX

B = Blok

ERRATA

in *The Life of Aleksandr Blok*, vol. I

Page	12, 18	Alexander II was assassinated in 1881, not 1882.
74	*Mir Bozhiy* was a legal Marxist, not a liberal journal.
111	The word used in the Orthodox prayers for the dead, misheard by the author as *novopredstavlennyy* ('newly presented'), is actually *novoprestavlennyy*, a Slavonic form meaning 'newly dead'.
115	The Greek word for ecstasy should read: εχστασις
131	Life nobility was awarded automatically to those attaining a certain rank in the military or civil services. The comparison with a knighthood is thus rather misleading.
150, line 5	*for* Leningrad *read* Petersburg
228, line 3 of note *e*	*for* brother *read* father
229	Ariadna Tyrkova-Williams was Duma correspondent, not head of the Kadet party.
231 and note	The word *kosnost'* comes not from *kosoy* ('bent' or 'squint') but from a Slavonic root meaning 'late', and is thus better translated as 'inertia' or 'torpor' than as 'distortion'.

I am grateful to those of my colleagues who have helped to pinpoint these inaccuracies and to suggest more correct alternatives, in particular to James Forsyth, Robin Milner-Gulland, and Kyril Zinovieff.

A. P.

August 1979